Sept 24

8.75

D0623330

THE
HARPSICHORD AND CLAVICHORD

The
Harpsichord and Clavichord

An Introductory Study

by

RAYMOND RUSSELL
F.S.A.

Second edition,
revised by Howard Schott

W · W · NORTON & COMPANY · INC ·
New York, New York

© 1973 Mrs Gilbert Russell

LIBRARY

JAN 2 1974

UNIVERSITY OF THE PACIFIC

274182

First published in 1959
by Faber and Faber Limited
Second impression 1965
Second, revised edition 1973
Printed in Great Britain by
R. MacLehose and Company Limited
The University Press Glasgow
All rights reserved

ISBN 0- 393- 02174-2 (USA)

CONTENTS

CONTENTS

2

ILLUSTRATIONS
at the end of the book

3

ILLUSTRATIONS

ILLUSTRATIONS

ILLUSTRATIONS

INTRODUCTION

This book has had a chequered and stormy childhood. The idea of writing it first entered my head in the late 1940's when it had become clear to me that the early keyboard instruments, despite their increasing popularity, had received a quite inadequate historical study. A good many books had been written, some good and some bad, but most of these were out of print and hard to find, and were largely taken from each other. They mostly derived from A. J. Hipkins' *The Pianoforte* (1896), a small book but far the best that has yet appeared in this field. It should be read by every student today.

In 1951 I began a methodical study of the principal foreign collections, starting with several months in France. There followed four visits to the Low Countries where lay the answer to so many problems (and the questions to so many more), and many other excursions into Switzerland, Germany, Spain, Austria, Italy and so on. During this period I disgorged a certain amount of material in a revised list of instruments from the Ruckers workshop at Antwerp, which appeared in *Grove's Dictionary*, 5th edition, 1954. But I did not yet feel ready to marshal my notes and thoughts into book form.

This part of the work got going through the kindness of Cecil Clutton in the winter of 1954. A publisher had asked him to write a book on all the keyboard instruments, stressing of course the organ, and he invited me to join him and take over the harpsichord and clavichord chapters. This offer I accepted, and I made a rough draft of what I thought was necessary; but as the greater part of what I wrote was new material, and as my approach was also new, we found that I needed more space than was allowed. Cecil Clutton then most generously withdrew, leaving the whole book for my own subjects.

I continued to travel, and visited more collections and single instruments; and the occasional purchase of a special instrument here and there (the first had been in 1939) gradually resulted in my possession of a large *armamentarium* in this field, demonstrating every national school, style, and period, better (I think) than does any other such collection in the world. The autumn of 1955 saw the first draft rewritten in book form with appendices, and Ralph Kirkpatrick with whom I was in Dublin most kindly read the whole of that typescript for me. His criticism necessitated the entire rewriting of the book, the translation of all foreign languages into English, and much other reorganization. His advice both at that time and since, on the many occasions when we have discussed the organization of this book, has been so clearly right that I have scarcely ever failed to take it.

So in the winter of 1955 I rewrote the book again, and during those months I examined a number of seventeenth and eighteenth century theoretical works, including several unknown to me until Ralph Kirkpatrick pointed out their importance. At this stage I decided to add at the end of each chapter a very brief outline of the types of decoration most commonly found, though these sections were not intended to be more than the most elementary guide. By the spring of 1956 this work had been done, and the whole text was then read by Donald Boalch, with whom I had been in constant touch for four years on this subject, and whose *Makers of the Harpsichord and Clavichord, 1440–1840* an indispensable book for every student and library, I had read in typescript and in proof.

The autumn of 1956 found me suddenly without a publisher, and I put the typescript away, hoping never to see it (nor a publisher) again. But it had to come out, and during the winter I rewrote the whole book once more, shortening the text, completely rewriting the plate commentaries, and reducing the number of plates by nearly half.

The book does not now cover as much ground as I had formerly planned; the text is shorter, the plates are fewer; but this may not be a bad thing. I have chosen the sub-title accordingly, and the sub-title means what it says. The book is meant for those who know nothing, or only a little, about the subject, though it will teach much that is new to the most experienced. It is a textbook of structure rather than of function. It shows what was built in every principal centre at all periods; but it no longer refers to musical details of function, and it will not tell you how to build an instrument, nor does it discuss details of the instrument maker's technique. Much information on those latter points will be found in Frank Hubbard's *Three Centuries of Harpsichord Making*. I have been at pains to stress the instruments in most general use; the primitive, the rarity, the decadent and the exception have been left without detailed comment unless they throw light on more general matters. At one stage I treated the modern harpsichord and clavichord in some detail, and received kind help from many instrument makers; but I removed the chapter as this activity is in a state of adolescence and (I hope) of change, and the remainder of the work is firm historical fact. Inclusion of such material would only shorten the useful life of the book.

Many text books today comprise a mass of undigested facts and references, borrowed from other writers, and unrelieved by original observations or new discoveries. The organization of this book is new, a great part of the factual contents and most of my interpretations are new; out of 109 illustrations only 18 have appeared before, and five of these, reproduced in Boalch (1956) with my glad permission, were specially taken for this book. Several hundred other photographs which had been specially taken were rejected from my final selection.

When a subject is so completely revised and so much is introduced that is new, it is probable that here and there a lack of balance may result. I have written about what I have seen and what I know, and I have stressed those things which in the light of my knowledge today seem important. But there is much which I do not know and have not seen, and no doubt I have passed over important trends without noticing them and have missed much while on my travels. This is inevitable; but the basic organization of the study is secure, and I hope that others will amplify and adjust the details from time to time. There is much interesting work to be done.

INTRODUCTION

Those readers who study the tables of scalings and plucking points should bear the following points in their minds. In the case of instruments with two eight foot stops the longer set of strings is that measured. The length of the shorter eight foot can therefore be obtained by subtracting *circa* $\frac{1}{2}$ inch from the measurements given. The eight foot plucking point is also taken from the longer set of strings, and this is by custom attacked by the principal eight foot of the upper manual, the plectra of which face to the player's left. In English harpsichords the two eight foot registers were always adjacent; in Continental instruments they were generally separated by the four foot register. Allowing a $\frac{3}{4}$ inch interval between the plectra of adjacent registers, the plucking point of the shorter eight foot can be adequately judged by adding $\frac{3}{4}$ inch in English harpsichords and $1\frac{1}{2}$ inches in Continental models, unless a different layout is specified in the text.

As this book is written both in English and in England the writer has judged it best to give all measurements in feet and inches. For those accustomed to the greatly preferable metric system the following conversion table may be of use:

$$1 \text{ inch} \quad = 2{\cdot}54 \text{ centimetres}$$
$$1 \text{ centimetre} = 0{\cdot}394 \text{ inches}$$

The following system of musical notation is used throughout, each sequence of letters embracing the octave immediately above:

It is a great pleasure to record the kindness and help I have received while at work on this study. Many individual owners of early keyboard instruments wrote to me, gave access to their harpsichords and clavichords, and allowed me photographs, and I am most grateful for their help. Museums were equally kind, and gave me special facilities for everything I wanted to do. In some of these I worked for several weeks and made repeated visits. I must in particular thank the Victoria and Albert Museum; the Antwerp City Museums; The Neupert Collection, Bamberg; the Belle Skinner Collection, Holyoke; the Musée du Conservatoire Royal de Musique, Brussels; the Deutsches Museum, Munich; the National Museum, Dublin; the Rück Collection, Erlangen; the Gemeentemuseum, the Hague; the Conservatoire National de Musique, Paris; the Kunsthistorisches Museum, Vienna; for exceptional facilities or photographic assistance.

Besides those already mentioned it is a pleasure to thank many others who have given me help: Noel Blakiston, Evelyn Broadwood, Mrs. George Crawley, Thurston Dart, Mrs. Arnold Dolmetsch, Carl Dolmetsch, Andrew Douglas who prepared the drawings for the two line blocks, Ralph Edwards, Dr. W. H. George, Hugh Gough, Dr. Rosamond Harding, John Hayward, W. G. Hiscock, Alec Hodsdon, Mrs. Eileen Jackson, E. C. Legg, John

Morley, Richard Newton, Vere Pilkington, the late Miss Olwen Pughe-Jones, Miss Gladys Scott Thomson, Miss Dorothy Swainson, Leslie Ward, the late James Wardrop; in France Marcel Asseman, Mlle. Marcelle Blanchard, la Comtesse de Chambure, Mme. de Jouvenel, Mme. Marcelle de Lacour, Marc Pincherle; in Spain J. Ricart Matas; in Austria Prof. Otto Erich Deutsch. Dr. Victor Luithlen; in Germany Karl Maendler, Dr. Hanns Neupert, Dr. Ulrich Rück, Konrad Sasse, Karl-Egbert Schultze; in Belgium Prof. Charles van den Borren, Dr. Auguste Corbet, Mme. Marguerite Reniers, the late Dr. J. A. Stellfeld, Dr. L. Voet; in Holland D. J. Balfoort; in the United States John Challis, Charles Fisher, Albert Fuller, Miss Fanny Reed Hammond, Frank Hubbard, Robert Johnson, Miss Sibyl Marcuse.

I owe a special debt to the late Professor Edward Dent through whose kindness I first had regular access to a harpsichord. He encouraged this study over a long period of time, wrote numerous introductions to help me on my travels abroad, and discussed and clarified many problems which arose.

Donald Boalch has most kindly read several typescripts and all the proofs, and his generous collaboration has been of the greatest help to me.

PREFACE TO SECOND EDITION

I t is hardly strange that a book which, when published in 1959, established itself immediately as the modern classic work on a wholly historical subject, should be thought to require a certain amount of revision a dozen years later. The need for a new edition was indeed recognized by the author before his untimely death in 1964. We know from his personal copy of the book that he contemplated making a number of small changes in the text to take account of the results of post-1959 research. It was in fact Russell's book more than anything else that laid the groundwork for all recent investigations into historical stringed keyboard instruments. One outstanding example makes this clear: when Frank Hubbard's *Three Centuries of Harpsichord Making*, a technical work which superbly complements Russell's book, appeared in 1965, its author acknowledged all the help and encouragement he had received from him.

The recent past has witnessed a spate of research papers amplifying our knowledge and clarifying our understanding of the harpsichord and clavichord. Many long-forgotten instruments have been brought to light. A few that had long been known have been shown to be different from what had been thought. Such constant re-examination of the historical evidence will inevitably continue, but the present moment seemed an appropriate one for producing a new edition of Russell.

My revisions are limited, and seek to correct and supplement the author's text only in matters of detail. The book remains in all essential respects as the author left it. Changes have been made reluctantly and, I sincerely believe, with great respect. From a practical point of view it was desirable to avoid resetting the book completely for reasons all too obvious in this world of rising costs. But, most important of all, the story of the harpsichord and clavichord down to the beginning of the modern revival remains substantially as Russell set it down.

A comparison of the new edition and the old will disclose a number of small alterations to the main text; some of these derive from Russell's own copy of the book. Both the list of collections of early keyboard instruments (pages 186 ff.) and the list of books of reference (pages 190 ff.) have been brought up to date. Many plates have been recaptioned, mainly to show the present ownership or location of the instruments depicted. New and clearer photographs of the instruments illustrated in Plates 31, 32, 39 and 40 have replaced the former ones.

Finally, thanks are due to those who have helped me complete the revision. Many of them, of course, knew Raymond Russell and were of service to him in the preparation of

PREFACE TO SECOND EDITION

the original edition. I am most indebted to Mrs. Gilbert Russell for authorizing and encouraging the production of the new edition of her son's book. Donald Boalch has been very generous and obliging in making the fruits of his own extensive research freely available to me while he was himself working on an enlarged second edition of his own *Makers of the Harpsichord and Clavichord, 1440–1840*. Derek Adlam, Gustav Leonhardt and Charles Mould have similarly been most helpful in answering my queries about instruments of which they have special knowledge.

The greater part of Raymond Russell's extensive instrument collection was given by Mrs. Gilbert Russell in 1964 to the University of Edinburgh 'in memory of her son and to fulfil a wish long entertained by him,' and some further instruments of his have since been added. Both John Barnes, who has restored and maintained a number of these, and Dr. Peter Williams, Director of the Russell Collection, merit special thanks for giving me access to the instruments and information about them. Geraint Jones, long a close friend of the author's, kindly read the final manuscript of the revised edition.

Mme. Janine Lambrechts-Douillez of the Vleeshuis Museum, Antwerp, and Miss Virginia M. Cline of the George F. Harding Museum in Chicago were of great assistance in providing the new photographs mentioned above. Many other institutions and their staffs have been of help; it is a pleasure to list those to which I am especially obliged: the Musée du Conservatoire Royal de Musique, Brussels, and Dr. N. Meeùs; the Yale University Collection of Musical Instruments, New Haven, and Richard Rephann; the Metropolitan Museum of Art, New York, and Edwin M. Ripin; the Germanisches Nationalmuseum, Nürnberg, and Dr. J. H. van der Meer; and the Musée Instrumental du Conservatoire National Supérieur de Musique, Paris, and Mme. de Chambure and Hubert Bédard.

Oxford, 1972   HOWARD SCHOTT

CHAPTER ONE

THE INSTRUMENT

HARPSICHORD

The history of the harpsichord, as the largest and most important domestic keyboard musical instrument of its day, covers the sixteenth, seventeenth and eighteenth centuries. Before those times it is known to us only from occasional references in manuscripts and from illustrations. The earliest authentically dated harpsichord on record is an Italian instrument of 1521 in the Victoria and Albert Museum (plates 5 and 6), while the latest dated specimen recorded by the writer is a Kirckman harpsichord of 1800 privately owned in England.

There is a tradition[1] that the last Kirckman harpsichord was dated 1809; but that instrument can no longer be traced.

The earliest forms of the harpsichord were the result of attempts to mechanize the psaltery, but no primitive examples have survived. However, a fairly detailed account of harpsichord construction is contained in a mid fifteenth century manuscript[2] in the Bibliothèque Nationale in Paris. This document was compiled by Henri Arnault of Zwolle, physician to the Duke of Burgundy, and in it Arnault discusses four different ways of attacking the string of the harpsichord. This suggests that the action of the instrument was by no means standardized by the middle of the fifteenth century. The general layout was, however, established; and a drawing of the same period,[3] but which does not show details of the action, is preserved in the Grand Ducal Library at Weimar. Another very early illustration of a harpsichord is a miniature in the Duc de Berri's *Très riches heures, c* 1485.[4] An English representation[5] of an early harpsichord is carved in the roof of the nave of Manchester Cathedral, and this has been dated *c.* 1465.

It can be seen from these examples that the harpsichord, in a primitive form, was in use in different parts of Europe by the middle of the fifteenth century. How standardized its form was we do not know; but by the turn of the century it had become, in all essentials, the musical instrument as made in 1800 or 1950. Mechanical refinements and certain details of materials and size are the only differences.

In general appearance the harpsichord is not unlike a narrow grand pianoforte, the latter

---

[1] Engel, 'Some account of the clavichord,' *Musical Times*, July 1879.   [2] MS. fonds Latin 7295.
[3] James, plate XI.   [4] Musée Condé, Chantilly, 65 (1284).   [5] Galpin (1910), figure 21.

instrument having evolved from basic harpsichord design. The keys are placed at one end, and on opening the lid we see the strings stretching away from the player in the familiar manner.

Immediately beneath the music desk we see the wrestplank; and in this are set the wrest or tuning pins, round which the proximal ends of the strings are wound. We also find on the wrest plank the proximal bridges or nuts, over which the strings pass, and at which point their vibrating length begins.

Beyond the wrest plank a strong wooden cover, the jack rail, covers the action of the instrument, which is placed in the usual position of the pianoforte hammers. In the harpsichord, however, there are no hammers, since a plucking mechanism is employed to set the string in motion.

The strings pass under the jack rail and continue their course to the far end of the instrument, where they are attached to the hitch pin rail, a narrow strip of hard wood running along the inner face of the bent side and of the end section of the case. Beneath the strings we see the soundboard with its bridges over which the strings pass. These bridges convey vibrations from the strings to the soundboard, which amplifies them; and at the point of contact with the bridges the vibrating length of the strings ends.

Having inspected the general appearance of the harpsichord we may examine the working of its action.

The instrument, in its most simple form, has one keyboard with a compass of perhaps only four octaves, and one string for each key. But, as with the organ, harpsichords have been built to many different specifications, and instruments with two keyboards and three strings for each key are common. We shall start with the least complex model.

On the distal end of each key stands a thin strip of wood called the jack; this contains the plucking mechanism, and is the unit of harpsichord action (plate 1). The dimensions of jacks vary with the exact design of individual instruments, but their height is from five to eight inches, their width about half an inch, and their thickness about three sixteenths of an inch. The top of the jack projects just above the level of the strings, and is just below the jack rail. At this level a small piece of felt is fixed to the side of each jack, and, projecting against the neighbouring string, acts as a damper.

A slot is cut in the upper part of each jack, and let into this is a small upright strip of wood, about one inch in height, called the tongue. Projecting from this tongue at right angles, and just below the adjacent string, is the plectrum, a small wedge of hard leather, or a strip of quill, about one eighth of an inch in length, which actually plucks the string. The tongue is pivoted on a pin inserted laterally through it, so that the upper part can be pressed back and away from the string, though it is normally kept upright by a small spring at the back, usually made of hog's bristle.

When a key is depressed the jack rises, and the plectrum plucks the string as it passes. When the key is released the jack falls back with it; but, when the plectrum reaches the string on its descent, the pivoted tongue is forced back, and this simple escapement allows the plectrum to repass the string without plucking it again. The hog's bristle spring then returns the tongue to its upright position, and finally the damper touches the string and silences it (pages 132, 133, and plate 17).

HARPSICHORD ACTION

It will be realized that this action depends on the key making the full journey of its course, for if an attempt is made to sound the note again before the key has fully returned, the plectrum will not yet be in position under the string to pluck it; hence it is clear that a carefully articulated finger technique is essential to harpsichord playing.

The jacks, one for each key, are held upright in position by passing through slots in two strips of wood or metal. The lower of these two strips is an inch or so above the keys, and is usually fixed in position; it is called the jack guide. The upper strip is level with, and placed between, the soundboard and wrest plank; this is called the slide. As its name suggests, it is capable of being slid to left or right, thus controlling the exact position of the jacks in relation to the strings. This decides whether the plectrum will engage the string or miss it when the key is depressed. The jacks are prevented from jumping out of place, when the instrument is being played, by the jack rail; and this bar also controls the depth of touch in many instruments.

A slightly more elaborate harpsichord than the one just described has a second set of strings. These are placed level and parallel with the first set, and are served by a second row of jacks, arranged with their plectra facing the opposite way to those of the first set. A lever attached to the end of each slide, and controlled by a hand stop, puts that row of jacks into the 'on' or 'off' position, thus enabling the player to select which set of strings he wishes to use. In modern harpsichords these movements are usually controlled by pedals.

If, as is common, a third set of strings is added, together with its own row of jacks and stop lever, it is tuned an octave higher than the other two sets; and, as the strings are much shorter, this octave or four foot stop has its own bridge on both wrest plank and soundboard, the strings and plectra being placed about half an inch lower than those of the unison or eight foot stops.

The largest modern harpsichords often contain a fourth set of strings, the sixteen foot stop, which is also, of course, provided with its own row of jacks; and this register is tuned an octave below the normal eight foot pitch. The sixteen foot strings and plectra are placed about half an inch above those of the unisons; the strings are occasionally provided with their own bridges, but more often use a super structure on the eight foot bridges. Though common in modern harpsichords the sixteen foot stop was, in the past, almost exclusively restricted to a few special German instruments.

Harpsichords with more than two sets of strings are usually provided with two keyboards. The upper keyboard controls one unison stop, while the four foot, the sixteen foot, and the other unison are played from the lower keyboard. The upper manual can be coupled to the lower in almost all modern, and in many old, instruments (figures 1 and 2, pages 56 and 78).

Two other stops in commom use must be mentioned here. The eight foot strings of the upper keyboard are often provided with a second row of jacks, which pluck the strings at a point very close to the nut; and this produces a very thin and brittle tone. It is known as the lute stop. Van Blanckenburg (1739) claims the invention of the lute stop as his own in 1708; but the date is very early for this register. Lastly there is the harp or buff stop, which consists of a series of small pads of felt or of buff leather; these can be slid against the various sets of strings at a point close to the nut, thereby muting them and producing a *pizzicato* effect. The harp stop is employed almost exclusively with the eight and sixteen foot strings.

The plectra of the modern harpsichord are usually made of hard leather, of the type employed for the soles of shoes and for the driving belts of machines. Before the modern revival of the instrument they were almost always made from the black tail and flight feathers of the crow or raven, though in early Italian instruments vulture quills, brass, and leather were occasionally used. Hard leather is favoured today because it is more reliable, and lasts longer, than quill; it also makes less mechanical noise as it touches the string on the descent of the jack; but it was little known until modern times. Quill, though less reliable than leather, is the material of tradition; and the experience of three hundred years led the old makers to believe that raven and crow quills were more reliable and less likely to break than those from most other birds. Modern makers, like the old Italians, sometimes use vulture quills; and these too have proved fairly stable. Tonally, the difference between leather and quill plectra is more apparent close to the instrument than when away from it. The two materials give two different touches to a harpsichord; but, while quill produces an effect of greater brilliance and clarity than leather when heard at close quarters, the two are very difficult to tell apart when the listener is away from the instrument, as in a concert hall.

The regulation of the plectra and the movement of the keys and jacks constitute the resistance to the finger known as touch; and on this depend many of the most fundamental aspects of refined harpsichord playing. In most old instruments each key is maintained in a horizontal position by the weight of the jacks on its distal end; and when these are removed the keys tend to fall forward as if depressed by the finger. In most modern harpsichords, however, the distal ends of the keys are weighted with lead, and so remain horizontal independent of the jacks. This means that the touch of most modern harpsichords is heavier than that of the old ones, since extra weight has to be raised by the pressure of the finger, the jacks often being weighted too.

Few early harpsichords had weights in either jacks or keys. Leads are occasionally found in the proximal ends of the lower keyboards of English instruments, but the purpose of this was to lighten the touch. They occasionally appear in the distal ends of the upper keyboards. Flemish, French, and German keyboards were not otherwise leaded. In Italy the pivot point of the keys was generally proximal enough to ensure that weights of any kind were unnecessary.

But in all harpsichords there is more for the finger to overcome than the weight of keys and jacks. Resistance is produced by the plectrum pressing upwards against the string before plucking it; and the longer, thicker, and less supple the plectrum, the greater the resistance. When the key of a harpsichord is depressed slowly, the finger feels an obstacle as the plectrum pushes against the string; then it effects the pluck and is past. The finger feels almost as though it were the plectrum itself, and an illusion of actual contact with the string is created.

If two stops are employed together, the resistance offered by the two sets of plectra against the strings is about twice that offered by one; and when, in a large instrument, four or five sets of jacks are all used together, the plucking resistance becomes very considerable.

16

Old harpsichords were generally very lightly quilled, and the touch should never be heavy; but in some modern instruments, often fiercely regulated, the resistance offered by the keys can be very great, especially when an elaborate coupling mechanism and overhead dampers add yet more weight.

The resistance from the plectra is partly overcome by the following important adjustment. Suppose we have a harpsichord with one manual and three stops: an octave and two unisons. We put these 'on', and very slowly depress a key. The four foot jack is generally adjusted to speak first; second the distal eight foot jack will act, that jack having moved through the greatest distance; and lastly the proximal eight foot jack. As a result the resistance from the three plectra is divided into three 'staggered' but normally unnoticed parts, and the touch is much less heavy than if all had acted exactly together. In a large instrument with sixteen foot and coupler the speaking order is usually: octave, lower manual eight, sixteen, upper manual eight; though some adjustments may in fact be made to this sequence.

The above description of the components of harpsichord touch is by no means academic. It is a matter of great practical importance to the experienced player, who feels acutely the movements described above, and keeps his instruments carefully adjusted. The actual depth of key movement and the manner of its regulation are also of importance to this basic matter; these have varied with the traditions of instrument making in different countries.

The compass of the keyboard has lacked standardization, as have most other parts of harpsichord construction. It has varied with the musical demands of the particular time and place of manufacture, and of various owners; and the compasses of individual instruments have often been altered during the course of their careers.

The earliest harpsichord known to us (plates 5 and 6) has an apparent keyboard compass of three octaves and a seventh: E to d^3 (originally c^3); but, by a system of tuning much employed until the eighteenth century, this keyboard actually represents a compass beginning at C. This was achieved by tuning the key E to sound C, F♯ to sound D, G♯ to sound E. Keys F and G were tuned normally, and the chromatic scale began on A. Thus this early harpsichord provided a complete chromatic compass from C to c^3, except for C♯, D♯, F♯, G♯. These four bass notes were very seldom required before the late years of the seventeenth century; accordingly they were often omitted from the keyboard.

Many early instruments show BB as the lowest key. This was tuned to sound GG, key C♯ to AA, D♯ to BB; then after C and D, the chromatic scale started at E. In this system we lack notes GG♯, AA♯, C♯, D♯, which were also seldom needed before the end of the seventeenth century. These two systems of tuning the bass notes are known as short or broken octave tuning; they explain the seemingly unusual bass keys on most early instruments. When an instrument is described as having a compass from GG, or from C, bass short octave, it means that the lowest apparent key is BB or E respectively, and that the appropriate tuning given above is employed (plate 2).

Another system of short octave must be mentioned, in which the two lowest accidentals, C♯ and D♯, or F♯ and G♯, are divided into two independent keys each, a front and a back section. The back part was tuned to its proper note, the front part to the short octave. This system was sometimes known as broken octave to distinguish it from the more common

17

short octave. It is a fairly common feature of keyboards built in the second half of the seventeenth century, when individual chromatic keys were developing in the bass, but while conservative treatment still retained the old proportion and appearance of the short octave keyboard (plates 2 and 3).

Around 1700 the full complement of accidental keys in the bass made its appearance (though key FF♯ was often omitted to the end of the eighteenth century), and the compass became a standard one of five octaves from FF. The largest harpsichord compasses were of five and a half octaves; but these are rare, and vary like all else. Shudi has employed CC to f³, Kirckman FF to c⁴, Joachim Swanen EE to a³. Further details of these matters are dealt with in the chapters below.

During the three hundred years covered by this study, from 1500 to 1800, pitch, or the frequency of a given note, was not standardized as it is now, and during the larger part of the period there was little or no conception of such an idea. In the first half of this time also, the notes which appeared on the stave in written music bore no relationship to any permanent level; they were movable up or down at convenience, and were therefore available to voices and instruments at whatever pitch level they sounded. Of course music was written with certain local singers and instruments in mind, but that did not prevent such music being performed elsewhere by other singers and by instruments using different pitches.

Musical instruments were built, during those years, at a great variety of pitch levels, according to local custom, convenience, and the rough practical methods of the instrument makers. Even if the idea of a standard pitch had existed there would have been no way of maintaining it. True there was the pitchpipe, a small stopped pipe, sometimes provided with a movable stopper; but this was only used for such purposes as setting the pitch level in church singing. Old pitchpipes are of no value as guides to the various groups of pitch level, and they vary in their own pitch with blowing pressure. The English invention of the tuning fork, a much more accurate instrument, dates from about 1711; but tuning forks were not in general use until the nineteenth century, and they varied in pitch like everything else. Organ pipes, and the measurements allotted them in early theoretical works, have often been examined with care, and local pitch levels of all periods and places have thus been calculated with every superficial appearance of great accuracy. This is a most misleading practice; it is quite impossible to show an *exact* pitch from such data; old organ pipes have often been altered and moved on the soundboards, and the variation permitted by actual tuning must itself defeat any attempt at accuracy. A. J. Ellis[1] did much work on these lines, but much of it is in need of correction. Certain pitch levels mentioned by Schlick (1511), Praetorius (1619), and others, have been examined with great care by Mendel (1948); and his provisional deductions for pitch levels, recommended or described for certain districts and at certain times only, are confirmed by such standards as contemporary wind instruments.

Where stringed keyboard instruments are concerned it is impossible to state with accuracy the details the reader would like to know. The scalings of these instruments varied exceedingly widely during the sixteenth and seventeenth centuries, though they were more settled by the middle of the eighteenth century. Besides these uncertainties, our lack of knowledge

[1] Ellis (1880).

of the tensile strength of the wire used for stringing, and the great variations permitted by tuning, make it impossible to say more than this: many—and all—pitch levels were used, both higher and lower than our modern pitch ($a^2 = 440$ c.p.s. at 68° Fahr.) during those times. Instruments kept alone, and not used with orchestral instruments or organs, were presumably tuned where they best stood in tune, there being in any case no standard by which to set their pitch.

A survey of mid eighteenth century scalings, when things were more settled, and bearing in mind that it is not difficult to discover how high an instrument can be tuned, and that the tensile strength of eighteenth century wire was certainly less than that of music wire today, enables us to believe that harpsichords and spinets were often tuned at a lower level in the eighteenth century than now.

But the writer believes:

1. That it is almost impossible to make even general statements of value about so intangible and fluid a matter as early pitches,

2. That it is impossible to fix, *precisely*, any early string pitch,

3. That pitch levels have never been generally 'high' or 'low', having varied widely in different—and the same—places, at different—and the same—times,

4. That all we can say with certainty is that pitch in general has gradually moved towards standardization, though neither particularly upwards nor downwards.

The scaling, or vibrating length of string, allotted by the maker to the various registers is of great importance, the whole instrument being built round these initial proportions. The eight foot vibrating length for c^2 has varied in different countries and workshops between about 10 and 15 inches, though 13 inches may be considered an average. By the theory of stretched strings the frequency of a note varies inversely as the length of the string; hence each octave below c^2 should, theoretically, be doubled in length, and each octave above should be halved. In the treble this is done, but in the lower registers an instrument of impractical proportions would result, and from g or so the length of the strings in relation to the proper scale falls off, but is compensated by strings of greater diameter, sometimes overspun, to slow down the vibrations by weight.

The wire used in the stringing was commonly of iron, steel, copper, and brass. Nürnberg has been a centre of wire drawing since the fourteenth century; but the old wire was of poor tensile strength. Later, iron wire was drawn in Berlin, and steel wire in England. A five octave harpsichord with eight and four foot stops was strung with copper and brass in the bass and steel or iron from the tenor upwards, the sizes varying from about 0·028 inches to 0·009 inches in diameter. The gauge numbers are often stamped or written on the nut in harpsichords, and on the wrest plank in clavichords, but it must be remembered that these numbers do not refer to our present day music wire gauge numbers. Berlin and Nürnberg wire both employed the same gauge numbers, but the English and French had their own systems. It has not proved possible to identify these numbers with actual diameter measurements. because in those early times there was no way of producing fine wire of exact and unvarying diameter.

For working purposes, however, stringing approximately that intended by the maker can be obtained by assuming that the wire used for the group of notes in the extreme treble is the finest commonly available for musical instruments. This wire is of diameter approximately 0·009 inches. Where old German and French instruments are concerned it will be observed that the gauge numbers run from between 7 and 12 in the treble to 00 or 000 in the bass, involving up to fifteen changes. But in English instruments the numbers run from 4 in the treble to 13 or 15 in the bass, involving ten or twelve changes. The lowest notes in an average five octave harpsichord require a string of diameter between 0·024 inches and 0·028 inches. If a change of string, increasing by 0·001 inches or 0·0015 inches, is made at each change of gauge number to cover the extreme measurements given above, the intentions of the maker will be adequately fulfilled. This does not necessarily apply to modern harpsichords where unusual scalings are often employed.

Of fundamental importance in determining the sound of a stop is the point at which the strings are attacked. The acoustic principle involved is simple. In theory, if the string is attacked at a node that node is abolished, and with it its corresponding partial. Thus, if a string is attacked at a point exactly one seventh of its length, the node at that point is destroyed and so is the seventh harmonic. If the string is plucked in the middle, its two halves will move in a similar manner, and the second and fourth harmonics, which must depend on dissimilar movement in the two halves, will be lost. The presence and comparative strengths of individual harmonics, and the rate of their growth and decay, are the principal factors involved in varying the quality of tone; the point at which a string is attacked is therefore fundamental where tone colour is concerned.

Since keys must be short and bass strings long it is clearly impossible to keep the proportionate point of attack constant. The most important section is in the treble, where the danger occurs of plucking the string centrally, thereby eliminating the second and fourth harmonics and their accompanying clarity. The actual points of attack must vary with each stop in an instrument; and the trend of individual makers must be examined with the rest of their work.

The casework of the harpsichord is designed, both in shape and construction, to provide a frame strong enough to withstand the tension of the strings which it houses, and to contain the action and soundboard. The longside traditionally consists of one length of hard wood; the bentside in modern instruments may be laminated. Further strength is provided by the solid underside, old harpsichords being closed underneath, and by hardwood bracings running the width and occasionally also the length of the instrument, below the soundboard. Bracing designs vary from maker to maker (plates 16, 38, 51, 74). The soundboard, made of pine or (in Italy) of cypress wood, is strengthened underneath by soundbars, which support it against the down pressure of the bridges, and assist in the transmission of the vibrations. The whole case and bracing of the classical harpsichord was constructed as lightly as possible within these limits to obtain the utmost resonance.

VIRGINAL AND SPINET

Contemporary with the harpsichord throughout its history was the group of smaller keyboard instruments known variously as the spinet and virginal. In sixteenth and early seventeenth century England the latter term was generically used to cover all keyboard instruments with plucking mechanism, no matter what their shape; yet it is in fact shape which differentiates the harpsichord from the spinet and the virginal. All three instruments have the jack action described above; but the virginal and spinet are to the harpsichord very much what the upright pianoforte is to the grand: the small model. Unlike the harpsichord their strings are arranged parallel or at a slight angle with the keyboard; the scaling in the bass is kept shorter; and there is, with rare exceptions, only one string for each key.

In England, apart from its generic use, the term *virginal* has particularly referred to the oblong form of the instrument, popular in the mid seventeenth century, while the word *spinet* has been applied almost exclusively to the wing shaped model which developed in the last quarter of the seventeenth century and continued in fashion for a hundred years. In Italy the word *spinetta* was used for all forms of the small model whether oblong, triangular, or polygonal; *clavicembalo* was reserved for the harpsichord proper. In France *épinette* was used for the small instruments; *virginale* is occasionally found; *clavecin* was *harpsichord*.

The Low Countries had various names for the rectangular instrument: *spinet* (or *vierkantig spinet*), *muselar*, *virginaal*. The harpsichord was usually called *clavicymbel*.

In Germany the small instruments were called *Spinett* and *Virginal*, while the harpsichord was *Cembalo*, *Flügel*, or *Klavier*. The latter two words were also applied to the pianoforte, and *Klavier* was often synonymous with *Clavichord*.

In the early years of these instruments the various names were very loosely applied, and in the early sixteenth century the words *clavichord* and *manichord* sometimes referred to instruments with jack action as well as to the real clavichord. In 1612 or 1613 there appeared in London a volume of keyboard pieces called *Parthenia or The Maydenhead of the first musicke that ever was printed for the Virginalls*. . . . Soon after, probably in 1614, there appeared another collection: *Parthenia In-violata, or Mayden-Musicke for the Virginalls*. . . . The title page of *Parthenia* shows a rectangular instrument, but the title page of *Parthenia In-violata* shows a harpsichord.

With these examples it is easy to see that care must be taken before stating exactly what instrument, if any, is intended where sixteenth or seventeenth century music is involved. It is also clear that the expression *virginal music*, which is often loosely used and suggests to many people the use of a rectangular instrument, is in fact synonymous with *keyboard music*, and that spinet, harpsichord, clavichord, or rectangular virginal, are equally indicated where the early compositions are concerned. In the words of Praetorius, '. . . In England all these instruments be they small or large are called *Virginal*. . . .'

The small instruments, whether oblong or wing shaped, have a different quality of tone from most harpsichords, and this is a result of the differences of scaling and of the point of attack of their plectra, as well as of the different shape and size of the soundboxes. They should not be regarded as important groups of instruments which have been specified by master composers in the past, but rather as the form of domestic keyboard instrument often owned by those who did not care for music, or who could not find money or space for a harpsichord. Musically good as many are, and tonally attractive in their own right, they

21

do not stand in the front rank as important historical solo instruments, any more than the upright pianoforte does today.

CLAVICHORD

Of all keyboard musical instruments the clavichord is the most simple in construction, and the most sensitive in its musical qualities. Unlike the harpsichord its design is bounded within narrow limits by the acoustic principle on which it is constructed, and this allows but little latitude to basic individual designs. Thus the difference between the early clavichords of mid sixteenth century construction and the products of a modern workshop is slight, while harpsichords of the same periods show greater changes in mechanical and structural detail.

The clavichord is in fact a set of monochords, one being provided for each note of the keyboard. Take a stretched string running between two bridges, and near one bridge wrap a piece of cloth round the string to damp it. Strike the string at any point away from the cloth damper with the back of a knife, keeping the blade in contact with the string after the blow has occurred. We now find the string divided into two parts, one on either side of the blade. That section where the damper is placed is silent; but the remainder of the string has become a system vibrating between the blade and the bridge, the frequency of the note emitted depending on the vibrating length of string which the blade has marked off, the mass of the wire per unit length, and the stretching force. Release the blade from its contact with the string. Immediately the cloth wound round the silent part influences the entire string, and the system ceases to vibrate. This is the principle of the clavichord.

The monochord, which has just been described, can obviously sound only one note at a time, though many different notes can be produced as we attack the string at one point or another. But, as we have said, the clavichord is a collection of monochords, one for each note. Take a keyboard of compass, let us say, four octaves from C, forty-nine keys, and place that number of strings above the keys, though naturally behind the keyboard, the strings running from left to right. Arrange the hitch pins for the strings to the left of the lowest key, a bridge to the right of the highest, and place a strip of cloth round the strings close to the hitch pins, and a soundboard beneath the bridge. On the end of each key place a small upright metal blade, the tangent, which will strike the string above it when the key is depressed; and let the lowest key have its tangent nearest to the player, so that the nearest string will sound the lowest note, while the furthest tangent is placed on the top key, so that the furthest string will sound the highest note.

Here is our clavichord (plate 4). With strings of suitable mass per unit length, and with proper tuning, we have only to ensure that the tangents mark off the required speaking length of string, and we shall have a set of monochords controlled by an ordinary keyboard of any compass we may choose. A left hand bridge is unnecessary since the tangent fulfils this function as well as setting the system in motion, and two strings are usually provided for each note. This is done to increase the tone of the instrument which is very faint, partly because of the small total mass of vibrating material, and partly because of the small velo-

22

city which the tangent can obtain during its journey of only some one eighth of an inch, a factor which greatly limits the amount of energy available to make the systems vibrate.

The earliest complete account of the clavichord at present known is to be found in the manuscript of Henri Arnault of Zwolle, mentioned above. Arnault draws and describes a clavichord of three octaves, B – b², which, though some five hundred years old, is perfectly workable and in keeping with present day methods. It cannot be otherwise, as the clavichord dictates its own design. Arnault wrote in the mid fifteenth century, and there is no reason for doubting that the clavichord was well established at that time. But the monochord from which it developed had been in use long before; and it seems likely that both monochord and clavichord were in early times used as aids to the singer. Certainly the earliest references in literature to these instruments are in connection with the voice and with minstrels.

The early German rules for the Minnesingers[1] or minstrels, drawn up by Eberhard Cersne in 1404, mention the *clavichordium*. In England the choirmaster of Lincoln Cathedral, William Horwood, was in 1477 appointed to teach the boys the clavichord.[2] In 1484 William Caxton published at Westminster his translation of Geoffroy de La Tour Landry, a writer of French about a hundred years before.[3] The following passage is quoted from Caxton's translation:

'A yonge man cam to a feste, where were many lordes, ladyes, and damoysels, and arrayed as they wold have sette them to dinner, and had on hem a coote hardye, after the manner of Almayne. He cam and salewed the lordes and ladys, and when he had done to them reverence, syre Geoffrey called hym before hym, and demanded hym where his vyell or clavycordes were, and that he should make his craft: and the yonge man ansuerd, Syre, I can not medle therewith. Haa, sayd the knyght, I can not beleve it; for ye be contrefaytted and clothed lyke a mynstrell.'

In Scotland the clavichord appears in the accounts of the Lord High Treasurer from early times:

'1497. Apr. 10. Item, to John Hert, for bering a pare of *monicordis* of the kingis fra Abirdene to Strivelin, ix s.'
'1504. Oct. 15. To the cheild playit on the *monocordis*, be the kingis command, xviij s.'

In England the Privy Purse Expenses of Henry the Seventh show:

'1502. Jan. To one that sett the Kinge's *Clevechords* xxiij s. iv d.'
'1504. March. For a pair of *Clavycords* xx s.'

while those of his wife Queen Elizabeth of York show:

'1502. August. Item, the same day to Hugh Denys, for money by him delivered to a straungier that gave the Queene a payre of *Clavycordes*, in crownes for his rewarde iiij li.'

As time went on the clavichord had a somewhat varied reception from one country to another, and its early general use may in part have been due to the simplicity and small cost of its construction, though we must remember that the word, like *virginal*, was loosely used.

[1] Grove, article 'Clavichord'.　　[2] Grove, article 'Clavichord'.　　[3] S.T.C. 15296.

THE INSTRUMENT

Despite frequent references to the instrument in sixteenth century England its popularity waned as the century went on, and its use here practically ceased, so that no authentic early English examples have survived. In the same way neither France nor the Low Countries seem to have left us an example, though they certainly used the instrument in early times. [1] For common use we must turn to Italy, Germany, and the Spanish Peninsula, all of which have left many clavichords dating from early sixteenth to early nineteenth centuries. These are described in their appropriate sections.

The earliest surviving clavichords are built with a keyboard of small compass: C to a² or c³, bass short octave, was common in the early sixteenth century, though a four octave compass is found in many instruments made in the countries listed above up to the end of the eighteenth century. These clavichords were sometimes single strung, though on account of their small tone they were more generally, as has already been said, provided with two strings for each note. Many instruments, however, did not have an independent string for each *key*, the tangents of groups of two or three adjacent keys attacking the same string at suitable points in its length. Among keyboard instruments this principle is one to which the clavichord alone lends itself; it was employed as a means of reducing the size and cost of an instrument, since the music seldom if ever demanded chords containing intervals of a second. The acoustic principle is not an unfamiliar one, and a parallel may be drawn with the fretted fingerboards of the lutes and viols. The clavichords described above were known as *fretted* or *gebunden*, while those with separate strings for each key were *unfretted* or *bundfrei*. Fretted clavichords are rarely seen after about 1750. They are much less restricting in performance than those unacquainted with them might imagine; and it is possible to play ornaments and decorative passages quite easily on adjacent keys governing only one string, provided the finger articulation is sufficiently clean to allow of damping before the next tangent hits the string.

By the mid eighteenth century, a period of clavichord composition in Germany which was to culminate in the work of C. P. E. Bach, the instrument had become much larger than its forerunner of a century earlier. It could boast a larger soundboard, and the certainty of two strings for each key, with sometimes a third tuned at four foot pitch for the lowest octave and a half. The compass was gradually extended to five octaves from FF, and this in turn advanced to c⁴, a compass often found from the last years of the eighteenth century onwards. Italian clavichords, however, remained small instruments of four octaves, and in this the Italians showed the same conservative attitude they adopted towards their organs and harpsichords. In Germany, the Spanish Peninsula, and in Scandinavia, however, the clavichord continued to increase in size until it was finally supplanted by the pianoforte.

From a purely musical point of view the clavichord offers possibilities and presents problems foreign to other keyboard instruments, though most are familiar to players of bowed stringed instruments. It is easy to understand that, when a note sounds on the clavichord, the finger of the player is in intimate contact with the string through the key and the tangent,

---

[1] The Brussels Conservatoire owns a clavichord for which early Flemish origin is claimed. This instrument is decorated with block printed paper which seems to be of later date. Another candidate is in the Rijksmuseum: Compass C – c³, bass short octave.

almost as the violin player stops the string directly with the finger. This intimate and direct relationship with the string allows the clavichord player to vary his finger pressure on the key when a note is already sounding, and hence to vary the pitch of that note as string players can do. This great aid to sensitive playing was known in Germany as *Bebung*, and it is perhaps the outstanding musical feature of the clavichord. Charles Burney, visiting C. P. E. Bach in Hamburg in 1772, describes[1] the effect of *Bebung* in good clavichord playing.

'The instant I entered (Bach's house), he conducted me upstairs, into a large and elegant music room, furnished with pictures, drawings and prints of more than a hundred and fifty eminent musicians: among whom there are many Englishmen, and original portraits, in oil, of his father and grandfather. After I had looked at these, M. Bach was so obliging as to sit down to his Silbermann clavichord, and favourite instrument, upon which he played three or four of his choicest and most difficult compositions, with the delicacy, precision, and spirit, for which he is so justly celebrated among his countrymen. In the pathetic and slow movements, whenever he had a long note to express, he absolutely contrived to produce, from his instrument, a cry of sorrow and complaint, such as can only be effected upon the clavichord, and perhaps by himself.

'After dinner, which was elegantly served, and cheerfully eaten, I prevailed upon him to sit down again to a clavichord, and he played, with little intermission, till near eleven o'clock at night. During this time he grew so animated and possessed, that he not only played, but looked like one inspired. His eyes were fixed, his under lip fell, and drops of effervescence distilled from his countenance. He said, if he were to be set to work frequently, in this manner, he should grow young again. He is now fifty nine, rather short in stature, with black hair and eyes, and brown complexion, has a very animated countenance, and is of a cheerful and lively disposition.'

Johann Freidrich Reichardt (1752–1814), the German composer and writer on music, visited C. P. E. Bach in 1774, and has left an interesting account[2] of his performance:

'Herr E. Bach plays not only a very slow and songlike *Adagio* with the most touching expression, to the shame of many players on other instruments who, considering the natural capacities of their instruments, might imitate the human voice with even less difficulty; he is also able to sustain in this slow *tempo* a tone of six quavers duration with all degrees of power and softness; and this he can do in the bass as well as the treble. But he can accomplish it probably only on his precious Silbermann Clavichord, for which he has also specially written some Sonatas, in which he has introduced such long sustained tones. The same remark applies to the extraordinary power with which he renders some passages. Indeed it is the strongest *fortissimo*; and any other clavichords but Silbermann's would be knocked to pieces by it. And then again we have the most delicate *pianissimo* which would be impossible to produce on any other clavichord.'

Those familiar with the clavichord will have no difficulty in picturing these scenes, in which we note that delicacy is not the only attribute of the instrument. However, the praise lavished on the Silbermann clavichord may well be exaggerated, and due more to

[1] Burney (1773).   [2] Reichardt (1774).

Bach's skill than to his instrument. Only two or three clavichords by Silbermann have survived. and they have proved a little disappointing.

Study of the clavichord is of great assistance in cultivating a sensitive approach to the other keyboard instruments, and this has been stressed by many accepted authorities. Johann Nicolaus Forkel (1749–1818), in his essay on J. S. Bach, tells us that 'he liked best to play upon the clavichord; the harpsichord, though certainly susceptible of a very great variety of expression, had not soul enough for him; and the pianoforte was in his lifetime too much in its infancy and still much too coarse to satisfy him. He therefore considered the clavichord to be the best instrument for study, and in general for private musical entertainment. He found it the most convenient for the expression of his most refined thoughts, and did not believe it possible to produce from any harpsichord or pianoforte such a variety in the gradation of tone as on this instrument, which is indeed poor in tone, but on a small scale very flexible.'

Bernard Granville, a friend of Handel, possessed a copy of Johann Krieger's *Anmuthige Clavierübung*, given to him by Handel himself. In this book Granville wrote[1] 'The book is by one of the celebrated organ players in Germany. Mr. Handel in his youth formed himself a great deal on his plan, and said thatKrieger was one of the best writers of his time for the organ, and to form a good player; but the clavichord must be made use of by beginners instead of organ or harpsichord.'

When Burney was in Vienna in 1772 he described[2] the following incident:

'From hence I went to Mr. L'Augier's concert, which was begun by the child of eight or nine years old, who he had mentioned to me before, and who played two difficult lessons of Scarlatti, with three or four by Mr. Becke, upon a small and not good Piano Forte. The neatness of the child's execution did not so much surprise me, though uncommon, as her expression. All the *pianos* and *fortes* were so judiciously attended to: and there was such shading-off some passages, and force given to others, as nothing but the best teaching, or greatest natural feeling and sensibility could produce. I enquired of Signor Giorgio, an Italian, who attended her, upon what instrument she usually practised at home, and was answered "on the clavichord".'

C. P. E. Bach also stressed this point in his work on keyboard playing; and the matter is not disputed among those who are really familiar with these instruments.

Finally it is necessary to stress another way in which the clavichord is capable of forms of expression in which the harpsichord is deficient: this is the ability to play loud or soft, and to produce *crescendo* or *diminuendo*, by touch alone, a quality the clavichord shares with the pianoforte, and which is reflected in music specially written for the instrument. Genuine clavichord music tends to be ill at ease when transferred to the harpsichord, though much harpsichord music can be satisfactorily transferred to the clavichord.

[1] Engel (1874).   [2] Burney (1773)

CHAPTER TWO

ITALY

A s in most branches of science and art Italy was far ahead of other European countries in her development of musical instruments, and in consequence sixteenth century organs, spinets, and harpsichords of Italian construction are relatively common. The oldest dated examples of domestic keyboard instruments made elsewhere, a Hans Müller harpsichord of 1537 in the Rome Museo Nazionale degli Strumenti Musicali, and a Joost Kareest spinet of 1548 in the Brussels Conservatoire, are apparently copies of contemporary Italian work; and the importance of Italy will become clear when we see the subsequent influence of the Flemish makers. About a dozen sixteenth century instruments from the Low Countries as well as that one German example have survived, and there is one English harpsichord of 1579 made by Theeuwes of Antwerp when working in London (plates 53 and 54); but there is nothing else from that century apart from Italian work.

The earliest dated harpsichord of Italian construction appears to be an instrument of 1521, now in the Victoria and Albert Museum (plates 5 and 6). The claims[1] of what might be earlier examples have been put forward from time to time, but the authenticity of their inscriptions is too doubtful for them to be accepted. One of these harpsichords is in private hands in Siena[2]; it is clear that the present nameboard was not made for the instrument, and the inscription is probably spurious. The faking of works of art has been an accepted trade in Italy for many years, and this must always be borne in mind when examining Italian musical instruments.

After the first quarter of the sixteenth century dated harpsichords and spinets of good quality become fairly common, and there are many organs of this period. The earliest surviving Italian keyboard instrument known to the writer is the organ built in 1470–1475 at San Petronio, Bologna, now much altered. Attention may also be drawn to those two organs built about 1500 in Siena, one in the chapel of the Palazzo Publico, the other in the church of Santa Maria della Scala. But we must bear in mind that these organs were by no means the earliest examples of their kind, and earlier references to the harpsichord may be found. In 1461, for example, Sesto Tantini, an instrument maker in Modena, applied in writing to Duke Borso d'Este for payment for a *clavicinbalo* which had been supplied to him.[3] But such early references are rare.

[1] A polygonal spinet in the Perugia Museum is signed with the name *Alessandro Pasi, Modena, 1493*; but the authenticity of both instrument and inscription is most doubtful. Similarly there is a spinet in the Museo Civico, Padua, signed *Giuseppe d'Organe, 1522*. The Cooper Union, New York, owns a doubtful upright harpsichord bearing the name *Sigismondo Maler, Venice*, and the date 1521.

[2] Compass C – d³, two unisons. Inscribed *Leo Papa X/Vincenti hoc opus est ex se rude. Deme Leonis/nomen erit mutum/nominis omnis honos/MVCXVI. XF.*   [3] Hipkins (1896).

ITALY

Italian instruments, having developed early and set the path along which other countries might follow, did not, however, arrive at the complex forms to be found in the rest of Europe. A parallel is to be found in the Spanish Peninsula. In Italy the violin, in Spain the guitar, and in both these countries the voice, were the normal means of musical expression; consequently neither country was particularly sympathetic towards the over developed harpsichords, striving in vain after the expressive possibilities of the pianoforte, which appeared elsewhere in the late eighteenth century. In these two peninsulas the native woods used for instrument making were different from those at hand further north, and the individual styles of harpsichord and spinet that resulted are easy to recognize.

Italian keyboard instruments of almost every shape have survived: harpsichords both horizontal and upright, spinets, and clavichords. The wood of choice was cypress, a hard and very close grained wood allowing of finely cut mouldings. It is very durable and scarcely ever attacked by worm, so that these instruments are generally preserved in good condition. Cedar was sometimes used for soundboards, but cypress is more usually found.

The instruments are always very lightly constructed; the casework is generally about a quarter of an inch thick, instead of the three quarters of an inch so often found in England and elsewhere. The oak wrestplank is covered with the same wood used for the soundboard, and this wrestplank often does not extend much further away from the keyboard than the line of the tuning pins themselves; hence the wrestplank bridge or nut is in fact a true bridge on a section of free soundboard, separated from the main soundboard by the jacks only. This principle of construction is common in spinets and virginals of all countries, but is rarely found in harpsichords made outside Italy (plates 54 and 56). Two other characteristics tend to appear in these harpsichords: slides placed diagonally, the jacks being further from the keyboard in the bass than in the treble; and a bridge which is curved in the treble, and is either angled for the bass strings, or else breaks off to allow a separate bridge in the bass, placed more or less parallel with the keyboard (plates 6 and 7).

The system of bracing employed in Italian harpsichords to strengthen the case against the tension of the strings is a characteristic which is not found elsewhere. In most countries the necessary strength was obtained by the use of wooden braces running between the bentside and the longside of the case, to which, in England, further braces running the length of the case were added in the first half of the eighteenth century. In addition the closed underside of the case provided much extra stability (plates 38, 51, 74). In Italy a different system prevailed (plate 16). A series of wooden buttresses were built all round the case, bracing the sides against the solid boards which form the underside of the instrument.

The usual model was a harpsichord with two unison sets of strings only. There was often no means of using these separately, the slides being fixed; but an extension of the slides was sometimes made to pierce through the right hand cheek of the instrument, a primitive method of stop control also employed in the Low Countries (plates 8 and 36). There was seldom a harp stop, and the writer has only seen one apparently original lute stop of the type found in England and Germany. [1] Harpsichords with one set of strings only are occasionally found; an unsigned example is preserved in the Benton Fletcher Collection (see page 125).

[1] Upright harpsichord in the Rück collection.

28

A four foot stop was uncommon, either in place of one of the unisons or as a third set of strings. We do not know when the four foot first appeared in the harpsichord or whether this development occurred in Italy. There are several sixteenth century Italian harpsichords containing $1 \times 8'$, $1 \times 4'$, but these could originally have been $2 \times 8'$. Harpsichords containing the former disposition were built in Antwerp at the end of the century, and the four foot stop may have originated there. On the other hand the London-made harpsichord organ of Theeuwes, 1579 (plates 53 and 54), contains $2 \times 8'$, $1 \times 4'$, and this seems to be the original disposition. But in Italy a four foot was at all times an unusual feature.

There are few Italian harpsichords with two manuals. They were, however, less rare than is sometimes supposed. The inventory of the estate of Cardinal Pietro Ottoboni (*d.* 1740) the well known patron of music in Rome, lists an organ, fourteen harpsichords, and a small spinet.[1] Of the harpsichords eight had a chromatic compass, the remainder presumably having bass short octave, two were small instruments with two stops each, six were large harpsichords with two stops each, and six remaining had three stops each, no doubt two unisons and an octave.

Sixteen foot stops were to all intents and purposes unknown. The Heyer Collection contains two such instruments: one is a double harpsichord by Giovanni de Perticis of Florence, 1683; the other example has one manual and is signed by Bartolomeo Cristofori of Florence, 1726 (page 37). Two other harpsichords attributed to Cristofori also contain a sixteen foot: one in the Deutsches Museum, the other in the Neupert Collection. But in none of these four cases is the sixteen foot an original feature. The author can trace no original sixteen foot stop in an Italian harpsichord.

There are about half a dozen Italian harpsichords with three keyboards:

1602, Simone Remoti -	- Württembergisches Landesgewerbemuseum, Stuttgart
1627, Stefanus Bolcioni	- The Russell Collection
n.d. Cristofori - -	- Michigan University
1779, Vincentius Sodi -	- Metropolitan Museum
1702, Cristofori - -	- Deutsches Museum
1703, Cristofori - -	- Neupert Collection

The reason for this unusual construction might be the advantage of having three levels of tone available without the necessity of changing the stops. The register of these instruments are usually disposed as follows:

Upper manual: $1 \times 4'$
Middle manual: $1 \times 8'$, $1 \times 4'$
Lower manual: $2 \times 8'$

Unfortunately the jacks and slides of these three manual harpsichords have been altered, and it is therefore impossible to ascertain the original disposition. Moreover features of their basic construction usually show alterations, and an extra keyboard has certainly been added to most of them at some time after they were built.

[1] Kirkpatrick (1953).

Care must be taken before accepting the inscriptions on these instruments, since unsigned work has been named and dated by unscrupulous dealers. References to three manual harpsichords appear in the works of Mersenne, Marpurg, and Adlung, and in various eighteenth century advertisements, but the only undoubtedly original example known to the author is the Hieronymus Hass harpsichord of 1740, described in chapter seven (plates 87 and 88).

Though Italian harpsichords are numerous, spinets seem to have been equally popular. In Italy the spinet had a very distinctive form, being almost always a polygonal instrument with five or six sides. The keyboard was placed more or less centrally, and projected from the front. The jacks were not placed in a slide, but in slots cut directly in the soundboard itself; and they tend to be further from the nut in the bass than is found in the equivalent English virginals and spinets. Very occasionally an example is found with two strings for each note, both of eight foot pitch, and such an instrument can be seen in the Benton Fletcher Collection. Octave spinets were common, and these were either rectangular or triangular, the keyboard sometimes projecting as in the larger model (plate 14). Octave harpsichords were also made; but few of these exist today. An example by Domenicus of Pesaro, dated 1543, is in the Paris Conservatoire (and see pages 36, 117 and 125).

Charles Burney toured Italy in 1770, and left this impression of the keyboard instruments he then saw: [1]

'To persons accustomed to English Harpsichords, all the keyed instruments on the continent appear to great disadvantage. Throughout Italy they generally have little octave spinnets to accompany singing, in private houses, sometimes in triangular form, but more frequently in the shape of our old virginals; of which the keys are so noisy, and the tone so feeble, that more wood is heard than wire. The best Italian harpsichord which I met with for touch, was that of Signor Grimani at Venice; and for tone, that of Monsignor Reggio at Rome; but I found three English harpsichords in the three principal cities of Italy, which are regarded by the Italians as so many phenomena. One was made by Shudi, and is in the possession of the Hon. Mrs. Hamilton at Naples. The other two, which are of Kirkman's make, belong to Mrs. Richie at Venice, and to the Hon. Mrs. Earl, who resided at Rome when I was there.'

Where Italy was concerned Burney had reason for his remarks. The instruments produced there are extraordinarily limited by the standards of Kirckman or Shudi, though they are excellent when used with strings or with the voice, as they have splendid blending and carrying power. As solo instruments they are not so versatile, though entirely adequate for Italian and foreign compositions of the sixteenth and seventeenth centuries.

A certain number of instruments in the form of upright harpsichords (*clavicytheria*), sometimes of unusual construction or dimensions, have come from Italy. Examples are to be found in the Donaldson Collection, the Heyer Collection, the Paris Conservatoire, the Metropolitan Museum, the Belle Skinner Collection, and elsewhere. While some are certainly examples of seventeenth or eighteenth century craftsmanship, others leave considerable doubt as to their origins. The early sixteenth century German musical writer, Sebastian

[1] Burney (1771).

CLAVICHORDS

Virdung, states in his *Musica Getutscht* published at Basel in 1511, that *clavicytheria* were provided with gut strings; but no concrete evidence of this has come to hand. However, the word *clavicytherium* means *keyed lyre*, and a lyre had gut strings by definition. A remarkable upright harpsichord is in the Rück Collection. This seventeenth or early eighteenth century instrument has two unisons, an octave, and a lute stop, this last being the only apparently authentic Italian lute stop known to the writer. The examples in the Paris Conservatoire and the Deutsches Museum are good representatives of their kind; but the few surviving Italian upright harpsichords are so far removed from the main stream of harpsichord making that they may be left without further examination.

Clavichords were made in considerable numbers in Italy (plates 11 and 12). They were of simple construction, usually fretted, and very seldom signed; they were apparently used by those who could afford nothing more elaborate, and they were consequently treated by their makers as something on which to waste no unnecessary time. They were, as usual, made of cypress wood, and were small instruments intended for standing on a table. They are very similar to, and often indistinguishable from, small German clavichords of the seventeenth century; both types can make good music, simple and unpretentious though they are.

A group of crudely faked clavichords, Italian by construction, but of mid or late nineteenth century date, and not sixteenth century as they pretend, can be identified by the style they have in common with one of their fellows, signed and dated *Alex. Trasontini 1537*. This is in the Metropolitan Museum, and is illustrated in James, plate XII. Others include a clavichord signed *Aloysius Ventura* and dated 1533, formerly owned by the late Miss Margaret Glyn; one signed *Alex Trasontini 1537* in the Claudius Collection, Copenhagen; and one the property of Marcel Salomon in Paris, bearing a picture of Venice in the lid. A spinet of similar type, signed *Aloysius Ventura* and dated 1533, is in the Gemeentemuseum. These are all made from pieces of old instruments, and the leather covers to some of their cases have been taken from early books; but the lettering of the inscriptions betrays them though collectors and museums have been deceived.

The compasses of Italian instruments, both harpsichords and spinets, fall into two basic categories: four and a half octaves with bass short octave, either $GG - c^3$, or $C - f^3$. The latter keyboard is far more common than the GG model. These two keyboards, differing by a fourth, suggest

1. that they are different members of the same family, one covering a lower range of notes than the other, *or*
2. that they cover the same range of notes, one model serving the purpose of a transposing instrument, a practice common in the Low Countries (see chapter 3).

Musically there are good reasons for both explanations. The two compasses are needed for solo and continuo playing; the transposition imposed on the accompanist, when playing with voices or instruments during the sixteenth and much of the seventeenth centuries, calls for a transposing keyboard. But it is not possible to demonstrate the exclusive use of either instrument for either purpose, since their scalings are extremely variable, eight foot models[1] showing a c² which ranges between about 10 and 15 inches, regardless of the overall compass. Bearing this in mind, and remembering the freedom allowed by tuning itself, which must always defeat any attempt at the precise location of pitch in these instruments, the writer can do no more than draw the reader's attention to these two types of keyboard and their various functions.

While these two keyboard compasses provide the framework and rule, there are of course many variations and exceptions. Throughout the entire history of early keyboard instruments in Italy the lowest octave is generally obtained by short octave tuning; but a chromatic keyboard is not rare, and makes its appearance regularly in the sixteenth century. A striking example is the Baffo harpsichord of 1579 in the Paris Conservatoire. This very large harpsichord (eight feet $3\frac{3}{16}$ inches) has a chromatic compass of nearly five octaves: AA – f³ (originally FF – d³), and the scaling is as follows:

$$AA \quad 83\frac{1}{2} \text{ in.}$$
$$c^2 \quad 11\frac{3}{4} \text{ in.}$$
$$f^3 \quad 4 \text{ in.}$$

Less common than a chromatic compass is the presence of the broken octave which appears in the late seventeenth century. The Paris Conservatoire owns two such instruments, both by Faby of Bologna (plates 2 and 3). The earlier is dated 1677 and has a compass of just over four octaves: C – d³, bass short octave, with the two lowest accidentals split; the later instrument is dated 1691, and is a GG – c³ harpsichord, bass short octave, the lowest two accidental keys split. The very early instruments tend to have a smaller compass, four octaves from C, bass short octave being common; but in later instruments the top note strays up to d³ and thence to f³.

An occasional instrument attempts the frankly experimental. Vito Trasuntino, an early seventeenth century maker, has left an instrument which was known as *Archicembalo* or *Large Harpsichord* (plate 13). This instrument is the property of the Liceo Communale in Bologna, and is on loan to the Museo Civico. It is a four octave harpsichord from C; but each accidental is divided into four keys, and there is an extra key divided in two parts between each of the natural key semitones, producing thirty-two keys to each octave, and a hundred and twenty-five to the keyboard. Such quarter tone instruments were, of course, experimental and scientific essays, and it is unlikely that the least worldly maker would have imagined that a market would be found for them; but it is interesting that such experiments were not infrequently made. Trasuntino's example was inspired by the composer and theorist Nicola Vicentino, whose *L'antica musica ridotta alla moderna prattica*, published at Rome in 1555, suggests a keyboard to include the three Greek systems: Diatonic, Chromatic, and Enharmonic. The matter was further discussed in *Il Desiderio* . . . of Ercole Bottrigari published in Venice in 1594.

The Brussels Conservatoire owns a harpsichord made a few years later, in 1619, by Boni of Cortona, in which each E♭ and A♭ key is divided into two parts. The lowest octave is

---

[1] Quint instruments were sometimes made, as we know from Praetorius and also from surviving examples. An Italian harpsichord exhibited at the Paris Exhibition, 1889, bore the inscription: 'fait à Milan pour sonner à la quinte; refait pour sonner au ton par J. J. Nesle, 1780.'

short, F♯ and A♭ being divided to give D and E at the front and a chromatic sequence at the back. Above this part of the scale each E♭ is divided to give D♯ at the front and E♭ at the back. Similarly each A♭ key gives G♯ at the front and A♭ at the back. This harpsichord has only one set of strings. These split keys were intended to avoid the interval known as the 'wolf': the dissonant fourth between keys E♭ and A♭ in mean tone temperament.

Attention may here be drawn to the use as a practice instrument which organists made of their harpsichords and spinets in Italy. The underside of the lowest octave or so of keys sometimes reveals attachments for strings to be connected to a pedalboard. Pedal pulldowns were found quite commonly in Italian organs though they were used in a very elementary way. The Jerome harpsichord of 1521 (plates 5 and 6) once had a pedalboard of this kind.

The simple instruments described in the preceding paragraphs satisfied the Italian market no less in the eighteenth than in the early part of the sixteenth century. A small book of 38 pages was, however, printed in Rome in 1775, which discusses many problems with which the advanced instrument makers of France and England were concerned, but which were left to the unambitious Italian to deal with in book form. This anonymous work: *Lettera dell' Autore del Nuovo Cembalo Angelico Inventato in Roma* deals with such devices as pedals to control the movement of the slides, the harp stop, and the use of buff leather for the plectra. A double jack with tongues facing in both directions is also discussed in detail, and a plate is included (plate 17); but few of these inventions were put into effect.

The author begins with a description of the essential feature of the *Cembalo Angelico*, which is said to consist of the substitution of soft leather plectra for the crow or vulture quills generally used in Italy. Six further sections complete the book (appendix 2).

The first section again confirms that jacks in Italy were usually furnished with quill plectra, and, as examination of old examples will often show, that the tongue was often kept upright by small springs of brass or of hen's quill instead of by hog's bristle springs. In the second section the author describes in great detail the method of making his leather plectra. These were constructed of ordinary thin sole leather, covered on top with a layer of thick but soft glove leather. This was to be stuck to the sole leather with the rough side uppermost, clove glue known as *cervonia* being the most suitable adhesive for the purpose. The name of this new plectrum was *polpastrello*; and an essential feature was that it was long and slanted downwards, so as to exert a stroking action on the string as it passed it. This leather must have been not unlike the buff leather sometimes used by Shudi, Kirckman, and Taskin for their lower eight foot stops.

As regards the changing of the stops we are told that most harpsichords with two registers had one fixed register and one movable, thus confining the player to two levels of tone. The fixed register was always quilled, and if the other was leathered its effect was lost, since it could not be played alone. But if each jack was fitted with two tongues facing in opposite directions, one containing a leather plectrum, the other a quill, the player had the advantage of using either or both sets of strings with either leather or quill plectra. This is explained as a great advantage, and a detailed description is given of how this movement of the two slides could be controlled by a pedal.

Section four describes the harp stop or *sordino*, and the method of fitting a pedal to it. In section five the common fault of mechanical noise is dealt with, and instructions are given as to the bushing—very unusual at this time—of the keys, both at the pivot point and also at the rear guide blade. This was to be done with soft leather, and the guides were to be similarly treated in order to prevent rattling jacks.

Lastly the author tells us that he has fitted organ pedals to his instruments, and he goes on to praise his invention. Tonally, he says, it was far superior to the harsh quilled harpsichord, and more like the hammer harpsichords (*cembali a martelli*), in that the touch could determine the loudness of the resulting note, a soft touch causing the plectrum to slide gently across the string while a sharp attack produced three times the volume. Mechanically the instrument was far superior to the hammer harpsichords of even Bartolo Fiorentino (i.e. Bartolo Cristofori of Florence), since the action was silent, it repeated efficiently, and it provided proper damping.

This interesting book tells us a good deal about contemporary Italian keyboard instruments; and it is strange that after centuries of stagnation an Italian instrument maker should suddenly concern himself with just those problems which were occupying the attention of the last harpsichord makers in France and England: the buff leather of Taskin, Abraham and Joseph Kirckman, and Broadwood, the machine stops and pedals of the English school, and the knee levers and pedals of Taskin and Erard.

Mention has already been made of the faking which Italian musical instruments have suffered in the past. It appears that much of this was the responsibility of one Leopoldo Franciolini who worked in the latter half of the last century in Florence, at Piazza Santa Maria Novella 6, and at Via de' Benci 14, and who was responsible for the sale to eager collectors of many instruments that he had 'improved' by the addition of signatures, dates, decoration, and so on. Anything connected with Italian instruments which does not seem to be in keeping with the style or musical practice of the period, and which is not obvious *bona fide* renovation or enlargement, must be viewed with suspicion. The spurious clavichords already mentioned have not with any certainty been tracked to this source, though it is by no means improbable that Florence was their birthplace. It must also be remembered that the great demand in the last two centuries for Italian works of art, whether sculpture, pictures, antiquities, or musical instruments, placed temptation in the way of many who were unable to resist it; and inexperienced buyers eagerly acquired what they believed to be unique works of art, and from which, happily, they derived much pleasure.

The earliest dated harpsichord which we now have is the small instrument of 1521 in the Victoria and Albert Museum, already mentioned. The maker, Jerome of Bologna (*Bononiensis*), who was working in Rome when his harpsichord was built, has not left anything else now on record. This instrument is typical of its kind. The compass is C to d^3 (originally c^3), bass short octave; there are two eight foot sets of strings, and two rows of jacks, both of which are fixed; the jackslides are parallel with the keyboard. The short treble scaling is also typical of Italy:

$$C \quad 57\tfrac{1}{2} \text{ in.}$$
$$c^2 \quad 10\tfrac{1}{2} \text{ in.}$$
$$d^3 \quad 4\tfrac{1}{2} \text{ in.}$$

This instrument, as already noted, at one time had pedal pulldowns attached to the lowest fourteen keys.

Giovanni Cellini of Florence (*c.* 1460–*c.* 1527) father of the more famous Benvenuto, was an architect who, according to his son, made musical instruments, though unfortunately none are at present known to have survived. In his autobiography Benvenuto says:

'At that time my father made wonderful organs with wooden pipes, and harpsichords (*gravi cenboli*) which were the best and finest that had ever been seen, as well as beautifully made viols, lutes and harps.'

In Venice Giovanni Antonio Baffo seems to have been working for a great many years, if the dates on all his instruments are genuine, as he has left dated work from 1523 to 1581. Fifty eight years of working life was an exceptional thing four hundred years ago, and it is possible that the first date is not authentic or that the later instruments may have been the work of a son. Eight possible instruments are recorded: two are spinets, six are harpsichords:

1523. Kunst und Industrie Museum, Vienna.
   This harpsichord disappeared during the 1939–1945 war.

1570. Musée de Cluny, Paris
   Spinet. C – f³, bass short octave.

1574. Victoria and Albert Museum.
   C – f³, chromatic. 2 × 8′.

1574. Nyack, New York, in private ownership.

1579. Conservatoire, Paris.
   AA – f³, originally FF – d³, chromatic. 2 × 8′.

1580. Heyer Collection, Leipzig.
   C – f³, chromatic. 2 × 8′.
   [Doubtful authenticity.]

1581. Messrs. Rushworth and Dreaper, Liverpool.
   Spinet. C – f³, chromatic.

1581. Historisches Museum, Basle.
   GG – c³, less AA♭.
   Two manuals. 2 × 8′, 1 × 4′.
   [Doubtful authenticity.]

Both the spinets have a compass from C to f³, though only the example of 1581 has a chromatic keyboard. The harpsichord of 1581 in Basle has two keyboards and includes a four-foot. If unaltered this is the earliest double harpsichord known; but there are reasons for thinking the upper keyboard and the four foot later additions, and for doubting the Baffo inscription. It is curious that so many of these instruments should be dated 1581, and a photographic comparison of the style of their inscriptions as a test of authenticity might be illuminating.

At the end of the sixteenth century there worked in Venice Alessandro Bertolotti, whose spinet of 1585 is in the Russell Collection (plates 9 and 10). The compass is $C-f^3$, bass short octave; and, as is sometimes found in Italian spinets, there is a spare string, jack, and slot for the lowest key, thereby allowing a dominant bass or low tonic final below C. Bertolloti built an organ and harpsichord combined which can be seen in the Brussels Conservatoire (plate 8). It is dated one year earlier than the spinet. The organ has three stops: an eight foot wood, a quint of wood, and a four foot metal. The harpsichord has one eight and one four foot. The compass of the organ is four octaves from C, while that of the harpsichord is $GG-c^3$. Such claviorgans were by no means unusual in Italy at this time.

Other Venetian instrument makers of the sixteenth century include Giovanni Celestini, whose earliest known spinet is in the Donaldson collection. It bears the date 1593 and has a large compass: $GG-f^3$, bass short octave. Several of Celestini's harpsichords are still in existence; his latest known instrument is a very fine spinet of 1610 in the Brussels Conservatoire.

Vito Trasuntino has already been mentioned in connection with his archicembalo of 1606. The Donaldson Collection contains a harpsichord by Alessandro Trasuntino, whom Hipkins thought to have been grandfather of Vito. This instrument is dated 1531; the compass is $GG-c^3$, bass short octave, and there are two unison registers.

A large number of harpsichords and spinets signed by Domenico of Pesaro (*Pisaurensis*) are in existence. These are dated between 1533 (a spinet in the Heyer Collection), and 1600, (a harpsichord sold by Sotheby and Co. on 11 February 1938, and now lost from sight). Sixty-seven working years suggest that either these instruments are the products of a family workshop or else that the dates are not authentic. Two of the instruments are clavichords: one dated 1543 in the Heyer Collection, the other dated 1547 in the Paris Conservatoire. The latter museum also contains the harpsichord by Domenico dated 1543 which is built at four foot pitch.

Compass: $C-c^3$, bass short octave
Scaling: C $32\frac{3}{4}$ in.
            c^2 6 in.
            c^3 $2\frac{3}{4}$ in.

Among other early makers are Francesco Portalupis of Verona, who made the spinet of 1523 in the Paris Conservatoire, and Francesco of Padua (*Patavinus*), a Hungarian. A spinet of 1527 by Francesco of Padua is in the Brussels Conservatoire, and a harpsichord of his, dated 1561, compass $GG-c^3$, bass short octave, is in the Deutsches Museum. This latter instrument contains $1 \times 8'$, $1 \times 4'$, originally perhaps $2 \times 8'$.

Among early seventeenth century makers is one whose instruments are represented by a three manual harpsichord dated 1627 in the Russell Collection, a spinet of 1631 in the Rhode Island School of Design, and a spinet dated 1629 now lost from sight. Stefano

Bolcioni of Prato lived in 1634 in the Via dei Servi, Florence, and in that year was admitted to the Instrument Maker's Guild. The writer has no doubt that the harpsichord of 1627 which has compass C – g^3, bass short octave, and three sets of strings: two unisons and an octave, has undergone alteration from its original form, when it probably had two keyboards only. Its inscription is of doubtful origin.

Milan produced a family of keyboard instrument makers in the Rossis. Annibale dei Rossi and his son Ferrante produced spinets from about 1550 onwards, and examples of their work can be seen in the Victoria and Albert Museum, in the Turin City Museum, and at Michigan University. These makers must not be confused with Toma Rossi of Viterbo, whose harpsichord of 1759 is in the Belle Skinner Collection.

A curious figure in the world of Italian instrument making is Father Theodoric Pedrini, a Lazarist priest, who was born in 1670. In 1702 Pedrini was sent from Rome to act as court musician to the Chinese Emperor K'ang Hsi (1662–1723). His journey must have been a most arduous one, as he did not reach Peking until 1711; but once there he remained until his death in 1745. Together with other duties Father Pedrini taught music to the Royal children, and made harpsichords and organs. Whether any of these have survived is unknown. The National Library in Peking has a set of eight sonatas for violin and figured bass by Pedrini, written under the pen name Nepridi.

At least four harpsichords have survived from the workshop of Nicolaus de Quoco, possibly father and son, at work in Florence between 1615 and 1694. The early instrument is in the Claudius Collection, Copenhagen; a double manual harpsichord dated 1690 is in the Lisbon Conservatorio; and two instruments bearing the date 1694 are in the Brussels Conservatoire and the Smithsonian Institution. Besides these four harpsichords are two more, dated 1640 and 1680, which passed through Franciolini's hands and are lost from sight.

Faby of Bologna has already been mentioned in connection with his two fine harpsichords of 1677 and 1691 in the Paris Conservatoire (plates 2 and 3), the only examples of his work known to the writer. Contemporary with Faby was Girolamo Zenti of Viterbo and Florence, whose surviving harpsichords and spinets show that he was at work between 1633 and 1683. Zenti came to England at some time in the 1660's and served as harpsichord maker to King Charles II. He was succeeded in this appointment in about 1668 by another Italian, Andrea Testa.

Bartolomeo Cristofori of Padua is an important figure in the history of instrument making because of his work in connection with the development of hammer action. Born on 4 May 1655, he had become by 1690 Court Instrument Maker to Prince Ferdinando de' Medici at Florence; and there he remained until his death on 27 January 1731. When the Prince died in 1713 Cristofori was appointed curator of instruments to his father, the Grand Duke Cosimo III, and in that capacity had charge of his eighty-four musical instruments. Of these over half were keyboard instruments, and among them were seven made by Cristofori (appendix 1). Hammer action was gaining ground in Cristofori's mind in the early years of the century, as in 1711 Maffei, in Vol. V of his *Giornale dei Letterati d'Italia*, states that Cristofori had made four *Gravicembali col piano e forte*, three of which were large in form and one small. [1] He persevered in this work, and Queen Maria Barbara of Spain possessed among other instruments five Florentine pianofortes, one of which had been built in 1731 by Cristofori's pupil, Giovanni Ferrini[2] (appendix 18). It is possible that the others were the work of Cristofori himself. That they were inadequate in mechanical design is suggested by the fact that according to the Queen's Inventory two had been turned into harpsichords. Cristofori's known instruments, or at any rate those which bear his name, are listed below:

1693. Heyer Collection, Leipzig.
        Spinet. $C - d^3$, chromatic. $2 \times 8'$.

1703. Deutsches Museum, Munich.
        Harpsichord. $C - f^3$, chromatic.
        Three manuals. $1 \times 16'$, $1 \times 8'$, $1 \times 4'$.
        Originally $2 \times 8'$, $1 \times 4'$.
        [Doubtful authenticity.]

1703. Neupert Collection, Nürnberg.
        Harpsichord. $FF - f^3$, chromatic.
        Three manuals. $1 \times 16'$, $1 \times 8'$, $1 \times 4'$.
        Originally $2 \times 8'$, $1 \times 4'$.
        [Doubtful authenticity.]

1720. Metropolitan Museum, New York.
        Grand pianoforte. $C - f^3$, chromatic.

1722. Count Giusti, Padua (1927).
        Grand pianoforte.

1722. Heyer Collection, Leipzig.
        Harpsichord. $C - c^3$, chromatic. $2 \times 8'$.

1726. Heyer Collection, Leipzig.
        Harpsichord. $C - c^3$, chromatic.
        One manual. $1 \times 16'$, $1 \times 8'$, $1 \times 4'$.
        Originally $1 \times 8'$, $1 \times 4'$, $1 \times 2'$.
        [Doubtful authenticity.]

1726. Heyer Collection, Leipzig.
        Grand pianoforte. $C - c^3$, chromatic.

n.d.   Heyer Collection, Leipzig.
        Harpsichord. $FF - f^3$, chromatic. $1 \times 8'$, $1 \times 4'$.
        [Doubtful authenticity.]

n.d.   Michigan University.
        Harpsichord. $C - d^3$, bass short octave.
        Three manuals. $2 \times 8'$, $1 \times 4'$.
        [Doubtful authenticity.]

[1] The author's copy of *Le Istitutioni Harmoniche* of Zarlino, 1558, contains a MS. account of an *Arpi Cimbalo del Piano e Forte* made by Cristofori in 1700. This was written by Federigo Meccoli, who was Director of Music to the Grand Duke Cosimo III in 1704.   [2] Kirkpatrick (1953).

DECORATION

This curious list contains instruments upon the genuine quality of which much doubt has been cast, and in view of the fact that several of these passed through the hands of Franciolini this doubt may well be justified. The Michigan instrument, which the writer has not seen, is generally discredited; and note should be taken of the three instruments with sixteen foot stops, two of which were originally built for two unisons and an octave only, while the example at Leipzig was intended for eight, four, and two foot registers. The third keyboard of the harpsichord in Munich is reported to have been constructed by Steingräber of Berlin;[1] that of the 1703 instrument in Bamberg is considered by Dr. Hanns Neupert to be a later addition, and the inscription is also under suspicion.

Another instrument with three manuals, sold by Franciolini (appendix 3), is signed *Simone Remoti fecit Ao 1602. Cimbalis bene sonantibus.* This harpsichord by an otherwise unknown maker is now in the Württembergisches Landesgewerbemuseum, Stuttgart; its authenticity is open to question.

Lastly attention must be drawn to the work of Alessandro Riva, an instrument maker of Bergamo, who was born on 5 February 1805, and died on 21 December 1868. The last spinet of the period before the modern revival known to the writer is Riva's instrument of 1839 in the Heyer Collection. The compass is from C to a^3 chromatic. This spinet serves as a reminder that the early keyboard instruments lingered on in unfashionable places for longer than is generally recognized.

DECORATION

Italian keyboard instruments, whether clavichords, upright harpsichords, polygonal spinets or ordinary harpsichords, can be identified by the cypress or cedar wood of which they are almost invariably made. They are of simple appearance, the sand coloured wood being undecorated except for mouldings and, in the more elaborate examples, studs of ivory placed round the upper edge of the case. The naturals are of boxwood, bone or ivory, and have arcaded fronts; the accidentals are often made of ebony or rosewood. The Italians generally left their instruments unsigned; but, when the maker's name and date appear, they are to be found written on the highest or lowest key or burned into the case above the keys by means of a branding iron. A rose of geometrical design, made of wood, leather, or varnished paper, was usually set into the soundboard; but Italian craftsmen do not appear to have incorporated their initials in the rose, as was the custom in the Low Countries, in France, and sometimes in England.

The instruments were provided with cases of much the same shape as themselves in which they were kept when not in use; but for playing they could be taken out of their cases and placed on a table. Polygonal virginals were usually fitted with an outer case of rectangular shape. The legs or stands of these instruments were separate from the case, and consisted of two separate trestle stands, sometimes elaborately carved.

The outer case received one of three forms of decoration: leather, fabric, or paint. Examples of leather covered cases include the Jerome harpsichord of 1521 in the Victoria

[1] Information from Dr. Ulrich Rück of Nürnberg, and from Herr Otto Marx, formerly of Leipzig.

and Albert Museum, and an unsigned spinet in the Fitzwilliam Museum, Cambridge. The leather was glued and nailed on to the wooden case, and it was usually decorated with gilt tooling. The use of fabric may be seen in the Victoria and Albert Museum in the unsigned hexagonal spinet which bears the arms of Queen Elizabeth I, the case of this instrument being covered with crimson velvet and lined with yellow silk. In view of the perishable nature of fabrics, early examples of this form of decoration are rare.

The great majority of outer cases were, however, painted. The outside of the case was usually fairly plain: perhaps garlands of flowers or draped designs on a coloured ground. Inside the lid there was often a painting, and family arms were sometimes incorporated. A few very elaborate instruments had cases decorated with jewels and marbles, and two well-known specimens are in the Victoria and Albert Museum. Such things are however rare; and rare also are fine pictures in Italian instruments. Farinelli had a harpsichord painted by Gaspard Poussin (1613–1675), and another instrument decorated by this painter is in the Palazzo Rospigliosi in Rome. The ordinary decorative painting found on Italian instruments usually lacks the refinement found on examples from other countries; but if the painting is less refined, it is also in keeping with the simple musical quality and the robust tone of the instruments made in Italy.

CHAPTER THREE

THE LOW COUNTRIES

T he history of harpsichord making in Europe is the history of two basic schools: one consisting of the independent but similar methods of Italy and the Spanish Peninsula, while the other school was inspired by Italy and founded in Antwerp. The two types of instrument always differed in construction, in tonal qualities, and in the materials from which they were made; and they retained these differences to the end of the eighteenth century. From the Antwerp school derive all the instrument makers of France, England, and Germany; and the background against which the Flemish masters worked must be considered here.

In the fourteenth century Bruges, owing to its position on the Zwyn, possessed what was perhaps the finest harbour in North Europe, and as a result of this was one of the greatest centres of commerce in its day. Unfortunately, in the first half of the fifteenth century the Zwyn began to silt up, and as the fortunes of Bruges declined those of Antwerp rose. The international trade of this great port brought a prosperity to the city in which artistic life flourished, and the Bruges schools of painting and architecture were soon transferred to Antwerp. It was thus natural that musical instrument making should have flourished in a city where craftsmanship of all kinds was much in demand.

An examination of the Antwerp city archives shows references to instrument making from the late years of the fifteenth century onwards, and it is clear that at this time harpsichords were part of the craft of the organ builder. Daniel van der Distelen is mentioned[1] as an organ builder in 1505, Hans van Cuelen (i.e. of Cologne) was making harpsichords in 1512,[1] Antonius Mors built *un clavicordium* for Eleanora, Archduchess of Austria in 1516.[1]

The craftsmen of Antwerp were supervised in the standard of their work by their Guilds; and the instrument makers, who had no Guild of their own, were obliged, in order to be allowed to decorate the cases of their instruments, to seek admission to the Guild of Saint Luke, which controlled the activities of the painters. Here their names appear, though not often designated instrument makers, during the first half of the sixteenth century.

To end this anomaly about ten makers petitioned the Deacons of the Guild in 1557, asking to be admitted as harpsichord makers and not as artists. Permission was granted, and in 1588 the magistrates of the city issued an ordinance establishing in detail the duties and rights of the petitioners (appendix 4). No one might set up in business as an instrument

---

[1] Stellfeld.

41

maker, nor trade in keyboard instruments, unless he had served a suitable apprenticeship and been examined and admitted to the Guild. After admission, however, he might enjoy all the privileges and liberties of full painter members of the Guild in his capacity as musical instrument maker.

All this was to have an important effect on instrument making. The craftsman's position had been established, and the standard of his work had been secured; apprentices were obliged to study in the masters' shops, and the basis of a national school was thus founded. By virtue of Antwerp's position as a great trading centre instruments made there were, by the end of the century and for a hundred years to come, exported to all the countries of Northern Europe.

Only three instruments made by the original supplicants for admission to the Guild of Saint Luke as instrument makers seem to have survived. One is the work of Joost Kareest, a son of Hans van Cuelen, who was admitted to the Guild as a painter in 1523. This instrument, now in the Brussels Conservatoire, is a hexagonal spinet with a compass of four octaves from C, bass short octave. The natural keys are of boxwood, and the instrument is much like an Italian spinet of the same period. It was made in 1548. The second instrument is a double virginal made by Martin van der Biest in 1580 for Alessandro Farnese, Duke of Parma, the Governor General of the Netherlands under Philip II of Spain, and it is in the Germanisches Museum at Nürnberg (plate 20). The main instrument is a large oblong virginal with a chromatic compass of four octaves from C, the keyboard being to the left. The right hand part of the instrument contains a drawer, extending under the wrestplank and soundboard, containing a small octave virginal of similar compass and decoration. The original compass of both these virginals was $C-c^3$, bass short octave; their present chromatic basses seem to be seventeenth century work. Double virginals of this kind are rare and seem to have been made exclusively in Antwerp. Only nine are known at the present time; in addition there are four examples of a harpsichord with a virginal built into the bentside, resulting in an oblong instrument with keyboards on two sides (appendix 5). The third instrument is the work of Lodewyck Theeuwes (page 65).

Little remains of the work of those who were first admitted to the Guild after 1558. Hans Moermans was admitted in 1570, and four harpsichords by him: two double and two single manuals, were sold at the Régibo sale of 1897; but only one, in private ownership in Redhill, Surrey, can now be traced. [1] Hans Grauwels, Master in 1579, was the maker of an undated virginal now in the Brussels Conservatoire (plate 19). This virginal is oblong, with the keyboard placed centrally, and it has a compass of three octaves and a sixth; $C-a^2$, bass short octave. A later double virginal of 1600 by Lodewijk Grauwels, probably the son of Hans Grauwels, is in the Metropolitan Museum. In 1579 Hans Ruckers was admitted to the Guild, and with him Flemish harpsichord making acquired its European fame.

The founder of this remarkable family of instrument makers was born at Malines, probably between 1550 and 1555, and he was the son of Franz Ruckers. On 25 June 1575 Hans Ruckers was married [2] to Adriana Knaeps in Notre Dame, Antwerp, and the marriage

---

[1] This harpsichord bears the date 1642, and it may therefore be the work of a son of Hans Moermans.
[2] Martin van der Biest was a witness at the marriage.

produced some ten children. Ruckers must have served an apprenticeship to one of the instrument makers already a member of the Guild of Saint Luke, for he was himself admitted in 1579; but he did not acquire citizenship of Antwerp until the following year. He died between July 1597 and December 1599. [1] But the years before had been occupied with the most industrious instrument making, as is shown by the constant references to Ruckers' work in diaries, inventories, sales, and collections, in all parts of Europe from his own time onwards. He was also responsible for some organ building and maintenance in Antwerp, though this was certainly only a small part of his work. Of his children we must notice two: Hans the younger, often called Jan (Jean), who was born in 1578, and Andries (Andreas), born in 1579.

Jan Ruckers, like Andries served his apprenticeship under his father, and he was admitted into the Guild in 1611. He married Maria Waelrant in 1604, and died in 1643. [2] His nephew, probably by marriage, was Jan Couchet, who was later trained by his uncle in the same tradition of harpsichord making.

Andries Ruckers was married in 1605 to Catherina de Vriese, and he was admitted to the Guild in 1610. In view of this date it is curious to note that the Russell Collection has a double harpsichord by Andries Ruckers dated 1608, a time when the rules of his apprenticeship must have forbidden his signing instruments personally. This example may, however, have been made under his father's direction and signed by him at a later date when repairing it. The year of his death is unknown.

Andries Ruckers had a son of the same name, baptized on 31 March 1607, who worked with him; and the later instruments bearing this name must be the work of Andries II and not of the father. He married Jeanne Flechts in about 1637, the year he was admitted to the Guild, and had three children. Hipkins, writing in Grove's *Dictionary*, attributed five instruments dated between 1655 and 1667 to Andries II; these have all disappeared, and it is difficult to know on what grounds Hipkins actually made his identifications, unless he considered Andries I too old to work in the latter years. The son was certainly producing his own instruments in 1644, as a single manual harpsichord of that date with original nameboard, now in the Vleeshuis, Antwerp, is signed *Andreas Ruckers den ouden me fecit Antverpiae*.

Finally, mention must be made of Christopher Ruckers, two of whose virginals in the family styles are preserved: one in the Metropolitan Museum, the other in the Archeological Museum, Namur. We do not know his relationship in the family, but these virginals are identical with the ordinary products of the Antwerp workshop.

We do not know how many instruments were made by the Ruckers. References to them are common throughout the seventeenth and eighteenth centuries, and they were in constant use a hundred and fifty years after they were made. Immediately after the French Revolution, for example, an inventory of keyboard instruments in good condition and formerly

---

[1] See Lambrechts-Douillez in Ripin (1971).
[2] The distinction achieved by members of this family may be demonstrated by the fact that in 1623 Jan Ruckers, together with Rubens, Jan Breughel, and certain others, were declared exempt from Civic Guard duties (Stellfeld).

the property of the nobility was prepared with a view to their being sent to the Conservatoire National (appendix 7). Of the sixty-two harpsichords and spinets listed in this last decade of the eighteenth century eleven were signed by the Ruckers, and others may well have been their work, though, as was often the case, unsigned except for a trade mark. In England Kirckman and Shudi, the best-known makers, were trading in Ruckers instruments and hiring them out, and this practice continued to the end of the eighteenth century. At the present time the writer knows the location of more than a hundred harpsichords and virginals by members of this family; and there are doubtless many others which are unrecorded.

The harpsichords built in the Ruckers workshop in Antwerp between about 1580 and 1650 were of two almost standard models: the single manual harpsichord had a compass of four octaves from C, bass short octave, and had one eight foot and one four foot stop; these were about six feet long. The double harpsichord also had one eight and one four foot stop, but was some seven feet four inches in length. This two manual instrument had four rows of jacks: two rows for each set of strings, thereby enabling either set to be played from upper or lower keyboard, there being no coupling mechanism. The (main) upper keyboard had the same compass as the small harpsichord; the (subsidiary) lower keyboard, however, had a compass of four and a half octaves, which *appeared* to be from C to f³, bass short octave. In fact, as it controlled the same two sets of strings as the upper keyboard, it actually sounded at the same pitch level. Thus if the top key of the upper keyboard were depressed (c³) that note sounded; if the top key of the lower keyboard (f³) were played the same note (c³) was heard, the top keys of the two keyboards being in alignment and attacking the same eight and four foot strings. The lower keyboard had, as we have seen, half an octave more of keys than the upper, and therefore had those extra strings to itself, the corresponding space at the bass end of the upper keyboard being filled in by a large key block. The strings peculiar to the lower manual were GG, AA, BB, F♯, G♯, and these were played from the keys which *appear* to be E, F♯, G♯, B, C♯, if short octave tuning is ignored. The three lowest notes provided useful dominant basses for the keys of C, D, and E; while F♯ and G♯ were denied to the upper keyboard where those keys sounded D and E, thereby accommodating the normal short octave. The lowest, third, fifth, eighth, and tenth jacks were not, therefore, provided for the two jackslides of the top keyboard, the slots being filled in. The lowest key of the upper manual, sounding C, was bent to the left, and the third and fifth keys, sounding D and E, had to cross over keys F, and F and G respectively, to the left, in order to get in alignment with lower keyboard F, G, A, and the appropriate strings which these keys sounded (plates 33, 34, 35).

There is good reason to believe that these two manual Ruckers harpsichords were the prototypes of all two manual harpsichords of later times, and we must here examine their purpose. The (main) upper keyboard, with its four octave C compass, was the counterpart of the keyboards of the one manual harpsichords and the Antwerp virginals. The lower manual, as we have seen, was a fourth lower in pitch than the main keyboard. This subsidiary manual was provided to help players in the routine transpositions down a fourth and fifth, with which they were commonly faced in the sixteenth and seventeenth centuries, when acting as accompanists. Details of these musical practices are beyond the scope of this chapter, but the writer will deal with them fully in another study. The reader is meanwhile referred to Bessaraboff[1] and more particularly to Mendel. [2]

Other examples of transposing instruments may be seen in single manual harpsichords and virginals, since keyboards pitched a fourth or a fifth apart from the scaling of the instruments were sometimes fitted at this period. There is an unsigned Flemish virginal of 1568 in the Victoria and Albert Museum (plate 18). This transposing virginal of normal string scaling has a keyboard compass of four octaves from F, bass short octave, 45 keys, the lowest being A; and music played on it in what would appear to be the key of F, would in fact sound about a fourth away in C. Another F keyboard may be seen in a small harpsichord of 1627 by Andries Ruckers in the Gemeentemuseum at The Hague (plate 37). This instrument has a scaling between eight and four foot pitch ($c^2 = 9\frac{1}{2}$ in.); and an examination of the keys and keyframe shows that the keyboard compass was originally four octaves from C, bass short octave. This arrangement was, however, changed to suit some early owner, and the keyboard is now of the same compass (F) as that described above. So this was originally a transposing harpsichord, but was later converted to unison pitch.

The writer knows of only one double harpsichord in which the transposing arrangement has been preserved intact to the present day: a Jan Ruckers of 1638 in the Russell Collection (plate 33). Many others, however, retain signs of their original transposing character, such as a mark at the bass end of the upper keyframe where the large keyblock was placed, or signs of rearrangement of the key pivots of the lower keyboard. [3]

As late as 1637 Jan Ruckers refused to provide a double harpsichord *without* transposing keyboards for King Charles I (page 68). Nevertheless the arrangement of keys we have been discussing fell into disuse in the mid years of the seventeenth century, and the advantages of contrasted tone available on two keyboards independently resulted in the alteration of the transposing Ruckers harpsichords. The two keyboards were brought into alignment, usually with a compass of four and a half octaves, GG to c^3, bass short octave, and a second set of eight foot strings was added for the top keyboard. The original eight and four foot sets of strings were played from the lower manual, and a simple mechanical coupler was added.

Ruckers harpsichords originally had the slides controlled by extensions which projected from the right side of the case. When the instruments were rebuilt this arrangement was generally altered to levers which ended in stop knobs piercing the front of the instrument over the keys, and therefore more conveniently placed for the performer. A harp stop of buff leather was in many cases originally provided both for harpsichords and virginals; and this was often divided into treble and bass sections, breaking about c^1. A similar slide, bringing metal hooks instead of buff leather pads in contact with the strings, was also occasionally used. An example may be seen in the Andries Ruckers virginal of 1610 in the Boston

---

[1] Bessaraboff (1941).   [2] Mendel (1948).

[3] Suitable examples for study include the instruments listed in Grove, article *Ruckers*, as follows: Hans Ruckers Nos. 16, 21, Jan Ruckers Nos. 3, 19, 21, Andries Ruckers Nos. 1, 8. The Jan Couchet of 1646 in the Brussels Conservatoire was also a transposing harpsichord (Meeùs 1970). Such instruments are also represented in contemporary paintings: a Jan Breughel in the Museo del Prado, Madrid, and a van Kessel in the Musée Municipal, Saint-Germain-en-Laye.

Museum of Fine Arts. Praetorius (1619) refers to this register as *arpichordum* (plate 26).

One more original feature of the harpsichords built in the Ruckers workshops must be mentioned; this was a very primitive attempt to get rid of the 'wolf'—the interval which in mean tone tuning was aggressively out of tune. This interval was usually a♭ – e♭, and for each e♭ the Ruckers provided two strings on both the eight and the four foot stops. These two strings ran, almost touching, over the nut, were plucked together by one jack, and were hitched together on the hitchpin rail. Signs of them can often be detected at these points and also at the tuning pins. The Ruckers always arranged the pins in two straight lines, one for the eight foot and one for the four foot, and at the e♭s a second pin standing forward from the first will often show where this crude system was in use. Van Blanckenburg (1739) tells us that Francisco de Salinas recommended quarter tones for keys e♭ and d♭, and says 'I have seen several large organs and clavecins of Ruckers with these additions. . . .'

The construction of a Ruckers harpsichord is a simple and apparently standard one (plate 38). Except for the wrestplank, which was made of oak, the casework and braces are of soft wood, usually poplar or lime. The braces run more or less parallel with the slides, and there are none placed lengthways from the header or counter wrestplank. Four are placed in the lowest part of the casework and their ends are let into it, while they are secured to the bottom of the instrument by wooden dowels. Between the two braces nearest to the keyboard there is a small compartment for tools, spare wire, etc., and this opens on the longside. Three other braces are placed just below the soundboard and are nailed to the case there. There are four battens or sound bars: two on each side of the rose hole at right angles with the longside; the cut-off bar runs parallel with the four foot hitch pin rail midway between it and the rose hole. In the soundboard is cut a hole to contain the maker's trade-mark or rose, and this bears his initials: H.R. for Hans, I.R. for Jan, A.R. for both Andries, C.R. for Christopher. Hans Rucker employed two types of rose, Jan used four; the others used one design each.

When examining a Ruckers harpsichord today we should remember that very few are in anything like their original condition. Though of rather crude construction they are of exceptionally good tone, and as a result were altered and enlarged rather than discarded in favour of new instruments. The first reconstruction they underwent has already been described. In the eighteenth century, and particularly in France, they were further enlarged by an extension of compass to five octaves from FF. This meant widening the case, and was accomplished by building a new bentside or by adding to the old one. The header and wrestplank were usually replaced, and a new lid was provided. The old bridges were either extended or replaced. Finally new keyboards, and, if it had not been done already, the second unison already mentioned, were installed. Despite these drastic measures the original quality of tone was often preserved, though little of the old instrument except the soundboard was retained; and this extensive alteration and enlargement was known in France as *ravalement* (pages 58 and 59).

Virginals (or spinets) were also built in the Ruckers workshop. Apart from a double virginal of 1581, now in the Metropolitan Museum, Hans Ruckers' earliest remaining example is a hexagonal spinet of 1591 in Italian style (plate 24). This is the only Ruckers example in this shape known today. Ruckers virginals are always oblong, though they were made in various sizes. Their compass is a standard one of four octaves from C, bass short octave, 45 keys, the keyboard being built within the case. Two important and tonally different designs were used (plates 25 and 26). In the one case the keyboard was placed to the left of the instrument, the jacks in consequence attacking the strings close to the left hand bridge and giving a bright quality of tone. In the other model the keys were placed to the right, and the strings were plucked much further from the bridge; in these virginals the point of attack in the bass is at about a third of the speaking length of the string, and these instruments have a much less incisive tone than those mentioned above. About twice as many Ruckers virginals have the keyboard to the right as to the left.

Douwes (1699) notices this important distinction, and says that the instruments with keyboard to the right were called *muselars*, while those with keys to the left were *spinetten*. Blanckenburg complains that the former instruments were difficult to control on account of the elasticity of the string when plucked far from the nut. Reynvaan (1795) substitutes the name *vierkanten* (i.e. rectangular) for the *muselars* of Douwes.

The keyboard compass of the virginals will be seen to be the same as that of the single manual harpsichord and the upper keyboard of the double harpsichords. Though a few virginals from the Ruckers workshop have now a compass of $C - f^3$, like the lower manual of the double harpsichords, the writer has seen no example which has not, in fact, been extended from the smaller compass. Only one virginal, a Hans Ruckers of 1598, has an original compass from GG to c^3, bass short octave (plate 25). This low compass was very unusual in the Low Countries, and the only other example seems to be the main keyboard of the Lodewijk Grauwels double virginal of 1600 in the Metropolitan Museum.

In addition to these eight foot virginals a small octave instrument was made, with its keyboard placed centrally and projecting from the case. These were sometimes made separately, but they were sometimes fitted into a drawer at the side of the keyboard of a large virginal, the two instruments combined being known as a *double virginal*. A slot was cut from the bottom of the small instrument under the ends of the keys, and by placing the octave spinet on top of its companion, with the latter's jackrail removed, the two played together from the eight foot keyboard, the jacks of the large virginal pushing up the ends of the keys of the octave instrument (plates 29 and 30). In six of seven surviving Ruckers double virginals the main keyboard is to the right. In the only other examples: the Martin van der Biest of 1580, the late sixteenth century Hans Ruckers in Milan and the Lodewijk Grauwels of 1600, it is to the left. Virginals of similar shape to the ordinary eight foot model were also made with scalings which suggest quint and octave pitch: i.e. $c^2 = 9\frac{1}{2}$ in., as in two examples by Andries Ruckers dated 1613; and $c^2 = 7$ in., as in one by Britsen. These three are in the Brussels Collection. [1]

Praetorius refers to the type of instrument just described under the heading *spinetta*. He says 'The spinetta is a small rectangular instrument tuned one octave or quint higher than the right pitch, and which one puts over or into larger instruments, though the big

[1] Praetorius (page 16) stated that harpsichords and symphonies by Hans Bos of Antwerp (fl. 1543–1557) were a third lower in pitch than German instruments.

rectangular as well as the small models are called without discrimination *spinetta* in Italy. In England all these instruments be they small or large are called *virginall*. . . .'

Ravalement was applied to virginals as to harpsichords, though the construction of the keyboard within the case usually permitted no more than the addition of extra notes up to f³ at the top or down to C chromatically at the bottom of the keyboard. The virginals did not, in their original form, have side blocks to the keys, and extra space had to be obtained by rebuilding the sides of the case at each end of the keyboard.

Tonally the Ruckers instruments are deservedly admired. In their original form they provided a bright eight and four foot on the upper keyboard, and when these were played on the lower keyboard they sounded rather less brilliant, as here the strings were attacked further from the nut. Originally always quilled throughout, they have lent themselves very well to the buff leather occasionally used in late eighteenth century France for the lower manual eight foot, and to the hard leather used in modern times. The brilliance of the upper keyboard provides a very satisfactory contrast to the sombre quality of the lower eight foot, and the bright octave stop blends into an ensemble of brilliance. The instruments are very sensitive to touch and have good carrying power. But, in spite of their adaptability, they were conceived as partners to accompany voices or other instruments, and to play the simple keyboard pieces of the early seventeenth century.

Employed in the Ruckers' workshop was Jan Couchet, the nephew of Jan Ruckers, who entered the Guild of Saint Luke in 1642. Later Couchet worked separately, and was assisted by his son, Peter Jan, who joined the Guild in 1655 or 6. Jan Couchet's instruments need not be described in detail as they exactly copy those of his master. The earlier harpsichords were small single manuals and transposing doubles, though the latter practice was abandoned by about 1650.

Mention must be made of Peter Daniel Bader, a German organ and harpsichord maker, who was resident in Antwerp and was admitted to the Guild in 1600; Joris Britsen, a family of three of the same name working from 1613 into the following century; and Cornelius and Simon Haeghens or Haquaerts, who entered the Guild in 1626 and 1641 respectively. The instruments of these makers are almost identical with the Ruckers models, in construction, decoration, and tone, and as with the Couchets it would be impossible to distinguish them from Ruckers instruments were they not signed.

The last surviving harpsichord from the Couchet workshop bears the date 1680, and there is no doubt that by that time Flemish harpsichord making had more or less come to a standstill. Instruments there were in profusion, the result of all the work of the preceding hundred years, but the craftsmen were now primarily occupied in converting them into a form more suited to the requirements of their own time. Not only do we lack new instruments made during the last quarter of the century, but no new maker of any great consequence appeared. Most of the seventeenth century work of *ravalement* was carried out anonymously.

In the early years of the eighteenth century the manufacture of harpsichords began again on the lines of the newly transformed Ruckers instruments. The second unison stop which these had been given became a permanent feature; but while some instruments retained the four rows of jacks of the early double model, many were now built with three rows only, one for each set of strings. In some double harpsichords with four rows of jacks the fourth row was employed to enable the octave to be used on either keyboard, without the assistance of a coupler. But sometimes it was used for attacking one eight foot at a point away from its normal row of jacks, in the furthest slide from the player, and sometimes with leather plectra instead of the quill which was still otherwise universally employed. In Germany and England the fourth row of jacks later appeared much nearer to the nut than the other registers as the Lute stop, almost unknown, however, elsewhere. The compass of the keyboard began to change, and the short octave fell into disuse. It is important to note that though *ravalement* was at this time often directed to an increase of compass *upwards* to f³, new instruments were more generally built with chromatic increase *downwards* to FF or GG, going no higher than c³; and this is significant, for it is obviously easier to increase the compass of an old harpsichord by building onto the treble than onto the bass; but the harmonic structure of contemporary harpsichord music required the lower compass of the keyboard more than ever before; and this extension downwards was the real musical trend.

Jacob van den Elsche was working in Antwerp at this time, and good double harpsichords of his with five octaves and three sets of strings exist at Charlottenburg (1710), and the Conservatoire Royal, Antwerp (1767). The former has four rows of jacks, while the later example, following the general Flemish and French trend, has only three. Jerome Mahieu was working in Brussels until his death in 1737, making harpsichords with one and two keyboards and a compass of either FF – f³ or GG – e³; these had only three registers. He has left one single manual harpsichord of 1732 with a five octave compass from DD; but the reason for this is obscure. This instrument was offered for sale in Paris in 1950.

An interesting relic of an earlier type of instrument occasionally made by the Ruckers workshop is to be seen in the Plantin Moretus Huis in Antwerp (plates 39 and 40). The contents of the home and workshop of the famous printers, Christopher Plantin and Jean Moretus, have remained there ever since the various buildings were erected, and they include a double harpsichord with an eight foot virginal built into the bentside. It was built in Roermond by the cathedral organist, Jan Joseph Coenen, and bears on the nameboard of the virginal the date 1735; the two roses however are dated one year earlier. The virginal has a chromatic compass of four octaves from C, though there is no C♯ while the harpsichord has 4½ octaves: GG – c³, bass short octave. There are the usual three sets of strings, but four rows of jacks; the bone topped ends of the slides project in the old style as stop knobs from the right side of the case.

A German from Hessen, Anton Dulcken, had a flourishing business as an instrument maker in Brussels in the early years of the eighteenth century. None of his instruments is known to the writer, though his son Jean Daniel has left a number of fine examples; the earlier ones were made in his Antwerp workshop, but about 1764 he moved back to Brussels. Dulcken's earlier instruments sometimes show him a conservative maker, as we find a short octave keyboard and stop knobs projecting from the right of the case; but his later work includes double harpsichords with a five octave compass from FF and three sets of jacks, and with stop levers over the keyboard. His articled pupil, Johann Peter Bull, produced similar instruments, both double and single, and with five octaves. The writer has seen instruments by Bull dated between 1776 and 1789. The last Antwerp man to note is Johann Heinemann, a blind harpsichord and lute maker. A small single harpsichord by Heinemann dated 1793 with, curiously enough, a short octave keyboard, C – d³, is in the Brussels Conservatoire.

Albert de Lin worked in Tournai. De Lin made spinets and harpsichords, both horizontal and upright (plate 41). The *clavicytherium*, as this latter instrument has often been called, was never as popular as its convenient shape might have ensured, probably because of the rather disagreeable effect produced by the jacks plucking directly in front of the player's face; and the noticeable mechanical noise from this, together with the complicated action needed to ensure the return of the jack with the aid of a spring instead of gravity, appears to have defeated the instrument. De Lin's instruments are dated from 1751–1770.

The school of keyboard instrument makers encouraged in sixteenth century Antwerp as a result of their recognition by the Guild of Saint Luke, and culminating in the Ruckers workshop and their pupils, supplied the larger part of the harpsichords required by musical Europe in the period before the eighteenth century. Subsequent makers were naturally to take these instruments as their model, as the Flemish harpsichords are of greater general musical use and adaptability than the Italian examples. Hence the influence of Antwerp is to be seen behind practically all later trends.

HOLLAND

Holland had no independent school of keyboard instrument making, relying on Antwerp for harpsichords; but a few instruments of native construction exist. An early maker, Nikolaus van Carpel, was born at Antwerp, and died in Amsterdam in 1637; but the writer has not found any of his work. Another maker, A. Leenhouwer, built a harpsichord with three sets of strings in his Leyden workshop in 1787, and this is now in the Gemeentemuseum; it preserves the old style of stop handle projecting from the side of the case. At Charlottenburg is a single manual harpsichord by Dirk van der Lugt, built in Amsterdam in 1770. The compass of this instrument is C – f³ chromatic, and there are three sets of strings. An eighteenth century maker at The Hague was Braütigam, but the writer has failed to trace any of his instruments. Lastly, a harpsichord in the Heyer Collection contains a rose with initials L.V., and the inscription *Amster(dam) Ao 1766*. There are three sets of strings, and the compass is GG – f³, bass short octave.

DECORATION

Just as few Ruckers harpsichords have escaped alteration, so few remain with their original decoration. A certain number have, however, been preserved, and similar instruments are shown in the paintings of the Flemish and Dutch artists of the seventeenth century. The best examples of untouched casework are to be found in the Vleeschhuis in

DECORATION

Antwerp. Nearly all the instruments in the Brussels Conservatoire have had the decorations renovated with copies of the old patterned paper that was formerly used. A good example in England of the original type of decoration is the harpsichord at Ham House, Petersham, inscribed *Joannes Ruckers me fecit Antverpiae* and dated 1634.

The stand, a separate construction on which the instrument was placed, was usually a good deal higher than we are now accustomed to, and contemporary paintings often show a performer standing to play. The legs were of turned wood, heavily framed both above and below, and often carved to a rather standard design (plate 36). Original stands at modern height are generally found on examination to have been cut down a few inches.

The outside of the case was sometimes painted a dark green with black or brown borders, but was often marbled, the favourite colours being green-blue and red-brown. Where marbling was used the edges of the case were generally painted in wide bands of dark green or brown to give the effect of panelling. Superimposed on the marbling a draped pattern can often be seen.

On opening a Ruckers instrument a most distinctive feature appears. Unless specially decorated, the space above the keys and the casework above the soundboard were nearly always covered with white paper, printed with designs in black. This paper was varnished, and now presents a yellow background; and the main lines of design were reinforced with vermilion paint. The interior of the lid was similarly decorated with a watered paper, edged with strips of the same designs as are found lining the case above the soundboard. Latin mottoes were stencilled in black paint on the watered paper, as was often the date. The origin of these papers and designs is obscure, but they may well have been inspired by Italian Renaissance decoration. Whether they were prepared by the Ruckers themselves or whether by Antwerp printers is unknown. Enquiries in Antwerp have failed to produce evidence that they were used for any other purpose than the decoration of keyboard instruments, and no suggestions as to their origin can be offered by the home of Antwerp printing, the Plantin-Moretus Huis. The writer has seen between twenty and thirty different designs, and these are variously used by the Ruckers, by the Couchets, and by Haghens, Cheerdink and Britsen. They cannot be considered the exclusive property of the Ruckers family.

The lids of the harpsichords were often made in one piece in the seventeenth century, though a hinged front section was sometimes used. Large eighteenth century harpsichords, and even early nineteenth century pianofortes, have appeared with seventeenth century Flemish paintings incorporated in the much larger lids, specially built to receive them. On measuring these paintings they may be found to be of the same size as the lids of Ruckers harpsichords, having been retained from earlier instruments and inset in their successors. Drop frontboards were attached to the instruments by hinges, but these prove most inconvenient if the player wishes to sit.

Original seventeenth century keys have bone or ivory naturals, and wooden accidentals stained black. The side blocks of the Ruckers' lower keyboards were oblong, but the upper ones were curved on top, both sets being moulded at the corners. The keys were numbered in ink. The keyframes and the top and bottom keys and jacks usually bear special numbers,

51

but the writer, despite much investigation, has failed to decipher their meaning. They appear in the instruments of Jean Couchet and Haghens as well (plate 35).

The maker's inscription appears in Roman upper case letters either on the nameboard above the keys or else on the jackrail; rarely on both. The form used was *Joannes Ruckers me fecit Antverpiae* or *Joannes Couchet fecit Antverpiae* usually without the date. The spacing of the lettering is very strange, as the inscription begins with large letters well spaced, and ends with the letters rather smaller and packed together, as though carelessly set out (plate 25). But this was the rule. The date, usually in large red or blue numerals, though sometimes smaller and set on a small white scroll as background, appears on the soundboard, and very rarely on the wrestplank. The scroll form was the speciality, though not the exclusive property, of Andries; when it was used, it was invariably placed between the rose and the longside. The soundboard and wrestplank were painted in *tempera*, with blue borders to the casework and bridges in a scallop design. The remaining surface of the soundboard was covered with tulips and other flowers, birds, fruit, and large red prawns. The Rose or Trade Mark was made of gilded lead; it contained the maker's initials together with a winged figure playing the harp. Several designs were used, and these trade marks were surrounded by garlands of flowers.

By the end of the seventeenth century taste demanded a different style of decoration for these instruments. The stand was usually replaced by a lighter model with curved legs in Louis XIV style. The marbled case was repainted black or red or green with panels in gold leaf, very often with a vermilion lining to the lid; but it might be covered with elaborate paintings, according to the means of the owner. The old keys were replaced by a new set with ebony naturals and ivory topped accidentals. The old lid, no longer large enough after *ravalement*, was discarded unless it contained paintings of particular value. The jack-rails and nameboard were replaced, for the old ones were too short for the widened instrument. Where an early Flemish harpsichord has been extended to five octaves and no joints can be seen in lid, nameboard, or jackrail, it is certain that these are replacements. Many paintings in whole lids of 5 octave width, attributed to Breughel, Paulus Bril, or others, must thus be discredited. Soundboard decoration was usually touched up and embellished when widening was carried out, and a new inscription in the maker's style of wording, though not with his lettering, was placed above the keys.

In England these instruments were more severely treated. The new stand was of the plain trestle kind employed by Kirckman and Shudi, and the outside of the case was veneered with walnut or mahogany. The soundboard decoration was allowed to remain, and so were the lid paintings, but the style of the case itself was toned down to the British taste of the period. Black paint was occasionally used on the outside of the case; and in one example, a single Jan Ruckers of 1637 in the Russell Collection, a coat of red paint with gold leaf decoration, and a trestle stand similarly treated, appear to be of early eighteenth century date. But such elaborate decoration was most unusual in England.

CHAPTER FOUR

FRANCE

It has not been possible to trace any surviving French keyboard instruments made before the early years of the seventeenth century. France is however the source of one of the earliest references to, and certainly the earliest technical work on, the harpsichord and clavichord. This is the manuscript in the Bibliothèque Nationale,[1] written by Henri Arnault of Zwolle in the middle of the fifteenth century (page 13). It deals with matters of instrument construction in a degree of detail otherwise quite unknown at that time. Arnault, a Dutchman by birth, took a medical degree in Paris, and spent most of his life at Dijon as physician and astronomer to Philip the Good, Duke of Burgundy. Near the end of his life he entered the service of Louis XI in Paris, where he died on 6 September 1466.

Arnault in his description of the harpsichord (*clavisimbalum*) speaks of an instrument with a compass of just under three octaves: B – a², and for this he offers a choice of four different actions. Three of these are forms of jack action, though none tally with practices known to us today; the fourth is a form of primitive hammer action, which does not seem to have met with success. It is interesting to note that Arnault used metal plectra for his jacks, though the MS. does contain one reference to quill as a plucking material. The scaling for the harpsichord appears to be: B 25 inches, c² 13 inches, a² 7½ inches, and this suggests a pitch similar to that in use today. For the clavichord Arnault gives a compass of three octaves: B – b², but it is difficult to be certain what scaling he intended. Another instrument, the *dulce melos*, is given the same compass as the harpsichord, but uses the fourth form of action. This primitive attempt at hammer action was identified by Galpin as an *echiquier* or *chekker*; and he constructed a model himself, but this failed to demonstrate any noteworthy musical qualities. The origin of the name *clavisimbalum* may be noted here: *clavis cimbalum*—a keyed dulcimer.

Though no harpsichords or clavichords of Arnault's time are at present known, nor any sixteenth century French examples, a number of early Italian spinets and harpsichords survive in France, together with at least six Ruckers instruments made before 1620. When we take into account the large number of instruments which were destroyed in the following centuries, it seems probable that a considerable part of the early French demand for keyboard instruments was met by import from Italy and the Netherlands. Many of these spinets and harpsichords continued in use up to the end of the eighteenth century, and they are often to be found disguised in eighteenth century casework.

[1] MS. fonds Latin 7295.

FRANCE

Among seventeenth century French instruments are spinets made by Richard. We know little of this maker, but a spinet in the Paris Conservatoire, which is signed *Fait par Richard, à Paris, rue du Paon, près Saint-Nicholas-du-Chardonet, 1693* gives us the address at which he worked. Another spinet with a similar inscription, but bearing the date 1690 (plate 44) was sold in Paris by Marcel Salomon of rue Boissy D'Anglas some years ago. The Rhode Island School of Design has a double harpsichord by Hans Ruckers, 1613, which bears a restorer's inscription under the soundboard: *Faict par Michel Richard 1688*.

At this time the Denis family was working in Paris. There was Jean Denis, organist of the church of Saint Barthélémy, and known to have been working between 1636 and 1653, and Philippe, either his son or his brother and also his successor as organist of the church. [1] A Louis Denis was at work a little later, as de Bricqueville has recorded the sale, on 9 April 1767, of one of his harpsichords dated 1702; but his relationship to Jean and Philippe is not known. No instrument by Jean Denis can be traced, though he has left us a book on tuning: *Traité de l'accord de l'espinette*, published by Ballard in Paris in 1650. A spinet by Philippe dated 1672 is preserved in the Paris Conservatoire; but, though both his name and that of Louis appear from time to time in eighteenth century sales, few other instruments are known to have survived. The late M. le Cerf of Paris, co-editor of the facsimile edition of Arnault's MS., owned a Philippe Denis harpsichord of 1674, enlarged and redecorated in the eighteenth century, but its present location is unknown. Another Denis appears as maker of a double manual mid eighteenth century harpsichord in the Musée Grevin, and he is also called Jean. It is of course possible that this is an enlarged instrument of seventeenth century origin.

The spinet of 1672 by Philippe Denis suggests that the common keyboard compass in the mid seventeenth century was GG – c³, bass short octave. This low bass seems to have been a fairly recent extension, if the compass offered by Mersenne is to be taken as standard French practice of forty years earlier.

Marin Mersenne (1588–1648), a French Minorite and renowned musical theorist, published among many other things his *Harmonie Universelle* which appeared in two volumes in 1636. This work, which contains many musical and other illustrations, includes detailed descriptions of contemporary musical instruments. From Mersenne it is not unreasonable to suppose that the French custom in the first half of the seventeenth century was to build harpsichords on the single manual Flemish model; that clavichords were also used in France; and that keyboard instruments (as he actually tells us) were manufactured there, as in the Low Countries, which sounded a fourth away from the normal standard of pitch.

But no French clavichords have survived. It seems that the instrument had no significant place in French musical history, though it is mentioned on the title page of Attaignant's organ books of 1530 as *manicordions*. [2] Closson has stated that the Denis family made them, but he offers no evidence in support of this. The *Encyclopédie Méthodique* does not assign an article to the clavichord; it is only mentioned in the article *clavecin*, written in 1791

---

[1] Boalch.
[2] The lack of interest which eighteenth century France showed in the clavichord may be illustrated by a sale advertisement of 5 May 1763 (de Briqueville): 'un manucordion allemand, sorte de petit clavecin. . . .'

by Hüllmandel, himself a pupil of C. P. E. Bach, as being a forerunner of the pianoforte.

Examples of the seventeenth century French harpsichord are very rare. Two examples in private hands have only one striking difference between them: there is a double curve bent-side to a harpsichord owned by the Comtesse de Chambure in Paris signed by Desruisseaux, a maker otherwise unknown; the other harpsichord, no longer extant, was unsigned and had an angled end (plate 42). Both are similar to the instruments by Vincent Tibaut of Toulouse, dated 1679 (plate 43), and 1681.

These harpsichords had the same original compass: GG – c³, bass short octave, and the same layout:

> Upper manual: 1 × 8′
> Lower manual: 1 × 8′, 1 × 4′, coupler.

This is the form the instrument had reached in France and also in the Low Countries by the end of the seventeenth century. Figure 1 (page 56) shows a cross section of the action of a French harpsichord, and the working of the coupler can be understood from that. The only difference between these early instruments and the French harpsichord of a hundred years later is to be found in an increase in compass and consequently in size.

Two other seventeenth century French makers must be mentioned here. In 1671 Pampes, who is otherwise unknown, supplied Louis XIV with a harpsichord, an organ, and a spinet; no one who was not well known and approved in his day would have received this royal patronage.[1] A double manual harpsichord by Nicholas Dumont dated 1697 is in the Paris Conservatoire. Brunold and others have maintained that this is the earliest example of a French five octave harpsichord. When it was built, however, this Dumont was not unlike the three harpsichords described above, for it underwent an enlargement at the hands of Pascal Taskin, and is inscribed on the wrestplank: *Refait par Pascal Taskin à Paris 1789*. It is certainly he who was responsible for the five octave chromatic compass.

In 1700 Jean Marius, an enterprising instrument maker, was at work in Paris. He is remembered today as a pioneer of pianoforte action, on which he was working independently in France at much the same time as Cristofori in Florence, and Schroeter at Nordhausen, and also for his *clavecin brisé* (plate 45). This was a portable harpsichord, built in three independent sections, hinged together. By folding the instrument at the hinges it was reduced to the appearance of a small wooden box, and thus proved very convenient for travelling. The *clavecin brisé* was normally made with compass GG – e³, bass short octave, the lowest E♭ key being split. It generally had two unison stops only, but the instrument owned by Frederick the Great, and carried by him on journeys and campaigns, has an octave as well. This is now in the Berlin Collection. Marius received a Royal Privilege or patent for his invention, and this was granted in 1700 for a period of twenty years. Of the five examples known to exist today[2] the earliest (1700) is in the Paris Conservatoire,

---

[1] Mederic Lorillat (fl. 1579) and Jacques Le Breton (fl. 1603–1656) were also Royal Instrument Makers.

[2] Paris Conservatoire (1700), Brussels Conservatoire (1709), Heyer Collection (1713), La Comtesse de Chambure (1715), Berlin (n.d.).

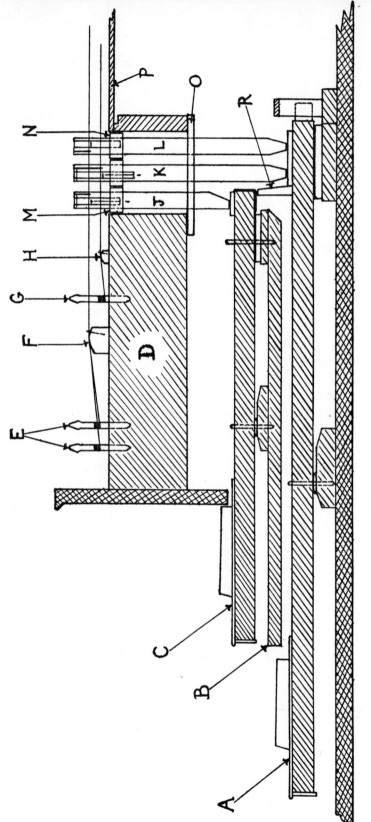

INCHES

0 1 2 3 4 5 6

Figure 1.   FRENCH HARPSICHORD, BY BLANCHET.   SECTION AT c¹.

A. Lower keyboard.
B. Upper keyframe.
C. Upper keyboard.
D. Wrestplank.
E. Eight foot wrestpins.
F. Eight foot nut.
G. Four foot wrestpins.
H. Four foot nut.

J. Eight foot jack, upper manual.
K. Four foot jack, lower manual.
L. Eight foot jack, lower manual.
M. Eight foot slide, upper manual.
N. Eight foot slide, lower manual.
O. Jack guide.
P. Soundboard.

R. Coupler, by means of which the lower manual keys depress those of the upper keyboard. If the upper keyboard and keyframe (B) are drawn towards the player—a movement of only $\frac{3}{8}$"—the uprights (R) will no longer engage the upper manual keys when the keys of the lower manual are depressed.

and the latest (1715) is in private hands in Paris; Frederick the Great's example is un-dated.

The writer has never seen an ordinary spinet or harpsichord by Marius; but a spinet attributed to him was lent by the Brussels Conservatoire for exhibition at the International Inventions Exhibition of 1885. No instrument at Brussels can now be identified as this spinet, and it is probable that the attribution was made on slender grounds.

In 1716 Marius presented a paper to the *Académie Royale des Sciences* in which he sug-gested four distinct actions for an instrument he called *clavecin à maillets*. Of these, actions one and two involved a very rudimentary hammer action; type three was nothing more than an unyielding pin set into the side of a jack, intended to strike the string instead of to pluck it; and the last action combined both harpsichord, played from a lower keyboard, and an elementary hammer action for use on an upper manual. But these inventions were quite primitive, and nothing came of them.

It is probable that Marius was stimulated in his work by a paper which had been read to the *Académie* in 1708 by another French instrument maker, Cuisinier. This inventor had proposed a harpsichord in which the tone of the vibrating string was sustained by revolving resined wheels, the strings being stopped by tangents called *maillets*. The incidental use of this word may well have led Marius's thoughts to hammer action. But the *clavecin brisé* was his most useful piece of work, and it is curious that after his patent had expired the instru-ment was not more generally used. The writer has seen only one of these instruments, un-signed and now in the Gemeentemuseum, which was not the work of Marius himself. [1]

At the beginning of the eighteenth century, as we have seen, the French harpsichord was complete in design, but still restricted in keyboard compass. During the first two decades the short octave keyboard became obsolete, and instruments were constructed with a chromatic compass from FF or GG. A fully chromatic bass was in demand by François Couperin, whose four books of harpsichord pieces, together with *L'Art de toucher le Clavecin*, appeared between 1713 and 1730. The upward extension of the keyboard to five octave compass followed rapidly, and was common by the time that Couperin's fourth book was published.

The French harpsichord was almost always built with two keyboards, the single manual instruments so often found in England being unusual in France, and there was a tendency to use three rows of jacks only. A certain number of harpsichords were, however, built with a fourth row of jacks, which duplicated the set employed for the lower eight foot, but attacked the strings with leather plectra instead of with the otherwise universal quill. In a few instruments, which were usually rebuilt Flemish work, the fourth row was used to enable the four foot or the upper eight foot to be used on either keyboard.

A new line of harpsichord makers now arose. The founder was Nicolas Blanchet, a native of Reims, who set up as an instrument maker in Paris in 1686. In the same year he married, and in due course his younger son, François Etienne, joined him in the workshop. François

[1] Jean Galland of Paris subsequently made these instruments. De Bricqueville quotes a sale of 16 Oct. 1775: 'Une épinette à grand ravalement de Edelman à Strasbourg, laquelle se replie en deux et se met dans une caisse.' Farinelli seems to have had two such harpsichords (Kirkpatrick 1953, p. 363), and there was another in the Medici collection (appendix 1).

Etienne Blanchet was married twice: the first marriage produced two children who died young; but a second marriage to Elisabeth Gobin in 1727 produced, in 1730, an heir to the business who was also called François Etienne. A daughter, Elisabeth Antoinette, born in 1729, married Armand Louis Couperin, the organist.

Until François Etienne's second marriage the instrument shop had been in Rue St. Germain l'Auxerrois, but the new Madame Blanchet had a share in a large family house in Rue de la Verrerie, and the Blanchet family removed there soon after the marriage. There, in 1731, Nicolas Blanchet died.

Young François Etienne grew up in his father's business, and in 1757 he married his cousin, Marie Geneviève Gobin. A son of this marriage, Armand François Nicolas Blanchet, continued in a junior position in the line. François Etienne the elder died in 1761, and François Etienne the younger died in 1766 at the age of only thirty-six. In the same year his widow married her late husband's apprentice, Pascal Taskin, a man who became the best-known instrument maker in France.

The Blanchet workshop was supreme in French harpsichord making, and its position was maintained and even enhanced under Taskin. Despite this, very few Blanchet harpsichords have survived. Two are double manual instruments with five octave FF compass, and three sets of strings. Both contain the rose of Nicolas Blanchet, but one instrument is undated, while the other bears the date 1730 and the inscription *N. et François Blanchet*. The writer acquired both these instruments in France. The 1730 harpsichord is now in private ownership in Boston, Mass. (plate 51); and the other in Paris.

A third Blanchet harpsichord, which the author saw in Paris in 1951, is a double manual with three sets of strings, but compass FF – c³ chromatic. It has the rose of François Blanchet, and the inscription *François Blanchet, Paris*.

The only recorded spinet from the Blanchet workshop is a candidate at Hever Castle. This instrument bears the name François Blanchet and the date 1709; there is much about it the author cannot accept.

There is no doubt that the scarcity of instruments by the Blanchets is due to the fact that much of their time was occupied in the restoration of harpsichords by the old Antwerp masters, and these instruments figure in the inventories of the Blanchet workshops which have been published by Hubbard and Hardouin (1957). A great many instruments were so restored, and a number of these are still in existence. No doubt it was such an instrument that Charles Burney saw in Paris in 1770:[1]

'After church M. Balbastre invited me to his house, to see a fine Rucker harpsichord which he has had painted inside and out with as much delicacy as the finest coach or snuff box I ever saw at Paris. On the outside is the birth of Venus; and on the inside of the cover the story of Rameau's most famous opera, Castor and Pollux; earth, hell, and elysium are there represented: in elysium, sitting on a bank, with a lyre in his hand is that celebrated composer himself; the portrait is very like, for I saw Rameau in 1764. The tone of this instrument is more delicate than powerful; one of the unisons is of buff, but very sweet and agreeable; the touch very light, owing to the quilling, which in France is always weak.'

[1] Burney (1771).

THE BLANCHETS AND TASKIN

Of Blanchet's own work we may take a contemporary account from the *Dictionnaire Portatif des Arts et Métiers* (Yverdon, 1767), volume 2, page 7:

'It is in the art of enlarging Ruckers harpsichords that Blanchet has done so well. To accomplish this it is necessary to remove the treble and bass parts of the case, and then to widen and lengthen the whole structure of the instrument. Next one must add some old and resonant pine, as near the same as one can get, to increase the soundboard to its new width and length. The wrestplank is entirely replaced in these instruments, which, taking all in all, retain from their original form only the soundboard, and some two and a half feet of the bentside. The various working parts, such as keyboards, jacks and slides, are now of far better workmanship and precision than those made by the Flemish masters a hundred years ago. A harpsichord by Ruckers or Couchet, carefully altered and enlarged, with jacks, slides and keyboards by Blanchet, is today considered a very precious thing.'

François Blanchet the elder, and later the younger, held the appointment of *Facteur de Clavessins du Roi*, and this honour fell in time to Pascal Taskin.

Taskin was a Belgian, born at Theux near Liége in 1723. The whole of his working life was spent in Paris where he died on 9 February 1793. His marriage on 27 November 1766 to Madame Blanchet resulted in his taking control of the whole business, and his trade card reads:

'Pascal Taskin, Facteur de Clavessins du Roi, élève et successeur de M. Blanchet demeure même maison rue de la Verrerie vis à vis la petite porte de St. Merry à Paris.'

In 1772 Louis XV offered him the position of keeper of the musical instruments in the Palace and Chapel Royal at Versailles, but Taskin was allowed to refuse this position, since it would almost certainly have meant giving up his business in Paris.

Like his master, Pascal Taskin has left few instruments by which we can judge him. The reason for this, as with Blanchet, is that most of Taskin's time was spent in the restoration of Flemish instruments made in the previous century. There are, however, eight harpsichords, a spinet, an *harpe couchée*, and three pianofortes. The list of good instruments confiscated from the nobility at the Revolution (appendix 7) contains only two Taskin harpsichords. One was dated 1770 and numbered 15, coming from the Menus Plaisirs, the branch of the Court responsible for musical entertainment; the other harpsichord was dated 1774 and was confiscated from the Farmer General Laborde. Closson tells us that Madame du Barry bought one for her use at Versailles, and that it cost three thousand livres, and that Madame d'Hibbert had another. But the proportion of Taskin's original work to his restorations is demonstrated by the fact that in the *Affiches, annonces et avis divers* between the dates 1752 and 1790 in Paris, forty nine Ruckers instruments were offered for sale, but not a single one by Taskin. His reconstructions of Flemish harpsichords were, however, in great demand, and it seems that these, together with his own instruments, were considered the best obtainable.

Late in life Taskin took to the study and construction of pianofortes, producing a new action in 1787. Three of these grands survive: one at Versailles dated 1790, another at Berlin dated 1787 and 1789[1] and a third undated one in the Yale Collection. After

---

[1] The Berlin Taskin pianoforte is inscribed on the lowest key: 'Vendue par Blanchet élève de Pascal Taskin rue de la Verrerie No. 167 . . . 1795.' This Blanchet was Armand François Nicolas.

Clementi's visit to Paris, when he brought a Shudi harpsichord and some rectangular piano-fortes with him, Taskin imported some of the latter from London, presumably for retail, as the following entry in Broadwood's books show:

'23 Oct. 1784. Pascall Taskain, for four Piano-forte, one plain, and three inlaid without stands, shipped to Paris.'

It is obvious that the plain English stand would not have been acceptable to French customers.

The *harpe couchée* mentioned above is an instrument with gut strings, shaped much like a harpsichord, but without stops or keyboard. It is a hybrid between a harp and a psaltery. Taskin's instrument is dated 1789 and is preserved in the museum of the Paris Conservatoire.

Of Taskin's harpsichords the two earliest are both dated 1769, one being in private hands in Paris, and the other in the Russell Collection; both are of identical construction. The latter instrument (plates 47 and 48) was obtained from the Taskin family in Paris in whose hands it had always been. Round the rose, which contains the initials *P.T.*, the maker has written *Pascal Taskin élève de Blanchet*. There are two manuals of five octave chromatic compass from FF; the natural keys are of ebony with arcaded boxwood fronts, and the accidentals are topped with bone or ivory. There are three sets of strings, and three rows of jacks:

Upper manual: $1 \times 8'$, harp
Lower manual: $1 \times 8'$, harp, $1 \times 4'$, coupler.

The upper eight foot is quilled, but the lower is furnished with soft buff leather in the manner favoured by Taskin in his later work. This material reduces the higher partials, and produces a tone quality that in many ways is more suggestive of the early pianoforte than of the plucked string; it is a great contrast to the incisive tones of the quilled register.

The tone of French instruments is full and robust, by no means displaying the fragile and delicate qualities so often associated with the popular idea of eighteenth century French harpsichords; and they are in many ways more resonant than their English equivalents. The bracing and soundbar arrangement of French harpsichords are similar to those of the Blanchet harpsichord of 1730 (plate 51). The large number of soundbars employed by French makers may be noted.

The use of buff leather or *peau de buffle* is often claimed as Taskin's invention, introduced for the first time in 1769. But buff leather was used in England at the same date, and it appears in an unrestored Kirckman harpsichord of 1768, formerly the property of the Salaman family, for whom Charles Burney personally selected it. The effect produced in France by this new tone colour, and the sensitive touch associated with it, was very real; but it is not impossible that Taskin exploited his *peau de buffle* with the skill which a good salesman must certainly have.

Another of Taskin's harpsichords is not a standard instrument in any way. It is dated 1786 and belongs to the Victoria and Albert Museum (plates 49 and 50). There is only one keyboard, with two unison registers and a harp stop. The compass is unusual: five octaves chromatic, with one extra note: EE – f³. This EE appears in at least five other instruments: the Taskin spinet of 1778 in the Yale collection, the Taskin harpsichord of 1780 in the Milan

Castello Sforzesco collection, a harpsichord by Andries Ruckers in the Rhode Island School of Design, which was rebuilt in eighteenth century France, though it is not known if Taskin was responsible for the work, the pedal harpsichord of 1786 by Swanen in the Conservatoire des Arts et Métiers, and the three manual harpsichord inscribed *Simone Remoti 1602* in Stuttgart. Key EE was probably tuned to sound CC. Taskin's harpsichord of 1786 is very unusual in that the keyboard is too small for the adult hand, an octave measuring $4\frac{3}{4}$ inches against Taskin's usual $6\frac{1}{4}$ inches. It is probable that this ornate little instrument was specially built for some noble child.

When rebuilding the instruments of the Flemish masters Taskin, while preserving the soundboard and adding to it where necessary, in fact converted the instrument to his own model. Occasionally knee levers were fitted in place of hand stops, in Taskin's later years (plate 22). Five or six of these levers were placed beneath the lower keyboard. Three or four controlled the slides of jacks; another was sometimes used to raise all the jacks of one eight foot register, thus allowing that set of strings to vibrate freely in sympathy with the others, in the same way as the English *celestial harp* (plate 79). Occasionally a further lever was used to cancel all stops except the buff leather eight foot and the harp, thus giving a *pianissimo* effect. It must be said, however, that the knee levers were not a great success and are very uncomfortable to manipulate; and they may in the first place have been an experiment on the lines of one Virbès who, in 1766, had fitted similar levers in Paris, but without securing any great fame or success for his invention.

Among the mass of dictionaries and encyclopedias which appeared in the second half of the eighteenth century in France, mention must be made of two. The *Encyclopédie des Sciences, des Arts et des Métiers*, appeared in Paris between 1751 and 1780, under the direction of Denis Diderot (1713–1784), who was himself an amateur musician and student of acoustics. A number of articles in this great work are devoted to musical instruments, and many were written by Diderot himself. Editions of the *Encyclopédie* were also published in Geneva and in Amsterdam; and Hubbard (1956) has examined the very different texts which appear in the various editions. While much that appears in these articles suggests a theoretical rather than a practical knowledge, they should be read by all students of early musical instruments.

Of less immediate interest where the harpsichord and clavichord are concerned, the second work is in fact most splendid in its own speciality. This is the treatise in four folio parts by François Bedos de Celles (1709–1779), a French Benedictine, entitled *L'Art du Facteur d'Orgues*. This most detailed work covers every aspect of organ building; in addition it discusses and illustrates the combination of both large harpsichord and rectangular pianoforte with the organ. This is dealt with in the fourth volume, plates CXXX–CXXXV, and pages 634–43.

Of the lesser figures of eighteenth century France a few are noteworthy. Louis Bellot was at work in Paris between 1729 and 1753; in the former year he built the small single manual harpsichord with two unisons only, now in the Bishop's Palace at Chartres (perhaps a speciality, as Corrette (1753) p. 84, refers to *petits Clavecins à deux Cordes de Bellot*), and in 1753 he is known to have provided a spinet for use at the opera (C. Pierre). An undated double manual harpsichord with three sets of strings is in the Metropolitan Museum. Both harpsichords have the early compass GG – e³ chromatic.

Guillaume Hemsch, working in the 1760's and 70's, and his kinsman, probably his brother, Jean Henri, who was at work between 1747, when he served in office in the Guild of Instrument Makers, and 1775, the date of his latest recorded harpsichord, are represented by standard double harpsichords in private ownership in France and the Boston, Mass., Museum of Fine Arts. Another family, perhaps of Flemish origin, was named Goermans, sometimes called Germain. Jean Goermans, born in 1703, the head of the family, and his son Jacques, both made fine instruments. Jean Goermans has left several recorded instruments; the earliest, dated 1748, is privately owned in Boston, Mass., while the latest, dated 1768, was sold in Paris just after the 1945 war. A harpsichord of 1754 is in the Metropolitan Museum. Marcel Salomon sold a full size harpsichord signed *Jacques Germain, 1735*, in the 1920's. Suspicion must be attached to the inscription of this harpsichord; Jacques was the youngest of seven children, and cannot even have been born in 1735, since Jean Goermans did not marry until 1730. A very good double harpsichord by Jacques Goermans with three sets of strings and four rows of jacks, dated 1774, is in private hands in Paris; a harpsichord dated 1785 was sold by Challis of Detroit in 1950.

Sebastian Erard (1752–1831) was founder of the well-known firm of that name. An Alsatian by birth, Erard went to Paris in 1768 and worked there throughout his life, except for a period of ten years from 1796 when he lived in London. His late harpsichords contain knee levers and pedals to control the registers. An instrument of this kind was exhibited at the South Kensington Exhibition in 1872; it was dated 1779 and at the time belonged to Mme. Erard. A similar instrument was formerly at Hever Castle, Kent.

Lyons had been a local centre of instrument making since the sixteenth century.[1] A harpsichord by Colesse of Lyons, dated 1768, is in private hands in Isère. In 1937 the Museé Historique, Lyons, was offered a double harpsichord made by Donzelague of Lyons, 1716, but declined it because of the instrument's dilapidated condition.

Another provincial maker of interest was Obert of Boulogne. A statement in the *London Chronicle* for 17–19 May 1753, announces the recent importation into England of some upright harpsichords by Obert; unfortunately none of these has come to light. Marseilles is represented by J. Bas, the maker of a harpsichord, sold at the Hôtel Drouot in 1902, which had been made in 1737. L. Bas, possibly a son of the above, made a harpsichord in 1781 which once belonged to de Bricqueville; and another of his instruments, possibly the same one converted into a pianoforte, was sold in New York in August 1949. A spinet by L. Bas dated 1786 is in the Musée Granet, Aix-en-Provence. Vincent Thibaut of Toulouse has already been noticed in connection with his harpsichords of 1679 and 1681.

Little has been said about the French spinet. While a number of these instruments are still to be seen in France they were much less popular than the large model harpsichord. In design they are similar to the English spinet of the eighteenth century, though the compass follows that of the French harpsichord. Few are signed, and it is possible that they were

[1] In early times Nicolas Bontemps worked in Lyons as a 'faiseur d'instruments et de manichordians' *c.* 1506–1516 (Valdrighi).

generally the work of smaller men than the Blanchets and Taskins of that time. They have no musical characteristics to require special explanation, and accordingly receive this brief notice only.

DECORATION

Seventeenth century French spinets and harpsichords were usually built in a case of oak, the outside being plain. The bentside was sometimes a double curve, but some instruments have a single curve and an angled tail. The lid of the harpsichord was often made in one piece, and the inner surface decorated with a painting. Following Flemish custom, the soundboard was painted with flowers and other designs in *tempera*, and the keyboard surround was also decorated. The natural keys were of ebony with arcaded fronts, the accidentals being topped with bone or ivory slips. The stand was composed of several turned or carved legs, framed together.

The eighteenth century saw a change of fashion in furniture which resulted in a new style of decoration for keyboard instruments. The framed stand was replaced by one supported by cabriole legs. The lid was hinged at the junction of the front part and the bentside, and the front board was attached by hinges to either the lid or to the left hand key cheek of the harpsichord. The keys were standard, the design remaining unchanged except for the addition of arcaded natural fronts of boxwood. The key slips of the upper manual were either moulded, or else provided with handles, to facilitate the movement of the keyboard for coupling and uncoupling.

The cases were painted inside and outside, and were then covered with a light clear varnish. Sometimes they were lacquered. In inexpensive instruments the outside colour was generally black or green (*merde d'oie*), and the interior of the lid was often painted vermilion, though other colours were also used. The mouldings were picked out with gold leaf, and the various surfaces of the instrument were decorated with bands of gold, about one inch wide, arranged in panels. More expensively decorated instruments had a painting inside the lid, and sometimes the outside was finely painted as well. For such elaborately decorated harpsichords a carved and gilt stand was often specially made. The soundboard was still painted with flowers and fruit in the Flemish style.

The maker's trade mark, usually a gilt metal figure holding a harp and containing his initials, was let into the soundboard. It was often surrounded by his name, though sometimes this appeared above the upper keys, and sometimes was omitted altogether. The date was painted on the soundboard or placed with the inscription. Blanchet and Taskin often signed and dated the top and bottom jacks and keys of their instruments. If the instrument was enlarged or restored, a second date was usually added to record the work. In Flemish instruments remade by these craftsmen, the original rose and initials remain in place, a new inscription to fit the widened instrument being placed over the keys. The name of the restorer is often to be found on the highest and lowest jacks and keys.

Many Flemish harpsichords enlarged in France are decorated with pictures erroneously ascribed to sixteenth and seventeenth century Antwerp masters. But if the instrument has at some time been extended to five octaves, it must of necessity have been widened some six inches, and probably lengthened the same amount. This may often be seen on the treble part of the soundboard, above the keyboard, on the lid, on the bentside, or the wrestplank. These parts, however, were often entirely replaced; so, if no tell-tale joints can be found, it must follow that these parts cannot ante-date the eighteenth century restoration, and consequently that they cannot bear authentic and untouched Flemish paintings of the seventeenth century.

Not only Flemish instruments were redecorated in this way. Numbers of Italian spinets and harpsichords exist in France which are enclosed in cases painted in the various styles of the eighteenth century. These however are not enlarged instruments, for the Italian types did not lend themselves to this treatment. An example of this, and also of the way in which people have always clung to some old instrument of good quality, rather than scrap it for some new but unknown quantity, is demonstrated by one formerly owned by the writer. By origin this is a seventeenth century Italian harpsichord. Later in the century it must have been in the Low Countries, judging by the style of its double keyboard and lid painting; later still it must have travelled to France where, towards the close of the eighteenth century, the outer case was entirely repainted with flowers and garlands on a lavender ground, and fluted legs were fitted to the case. The old cedar and cypress harpsichord was then fixed permanently inside the case, and the soundboard was painted in the same manner as the case itself. Such altered instruments are by no means rare; and they clearly demonstrate how necessary it is to examine the history of early keyboard instruments very carefully before accepting or offering any attributions regarding their dates or origins.

CHAPTER FIVE

THE BRITISH ISLES TO 1730

The names of nearly twenty keyboard instrument makers resident in London and the Provinces in the sixteenth century have been preserved in Parish Rate Books and other records;[1] but only one instrument made in England in that century is known to exist to day. This is an organ and a harpsichord combined (plates 53 and 54), and it is the work of Lodewijk Theeuwes, a Fleming who had been admitted to the Guild of Saint Luke in Antwerp in 1557. He came to London, and was living in the Parish of Saint Martin's le Grand in 1568. Little of the organ remains, but there is no reason to doubt that the harpsichord is typical of the larger domestic instruments of that time, though no doubt the smaller virginal or spinet was more often to be found.

This instrument was built in 1579 and had one keyboard. The compass was forty nine keys: either a chromatic compass of four octaves from C, or more probably a four and a half octave compass from GG, bass short octave. There were three sets of strings: $2 \times 8'$, $1 \times 4'$, and this is the earliest harpsichord with a four foot stop known to the writer (page 36). The keyboard, the four foot bridge, and the lower part of the eight foot bridge are now missing, but the scaling appears to have been $c^2 = 13\frac{7}{8}$ inches. One jack pierced for quill remains. Flemish influence had long been at work in England,[2] for Jasper Blanckart had also come over from the Low Countries, and after serving an apprenticeship to William Treasurer, the instrument maker and tuner to the Queen, he set up in Aldgate, where he lived from 1566 to 1582.

No harpsichord seems to have survived between the Theeuwes of 1579 and an instrument which is at Knole Park, Sevenoaks (plates 55 and 56). This was built by John Haward in 1622, and is also a single manual. It is more dilapidated than the instrument described

[1] William Betton (fl. 1538–1553), Jasper Blanckart (fl. 1566–1582), Thomas Blunte (fl. 1594), Thomas Browne (fl. 1508 Cambridge), Paul Defield (fl. 1568–1582), Gregory Estamproy (fl. 1526), Nicholas Farnaby (fl. 1587–1630, father and son), William Goodman (at Chester), Robert Gundet (fl. 1551), Thomas Hartwell (fl. 1589–1592), John James (fl. 1571), John de John (fl. 1526–1531), William Lewes (fl. 1530), Andrew Marsam (fl. 1579–1580 at Leicester), Sir Michael Mercator (1491–1544, also of Venloo, Virginal maker to King Henry VIII and to Cardinal Wolsey), William Norton (fl. 1594), Edmonde Schetz (fl. 1587–1601), Ludovic Theeuwes (fl. 1558–1579), William Treasurer (fl. 1521–1576).

[2] Dr. Nelly J. M. Kerling has found an entry in the Customs Accounts of Kingston upon Hull, for the year 1485, showing the import of '22 scok Lutestrynges' and 'Una parva clavy symball . . . valor £48'. (Dutch or German *Schok* equals three score.) The ship bearing these goods sailed from Danzig, stopping at unspecified Hanse ports on the way. (*See* Public Record Office El22/63/1.)

above, the soundboard having disappeared, but it can be seen from the wrestplank that the compass was fifty three keys. There were three sets of strings; but, most unusually, one of these was of lower pitch than the other two. Thus the tuning may have been $1 \times 16'$, $2 \times 8'$, or $1 \times 8'$, $2 \times 4'$, or it is possible that the two short sets were tuned at unison pitch, while the longer set was a fourth or fifth lower, to facilitate the accompanying of variously pitched voices and instruments.

A certain Italian influence is to be found in both these early harpsichords. The wrestplank bridges or nuts of both the Theeuwes and the Haward are placed, not above the oak wrestplank containing the wrestpins, but on a section of free soundboard a little closer to the jacks, a practice very generally employed by the Italian makers. At Knole the sharp curve of the bentside suggests a short scale in the treble, perhaps no more than $c^2 = 10$ inches, and this again is reminiscent of Italian practice.

It is evident from these two harpsichords that English players of 1575 to 1625 were not confined to a simple spinet or virginal for the performance of keyboard music, but enjoyed facilities equal to those offered by many harpsichords built a hundred and fifty years later. The Theeuwes and the Haward were capable of various changes of tone and of pitch, and there is no reason to think that such changes are foreign to the style of English keyboard music of the period. Yet such a belief persists; and there are many who are under the misapprehension that an authentic performance of early English music can only be given on a simple rectangular virginal (page 21). It is probable that this mistaken idea originates from a misinterpretation of the word *virginal*, a generic term in the period under discussion for all domestic keyboard stringed instruments with jack action, though nowadays it is generally reserved for the rectangular type. An examination of these surviving instruments and of the title page of *Parthenia In-Violata*[1] shows clearly that the larger harpsichord was already in full use.

Against the background provided by these two instruments the previous and subsequent history of harpsichord making in England can be unfolded. Though examples of earlier work have not survived, it is interesting to consider what types of instrument were in fact in use at the beginning of the sixteenth century.

Several references to keyboard instruments appear in the Privy Purse Expenses of members of the Royal Family. The accounts of Henry VII show the following:[2]

> 1502. (Jan) To one that sett the Kinge's Clevechords xiii s. iv d.
> 1504. (March) For a paire of clavycords   xx s.

and examples of a similar nature appear from this time on. It must be borne in mind that the word *clavichord* was sometimes used generically in very early times, and thus covered plucked instruments as well as the real clavichord.

Henry VIII possessed at least one elaborate instrument, as in his Privy Purse expenses for 1530 we find:[3]

[1] The only recorded copy of this work, printed in London *c.* 1614, is now in the New York Public Library. (*See* Boyd (1940), frontispiece.)
[2] *Privy Purse Expenses of Henry the Seventh. B.M. Ad. MSS. 7099.*
[3] *Privy Purse Expenses of King Henry the Eighth.* Ed. Sir N. Harris Nicolas, 1827.

'(April) Item the vj daye paied to William Lewes for ij payer of virginalles in one coffer with iiij stoppes brought to Grenewiche iij li. And for ii payer of virginalls in one coffer brought to the More other iii li. And for a little payer of virginalls brought to the More xx s . . . vii li.'

The More was the Royal palace in Hertfordshire; but it is the first instrument at Greenwich that excites our attention. This appears to have been a double harpsichord with four stops. 1530 is very early for such an instrument;[1] but no other meaning for the entry seems possible.

Keyboard musical instruments were not lacking in the early years of the sixteenth century; the astonishing inventory of Henry VIII's instruments (appendix 8) shows among many other things: one virginal, and one virginal and regall combined at Greenwich; two virginals and regalls combined, fourteen other virginals and two clavichords at Westminster; nine virginals at Hampton Court; and more at Newhall and the More. To what extent these instruments were of English make it is impossible to say. In the Victoria and Albert Museum there is an Italian hexagonal spinet which bears the arms and device of Queen Elizabeth I; like almost all Italian instruments, it is made of cypress, and several of Henry VIII's virginals are also described as being made of this wood. It is not unreasonable, therefore, to assume that harpsichords and spinets were imported from Italy, and this idea is strengthened by the fact that numbers of good Italian instruments exist in England today, though some of these have no doubt been imported in more recent times.

Queen Elizabeth's skill as a musician is well known, and an account of her playing has been preserved in the Memoirs of Sir James Melville (1535–1617), who acted as Mary Queen of Scots' Ambassador to Elizabeth. The English Queen questioned Melville about Mary:[2]

'She asked what kind of exercises she used. I answered that when I received my dispatch, the Queen was lately come from the Highland hunting; that when her more serious affairs permitted, she was taken up with reading of histories; that sometimes she recreated herself in playing upon the lute and virginals. She asked if she played well. I said, reasonably for a Queen. That same day after dinner my Lord of Hunsdean drew me up to a quiet gallery, that I might hear some music, (but he said that he durst not avow it) where I might hear the Queen play upon the virginals. After I had hearkened awhile, I took by the tapestry that hung before the door, I entred within the chamber, and stood a pretty space hearing her play excellently well. But she left off immediately, so soon as she turned her about and saw me. She appeared to be surprised to see me and came forward, seeming to strike me with her hand; alledging she used not to play before men, but when she was solitary, to shun melancholy. She asked how I came there. I answered, As I was walking with my lord of Hunsdean, as we passed by the chamber door, I heard such melody as ravished me, whereby I was drawn in ere I knew how. . . . She enquired whether my Queen or she played best. In that I found myself obliged to give her the praise.'

[1] One double manual harpsichord said to be of 1590 and by Hans Ruckers is in private ownership in Brussels.
[2] *Memoirs of Sir James Melville*. Ed. George Scott, London 1683.

Musical instruments were by no means confined to the palaces of Henry and Elizabeth. In January 1525 the account books of the Earl of Rutland show:[1]

'Item payde be my Lorde's commaundement for the residewe of a paire of virgynals bought at my Lorde Mountjoye's, iij s. iiijd.'

Robert Dudley, Earl of Leicester, possessed at Kenilworth in 1583:[2]

'. . . an instrumente of organs, regalles, and virginalles covered withe crimson velvett and garnished withe golde lace. . . . A faier paire of double virginalles. A faier paire of double virginalles, covered with blacke velvett. . . .'

And in 1603, at Hengrave Hall, Sir Thomas Kitson possessed:[3]

'Item, one payer of little virginalls. One wind instrument like a virginall. . . . One great payer of double virginalls . . . one payer of virginalls with irons . . . a payer of virginalls with irons. . . .'

At Hengrave John Wilbye (1574–1638) was employed as resident musician from about 1595–1628, and during this period much of his work was produced.

Charles I, like Elizabeth, included instruments of foreign make among his possessions. A harpsichord was ordered from the Ruckers family in Antwerp, and the Resident there, the painter Balthazar Gerbier, wrote to Sir Francis Windebank, Secretary of State, in January 1637 to describe it:[4]

'The virginall I do pitch upon is an excellent peece, made by *JOHANNES RICKARTS* att *Antwerp*. Its a dobbel staert stick as called hath four registers, the place to play on att the side. The virginall was made for the latte Infante, hath a faire picture on the inne side of the Covering, representing the Infantas parks, and on the opening, att the part were played, a picture of *Rubens*, representing Cupid and Psiche, the partie asks £30 starling. Those virginalls which have noe pictures cost £15.'

The virginal, or large double harpsichord as we should call it, in due course arrived, but it proved to have transposing keyboards (page 44, and plates 33–5), and a complaint was sent off to Gerbier:

'The workman that made it, was much mistaken in it, and it wants 6 or 7 keys so that it is utterly unserviceable. If either he could alter it, or wolde change it for another that may have more keys, it were well: but as it is, our music is marr'd.'

Jan Ruckers, however, proved unyielding, and Gerbier reported that he would neither alter it nor make one to a different design: 'This virginall cannot be altered, and none else made on sale' (appendix 9).

This interesting correspondence suggests that as late as 1637 the Ruckers family were still building their large harpsichords on the transposing keyboard model only; though the writer has sometimes doubted whether this was really so. Why they would not adapt one, when the operation was so simple, it is difficult to understand; but their views changed within a few years of this incident. There is no doubt that Flemish instruments were much imported at this time, and a number have survived in England to this day.

[1] *Historical Manuscripts Commission* 24. Rutland MSS. IV.
[2] *Historical Manuscripts Commission* 77. de L'Isle MSS. I.
[3] Woodfill (1953).
[4] *Original unpublished papers illustrative of the life of Sir Peter Rubens*, London, 1859.

King Charles had, however, an English instrument maker in London: Edward Norgate. The Lord Chamberlain's warrants for 1632 show a payment to Norgate of £42 for work on the organs and virginalls. [1]

From surviving instruments we cannot trace a continuous course of keyboard instrument making in England from a date earlier than 1641. In that year Gabriell Townsend made a rectangular virginal, now in the Brussels Conservatoire, which is the oldest survivor of some twenty instruments of similar construction. Whether rectangular virginals had been made in this country for many years before the Civil War we do not know; [2] but they seem to have become obsolete by the last quarter of the century, the latest dated example being the Charles Rewallin virginal of 1679 in the Royal Albert Memorial Museum, Exeter. That they were common enough is shown by the following entry in Samuel Pepys's diary during the Great Fire:

2. Sep. 1666.

'River full of lighters and boats taking in goods, and good goods swimming in the water, and only I observed that hardly one lighter in three that had the goods of a house in, but there was a pair of Virginalls in it.'

These instruments are remarkably alike in design and construction, and the author believes that they derive from the virginals made in the Ruckers workshop, which they resemble closely. All are scaled at eight foot pitch and the keyboard is placed to the left of the centre. This important characteristic means that the plectra attack the strings at a point very close to the nut, and the tone is consequently brighter than in those Flemish instruments where the keyboard is placed to the right of the centre and the plectra attack further from the nut (page 47 and plates 25 and 26). The majority of English virginals have a keyboard compass from GG by short octave, the top note varying between c^3 and f^3. None has split keys. Only two instruments descend to FF chromatically, [3] though neither has FF$\sharp$ (plates 57 and 58), and five descend chromatically to C, which is in no case reached by short octave. The bright tone of these virginals carries unusually well, and the lightness of their construction gives a resonance which allows them to sound more powerful when played alone in a large concert hall than a full size modern harpsichord or one by Shudi or Kirckman.

Harpsichords contemporary with these oblong virginals have not survived, unless an unsigned and undated instrument in private possession in Los Angeles is accepted as English (see Boalch, plates 21 and 22). This tentative attribution is made partly in view of the decoration, which is very similar to the conventional decoration of the English virginals, and partly on account of certain Italian features of construction which are similar to the Knole harpsichord, and to the next dated English example: a Charles Haward of 1683, now at Hovingham Hall, Yorkshire.

[1] State Papers (Domestic), Vol. 229, No. 67.
[2] Parthenia, published in London c. 1613, shows a rectangular virginal on the title page.
[3] One made in 1664 by Robert Hatley (Fenton House, Hampstead), the other by Stephen Keene 1668 (Russell Collection).

The Los Angeles harpsichord has a chromatic compass from AA to f³. There are two eight foot registers and, in Italian style, the jack slides are not placed parallel with the keyboard but are further away in the bass. Also in Italian style, the sharp curve of the bentside gives a very short treble scaling, almost too short to suggest eight foot pitch:

C	$51\frac{1}{4}''$
c	$33''$
c¹	$17''$
c²	$8\frac{7}{8}''$
c³	$4\frac{1}{2}''$

The design of the two roses in the soundboard, the *tempera* decoration with which it is painted, the stamped and gilt paper over the keys, and the mouldings of the wood, are strongly reminiscent of the English virginals. But this may be an Italian harpsichord with English decoration.

The Charles Haward harpsichord of 1683 at Hovingham is of more restrained appearance, despite marquetry above the keys (plate 61). It has a sharply curving bentside, two eight foot registers, and jack slides diagonally placed. The compass is FF – d³, but there is no FF♯. This instrument is unusual in that it at one time had a lute stop, probably very early in its career. It is not known when this was removed; but a lute stop would have been an unusual feature in the late seventeenth or early eighteenth century, though it must in fact have been discarded at some time during the latter.

About this time an attempt was made to popularize a harpsichord with pedals instead of hand stops. In his *Musick's Monument*, published in 1676, Thomas Mace, Clerk of Trinity College, Cambridge, described a harpsichord with pedals:

'. . . the *Pedal*, (an *Instrument* of a *Late Invention*, contriv'd (as I have been inform'd) by one Mr. *John Hayward* of *London*, a most *Excellent Kind of Instrument for a Consort*, and far beyond all *Harpsicons* or *Organs*, that I yet ever heard of, (I mean either for *Consort*, or *Single Use*;) But the *Organ* far beyond It, for *Those other Performances* before mentioned.

'Concerning *This Instrument*, (call'd the *Pedal* because It is contriv'd to give *Varieties* with the *Foot*) I shall bestow a few *Lines* in making mention of, in regard It is not very commonly used, or known; because *Few make of Them Well*, and *Fewer* will go to the *Price of Them*: *Twenty Pounds* being the *Ordinary Price of One*; but the *Great Patron of Musick in his Time*, Sir *Robert Bolles*, (who, in the *University*, I had the *Happiness* to *Initiate*, in *This High Art*) had *Two of Them*, the one I remember at 30 1. and the other at 50 1. very *Admirable Instruments*.

'*This Instrument* is in *Shape and Bulk* just like a *Harpsicon*; only it differs in the *Order* of *It*, Thus, *viz*. There is made right underneath the *Keys*, near the *Ground*, a kind of *Cubbord*, or *Box*, which opens with a little *Pair* of *Doors*, in which *Box* the *Performer* sets *both his Feet*, resting them upon his *Heels*, (his *Toes* a little turning up) touching nothing, till such time as he has a *Pleasure* to employ them; which is after this manner, *viz*. There being right underneath his *Toes* 4 *little Pummels of Wood*, under *each Foot* 2, any one of *Those* 4 he may *Tread* upon at his *Pleasure*; which by the *Weight of his Foot drives a Spring*, and so *Causeth the whole Instrument to Sound*, either *Soft* or *Loud, according as he shall chuse to Tread any of them down*; (for without the *Foot*, so us'd, *Nothing Speaks*.)

'The *out-side* of the *Right Foot* drives *One*, and the *In-side* of the same *Foot* drives other; so that by treading his Foot a little awry, either outward or inward, he causeth a *Various Stop* to be heard, *at his Pleasure*; and if he clap down his Foot Flat, then he takes *Them both*, at the same time, (which is a 3d. *Variety*, and *Louder*.)

'Then has he ready, under his Left Foot, 2 other *Various Stops*, and by the like *Order* and *Motion* of the Foot he can immediately give you 3 other *Varieties*, either *Softer* or *Louder*, as with the *Right Foot* before mentioned, he did.

'So that thus you may perceive that he has several *Various Stops* at Pleasure; and all *Quick and Nimble*, by the *Ready Turn* of the Foot.

'And by *This Pritty Device*, is *This Instrument made Wonderfully Rare, and Excellent*: So that doubtless it *Excels* all *Harpsicons*, or *Organs* in the World, for *Admirable Sweetness and Humour, either for a Private, or a Consort use.*

'I caus'd one of *Them* to be made in my *House*, that has 9 several other Varieties, (24 in all) by reason of a *Stop* (to be Slip'd in with the *Hand*) which my *Work-man* calls the *Theorboe-Stop*; and indeed It is not much unlike It; But what It wants of a *Lute*, It has in Its own *Singular Prittiness*.'

That Mace himself possessed such an instrument is shown by a handbill[1] he published when he wished to sell his 'musical furniture' at Cambridge, because of his increasing deafness and poverty:

'There is a *Pedal Harpsicon* (the absolute best sort of *consort harpsicon* that has been invented); there being in it more than 20 varieties, most of them to come in with the foot of the player, without the least hindrance of play (exceedingly pleasant): and, also a *single harpsicon*.'

It is probably a similar instrument which is mentioned in the Lord Chamberlain's Records for 1664, when John Hingston, Keeper of the King's Instruments, was paid for 'repairing the organs, harpsichords and pedalls'. In 1678 he received £1.10.8 for 'strings for the harpsichords and pedall for three years and a quarter', and in 1683 £3.10.0 for the same work for four and a half years. [2]

Hingston, in his early life, was a pupil of Orlando Gibbons, and so became a practical musician. Whether he actually made musical instruments we do not know.[3] He seems to have done considerable work, as he received £56.16.0 on 29 May 1670 'for stringing and repairing the harpsichords . . .' and for strings for the virginals. In 1673 he received: 'for repairing and mending two harpsichords for the practice of the private music in the Great Hall . . . £1.10.0. For repairing and amending two harpsichords and carrying them to the playhouse £0.10.0.'

In 1673, at the age of fourteen, Henry Purcell was admitted 'Keeper, maker, mender,

---

[1] Harleian Collection, No. 5936. Trinity College, Cambridge.   [2] Lafontaine.
[3] During this period Girolamo Zenti of Florence and of Viterbo (fl. 1633–1683) became harpsichord maker to Charles II. He was succeeded by another Italian, Andrea Testa (page 37).

repayrer and tuner of the regalls, organs, virginalls, flutes and recorders . . . without fee . . . , and assistant to John Hingston, and upon the death or other avoidance of the latter, to come in ordinary with fee.' In 1683 Hingston died, and Purcell succeeded him in the following year at a salary of £60 a year. [1]

Charles Haward, maker of the Hovingham harpsichord, who lived in Aldgate Street, and his contemporary John Player were well known spinet makers in the last quarter of the seventeenth century, and a number of their spinets are still in existence. These represent the form which the small domestic keyboard instrument then assumed (plates 59 and 60). In shape they can be compared with a small harpsichord in which the strings and longside are no longer at right angles with the keyboard, but have been brought round to form an angle of about 35° with it; the bentside remains, and the keyboard projects from the front of the instrument. The spinet, with very rare exceptions, contains only one set of strings and one row of jacks; the strings are arranged in pairs, and the jacks for each pair of strings face each other, and consequently are not amenable to the movement of a slide for 'on' and 'off' purposes. It is really a small harpsichord of the most simple musical content, and of modified shape convenient for small rooms which cannot comfortably house the larger instrument Charles Haward's surviving instruments date from 1683; they are built with a compass from GG by short octave, and in some cases with split keys. The highest note is either c^3 or d^3. This compass is reflected in the keyboard music of the late seventeenth century, though the music of Henry Purcell requires a fully chromatic compass from AA, with GG as well. Spinets of similar disposition have come down to us from other instrument makers of the period, but those of Charles Haward are the most numerous.

Samuel Pepys bought a spinet from Haward, as the following entries in his diary show:

4 April, 1668. 'Up betimes, and by coach towards White Hall, and took Aldgate Street in my way, and there called upon one Hayward, that makes virginalls, and did there like of a little espinette, and will have him finish it for me: for I had a mind to a small harpsichon, but this takes up less room, and will do my business as to finding out of chords, and I am well pleased that I have found it.'

10 July, 1668. '. . . Home to dinner, and thence to Haward's to look upon an Espinette, and I did come near the buying one, but broke off. I have a mind to have one.'

13 July, 1668. '. . . I to buy my espinette, which I did now agree for, and did at Haward's meet with Mr. Thacker, and heard him play on the harpsichon, so as I never heard man before, I think.'

15 July, 1668. 'At noon home to dinner, where is brought home the espinette I bought the other day of Haward: costs me £5.'

Tonally the English spinets conform to a fairly standard pattern. The scaling is short, c^2 being generally about $10\frac{1}{2}$ inches though a length of 12 or 13 inches is occasionally found. In seventeenth century models the jacks attack the strings close to the nut, and the tone is thus bright and crisp, but in the larger eighteenth century instruments the plucking point is further from the nut, and the tone is consequently less incisive, particulary in the lower octaves. The strings are never plucked centrally in English or in continental spinets or

[1] Lafontaine.

virginals, though the centre point is of necessity approached in the highest notes. In England the tendency in both virginals and spinets was to pluck the lowest string at a point about a tenth of its length, and the highest at about a third.

The John Haward harpsichord of 1622, the Charles Haward of 1683, and, perhaps, the Los Angeles harpsichord, are the only seventeenth century examples to have survived. The early years of the eighteenth century have left little record of harpsichord making in England;[1] the spinet was evidently the instrument of choice. The period 1700–1730 can claim a Thomas Barton of 1709, a Tisseran of *c*. 1712, a Thomas Hancock of 1720, a Tabel of 1721, and a Shudi of 1729; two undated harpsichords: a Thomas Hitchcock and a Francis Coston, may be cautiously assigned to the end of the period.

The Tisseran harpsichord is at Woollas Hall, Pershore, and has been in that house since 1712 when it was purchased. It bears the inscription *Josephus Tisseran faciebat Londini*, and is a double harpsichord with three sets of strings, and three rows of jacks: $2 \times 8'$, $1 \times 4'$. The compass is four and a half octaves from GG, broken octave. Tisseran has left no other instruments. Preserved with this harpsichord are two contemporary letters describing its purchase and the manner of its transport from London, together with instructions about regulation and repair:[2]

1. Tho. Day, (London), June 10, 1712, to Mr. Edw. (Hanford, Woollas)

'I have been this morning to see another harpsichord: it is of Player's making, with split or quarter notes like Mrs. Stratford's . . . the upper sets of keys is an Eccho, very soft and in my opinion a little snaffling; but the other sett has two unisons like Mrs. Stratford's belonging to it, but a more noble sound. The man asks 30 guineas; I believe that the Excellent Harpsichord of 45 guineas will come at 40 if not for 40 lb. It is handsomely vernish'd, with mixt gold and black, and must have a leather cover which will come to 24 sh: the first I mention'd is plain without and has a leather cover to it, tho' not very handsome . . . the Harpsichord I saw today has the full compass that Mrs. Stratford's has above; a long octave to F below. The other Harpsichord is just of the same compass as hers but of a sound and make that is beyond exception . . . I do not find any difference between it and those that cost 80 and 100 guineas.'

2. Th. Day (London) Aug. 23, 1712, to Mr. Ed Hanford (Woollas)

'I sent you word when I went to Mrs. Hanford that I had bought you a Harpsichord. . . . I saw it safely put in the wagon. . . . You will be pleased to send a cart for it to Pershore, and that, before the wagon can be there, for fear there should not be due care taken in unloading it; for it is heavy and requires strong hands as well as care. When you have got it into the room you design for it, and have taken off the cover and Cross Bars that are within the case, you will lay it down as softly as can be, with the openside of the case downwards and then take up the case from the Harpsichord. Among the shavings you will find the stick and key tied to it. . . . I fear one of the nails has razed the leather cover. . . . The pins

---

[1] Christ Church Library, Oxford, has a MS. (1187) of *c*. 1690–1700 written by Henry Aldrich and James Talbot, giving details of many contemporary instruments. The harpsichord is described as a single manual, compass C – c³ chromatic, with two unisons and an octave. The scaling is Italian rather than English:

C 60", c 37", c¹ 21", c² 10", c³ 5"

[2] Sold by Sotheby and Co. together with the harpsichord, 16 Dec. 1949.

are tied with Packthread but I hope to have an occasion to send you some sattin lacing for that purpose. . . . The lid of the Harpsichord opens in two places; the first will do best for your usual practice because the more you open it the sooner it will be out of tune. I hope you design to keep it in the grey room, that being as I take it the dryest. . . . There are three setts of strings, which may be played on either all together, or every one by itself. One Set is an Octave to the other two. All together are only a thorough-bass to a Consort: for Lessons any two sets of the three are more proper. . . . If any Jack does not speak it is commonly by reason of the pen (i.e. the quill) hanging on the string; and the way is not to beat the key or shave the Jack, but take your penknife and scrape the underside of the pen towards the point as lightly as ever you can; then smooth it with three or four strokes of your penknife haft. And if any Jack should not slip down, never shave it, but thrust it up and down, and at the most scrape it gently.'

The 'split or quarter notes' seen in the Player harpsichord were, of course, the divided C♯ and D♯ keys of the broken octave.

The second of these early eighteenth century harpsichords is a small instrument, in the Russell Collection, which is signed *Thomas Hancock fecit 1720*. There is one manual with compass GG–e³, chromatic; the keyboard is decorated with ebony naturals and ivory accidentals each inlaid with a central ebony slip. There are two unison registers. This harpsichord is interesting as it still demonstrates the Italian features we have seen in seventeenth century English work: the jackslides placed diagonally, and the scaling very short in the treble, but it seems to be the last instrument to show these characteristics. The scaling is as follows: GG: 65″, c²: 10″, e³: 2½″.

Apart from the Tabel harpsichord of 1721 and the Shudi of 1729, with which we shall deal in the next chapter, the only remaining claimants to early eighteenth century English origin are double harpsichords by Thomas Hitchcock and Francis Coston.

The former of these is in the Victoria and Albert Museum, and is signed *Thomas Hitchcock fecit Londini* (plates 63 and 64). It almost certainly belongs to the first thirty years of the eighteenth century, though it has generally been assigned to the period *c.* 1690. This harpsichord has three sets of strings and four rows of jacks, and the disposition is:

Upper manual: $1 \times 8'$
Lower manual: $2 \times 8'$, $1 \times 4'$.

The system whereby the upper manual eight foot is also available on the lower manual, but without the assistance of a coupler, a system universal in eighteenth century English harpsichords, will be understood from figure 2, page 78.

This harpsichord has four unusual features, though the basic specification is that followed throughout the eighteenth century in double manual English instruments. (1) The compass is five octaves chromatic: GG–g³, a compass common among spinets, but very rare among harpsichords, where an FF compass was almost invariable. The Hitchcocks, however, were really spinet makers, accustomed to a GG keyboard, and the only other Hitchcock harpsichord known: an undated John Hitchcock of rather later period, at Lyme Park, Cheshire, also has a GG compass. (2) The grain of the soundboard is laid diagonally (plate 64), though it is normally always laid lengthways. (3) This harpsichord has a double curve bentside, rare in England. (4) The four foot hitchpins are on a hitchpin rail visible above the soundboard, instead of being driven through the soundboard into a rail concealed beneath it in the usual manner.

It will be noticed that there is no harp stop. This stop is often absent from English harpsichords until the latter forty years of the century, as the effect is available by other means. Put 'on' the upper eight foot and the lute stop only, and play on the lower manual. The upper eight foot will sound, as this row of jacks plays on both keyboards. But the lute stop only plays from the upper manual, and will not be affected by the movement of the lower keys. Thus the upper eight foot jacks will pluck a set of strings damped by the dampers of the lute jacks, and a *pizzicato* will result, very similar to that produced by the more conventional harp stop.

This Thomas Hitchcock harpsichord, together with the organ harpsichord of Theeuwes, came from Ightham Mote in Kent.

Francis Coston was at work in Brownlow Street, Drury Lane, between *c.* 1700 and 1738, in which year he sold his stock. His only surviving harpsichord was shown at the International Inventions Exhibition in London in 1885, and later passed into the Boddington Collection; its present location is not known. It has three sets of strings and a complete five octave compass from FF. The case is oak with some satinwood (perhaps harewood) inlay, the latter possibly a subsequent addition; and there is an early turned stand similar to that of the Thomas Hitchcock instrument. It is undated, but was probably made about 1730.

As little harpsichord making was taking place in England at this time, the instrument was still much represented by the work of men abroad. Zacharias von Uffenbach, the German traveller whose experiences in London were first published in 1753, wrote of a day here (1 Nov. 1710):

'To Gerard Street at the Romer tavern, where the host, a Frenchman called Binet, holds a weekly concert. There is a large room with a small one adjoining it where there hang a great quantity of choice musical instruments. The most notable of these are two magnificent clavearis, which are considered the best in all England, each being valued at two hundred pounds sterling. They are over a hundred years old and are by two of the most famous masters in Antwerp. The best is by Hans Rucker and the other is by his son who signed himself Jean Rucker to avoid confusion. Both have double keyboards.'

In 1720 John Christopher Pepusch compiled an inventory of musical instruments at Cannons, the palace of the Duke of Chandos, Handel's patron; here we find:[1]

'1. A chamber organ, 3 rows of keys, 18 stops, made by Jordan.

2. A four-square harpsichord, 2 rows of keys at one end, a spinet on the side; painted on the lid, Minerva and the nine Muses, by A. TILENS 1625, made by J. RUCKERS, Antwerp.

3. Harpsichord: 2 rows of keys made by HERMANUS TABLE London.

4. Spinet. Made by THOMAS HITCHCOCK.

5. Double bass, with case. Made by MR. BARRETT.

[1] Stow MSS. No. 66. Huntington Library, San Marino, California.

6. Violoncello or bass violin. Made by MR. MEARS.
7. Tenor violin. Made by Mr. MEARS.
8. Violin: and case: made by JACOBUS STAINER. An inscription:
     "In Absam proper Oeni Pontium (i.e. INNSBRUCK) 1660"
9. Violin similar inscription, date 1676, made by JACOBUS STAINER.
10. Violin similar inscription, date 1665, made by JACOBUS STAINER.
11. Violin similar inscription, date 1678, made by JACOBUS STAINER.
     "besides these mention 2 more made in London."
   The following are in Albemarle Street:
12. Bass viol made by HENRY JAY, Southwark, 1623.
13. Harpsichord, 2 rows of keys.
14. Spinet.
15. Harpsichord with gut strings—made by MR. LONGFELLOW, of Pembroke Hall, Cambridge.
     "This stands at my house in Boswell Court." '

From this we can see that the Antwerp harpsichords were still much in use in the early eighteenth century. Unsigned instruments were common then as now, and are not necessarily the result of long lost name boards. The Ruckers double harpsichord and virginal is now lost from sight.

By the second quarter of the eighteenth century the spinet less frequently exhibited the double curve bentside often used by Haward and the Hitchcocks (plate 65), and took on the angular tail of the common harpsichord. The compass was increased, and the bass notes were obtained by conventional chromatic keys. In English spinets, as we have seen, the full keyboard compass often became five octaves chromatic from GG, 61 keys, while the equivalent harpsichord compass (joined by some spinets) was five octaves from FF (no FF$\sharp$), 60 keys. Why this was so it is impossible to explain. Towards the end of the eighteenth century the harpsichord generally received its lowest accidental; but the GG compass of the spinet is musically the more useful. The two Hitchcock harpsichords with their complete five octave GG compass are almost unique. Ferdinand Weber and Henry Rother of Dublin built some instruments with compass from FF or GG to g^3 (plates 77 and 78). From about 1765 Shudi built a few harpsichords with compass CC to f^3 chromatic (plates 75 and 76) (appendix 10), and in 1772 Kirckman produced one instrument of compass FF to c^4 (plates 71–4). But five octave FF compass became the standard and almost invariable rule for harpsichords.

CHAPTER SIX

THE BRITISH ISLES FROM 1730

At work in London in the early eighteenth century was a harpsichord maker named Hermann Tabel (or Table). Very little is known about him; J. S. Broadwood[1] is said to have stated in 1838 that Tabel was a Fleming who had served his apprenticeship in the workshop of 'the successors to the Ruckers family', and this has been accepted as meaning the Couchets. There is, however, no confirmation of this in the records of the Guild of St. Luke in Antwerp, where Tabel's name cannot be found. His importance to us lies in the fact that Shudi and Kirckman, the men responsible for almost all the harpsichord making in eighteenth century England, served their apprenticeship in his workshop, and it is likely that the standard large harpsichord made in this country derived from his designs. It is also possible that a special feature of design in double manual English harpsichords: the upper manual eight foot which is common to both manuals (figure 2, page 78) was an invention of Tabel's, but this design was also used in Hamburg at least as early as 1723.[2]

Almost all we know of Tabel is found in a notice in the *Evening Post* of 30 May 1723:

'Mr. Tabel the famous harpsichord maker has 3 Harpsichords to dispose of, which are and will be the last of his making, since he intends to leave off Business. At his House in Oxendon Street over against the Black Horse in Piccadilly, N.B. he has some fine Airs-wood (harewood) for furnishing the Insides to dispose of.'

In fact he did not retire but continued in business until his death in 1738. At that time his Foreman was Jacob Kirckman, who made haste to marry Tabel's widow.[3]

Only one Tabel instrument is known today.[4] This is a double manual harpsichord of five octave compass from FF:

> Upper manual: 1 × 8′, lute.
> Lower manual: 2 × 8′, 1 × 4′.

Broadwoods restored it in the mid nineteenth century, apparently adding the present inscription and putting in new keys and jacks. The rose in the soundboard is a cipher sur-

[1] Dale (1913).
[2] Harpsichord by Hieronymus Hass in the Musikhistorisk Museum, Copenhagen (see pages 101 and 103).
[3] Further details can be found in Boalch (1956).
[4] Dale's account of this harpsichord is misleading. See Mould in Ripin (1971).

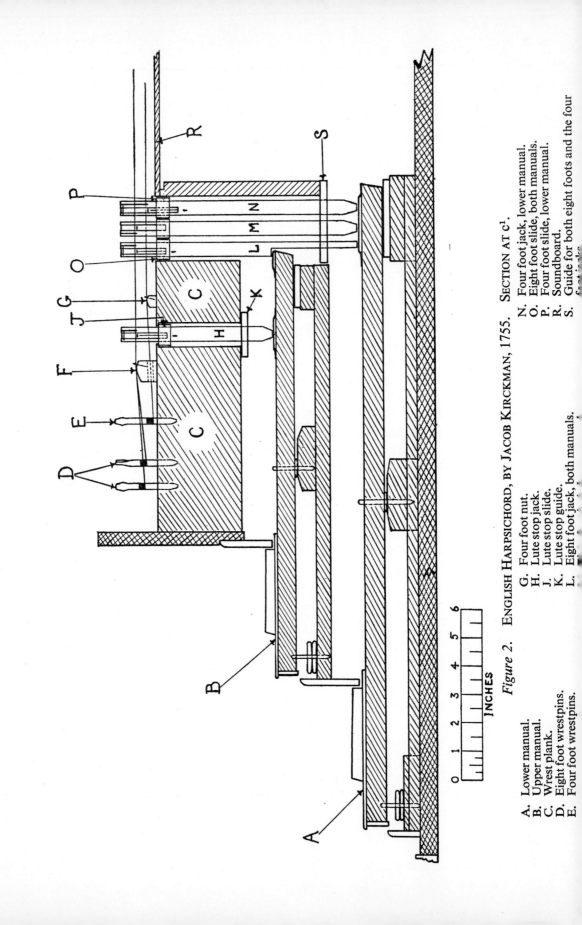

INCHES

0 1 2 3 4 5 6

Figure 2. English Harpsichord, by Jacob Kirckman, 1755. Section at c[1].

A. Lower manual.
B. Upper manual.
C. Wrest plank.
D. Eight foot wrestpins.
E. Four foot wrestpins.
F. Four foot nut.

G. Four foot nut.
H. Lute stop jack.
J. Lute stop slide.
K. Lute stop guide.
L. Eight foot jack, both manuals.

N. Four foot jack, lower manual.
O. Eight foot slide, both manuals.
P. Four foot slide, lower manual.
R. Soundboard.
S. Guide for both eight foots and the four

mounted by an Earl's coronet; but there is no original feature to suggest the work of Tabel in particular nor of the Low Countries in general, and there is no record to show why it was necessary to replace the maker's inscription with one which the late Mr. James Wardrop considered to show nineteenth century lettering. Two Tabel harpsichords were sold at Christie's in 1793; and Shudi's MS. books contain an entry for 18 March 1777: 'Lady Howe bought a second hand harpsichord made by Table.' But we have little real knowledge of the man or his work.

The two best harpsichord makers in England in the eighteenth century were Burkat Shudi (or Tschudi) and Jacob Kirckman.

Shudi was born at Schwanden, Glarus, in Switzerland on 13 March 1702, and died in London on 19 August 1773. He came to London as a joiner in 1718, having learned this trade from his uncle, and shortly after his arrival was articled to Tabel in Oxendon Street. We do not know when Shudi left his master and set up his own workshop, but a harpsichord dated 1729 and signed by him is in private possession in Copenhagen. This instrument has the same specification as the Tabel described above, and it must have been one of Shudi's earliest instruments. In 1739 he took a house in Meard Street, off Dean Street, Soho, and there he remained until 1742 when he moved to Great Pulteney Street; this address remained the family headquarters until 1904. The date of Shudi's marriage is unknown; but his wife, Catherine Wilde, was also a native of Schwanden, and bore him children among whom were Burkat Shudi the younger (d. 1803) and Barbara (bapt. 1748, d. 1776).

In 1761 Shudi took as apprentice a Scottish cabinet maker from Cockburnspath, John Broadwood (born 1732), who in 1769 married Barbara, and was taken into partnership by his father-in-law shortly afterwards. In 1771 Shudi retired, leaving his son-in-law in charge of the business; details of the agreement are to be found in appendix 11. Burkat Shudi died at his house in Charlotte Street on 19 August 1773. The *Public Advertiser* for 21 December 1773 gives details of Broadwood's plans for the future:

'John Broadwood, late Partner of Mr. Burkat Shudi, Harpsichord Maker, deceased, begs leave to acquaint the Nobility and Gentry that he has the assignment of the Patent for the new improvement of the Harpsichord, so much admired by all lovers of Music, and continues the business in Great Pulteney Street, Golden Square, with Burkat Shudi, only son of the deceased; where they humbly hope for the continuance of the favours conferred on the late Mr. Shudi as it will be their constant study to deserve such favours, and will take care to execute the commands of the Nobility and Gentry with the utmost punctuality.

'N.B. Harpsichords tuned and put in order on the most reasonable terms, at the shortest notice.'

John Broadwood retired in 1811 and died during the following year. The firm continues today as the pianoforte makers John Broadwood and Sons.

Shudi's harpsichords are built to certain fairly rigid specifications; with the exception of a few special instruments, they have a compass of five octaves from FF, the earlier ones lacking FF♯. Single manual harpsichords have two unisons and, almost always, an octave, controlled by three, or when a lute stop is present, by four rows of jacks. The double harpsichords have the latter content, disposed in the standard English way:

Upper manual: $1 \times 8'$, lute.
Lower manual: $2 \times 8'$, $1 \times 4'$.

A harp stop of buff leather was usually provided for the lower unison after about 1760.

Later instruments were often equipped with a *machine* stop worked in conjunction with a pedal, the stop lever for the mechanism being placed in the left hand key cheek of the case. This mechanism probably dates from about 1765 when it appeared in a harpsichord made for the King of Prussia.[1] When this stop is put 'on' the mechanism engages the upper unison and the octave; the lower manual unison must be added separately. On depressing the pedal this combination is changed to give the lute on the upper manual, leaving the one unison on the lower. In instruments with one keyboard, pressure on the pedal takes off the first eight foot and the octave, leaving the second unison only. The mechanism for this action is contained in a box on the left of the case.

On 18 December 1769 Shudi patented a Venetian swell mechanism for his harpsichords, which was similar to the swell box of the organ. This consists of an inner lid to the harpsichord, fitted with hinged shutters. Pressure on a pedal causes the shutters to open and allows of *sforzando* and *crescendo* effects. But the *open* and *closed* effects in harpsichords incorporating the swell differs as much in tone colour as in volume. Upper partials are suppressed in the *closed* position, and a muffled sound is produced compared with the brilliance of the *open* effect. The invention was useful in giving expression to a note already sounding, as well as in providing some *crescendo* and *diminuendo* in the harpsichord's fight for survival against the pianoforte. The swell lid can be put up with the main lid of the harpsichord if the device is not wanted. Weber of Dublin was fitting a swell of almost the same design at about this time,[2] and Kirckman and others hastily took up its construction. The earliest form was the *Nag's Head* swell, a simple flap in the lid which could be opened or closed by means of a pedal; but this was a much less effective Nag's Head swell than that fitted to the organ.[3]

From the 1760's Shudi occasionally made a harpsichord with a compass of $5\frac{1}{2}$ octaves from CC to f^3; and these were the largest model of harpsichord produced in England (plates 75 and 76). It is not known how many were made, but several can still be traced (appendix 10). They are built to the same specification as the ordinary two manual harpsichord. The scaling of the lowest (CC) eight foot string is usually about 82 inches, and these instruments are consequently nearly nine feet long.

Shudi appears to have made at least one harpsichord with a sixteen foot stop, as the following advertisement from the *Morning Herald* shows:

[1] Harpsichord bearing the number 496, until 1945 in Wroclaw Castle. The machine is also found in two more harpsichords built for Frederick in 1766, numbered 511 and 512. These have always stood in the Neues Palais, Potsdam; but harpsichord No. 512 disappeared at the conclusion of the 1939–1945 war. A machine stop fitted to Shudi's harpsichord No. 120 of 1742 at Chirk Castle appears to be a later addition.

[2] Halfpenny (1946).

[3] Nag's Head swell boxes are still preserved in Broadwood Kelly Church, Devonshire, (Telford), Teigngrace Church, Devonshire (maker unknown), and in Cobham Hall, Rochester (Snetzler 1778).

'Handel's Harpsichord, at Mr. Cross's opposite the Town Hall, Oxford. On Thursday, the 26 June 1788, at Two o'clock in the afternoon. A capital double key'd harpsichord by Bureat [*sic*] Shudi made for the immortal Handel and used by him till his death, at the different Concerts in London. It consists of four stops, which are as follows: two unisons, an upper and lower octave, has a powerful tone and is well calculated for Concerts.'

What has become of this instrument is not known.[1]

The question of Handel's harpsichord has led to many claims and traditions. Some of these are supported by evidence, others rest on very slight foundations. The chief claimants are examined in appendix 12.

The string scaling and plucking points of the various registers of Shudi's harpsichords bear a strong resemblance to those employed by Kirckman. But after John Broadwood became Shudi's partner, these details changed; the scaling of the bass strings was increased, FF often reaching 76 inches, as opposed to the old 68 or 70 inches, and the plucking point of the jacks was moved further from the nut. This no doubt resulted from Broadwood's desire to treat more scientifically matters of harpsichord design that had previously been settled by practical experience in instrument making alone. In the 1780's according to MS notes in the possession of Messrs. Broadwood, he took professional advice from Dr. Gray of the British Museum with a view to equalizing tension throughout the scale, and adjusting the point of attack of the strings. Among the changes which resulted from these discussions was an attempt to place the point of attack at about a ninth of the string's vibrating length, though practical reasons prevent this being constant throughout the scale. Consequently the tone of the late Shudi instruments is less incisive than that of the Kirckmans, and lacks much of the latter's brilliance. The last harpsichord from the Great Pulteney Street workshop is a single manual harpsichord of 1793, No. 1155. Various structural features suggest that it occupies a case which had been designed to contain a grand pianoforte, and its tone is so lacking in brilliance that early hammer action is suggested to the ear. It seems to be the only harpsichord signed by John Broadwood alone.

From 1770 onwards the instruments bear the name of both father and son-in-law; after the death of Shudi in 1773 young Burkat's name appears with that of Broadwood. The last recorded example so inscribed is a single manual harpsichord of 1791, No. 1148, in the Manchester Central Library. Four instruments exist which do not fit into this classification: the John Broadwood of 1793 described above; a double manual of 1769, which is signed by Bernard Shudi, whose relationship to Burkat it has proved impossible to determine. The two other instruments, which are also double harpsichords, are dated 1773 and 1776 and bear the signature of Joshua, nephew of Burkat, who had quarrelled with his uncle and set up his own business in 1766 (appendix 13).

A single manual Shudi in the 1770's cost 35–40 guineas, but the price was 50 guineas if a swell was added. A double harpsichord with swell cost about 80 guineas; but the 5½ octave model could be as much as £110. A machine stop was some 10 guineas extra. The Shudi

---

[1] The notice has been interpreted to mean that there was a four foot on each keyboard, and this meaning is also possible.

output from 1729 to 1793 seems to have been 1155 harpsichords, if these were numbered consecutively.

Jacob Kirckman was eight years Shudi's junior. An Alsatian, he was born in 1710 at Bischweiler near Strasbourg. Kirckman must have come to London in the 1720's, as he served an apprenticeship and became Foreman to Tabel, whose widow he married in 1738. The following advertisement, which appeared on 8 May 1738 in the *Daily Gazetteer*, suggests that Tabel had died only a short time before.

'Whereas Mr. Hermann Tabel late of Swallow Street, the famous Harpsichord maker, dead, hath left several fine Harpsichords to be disposed of by Mr. Kirckman, his late Foreman; this is to acquaint the Curious, that the said Harpsichords, which are the finest he ever made, are to be seen at the said Mr. Kirckmann's the corner of Pulteney Court in Cambridge Street, over against Silver Street, near Golden Square.'

Kirckman's marriage, as might be expected, was not a fruitful one; and by 1772 he had taken into partnership his nephew Abraham, with whom his instruments were then jointly signed. He died at Greenwich in 1792 and was buried in Saint Alfege's Church on 9 June. Abraham, who had been born at Bischweiler in 1737, outlived his uncle by only two years; he died at Hammersmith in 1794, and was buried in the same church as Jacob on 16 April. Abraham's son, Joseph, took over the firm, which continued as pianoforte makers throughout the nineteenth century. The business was amalgamated with Collard's in 1896, who in their turn were taken over by Chappell and Co. Ltd.

The design of Kirckman's harpsichords is not unlike that of Shudi's, and there can be little doubt that both were modelled on Tabel's instruments; there have survived however about twice as many Kirckman as Shudi harpsichords. Kirckman built some single manual harpsichords[1] with two unisons only, and others with an octave as well. He does not seem to have included a lute stop in these single instruments. His double harpsichords have the same specification as those of Shudi. A buff leather harp stop was generally included after about 1760; there is often a machine stop and, in some instruments, a swell. These two devices were sometimes added to early instruments some years after their manufacture, as is demonstrated by a double harpsichord of 1754, built in a case veneered with figured walnut. The swell and machine, however, are later additions and are not of walnut but of mahogany. Kirckman's early machine stops are of crude design compared with those of Shudi, though in his later work he used a similar mechanism.

Until 1772 Kirckman harpsichords were signed by Jacob alone; but in that year the name of Abraham was included, the form being *Jacobus et Abraham Kirckman Londini fecerunt*. A few instruments from 1789 to 1791 are signed by Abraham and Joseph; and the last few, from about 1798, bear Joseph's name only.

The earliest surviving Kirckman at present known was made in 1744 as against Shudi's harpsichord of 1729 in Copenhagen. But Kirckman made harpsichords for some years after Broadwood had left off; there are two of 1798 and another of 1800.[2] Kirckman, at

---

[1] Robert Smith (1689–1768), Astronomer, and Master of Trinity College, Cambridge, stated in his *Harmonics* (1762) that he possessed an enharmonic harpsichord by Kirckman, single strung.
[2] Engel believed the last Kirckman harpsichord was made in 1809 (*Musical Times*, July 1879).

least in his early days, made spinets as well as harpsichords. Four of these are known at the present time.

A remarkable claviorgan: a harpsichord by Kirckman and an organ by Snetzler, is in the possession of the Earl of Wemyss. The harpsichord is signed *Jacobus Kirckman fecit Londini*, and is a double manual with five octave compass from FF:

Upper manual: 1 × 8', lute,
Lower manual: 2 × 8', 1 × 4'.

The organ is signed *Johan Snetzler fecit Londini 1745*, and is playable from the lower manual, from which it can, however, be disconnected by moving two levers. It has the following composition:

8', stopped wood diapason (GG to b)
8', open wood diapason (c¹ to f³)
4', stopped wood flute
2', open metal fifteenth
Open metal mixture II (19, 22; from c² 12, 15).

There are two blowing pedals (for use in different positions), a swell pedal which opens a door at the side of the organ, and a pedal to cancel the principal and mixture. The case of figured walnut and of marquetry in sycamore is of exceptional quality.

Charles Burney stated that claviorgans were sometimes produced by Shudi and Snetzler,[1] though no example can now be found. The harpsichord organ figures in Shudi's books quite commonly, but the organ builder is not named.[2] The only examples made in England and at present known to survive are the Kirckman Snetzler, the Ludovic Theeuwes dated 1579, and one dated 1745 by Crang, formerly at Nettlefold Castle. This instrument was subjected to an unfortunate rebuild in London in 1953, when the interesting organ was discarded and its casework and decoration were altered and spoiled.[3]

The command which Shudi and Kirckman exercised over the harpsichord trade in London was so great that examples from other workshops are comparatively few. Longman and Broderip, a retail music and musical instrument shop, was founded in the 1760's by James Longman at 26, Cheapside. He was joined in 1771 by a man called Lukey, and the

[1] Snetzler was an executor of Shudi's will, according to a Deed dated September, 1773 (John Broadwood and Sons). The writer cannot trace this statement of Burney's, which is given by Rimbault (1860) page 89.
[2] There are, however, the following entries: '9 April, 1783: Lord Howe sent an organ to be sold.' '16 April, 1783: Mr. Green tuned Lord Howe's organ.' It is possible that Shudi did some work with Samuel Green (1740–1796). Such entries as '21 Feb. 1776: Lady Luisa Manners Harpd. Organ repaired & sent home: £3. 16. 6.', or '23 Sep. 1777: Shipped two harpsichords and organs' occur several times a year.
[3] The remaining part of this instrument was offered at Christie's on 18 July 1957. An inscription above the upper manual, set in carved panels which have been much cut about, states: 'This Organ and Harpsichord were a Present from Beeston Long Esq. to his Sister Mrs. Drake.' Compass: FF – f³, lacking FF♯.

Upper manual: 1 × 8', lute,
Lower manual: 2 × 8', 1 × 4'.

firm bore both names until 1778 when Francis Broderip was taken into partnership. Lukey left the following year, and the firm was thereafter known as Longman and Broderip until it was declared bankrupt in 1795. Wind instruments as well as harpsichords, spinets and pianofortes, were retailed there; and the nameplate of the firm concealed the work of Thomas Culliford, Baker Harris, and other spinet and harpsichord makers. Longman and Broderip also supplied organs. The harpsichords, at least twenty of which survive, follow the various designs of Shudi and Kirckman, and range from single keyboard instruments with two unisons only, to full size double harpsichords with machine and swell. The firm also had rooms at 26 Haymarket, where music was published.

Joseph Mahoon has left several harpsichords and spinets, and was certainly one of the more popular of the smaller makers. A harpsichord by Mahoon is illustrated in Hogarth's *Rake's Progress* (plate 2), and this shows that he was working in 1735. A Mahoon spinet in the Victoria and Albert Museum was made in 1771.

Harpsichords with pedals are mentioned in an auction advertisement of 11 February 1772. The mechanism there referred to is probably a different one from that of the machine stop described above: possibly a pedal board for trackers, or a separate pedal harpsichord as made in Germany.

'To be sold by auction by Mr. Christie, at his Great Room, late the Royal Academy, in Pall Mall, Tomorrow and Thursday; Fifteen fine toned harpsichords, with double and single keys, several of which, with double and single bass pedals, etc, being the stock in trade of Frederick Naubauer [*sic*], Harpsichord maker, together with a *Lyrichord*, a capital melodious instrument made by the famous Rutgerus Plenius. To be viewed this day. Catalogues may be had as above.'

Frederic Neubauer, worked in London between 1763, when he is mentioned in John Coote's *Universal Director*, and his death in 1774. Coote describes him as:

'Maker of double-basset and treble-key'd Harpsichords, with six stops, and of Pianofortes, Lyrichords, Classichords, etc., living in Compton Street, St. Anne's, Soho.'

Sixteen foot stops, three manual harpsichords, and clavichords, are possible interpretations of the terms used in this advertisement. But there is no certainty in this curious terminology, and no example of Neubauer's work survives. His daughter, Charlotte, married Abraham Kirckman, and with her sister was responsible for the administration of her father's estate after his death. His instrument making was therefore probably absorbed into that of the Kirckmans.

The *lyrichord*, referred to in both quotations given above, was originally patented by a musical inventor and instrument maker, Roger Plenius, in 1741. It consisted of the application to the harpsichord strings of revolving wheels covered with resin, in an attempt to prolong the sustaining power of the instrument. It was claimed that the Lyrichord would not go out of tune, and that the sounds of bowed instruments could be effectively imitated. No example has survived; but see plate 103.

Spinet makers flourished in England in the eighteenth century, and a great many examples of their work have survived. The most important firm was the Hitchcock family (pages 74 and 76). There were three active instrument makers here: Thomas Hitchcock the elder, who signed a spinet which bears the early date 1660;[1] Thomas Hitchcock the younger, a son of the above; and John Hitchcock who died in 1774 and therefore may well have been a son of Thomas the younger. Spinets by the Hitchcock family were seldom dated, but are usually numbered, and the numbering suggests many were made. A spinet of Thomas the younger numbered 1425 bears the date 1733; the highest number on any known instrument of his is 1547. John Hitchcock has left a spinet numbered 2012 which is the highest recorded number for him. When examining spinets by the Hitchcock family it is important to be sure that the number on the top or bottom key or jack (or on the nameboard) is not misinterpreted as the date, a mistake which has sometimes occurred in the past, as when Hipkins[2] described a spinet by John Hitchcock, of obvious eighteenth century construction, as being dated 1630. Attention has already been drawn to the five octave GG compass of Hitchcock spinets, for which no explanation is available.

The names found on English spinets are often confusing. Signatures which appear on keys and jacks alone at one moment, suggesting a keymaker or Foreman, reappear on the nameboard of another instrument, suggesting an independent instrument maker. But these difficulties are solved when we remember that large scale makers, such as the Hitchcock family, must have employed several workmen and apprentices, who often left a personal record on keys and jacks. Later some of these men worked independently, when they signed their work on the nameboard. Similarly when instruments were sold by retailers, such as Longman and Broderip, who did not make instruments, the names of these retailers appear on the nameboards, though the actual maker's name can be found on the keys or jacks.

The writer suspects that component parts of keyboard instruments (e.g. jacks and keyboards) were sometimes made by specialist workmen who were independent of the workshops of the instrument makers, and that the latter bought these parts and assembled them in the instruments they had made to their various designs. No proof of this can be offered, but the custom persists today in pianoforte making for keyboards and for actions.

Little work by John Joseph Merlin has survived, but he is an interesting figure. Born at Huys near Liége in 1735, he came to England as a member of the Spanish Ambassador's court in 1760. Where he learned his instrument making is unknown; but in 1774 he took out a patent for a combined pianoforte and harpsichord. In this instrument the harpsichord contained two unisons and an octave, and the pianoforte hammers, which were brought into action by means of a pedal, attacked one of the unisons. The second unison and the four foot could be added, one at a time, by means of another pedal. One Merlin harpsichord only has survived, and it is the only eighteenth century English harpsichord at present known which has an original sixteen foot (plate 79).[3] This instrument is in the Deutsches Museum and bears the number 80 and the date 1780. It has one manual, compass FF – f³

[1] The transverse spinet was at that time a newcomer to England, and the rectangular virginal was commonly made here. Samuel Pepys (14 June 1661) refers to a 'Triangle Virginal', which demonstrates that the spinet was then relatively unfamiliar.

[2] *Grove's Dictionary*, 3rd Edn. (1927), article *spinet*.

[3] Another English example of the harpsichord pianoforte is in the Smithsonian Institution. The upper manual is for the pianoforte, the lower for the harpsichord. This instrument is by Robert Stodart and is dated 1777.

chromatic, and it contains a harpsichord with three registers: sixteen, eight and four foot, and a down striking pianoforte action with one string of its own for each note. There is also a shorthand recording machine, worked from extensions above the four foot jacks, which takes down the performance on a roll of paper revolving by clockwork. The recording device is built in a frame fitted inside the case above the strings; it can be removed if not required.

Charles Burney ordered a special pianoforte from Merlin in 1777 with the then unknown compass of six octaves from CC; and in his will he states, on leaving the instrument to his daughter Esther, that it was made for playing duets. This pianoforte is now lost, but two others are in the possession of Sir Albert Richardson, dated 1783 and 1786. Merlin died in May 1804. His interest to us is in the way he sought to increase the expressive power of the harpsichord in terms of dynamic control; but like others of his time he did not realize that these qualities were inherently part of hammer action, and he sought to experiment with modifications of the harpsichord that were musically unsound and mechanically too complicated to succeed. Like the swell and the machine stop, which appeared in England in the second half of the century only, Merlin's invention testifies to the failure of the harpsichord when faced with competition with the pianoforte. We must remember that these devices have nothing to do with the classical harpsichord literature of Bach, Handel, Couperin, or Scarlatti, which was in existence before this period of transition.

London was not the only place where keyboard instruments were made, though little of importance seems to have been done elsewhere. John Loosemore (1613–1681), an organ builder of Exeter, made regals and virginals; and instruments by him and by his fellow townsman and contemporary, Charles Rewallin, have survived. In Edinburgh John Davidson and Alexander Adam made virginals in the seventeenth century; spinets and pianofortes were made by John Smith, John Johnston, James Logan, and by Neil Stewart who was also a retailer, between 1760 and 1791. Spinets, and at least one harpsichord which is now in the Castle Museum, York, survive from the workshop of Thomas Haxby of York (*c*. 1737–1777). John and Joseph Kirshaw of Tib Lane, Manchester, have left good spinets of conventional pattern, built in the 1770's. In Bristol John Kemys, Brice Seede, Maddey and John Smith Kemp were eighteenth century makers, repairers, and probably retailers. None of their instruments is at present known. In Wigan there was John Longshall who has left spinets made about 1760. There was Thomas Warn in Gloucester (fl. 1740), Thomas Underwood in Bath (fl. 1746–1760) and Ruive in Liverpool.

IRELAND

According to Flood[1] virginal making in Ireland is recorded from 1515. The earliest known Dublin virginal maker is Adrian Strong, who was at work between 1639 and 1655. None of his instruments are thought to survive.

In the early eighteenth century John Woffington and Thomas Hollister were both well known in Dublin as organ and harpsichord makers, and they can be traced from about 1728. John Woffington was succeeded by his son Robert, and this firm continued until 1836.

[1] *Jnl. of the Royal Society of Antiquaries of Ireland*, Vol. 19, 1909.

IRELAND

The best known harpsichord maker in Ireland was Ferdinand Weber, who came over from Germany in 1739, and opened his workshop at Dublin in Werburgh Street. Weber had previously served an apprenticeship of seven years to Johann Ernst Hähnel, an organ builder in Meissen. A number of instruments survive: upright harpsichords, horizontal harpsichords, spinets, pianofortes and organs.

Weber's work, though not unlike that of his London contemporaries, is unusual in that his harpsichords often show a compass of FF to g^3. He used a swell mechanism, slightly different from that patented by Shudi,[1] from about 1769, and also various forms of machine stop.

Flood tells us that Weber made harpsichords for Thomas Roseingrave (1752), and later for Dean Delaney, Lord Grandison, Lord Mornington, and Lord Normanton, Archbishop of Dublin (1768–1769). The latter instrument is now in the National Museum of Ireland. In addition, Weber's books show the following harpsichord sales:

Dec. 1764	Mr. Lyster	£34	2	6
Jan. 1772	Mr. Thomas	£22	15	0
Jan. 1776	Mr. Skerrett	£36	8	0
Jan. 1778	Bishop of Ferns	£34	2	0
Apr. 1778	Countess Glandore	£25	0	6

This list is by no means complete. There is a single manual harpsichord, dated 1751, in the Brussels Conservatoire, and other single manual instruments exist in England and Ireland, though the writer knows none with two manuals. A harpsichord sold by Sotheby and Co. on 16 March 1956, was signed *Ferdinandus Weber Londini fecit 1746*, and this serves as a reminder that between 1746 and 1760, in which year Weber hired out a harpsichord to the Duchess of Bedford at Woburn Abbey,[2] he was working in London, at least for part of the time. His death occurred in Dublin in 1784.

Another maker of harpsichords was Henry Rother, and an upright harpsichord from his workshop is preserved in the National Museum of Ireland. The instrument has the same compass: FF – g^3, which often appears in Weber's work; and this feature, together with the manufacture of the upright harpsichord, are special Irish characteristics of the eighteenth century.

Other Dublin makers with the dates of their work are William Gibson (1764–1790), and the MacDonnell family represented by Alexander, James, and Daniel (1790–1804). Instruments were imported a good deal from England, the chief agents being William Ware of Belfast and Henry de la Maine of Cork.

THE CLAVICHORD AND EARLY PIANOFORTE

The clavichord was very little used in the British Isles.[3] The only example which claims old English construction is a small fretted instrument, compass C – d^3 chromatic, and signed

[1] Halfpenny (1946).

[2] The accounts for this hire are preserved at Woburn Abbey together with other bills from Shudi and Hitchcock.

[3] Thurston Dart owned a late seventeenth century English MS. of keyboard music, which includes two 'Allemandes fitt for the Manichord'.

87

Peter Hicks Fecit, in the Victoria and Albert Museum. This clavichord was at one time believed to be an early eighteenth century instrument, but it is impossible to accept this. There is no doubt however that clavichords were sometimes imported from Germany in the eighteenth century. A number of the best German instruments exist in this country, including at least seven from the Hass workshop at Hamburg. We do not know when they were brought over, but it is clear that the instrument was not unknown here. Contemporary references are rare, but Handel's friend Mrs. Delaney, writing on 27 March 1756, refers to her daughter practising the clavichord in the dining room of her house in Spring Gardens. [1] Shudi's books for 9 October 1773 show: 'Count Brahl went for No. 3.4.5.6.7.8.9.10.03 Brass wire for a Clavichord.'

Though pianoforte making was common in London from the late 1760's, the harpsichord continued in use until the turn of the century, though during these years it lost more and more ground to its fashionable successor. The last harpsichord from Broadwood's was, as we have seen, made in 1793; and Carl Engel (1818–1882) writing in the *Musical Times* for 16 June 1878, stated 'the late Mr. Kirckman told me that he, with his father, constructed the last harpsichord in the year 1809'. Engel was of course referring to the Joseph Kirckman (*c.* 1790–1877), son of Joseph Kirckman, and grandson of Abraham. That the instrument was retained in use by a few conservative people in the early nineteenth century is obvious; but the general position is demonstrated by the fact that when Charles Dibdin, the composer (1745–1814), sold his theatre in Leicester Place in 1805 and its contents were auctioned, a fine Shudi harpsichord was offered but there was no bid for it; a Hancock grand pianoforte fetched £70.

AMERICA

It is convenient to discuss instrument making in North America here, as that country was under British rule up to the last twenty years of the eighteenth century. The demand for musical instruments was in part met by the import of English harpsichords and spinets; but a certain number were built in the country, and though some were the work of immigrants, there were also native instrument makers.

Johann Gottlieb Klemm (1690–1762) was born in Saxony. In 1736 he emigrated to America and settled in Philadelphia. In 1745 he moved to New York, and remained there until 1757. An early spinet by Klemm has been preserved, and is now in the Metropolitan Museum; [2] the compass is FF – c^3, and the inscription: *Johannes Clemm fecit Philadelphia 1739*. Gustav Hesselius was also working in Philadelphia about this time but none of his work is known today.

A native instrument maker of this period was Samuel Blythe, who was baptized in 1744 at Salem, Massachusetts. A spinet dated 1789 is in the Essex Institute Museum, Salem, [3] and has a compass GG–f^3, bass short octave. It is signed over the keys *Samuel Blyth, Salem Massachusetts fecit*. Blythe appears to have worked in his native town all his life, and there he died in 1795.

On 12 October 1761 George Washington wrote from Mount Vernon to John Didsbury,

[1] Deutsch (1955), page 771.   [2] Boalch (1956), plate 32.   [3] James (1930), plate 32.

probably an agent, in London, asking for the despatch of a large variety of stores. Among these he wanted:

'one very good spinet, to be made by Mr. Plinius, Harpsichord Maker in South Audley Street, Grosvenor Square. Note it is beg'd as a favour, that Mr. Cary (the shipper) would bespeak this instrument as for himself or a friend, and not let it be known that it is intended for Exportation. Send a good assortment of spare strings to it.'

But this order came to nothing. Roger Plenius had been declared bankrupt in 1756 and was out of business in 1761. He had had a checkered career as a musical inventor, producing among other things his Lyrichord (page 84), but no examples of his work have survived. Much time elapsed before Washington finally obtained, in 1773, a harpsichord by Longman and Broderip (page 83); this instrument is still preserved at Mount Vernon. It is a double manual harpsichord, and bears the maker's number 735. Washington was not the only celebrated American of his time who sent to England for a harpsichord; in 1758 Benjamin Franklin wrote from London to his wife, telling her of his efforts to find a good harpsichord to bring home to Philadelphia with him.

In 1768 a well known London spinet maker, John Harris, emigrated to America. The son and successor in business of Joseph Harris, he worked from about 1730 in Red Lion Street in London, and undertook experimental work in harpsichord making as well as his every-day business. On his arrival in America the *Boston Gazette* for 18 September 1768 announced:

'It is with pleasure that we inform the Public, that a few days since was shipped for Newport, a very curious Spinnet, being the first ever made in America, the performance of the ingenious Mr. John Harris, of Boston, (Son of the late Mr. Joseph Harris of London, Harpsichord and Spinnet Maker), and in every respect does Honour to that Artist, who now carries on Business at his House, a few Doors Northward of Dr. Clark's, North End of Boston.'

On the 14 November 1768 the *Boston Chronicle* stated:

'John Harris, who arrived in Capt. Calif from London begs leave to inform the public that he makes and sells all sorts of *Harpsichords* and *Spinnets*. Likewise mends, repairs, new strings, and tunes the said instruments, in the best and neatest manner. Any Gentlemen and ladies that will honour him with their custom shall be punctually waited upon. He lives at Mr. Gavin Grown's Watch-Maker, North side of King Street.'

There are spinets by Harris in the Horace Jackson collection at Lewes, and at Birmingham, Michigan; a third example was sold by Sotheby and Co. on 22 March 1934. The spinet in Michigan is the only one which may have been made in America.

Francis Hopkinson, the Philadelphia lawyer and musician, was much interested in improving defects in harpsichord construction, and between 1783 and 1787 he read four papers on harpsichord plectra before the Philosophical Society of Philadelphia (appendix 14). His first experiments were concerned with attempts to prevent quill plectra from breaking, and when he had satisfied himself with this work he communicated the results to the Society on 5 December 1783. At about the same time Hopkinson sent to England for a Shudi and Broadwood harpsichord, and instructed the maker to incorporate in it his new method of quilling.

The entry for this harpsichord in Shudi and Broadwood's books is dated 28 June 1783, and reads:

'Mr. Robert Bremner (the shipper) for a Double Key'd Harpsichord with five stops, two pedals, patent swell, etc. Mohogony Case.

	73	10	0
To three extra rows of jacks (leather plectra)	3	3	0
To a sett of tuning forks	1	1	0
To a leather cover	1	11	6
To 50 Raven Quills		7	6
To 500 Crow Quills		3	0
To a pair of Plyers		1	3
To 13 yards of Red flanel		18	0
To a Packing Case & matts	1	2	0
	81	17	3

'Sent to Mr. Hopkinson, Philadelphi.'

In 1784 Hopkinson reported to the Society that the new double harpsichord had arrived, and that Broadwood had further improved his invention in the quilling of it. At the same time he reported that he had just had twelve semitonal tuning forks made up as a set, to encourage amateur musicians to tune their own instruments by enabling them to set the scale. That Hopkinson was much occupied by his researches is demonstrated by four letters exchanged between him and Thomas Jefferson in 1785 on the subject of plectra (appendix 15). In these letters Hopkinson makes it clear that, in his researches for a more reliable plectrum than quill, he had himself chanced on leather, and after much experiment had put sole leather in the first unison, soft Morocco leather in the second unison, and wooden plectra in the octave of his new harpsichord. He was so well satisfied with the results of his experiments that he determined to sell the invention in England. Writing to Jefferson on 31 December 1785 he says:

'... Crow quills will hereafter be totally thrown aside. I sent this discovery to a friend in England, he was to offer it for £50, but writes in answer that my invention has been anticipated. I see I am to be defrauded both of the Money and Credit.'

Hopkinson communicated his researches on leather plectra to the Society in Philadelphia on 28 January 1786.

On 9 May of that year Jefferson, who had gone to Europe, wrote to Hopkinson from Paris saying that he had lately been in London and had called on Broadwood to talk about all these things. Broadwood had shown him that he had, from time to time, used leather plectra of various types for some years past. Jefferson also visited Adam Walker, a pianoforte maker of 8 Great Pulteney Street, Golden Square, and was shown the *celestine* attachment for harpsichords which Walker was making, and which he had patented as No. 1020. The celestine consisted of a downstriking hammer action, which attacked the strings at a point where a silken band revolved against them. The band was actuated by means of a treadle, and was intended to increase the sustaining power of the strings. This attachment cost eight guineas. [1]

On 25 May Jefferson, still in Paris, determined to buy a Kirckman harpsichord with Walker's Celestine attachment, and wrote to London to order the instrument. His enthusiasm was clearly excited, and a correspondence on the subject developed with Dr. Charles Burney. Writing to Burney on 10 July 1786, Jefferson makes it clear that Kirckman did not much like the incorporation of the Celestine in his instruments; and they were sent away to Walker for that work to be done. Meanwhile Hopkinson had addressed his Society for the last time on harpsichord plectra in a communication of 1787. He had been experimenting with plectra of velvet cork, covered with soft leather, and wished to inform his fellow members that the resulting touch was better than that provided by leather. Unfortunately neither Hopkinson's Shudi and Broadwood of 1784 nor Jefferson's Kirckman of 1786 can now be traced.

At the end of the century two more names appear in eighteenth century American instrument making. Charles Trute, who lived in London at Broad Street North, Golden Square, from 1782–1789, emigrated to America, taking into partnership a man called Wiedberg. An early grand pianoforte by Trute, thought originally to have been a harpsichord, has lately been converted to jack action by John Challis. This instrument is signed *True and Wiedberg Makers, Filbert Street, Philadelphia*. The Ford Museum, Greenfield, Michigan, has a rectangular pianoforte made in London by Trute; another belonged to E. C. Legg of Cirencester in 1954. A fourth pianoforte, owned by Mrs. G. Cappella, bears the address *Wilmington, Delaware*, but it is not recorded when Trute lived in that town, and nothing more is known of him. In Boston, at about this time, lived Benjamin Crehore, born at Milton, Massachussets. He made pianofortes, violins, and possibly spinets as well; he died in Boston in 1819.

DECORATION

The decoration of English keyboard instruments falls into four periods. In the sixteenth and seventeenth centuries oak was the wood of choice. Walnut had been used in this country for special pieces of furniture from the middle of the sixteenth century (page 158), and we might expect to find musical instruments built with this wood; but in fact oak seems to have been used almost exclusively until the last quarter of the seventeenth century. Walnut then made its appearance, and became increasingly common. It was used in solid pieces for lids, and in view of an increased use of veneer in the last quarter of the century, the sides of the instruments were covered with walnut in this way. Some of this wood was of English origin, but some was shipped from Virginia. From about 1720 mahogany began to appear in increasing quantities, imported from the West Indies, and later on from Central America also. Like walnut it was at first used for lids, but it rapidly gained in popularity, and was soon applied as veneer, sometimes alone, sometimes as cross banding for walnut panels. Walnut itself

[1] Shudi also employed the *celestine* as his books show, i.e., '5 March 1777. Mrs. Sanderson had a Celestina Harp^d. 7 March 1778. Made a Celestina & sent (it).'

quickly lost ground, and disappeared in the 1770's, except for special uses such as panels of burr walnut as decoration round the keyboard. The fourth period is that in which satinwood made its appearance. Though veneers of this wood had been in use for furniture from the 1760's, it seldom appeared in musical instruments until some twenty years later. Satinwood was imported from the East and West Indies, and was not at first plentiful enough to be used in solid pieces. It is common in harpsichords from about 1780 onwards, its usual place being as cross banding for mahogany panels. In the early years of the nineteenth century, however, its use became lavish.

It will be realized that these divisions overlap, and are no more than rough guides; but they may be set out as follows: Oak until *c*. 1700; Walnut from *c*. 1680 to *c*. 1770; Mahogany from *c*. 1720; Satinwood from *c*. 1780.

Other forms of decoration appeared from time to time, and two of these require mention: marquetry and harewood. Marquetry was introduced soon after the Restoration, and was used in the more expensively decorated spinets and harpsichords. Its use in the old fashioned style of eighty years before is found as late as the 1760's, boxwood, sycamore and holly being favourite materials. Stringing of conventional pattern, using ebony with boxwood, sycamore or holly, was in constant use from the early years of the eighteenth century. Harewood (that is sycamore or maple treated with iron oxide which gives a green tint to the wood) was used for special purposes, such as decorative keyboard surrounds, from the 1720's, and plain sycamore and maple were occasionally used in the same way.

English instruments were seldom painted. The exceptions are the interiors of the seventeenth century rectangular virginals and some of the Flemish harpsichords that were enlarged in England. These latter were often veneered, but they were sometimes given a coat of paint. Shudi, on 24 December 1774, seems to have sold a painted instrument, for his books contain the entry: 'Miss Skeine bought a octava harpsichord, Blew bordered, No. 710'; but the writer has never seen an original painted English harpsichord, unless the Tisseran (page 73) at Woollas be so considered.

Both the Theeuwes harpsichord of 1579 (plates 53 and 54) and the Haward harpsichord of 1622 (plates 55 and 56) are built in oak cases. The Knole instrument has an original stand of ten fluted and arcaded legs, the whole being framed; it is a unique example of its kind, since there is nothing like it except in the Low Countries.

Virginals of the mid seventeenth century are the only real examples of English painted instruments. They are enclosed in oak cases, the drop front attached by hinges, the lid sometimes flat, sometimes domed. All this is plain wood. Inside, however, they present a mass of colour. The drop front and the lid are covered with paintings in *tempera*; these usually represent groups of figures walking in a country scene, and this setting is often formally described as 'St. James's Park'; but it is fantasy. The soundboards are painted with flowers and fruit and geometrical patterns, and there are carved roses or sound holes made of metal or varnished leather. The front and the inside of the case above the soundboard are always covered with gilt paper, embossed with one or more of several standard designs. Varieties of Royal arms are sometimes used, possibly taken from a coin or medal; but there is no reason to think that this denotes a Royal owner, for the practice is not uncommon. Most of the original stands with their turned and framed legs are lost, but a few old ones are preserved: i.e. in the Yale Collection and the Ashmolean Museum, both the work of Adam Leversidge, and dated 1666 and 1670 respectively. The keys of these instruments, and of most others until about 1700, have ebony naturals and ivory accidentals, the fronts of the naturals being gilded or covered with embossed paper. Boxwood naturals and rosewood accidentals are occasionally found.

The fashion for spinets in England dates from the last half of the seventeenth century. At first they were made of oak or walnut, often with a cross banding of the same wood. Marquetry was set above the keys of the more elaborate examples, and a handful have this decoration inside the case as well. The stands, like those of the virginals, were turned and framed, but original examples are not common.

With the turn of the century the general appearance of both spinet and harpsichord took on a lighter effect. The stands were still provided with turned legs, but these were more delicate than formerly. Oak disappeared, and cross banded walnut became the rule. A stringing of boxwood or holly, combined with ebony to form a herring bone or similar design, lightened the effect of these instruments; and the provision of handsome hardware fittings of brass was usual.

Ebony natural keys went out of fashion in England soon after the turn of the century. Examples occasionally appeared later on, but made to special order, as they are rare. The standard keyboard throughout the eighteenth century had natural keys covered with ivory, the fronts faced with boxwood mouldings; the accidental keys were of ebony. Occasionally a particularly handsome keyboard makes its appearance, possibly from some keymaker who specialized in such things, in which the ivory naturals have ivory arcaded fronts, while the accidentals are made of ebony with a slip of ivory in the centre. The Hitchcocks used these keys a great deal; Kirckman, Crang and Mahoon but rarely; Shudi put them in the two harpsichords of 1766 made for Frederick the Great; Snetzler used them for some organs. A specially fine keyboard is to be seen in Thomas Hitchcock's spinet No. 1547, his last known instrument, which was made c. 1740. This has ebony naturals with ivory arcaded fronts, and ivory accidentals with a slip of ebony let into the centre. A similar keyboard is in Thomas Hitchcock's spinet No. 1518 in the Metropolitan Museum.

The two hundred or more English harpsichords which survive from the eighteenth century provide many variations of detail within this outline of materials. The oldest surviving Shudi remains a keyboard with ebony naturals, though he soon after changed to the more usual style. The third oldest Shudi that we have: No. 120 dated 1742, at Chirk Castle, has elaborate marquetry decoration very like that used by Kirckman in 1755 (plate 66). But this is Shudi's only recorded example of such marquetry, while Kirckman used this decoration in several cases, from the very elaborate example of 1755 to instruments with a plain stand and a little marquetry above the keys only. A double harpsichord dated 1754, with walnut veneer, has a silver trophy of musical instruments above the keys; and this design, but made in marquetry, was sometimes ordered by Longman and Broderip thirty years later.

The stands of harpsichords and spinets of this period were usually plain, consisting of four legs of square section, joined by struts, with, occasionally, a shelf for music. Claw and ball feet are rare, being reserved for the most elaborate designs only, and they are used more often by Kirckman than by Shudi. Few instruments were made with music desks, and an examination of most will show that there is no space in which to put one. But occasionally a harpsichord was made half an inch deeper than usual, and then a music desk of mahogany will be found; walnut does not seem to have been used for this purpose.

Very few English harpsichords, and probably no spinets, were made to stand away from the wall, and the longsides were left without veneer. The Shudi of 1742, which has marquetry and a claw and ball stand, is an exception to this, but only one or two of the most decorated Kirckmans have veneer on the longside. The Shudi harpsichords of five and a half octaves are thus veneered, and the last instrument from this firm, the Broadwood of 1793, is also fully veneered. So is Kirckman's harpsichord of 1800, the last of his instruments now recorded as extant; but the ordinary harpsichord was not so veneered.

Compared with French or German instruments the decoration of English spinets and harpsichords was restrained; but within the wide possibilities offered by a few woods, with carefully selected panels for veneer, with various designs of stringing, and with crossbanding, these instruments achieve a fine effect; while Kirckman's most elaborate walnut and marquetry harpsichords are among the most magnificent pieces of furniture of any period.

CHAPTER SEVEN

GERMANY

Germany has left us more books on the construction of musical instruments in the sixteenth and seventeenth centuries than any other country; nevertheless very few German domestic keyboard instruments dated before 1700 have survived, and most of these appear to have been constructed in the latter part of the seventeenth century. Germany produced in the eighteenth century some of the best domestic keyboard instruments of all time, both harpsichords and clavichords, while organ making was equally high in quality; but the history of German instruments as seen from surviving examples is really the history of the eighteenth century only, and apart from organs nothing of much importance has survived from earlier times except the 1537 Müller harpsichord in Rome.

German literature on musical instruments is extensive, and begins with *Musica getutscht* of Sebastian Virdung, a German musician who published this book, the first of its kind, at Basel in 1511. It was printed in German, but a Latin edition was produced in 1536 by Luscinius, an Alsatian who had been organist of Strasbourg Cathedral. *Musica getutscht* (i.e. *gedeutscht*, or written in German) describes the keyboard, monochord and clavichord, pedal clavichord, virginal, harpsichord, clavicytherium, organ and other instruments, together with their tablatures, and woodcuts are provided. The clavichord is shown as a fretted instrument with all strings of the same length: a legacy from the monochord; and on the same page is illustrated a virginal in rectangular form. Both virginal and clavichord are shown with a compass from F to g^2, without F$\sharp$. The *clavicimbalum* is shown with a keyboard from B$\natural$ to d^2, and in appearance it is similar to the virginal. The clavicytherium has a compass from F to g^2, and we are told that it was a new invention with catgut strings. The blocks were, for some reason, not cut in reverse; hence these woodcuts are printed back to front, the treble and bass appearing at the wrong end. Agricola, Luscinius, and Rimbault, who reproduced the illustrations, failed to notice the error, but Hipkins (1896) drew attention to it. Virdung was reprinted in *facsimile* by Robert Eitner in Berlin in 1882, and by Bärenreiter Verlag, Kassel, in 1931.

In 1529, eighteen years after the appearance of Virdung's book, Martin Agricola produced his *Musica Instrumentalis Deudsch*. Agricola was born at Schwiebus on 6 January 1486, and besides producing some half dozen works on musical theory he was Cantor of the protestant school at Magdeburg, where he died on 10 June 1556. *Musica Instrumentalis*

Deudsch is written in German, and contains the same woodcuts which Virdung had used; but it tells us little of the early keyboard instruments. A reprint of Agricola appeared in Leipzig in 1896.

Michael Praetorius (or Schultz) was born at Kreutzberg, Thuringia, on 15 February 1571. He was a composer who left a large number of works, together with an important book: *Syntagmatis Musici . . .*, which was planned in four volumes, though only three appeared. Volume II, entitled *Organographia*, was published between 1618 and 1620, and it contains much detail relating to musical instruments at that time, with forty two woodcuts illustrating many different types. Of these the harpsichord is shown as a single manual with one eight and one four foot, and a compass which is probably intended to be four octaves from C, bass short octave. This compass is also given to the clavicytherium and to the clavichord. A polygonal spinet and a clavichord, both described as Italian, have the compass we would expect: C to f³, bass short octave; while a small clavichord and polygonal octave spinet have C to a², without a²♭, both with bass short octave. An oblong virginal has C to d³, broken octave, the two lowest accidentals and each e♭ being split.

Praetorius gives special sections to certain keyboard instruments, of which the first is the monochord. He next deals with the clavichord, which he describes as the fundamental member of the family of keyboard instruments. He recommends its employment as a practice instrument to students; he also deals with the problems of fretted clavichords and clavichords with quarter tone keyboards.

The next instrument described is the *symphony*. The terminology is very obscure here, but the present writer is inclined to think that it was a term reserved for the rectangular and polygonal spinets of eight foot pitch, shown in Praetorius' Plate XIV. But this is not certain, and he would do no more than direct attention to the possibility. Here Praetorius warns the reader against using the word *instrument*, instead of stipulating the exact keyboard instrument referred to.

The *spinetta* is described as being a small virginal, tuned at quint or octave pitch, and often placed in or on top of an eight foot virginal (page 47 and plate 29). We are told that in Italy both the large and the small instrument are called *spinetta*, that in England all are called *virginall*, in France *épinette*, in the Low Countries *clavicymbel* or *virginall*; but that in Germany *Instrument* referred to all musical instruments as a species, or to the *spinetta* in particular (*Instrument in Specie, vel peculiariter sic dictum*).

Praetorius then deals with the *clavicymbalum*, the instrument we know today as the harpsichord. Some people, we are told, call it *flügel* on account of its wing shape, while the vulgar call it *schweinskopf* (pig's head) on account of its shape suggesting a boar's snout. It is double, triple or quadruple strung; and Praetorius has seen an example with two unisons, a quint, and a four foot.

Next we are told about the *clavicymbalum universale*, a harpsichord with split keys designed for playing in the Diatonic, Chromatic, or Enharmonic systems at will. This was a favourite theme among the musical theorists of the late sixteenth and early seventeenth centuries (page 32 and plate 13). Short sections follow on the *clavicytherium*, the *clavi-*

organum, and the *arpichordum* (plate 26); the latter being a virginal with a sliding batten of brass hooks (*messingshäcklin*) instead of the usual buff leather harp stop. [1]

Lastly Praetorius describes the *geigenwerk* (plate 103). Impetus was given to this invention by the publication of a small book in Nürnberg in 1610 by Hans Haiden, from which Praetorius quotes. The *Nürmbergisch geigenwerck* was an instrument shaped like a harpsichord in which the strings were brought into contact with revolving wheels covered with resined parchment. It is interesting to note that the bass strings of this instrument were made of thick brass or steel, covered with windings of parchment: an early use of the covered string.

Praetorius contains a mass of information about the music of the early seventeenth century: he is an essential study for the specialist student.

Athanasius Kircher was a Jesuit who was born at Geisa, near Fulda, on 2 May 1602, and died in Rome on 28 November 1680. His *Musurgia universalis sive ars magna consoni et dissoni* appeared in two volumes in Rome in 1650. In the first volume, amid much that is untrustworthy, we have illustrations of musical instruments, including a single manual harpsichord with one eight and one four foot, and four octaves from C, chromatic, which is reproduced from Mersenne's book of 1636 (page 54). Far more valuable is Jacob Adlung's *Musica Mechanica Organoedi*, published in two volumes in Berlin in 1768. Adlung, born at Bindersleben, Erfurt, on 14 January 1699, was a theologian and a musician who gave practical instruction as well as making clavichords, though none of these is known to have survived. His work deals at length with the organ and harpsichord, but other matters are also included, and in the second volume there is a detailed account of the *cembal d'amour* (page 105). A facsimile of Adlung's book appeared in 1931 at Kassel, edited by Christhard Mahrenholz.

The bevy of musical instruments expected from a country which produced so many technical works is not to be found, and with the exception of the organ we have little of importance as far as keyboard instruments are concerned until the early eighteenth century. These were certainly imported in early times from Italy and the Low Countries; but in the sixteenth and seventeenth centuries instrument making was also carried on in a simple and unpretentious way by musicians and others with little knowledge of fine cabinet making. Such instruments: the typical small fretted clavichord of the seventeenth century, are of rough construction; and Andreas Werckmeister (1645–1706) the German organist, composer, and writer, states in his *Orgelprobe*, 1698, p. 56: 'such are not worth bothering about, for they are only fit to be used as firewood for cooking fish.' These small instruments are very difficult to distinguish from their Italian contemporaries. They are fretted, several adjacent keys attacking the same strings with their tangents; the compass in early examples is four octaves from C, bass short octave; but this compass often becomes chromatic towards the end of the seventeenth century. Despite the comments of Werckmeister these simple clavichords are often sensitive musical instruments, though their meagre dimensions and scaling can only result in rather poor tone.

The clavichord always remained the popular instrument in Germany, and this is demonstrated by the fact that, while only about twenty German harpsichords are known, the

[1] An arpichordum by Andries Ruckers of 1610 is in the Boston Museum of Fine Arts (Bessaraboff, fig. 62).

number of clavichords is very considerable. The reason for this is simple. Harpsichords are much more expensive than clavichords, and we must remember that Germany was unsound both politically and economically during the period when these instruments were built. Harpsichords existed for use in the theatre and opera, in large churches, and in the palaces of the nobility; and the sumptuous decoration of the survivors suggests that their owners were people of unusual means. Further, the lack of native harpsichords in Germany may not be unconnected with the ruthlessness with which everything savouring of the old was swept away in the first half of the nineteenth century, in preparation for new styles of decoration.

The primitive German clavichord began to give way, in the early eighteenth century, to the fine work of a number of skilled craftsmen. The old four octave instrument had been very small: not more than about three feet six inches long, and one foot wide; and this model continued to be made in the eighteenth century; but in addition a larger clavichord appeared, often reaching a five octave compass from FF. These instruments were the commonly built model from the 1720's onwards, and they were often strengthened in the lowest octave and a half by the addition of a third set of strings tuned at four foot pitch. Later, the compass was again extended, this time upwards only, and from the 1780's a^3 or c^4 was not uncommon.

Organists made use of their clavichords for the purpose of practising organ pieces,[1] a great convenience when churches were unheated, and organ blowing depended, in large instruments, on the services of several men. The clavichord was accordingly often fitted with a pedal board attached by trackers to the underside of the lowest keys; sometimes a separate pedal clavichord was built beneath the main instrument. An example of this kind with two manuals is in the Heyer collection (plate 89). It consists of two clavichords placed one on the other, thus giving two manuals, and a third instrument placed below with sixteen and eight foot strings and worked by means of a pedal board. Few of these pedal clavichords have survived: a one manual and pedal clavichord by J. P. Kraemer of Göttingen was destroyed in the 1939 war, but was formerly in the Germanisches Museum, Nürnberg. An example by Glück of Friedberg is in the Deutsches Museum, Munich (plate 90). Another is in the Bach Museum, Eisenach; and this is also a single manual with independent pedals, and is said to have been built by an unknown maker about 1800. It has a six octave keyboard from CC: an exceptional compass. Pedal harpsichords were also made. They are now very rare, but an interesting example with independent pedals is an instrument built in 1786 by Joachim Swanen, an Alsatian. The pedal action in this harpsichord has a hammer and not a jack action, and it is possible that it is a later addition. It is in the Conservatoire des Arts et Métiers, Paris (page 109).

About twenty German harpsichords made in the eighteenth century are preserved. Seven of these are the work of the Hass family, father and son, in Hamburg, the remainder being mostly isolated specimens from various workshops. In compass they range from just over four octaves: $C - d^3$, to over five octaves, the Joachim Swanen in Paris having the compass $EE - a^3$ chromatic. In specification they vary from $2 \times 8'$, $1 \times 4'$, to $1 \times 16'$, $2 \times 8'$, $1 \times 4'$,

---

[1] Jeans (1950).

$1 \times 2'$. Germany seems to have been the only country where the two foot stop was employed (but see page 38), and the only place where the sixteen foot was found at all regularly; of the German harpsichords known today, five have this as an original feature. [1]

A variety of unusual instruments for which German parentage is claimed are to be seen in the Heyer collection. These include various octave virginals, one with two manuals, clavicytheria, and so on. These are however of little importance where the history of instrument making is concerned, since they are for the most part unique specimens, and had no general musical position. A group of very small virginals are in existence, more toys than anything else, and too small for the adult hand to play. One is in the Victoria and Albert Museum, several are in the Heyer collection, two are in the Paris Conservatoire, one of the latter bearing a spurious inscription of Hans Ruckers, 1620. They are probably of German or Italian origin. They are in many ways similar to some of the ordinary and the automatic spinets of Samuel Biderman of Augsburg (1540–1624), though there is no reason to suppose he was their maker.

In the International Inventions Exhibition of 1885 there was exhibited what seems to be the second oldest German harpsichord, an instrument then attributed to *c.* 1700, but now lost from sight. It was the work of Friedrich Ring of Strasbourg, and had two manuals. There were four sets of strings: two unisons and two octaves, but one of the octaves was for sympathetic vibration only. The writer has not come across anything else by this Alsatian. Hermans Willen Brock of Hanover has left a harpsichord organ, now in the Metropolitan Museum. This claviorgan has a compass GG – c³, without GG♯, but hammer action has been substituted for the jacks. The instrument was made in 1712 by order of the Elector of Hanover, later King George I, for presentation to his Regimental Chaplain. There are two keyboards, and the organ is represented by a set of *gedact* pipes. This instrument shows the common German custom of a double curve bentside. Originally the harpsichord had two unisons and an octave.

Of this period is Johann Heinrich Harrass of Gross Breitenbach, who died in 1714. Adlung stated in his *Musica Mechanica Organoedi* (Vol. 2, p. 110) that Harrass made double manual harpsichords with sixteen, eight, and four foot stops, the eight foot being on the upper manual, the other two registers on the lower. A harpsichord by Harrass was, in 1924, in the library of the Court Chapel at Sondershausen, but the specification is not recorded.

On 1 December 1689 Hieronymus Albrecht Hass was baptized at the church of St. Jacobi in Hamburg. Hass, with his son Johann Adolph, constituted the most important family of harpsichord and clavichord makers in Germany, both on account of the number of surviving specimens of their work, and of its unusually high quality. Hass was married on 12 October 1711, and was described as *Instrumentmacher*. Three years later he was admitted *Bürger*, being listed on 23 March 1714; at the baptism of his first child, Maria Johanna, at St. Jacobi's on 3 April 1715 he was described as *Klaviermacher*. The date of the birth of Johann Adolph Hass has escaped search; but he was admitted *Bürger* on 28

---

[1] The Hass harpsichords of 1734 (Brussels), 1740 (Paris), 1770? (Yale); the Stein 1777 (Verona); the Swanen 1786 (Paris). Forkel stated (*Strassburger Gelehrte Nachrichten*, 1783) that J. H. Silbermann also made sixteen foot harpsichords.

October 1746, when his father was still alive. Hieronymus Hass's father was Conrad Hass, unknown in any musical connection; but the wife he had married in 1711, Margreta Doratea von Höffen, with all her brothers and sisters, claimed among their godparents Abraham van Driel, an instrument maker, and Kortkamp, an organist. Johann Adolph married Anna Elisabeth Tramnitz, daughter of a grocer, on 22 November 1746, and there were seven children, all of whom were called Hieronymus or Albrecht among their other names. It seems that old Hass was no longer alive when a grandson, Johann Albrecht, was baptized, on 31 May 1761, nor his wife on a similar occasion on 31 May 1753. One of Johann Adolph's daughters married an instrument maker named Johann Christoph Krogmann.

Hieronymus Albrecht Hass has left us five harpsichords dated between 1721 and 1740, together with at least four clavichords built between 1742 and 1744. A harpsichord attributed to him, now in the Yale Collection, bears an inscription which has been interpreted as *I. A. Hass, Hamb. Anno 1710*. Something is wrong here; the younger Hass was not yet born, and the father was only twenty-one years old in 1710, a time at which he would scarcely have made one of the most sumptuous harpsichords in existence, and one which is of a much later style of decoration, musical content, and workmanship. This instrument is perhaps the work of Hass the younger, and the date may have been damaged and incorrectly restored. J. A. Hass has left one other harpsichord, dated 1764, and some fourteen clavichords dated from 1747 to 1786.

The clavichords are almost all of complete five octave compass from FF, and are seldom fretted; the writer knows only two smaller instruments[1] one GG – d³, the other C – f³, and none larger than five octaves. These clavichords, the traditional large eighteenth century German instrument, the instruments to which we indirectly refer when we speak of 'clavichord music', are very large compared with the little products of most of our contemporary makers; they are usually about five feet eight or ten inches long, and about one foot ten inches deep. The tone is brighter and more sustained than that obtainable from small clavichords, and the length of the instrument makes it unnecessary to use covered strings, though these were not unknown in Germany at that time. The Hass clavichords are double strung, and many of them have the addition of a third string at four foot pitch in the lowest octave and a half. The tuning pins of these octave strings are on the left side of the instrument, and after passing over their own bridge on the soundboard they are hitched to the latter as in the harpsichord. The amount of tone added by this four foot is very small, but it gives a slight extra brilliance to the lower register which is very advantageous there. An exceptional clavichord in the Musikhistorisk Museum in Copenhagen is signed *J. A. Hass, Hamb. Anno 1755*. The compass is FF – f³, and the octave strings extend from FF – c¹. Above this point they assume eight foot pitch, so that the instrument has three unison strings for each key from c¹♯ to f³. Some of these instruments are also provided with a second soundboard which is placed below the keys, and which is intended to amplify vibrations transmitted through the casework (plate 94).

The earliest harpsichord by Hieronymus Albrecht Hass is in the Göteborg Museum and is dated 1721. It is a large instrument, eight and a half feet long, and the compass is FF – d³

[1] At Berlin, and in private hands in Ghent.

chromatic. Originally it was a double manual with two unisons and an octave, but at some time in the past the jacks were removed and hammer action substituted; the upper keyboard was then discarded. The original lower keyboard is, however, still in place, and the natural keys are covered with tortoiseshell, a form of keyboard decoration much employed by the Hass family both for harpsichords and clavichords, though only, it would appear, for the more elaborately decorated examples.

The Göteborg harpsichord is followed by one dated 1723, now in the Musikhistorisk Museum in Copenhagen. The compass is FF – c³, there are four sets of strings, three eights and a four foot, and four rows of jacks; there are two eight foot rows for the upper manual, one of these playing from both manuals, and one eight and one four foot row for the lower manual. The keyboards can be coupled by pulling the lower manual out. Both these harpsichords, and all others by the Hasses, have a double curve bentside; the four foot is never playable from the upper keyboard.

A harpsichord in the Kunstindustri Museet in Oslo is inscribed *Hieronymus Albrecht Hass, fecit Hamburg Anno 1732*. It is a smaller example than the two already described, having one manual, C – d³, two unisons, an octave, and a harp stop. It is seven feet two inches in length, and has natural keys of ivory. It seems likely from these two or three harpsichords that the Hasses did considerable trade with Scandinavia, where a number of the clavichords are also to be found.

The next three harpsichords are much larger instruments, all having a sixteen foot stop. This register was provided by Hass in a way which was not employed by any other instrument maker. He first constructed the four and eight foot parts of the instrument in his usual fashion, with a double curve bentside, but this was not so high as usual, rising only about a quarter of an inch above the soundboard; to this bentside were hitched the eight foot strings. Beyond this Hass placed a second soundboard, with a bridge for the sixteen foot strings. Lastly a second double curve bentside and hitchpin rail to which these strings were hitched completed the instrument. Thus, starting with such an instrument as that in Copenhagen or Göteborg, Hass added a second S shaped soundboard beyond the bentside, and a second bentside to complete the case.

The result of this is good. The extra length of the sixteen foot strings, placed on their own bridge, allows the use of uncovered strings throughout the compass, with advantage to the quality of tone in the bass; the tension of the eight foot and sixteen foot strings is more generally spread over the casework, being taken by two bentsides instead of one; the down pressure on the main bridge is reduced; and this allows the eight foot strings a much more sensitive soundboard; and the extra vibrating area provided by the sixteen foot soundboard allows a freer tone to that register than in instruments where the sixteen foot strings are placed on the same bridge as the eight foot.

The first of these large harpsichords is in the Museum of the Brussels Conservatoire (plates 85 and 86). It is dated 1734, and is just under nine feet in length. The compass of the two manuals is GG – d³ chromatic. There are four sets of strings: sixteen, two eight foots, and four foot, and harp stops for the sixteen and lower eight. As in all instruments from this workshop, the stop handles do not pierce the case above the keys, but are placed on the left and right sides of the wrestplank, while the harp stops are controlled by handles on the ends of the slides themselves.

> Upper manual: $1 \times 8'$, lute,
> Lower manual: $1 \times 16'$, $2 \times 8'$, $1 \times 4'$, two harp stops, coupler.

The upper manual eight foot, as was Hass's custom—and a common one among German builders—plays from both manuals as in the English harpsichords. But the Hass dogleg jacks could be disconnected by pulling the lower manual forward. (The present coupler is a later addition.)

The scaling of the unisons in the large Hass harpsichords is very similar to that employed by Kirckman; the octave has however some seven inches more of speaking length in the bass than is found in English instruments. The sixteen foot is double the eight foot scale down to the middle of the keyboard, and even on the lowest string has some sixteen inches more than the unisons. The jacks attack the strings at a point nearer the nut than was customary in instruments made elsewhere, and this gives a Hass harpsichord its somewhat impersonal and incisive tone, a medium where the extremes of contrast attempted in late eighteenth century France and England find no place. This instrument belongs to the great eighteenth century period of harpsichord composition; it did not have to face competition with the pianoforte.

In private ownership in France is an instrument of 1740 which appears to be not only the largest of Hieronymus Hass's instruments, but the most complete harpsichord on record (plates 87 and 88). It has three manuals, with a compass of five octaves from FF, though there is no FF♯. The lowest keyboard is built like a drawer which can be pushed right into the instrument if it is not wanted, and it projects beyond the front of the casework when in use. There are five sets of strings: sixteen, two eights, four, and two foot, six rows of jacks, and a harp stop for the sixteen foot.

> Top manual: $1 \times 8'$, lute,
> Middle manual: $2 \times 8'$, $1 \times 4'$, coupler,
> Bottom manual: $1 \times 16'$, harp, $1 \times 2'$, coupler.

Here, again, the top eight foot is common to two manuals, and the coupler can only serve the lute stop. The bottom keyboard couples the middle to it, if pulled right out; but if pulled only to veneered marks on each keycheek—about half an inch short of its full movement—it is uncoupled. These veneered marks are indicated in plate 88.

As a harp stop is always provided for the sixteen foot it seems probable that Hass expected this stop to be sometimes used for accompaniment, in which it is very effective. The two foot fills the same function in the harpsichord as does the octave in the clavichord, and this set of strings goes up to c^1. There is, of course, a practical reason also for this, since it would be impossible to carry this stop up to its highest notes with the length of string dictated by the width of five slides, even though these ($\frac{5}{8}$ inch each) are narrower than usual. Again, the two foot is placed furthest from the player to overcome this same difficulty in the treble where the four foot is concerned. The scaling and plucking points in this harpsichord will be seen to be similar to those of the instrument of 1734.

HASS

Of the two harpsichords of Johann Adolph Hass one has already been mentioned above, and it constitutes the third of the large instruments. That there must be a fault in the inscription, which is dated 1710, seems clear. The signature is undoubtedly that of the son, who always signed his soundboards with initials: *I. A. Hass* and the date and place (Hamburg). Old Hass with one exception—the Göteborg harpsichord of 1721 where he signs *H. A. Hass* —always wrote his Christian names in abbreviated form, i.e. *Hieron. Albr. Hass*, or else in full. And it has already been pointed out that the son was not born in 1710, and the father was only twenty-one. The style of this harpsichord is certainly that of the second half of the century, and it is reasonable to feel that it may perhaps belong to 1770 and not 1710.

However that may be, the Yale harpsichord is a double manual with five octaves from FF, chromatic. There are five sets of strings: sixteen, two eights, four, and two foot, and six rows of jacks, all being placed together under one jack rail.

> Upper manual: $1 \times 8'$, harp, $1 \times 2'$ (to c^1 only),
> Lower manual: $1 \times 16'$, harp, $2 \times 8'$, $1 \times 4'$, $1 \times 2'$ (to c^2), coupler.

Why the two foot register is provided with a separate row of jacks for each manual, and with an extra octave on the lower manual, is obscure. Scaling is similar to that used in the two other large harpsichords.

Lastly there is a single manual harpsichord by Johann Adolph Hass, of 1764, in the Russell Collection. The compass is FF – f^3 chromatic, there are three sets of strings: two unisons and an octave, three rows of jacks, and a harp stop. The scaling is very like that of a Kirckman, though the four foot is six or seven inches longer in the bass.

Summing up the work of the two Hasses it can be said that the extent and quality of their surviving work must place them first in German instrument making. How many instruments they made we do not know; but Stein's formidable list of (apparently) one year's work (appendix 17), shows a very busy workshop, from which, however, only two harpsichords have survived. From that it would seem that the Hasses may have produced a very great number of instruments. They were first of all clavichord makers, and the dates of their instruments suggest that they were the pioneers of the five octave instrument later championed by Carl Philip Emmanuel Bach. They seem to have introduced the four foot string in the instrument, and this became fairly standard in Germany and Scandinavia, though C. P. E. Bach did not like it (page 105). They worked at a time before it was necessary to increase the compass of the instrument above f^3.

Hass harpsichords, each made to a different specification, suggest that these were only made to special order; they are certainly work of the front rank, both in musical quality and in construction. In harpsichord making the Hasses are the first to have produced instruments with sixteen foot stops and almost the only people to have built them at all; they were also the only ones who used a two foot. The early use of a jack which makes the upper eight foot common to both manuals is important, and it raises the possibility that this system was started by the Hasses, and not by the English, as has generally been assumed up till now. They do not seem to have been noticed by their contemporaries in any accounts which have come down to us, though Ernst Ludwig Gerber in his *Historischbiographisches*

Lexicon wrote in 1790: 'Hass both father and son, were organ makers in Hamburg. They made excellent harpsichords (*Flügel*) and clavichords (*Klaviere*) which are still to be met with.' It has hitherto always been customary to name the Silbermanns as the great German harpsichord and clavichord makers; this detailed account of the work of Hieronymus Albrecht and Johann Adolph Hass of Hamburg is intended to adjust that tradition.

Hamburg was also the home of other instrument makers. Christian Zell was admitted a *Bürger* of Hamburg in 1722, and in the same year he married Florentina, the widow of Carl Conrad Fleischer. Fleischer was a member of another family of harpsichord makers, and he has left a single manual harpsichord of 1720, compass GG – c³, in the Museo de Musica, Barcelona. Zell made a very sumptuous double harpsichord in 1728, compass FF – d³, with double curve bentside, which formerly belonged to Amédée Thibout in Paris, [1] but is now in the Hamburg Museum für Kunst und Gewerbe. In appearance it is much like the large instruments which have been described above, and, possibly, it owed something to the influences of Hass's work. A single manual harpsichord by Zell, dated 1737, is in the Barcelona Museum and another of 1741 in the East Frisian Museum, Aulich.

Johann Christoph Fleischer, brother of Carl Conrad, was also at work in Hamburg, where he made lutes and viols, as well as keyboard instruments. Born in 1675, the son of Hans Christoph Fleischer, also an instrument maker, he obtained his citizenship in 1705. In 1718 J. C. Fleischer invented a *Lautenclavecin* which had two registers with gut strings, and also a *Theorbenflügel* which had two registers strung with gut and a third strung with metal. He also made clavichords. His harpsichords are recorded by Walther in his *Musicalisches Lexicon* of 1732 as costing between 60 and 100 thalers. There is an unsigned harpsichord in private hands in New York, dated 1710, which was restored in 1724 by J. C. Fleischer. It has a double curve bentside, two unisons, an octave, and a harp stop.

Gottfried Silbermann was born at Kleinbobritzsch on 14 January 1683 and died at Dresden on 4 August 1753. With his elder brother, Andreas, he was a well known organ builder of his day, and their organs are still in use. But his work as regards domestic keyboard instruments must have been secondary to his output as an organ builder, since very few examples have survived. Gottfried Silbermann's clavichords were highly thought of in his day, but it is probable that the extent of his work and its excellence have been magnified by the often repeated fact that C. P. E. Bach possessed a Silbermann clavichord. Charles Burney heard him play this instrument in Hamburg in 1772 (page 25).

Only six domestic keyboard instruments made by Gottfried Silbermann have been preserved: two of the grand pianofortes ordered for Potsdam by Frederick the Great; a clavichord is in the Gewerbemuseum at Markneukirchen; there is a spinet dated 1723, compass GG – f³, in the Göteborg Museum; a double harpsichord is in the Bach Museum, Eisenach. This latter is an instrument of compass FF – f³, and it has three sets of strings: two unisons and an octave, a coupler and a harp stop. One of the unisons is now strung to give sixteen foot pitch, but this is not in accordance with the maker's design. The Göteborg spinet is the forerunner of a group of six similar instruments made by Gottfried's nephew, Johann Heinrich Silbermann, an instrument maker of Strasbourg (1727–1799). These

[1] Illustrated on page 48 of Paris (1900) Catalogue.

instruments are shaped much like the large eighteenth century English spinet, and are good examples of their kind. Two are in the Bach Museum at Eisenach, one is in the Instrumental Museum at Basel, another is in the Heyer collection, one is in the Gemeentemuseum, and one—the only dated example (1767)—is in the Neupert collection (plate 91). All have a five octave compass from FF. A five octave clavichord dated 1775 is now in the Instrumentensammlung, Berlin.

The work done by Gottfried Silbermann on pianoforte action is outside the scope of this survey, but he may be mentioned as a pioneer in this direction after Cristofori, whose action he copied with small modifications. He also produced a clavichord with strings of double the normal speaking length, the tangent striking centrally, and with bridges and soundboards both to the right and the left. This instrument was the *cembal d'amour* (page 97); but it never found favour, and no specimen has survived. Adlung deals with the construction in *Musica Mechanica Organoedi*, Vol. II, p. 123, and the State and University Library in Hamburg contains a detailed drawing by Mattheson of a similar instrument. Oppelmann of Hamburg is also said to have made these instruments in the eighteenth century. [1]

Several keyboard instruments have survived from the workshops of the Friederici family (originally Friedrichs), natives of Meerane, who worked at Gera. Christian Ernst Friederici (1709–1780) made two instruments called *Pyramidenflügel* in 1745, one of which is preserved in the Brussels Conservatoire and the other in the Goethehaus in Frankfurt; another example, dated 1750, is in the Neupert collection. These very early vertical pianofortes are shaped as their names implies, and the bass strings run at an angle with the keyboard and are hitched centrally at the highest part of the case. A clavichord by this maker, dated 1772, is preserved in the Kunsthistorisches Museum in Vienna. C. P. E. Bach owned a clavichord and a pianoforte by Friederici; [2] and in a letter to Forkel on 10 November 1773 he states his preference for this make to the clavichords of Fritz and Hass, finding them better constructed and preferring instruments without octave strings in the bass. Christian Gottlob Friederici (1750–1805), a nephew of Christian Ernst, was also a prolific clavichord maker. An example of his work is in the Heyer collection, where a rectangular pianoforte dated 1804 and a grand pianoforte combined with an organ are also preserved.

Contemporary with this family was Barthold Fritz (1697–1766) of Brunswick. Fritz was the author of a successful book on the tuning of musical instruments, which was published by Breitkopf of Leipzig in 1756 with a dedication to C. P. E. Bach. There were five editions of this work, together with a Dutch translation which appeared in Amsterdam. The second edition (1757) contains a list of all Fritz's instruments with the names of their owners. A large clavichord dated 1751 is in the Victoria and Albert Museum: compass FF – a³, chromatic, and with octave strings from FF to c.

[1] This name has also been rendered *Cembal d'amore* and *Clavir d'amour*. Johann Ulrich König (*Breslauische Gedruckte Sammlungen*, 1721) stated that the name derived from the unusual blending power of the instrument with the viola d'amore.

[2] At his death the inventory of C. P. E. Bach's instruments listed one *Flügel* in a walnut case, a clavichord by Jungcurth, and a clavichord and a pianoforte, both in oak cases, by Friderici of Gera. Bach had parted from his Silbermann clavichord in 1781, which is strange if the Silbermann really was his favourite instrument.

GERMANY

Christian Gottlob Hubert (1714–1793) was one of the best known clavichord makers of his time. Born in Poland, Hubert moved to Germany, working in Bayreuth and Anspach; there he produced many clavichords as well as pianofortes in various shapes. A good many of Hubert's instruments have survived, and a fine example can be seen in the Heyer collection, dated 1772, compass FF – a³; Berlin has two: a fretted clavichord of 1776 and an unfretted instrument of 1782, both with compass C – f³; clavichords of 1782, compass C – g³ are in both the Basel and the Metropolitan Museums; Messrs. Rushworth and Dreaper have an example of the following year with this same compass.

Employed in Hubert's workshop was Johann Wilhelm Hoffmann (1764–1809) who took over the business on the death of his master. He is not to be confused with Christian Gotthelf Hoffman of Ronneburg, whose clavichords may be seen in the Yale collection, dated 1784, compass FF – f³, and in the Heyer collection, dated 1763, the latter a fretted instrument of four octaves from C.

The Horn family of Dresden were also clavichord makers, the best known members being two brothers. Gottfried Joseph Horn (1739–1797) worked with Schwarze, a pupil of the Silbermanns, and took over his master's business on his death. Gerber (1812) tells us that G. J. Horn made 464 clavichords between 1772 and 1795, often built with the compass FF – g³. He was known as 'Senior' to distinguish him from his brother Johann Gottlob Horn (1748–1796), who was a pupil of Stein in Augsburg and of Friederici in Gera. This brother settled in Dresden in 1779, working for a time with Heinrich Ludolph Mack, who set up on his own in 1799 and died in 1807.

Another family of clavichord makers was called Lemme. There we find Friedrich Carl Wilhelm Lemme (1747–1808) of Brunswick, and his son Carl (1769–1832). Clavichords by the father are preserved in the Deutsches Museum, dated 1766, and in the Heyer collection, dated 1787, compass FF – a³. [1]

Zacharias Hildebrand of Leipzig (1680–1755), an organ builder who had studied with Gottfried Silbermann, is best remembered on account of his having built a *Lautenklavizymbel* for J. S. Bach. This harpsichord had two unison registers, gut strung, and a four foot with brass strings. Adlung (II, 139) described this type of instrument, and says that Friederici also made them. We have already seen that J. C. Fleischer was making the *Lautenclavecin* at Hamburg in 1718 (page 104).

Lute harpsichords were however largely experimental efforts, and J. S. Bach left two on his death (appendix 16). As elsewhere, German makers experimented with harpsichord design from time to time. In 1756 Joseph Glonner of Munich built a three manual clavichord (*ein dreifaches Clavichord*) for the Electress of Bavaria for 60 florins, also supplying the Court with three double harpsichords at 200 fl. in 1753, and two small ones at 60 fl. in 1757. [2] Hofmann of Gotha built in 1779 a *doppeltes Klavizymbel* for the Duke of Saxony, which had two keyboards at each end; [3] and Peter Johann Milchmeyer of Frankfurt a/M (1750–1813) built a three manual harpsichord with 250 changes of tone in 1780. [4] These experimental instruments have vanished; but they have parallels in most other countries

---

[1] F. C. W. Lemme made laminated soundboards for his clavichords from 1772. See Lemme (1802).
[2] Bierdimpfl (1883). [3] Fétis. [4] *Magazin der Musik* (Hamburg 1783).

where self advertisement, and a desire to increase the expressive powers of the (by then decadent) harpsichord, according to the trend of that time, sought an outlet in these complicated instruments. [1]

Three makers remain to be mentioned: the Gräbners, the Steins, and Joachim Swanen of Strasbourg.

The Gräbners of Dresden were Johann Christoph, a late seventeenth century organ builder, his son Johann Heinrich, and the sons of the latter: Wilhelm (b. 1737) and Carl August (b. 1729). A harpsichord by Johann Heinrich Gräbner, dated 1722, is in the Villa Bertramka, Prague. It has two unisons and an octave, and the compass of the two keyboards is EE to e³, five octaves. The keyboard can be shifted a semitone for transposing purposes. Two harpsichords of almost identical appearance are preserved: the one by Carl August, dated 1782, is in the Rück Collection at Nürnberg (plate 92); the other, dated 1774, is in the Heyer collection at Leipzig. These two double manual instruments have a compass of FF – f³ and three sets of strings: two eights and a four foot, together with a coupler and a harp stop. Dr. Rück's harpsichord has that curious feature which has been noticed above: the upper manual eight foot is common to both manuals, though nevertheless a coupler is provided. In the Leipzig instrument, however, one unison has been strung to sixteen foot pitch, and the octave has been placed by itself on the upper keyboard, though this is not the maker's plan.

It is so often said that German harpsichords always had the four foot on the upper-keyboard, and this statement has been repeated so blindly and resolutely, that it is now accepted as absolute fact; but it must be understood that this is not so. Apart from this altered Gräbner the only old German harpsichord with the four foot on the upper manual (and this disposition is also not original), seems to be an unsigned and undated double manual instrument at Berlin. [2] This is a five octave FF harpsichord with the following disposition:

Upper manual: $1 \times 8'$, $1 \times 4'$,
Lower manual: $1 \times 16'$, $1 \times 8'$, coupler.

There is also a harp stop. The sixteen foot strings pass over the ordinary eight foot bridge on the soundboard, and use a superstructure above the eight foot nut. Herr Hartmann, a former technician to the collection, held that this register was a later addition. Frank Hubbard, who examined the instrument most thoroughly in 1957, believes that the original disposition was the same as that of the Hass harpsichord of 1723 in Copenhagen (page 101):

Upper manual: $2 \times 8'$ (one common to both manuals),
Lower manual: $2 \times 8'$, $1 \times 4'$, coupler.

At Copenhagen there are four sets of strings, one of the three unisons being placed at a higher level than the other two: that is, in the position occupied in the Berlin harpsichord (and in most modern ones) by the sixteen foot.

[1] Marpurg (1755) records that in 1757 Mathias Koch of Strasbourg built a three manual harpsichord with three unisons, an octave, and a divided harp stop.
[2] Grove, vol. 4, plate 25.

A modern tradition has it that this instrument was J. S. Bach's own large harpsichord, mentioned in the inventory of his house after his death as being veneered (*fournirt clavecin*); but the Berlin harpsichord is in a plain case painted black, with a little inlay over the keys only. This instrument first attracted attention when Wilhelm Rust, writing in the Introduction to the Collected Works of Bach, 9th year, 1860, briefly described the instrument, but only as generally illustrative of a harpsichord. It then belonged to Graf von Voss of Berlin. Rust claimed nothing for the instrument's past, other than recording its owner's statement that Friedemann Bach, from whom his family had acquired some of J. S. Bach's manuscripts, had visited their house and had played on it. Rust later obtained the instrument, but never said that it had belonged to J. S. Bach, though he was himself Cantor of St. Thomas's, Leipzig.

The 'tradition' appeared in March 1890 when an unreliable Dutch writer, dealer, and collector, Paul de Wit, acquired the instrument; and the myth was started by an article in the *Zeitschrift für Instrumentenbau*, of which de Wit was a founder, (10th year. No. 36). The same year, at the dispersal of de Wit's second collection, Philipp Spitta arranged for the sale of the instrument to the Hochschule für Musik in Berlin, the price being ten thousand marks.

In the Museum Catalogue of 1892 (page 111), Oscar Fleischer stated that a belief that the instrument had belonged to J. S. Bach, that it had been given by him to his son Friedemann, and later sold to von Voss, and an attribution to Gottfried Silbermann as maker, rested on verbal tradition only. Fleischer then wrote an article in the *Zeitschrift der IMG*, (l. 161), describing C. P. E. Bach as the only son of Johann Sebastian, and quoting Ernst Ludwig Gerber as authority for a statement that when C. P. E. Bach went to Berlin in 1738 his father gave him a Silbermann harpsichord. This reference comes from Part II of Gerber's *Tonkunstler-Lexikon*, where the instrument referred to is called *Klavier*, a term which at the end of the eighteenth century was generally synonymous with *Clavichord*. (For an inventory of C. P. E. Bach's instruments at his death see page 105).

In the 1922 Catalogue of the Berlin Collection Curt Sachs repeated these statements and said that the instruments had also been the property of Friedemann Bach. In *Das Klavier*. (1923) page 19, he doubted if Silbermann was the maker, but said the instrument was J. S. Bach's 'in his own most mature period.'

It will be seen that this tradition is based on fantasy, and that there is no evidence on which to assume that this harpsichord, now at Charlottenburg, belonged to J. S. Bach. Nothing seems reliable in these accounts apart from Rust's original and uncoloured statement. There have been unfortunate repercussions from this display of poor scholarship, for modern German harpsichords have almost always been designed on the lines of the spurious Bach harpsichord, and are inconveniently unusual in having the four foot on the upper keyboard. Let this be a lesson to us.

Several interesting instruments, the work of Johann Andreas Stein of Augsburg (1728–1792), can be seen in European museums. Stein was born at Heidelsheim in Baden, and learned his trade from J. A. Silbermann and also in Paris. He set up his workshop in Augsburg where he built organs, harpsichords, and pianofortes. Stein had the advantage of being a practical musician; he was organist of the Barfüsserkirche, and built the new organ for that church and also for the Kreuzkirche. A glance at Stein's list of instruments said to have been made in one year (appendix 17) will show his astonishing success; but the writer knows only two Stein harpsichords at the present time.

A certain number of small pianofortes by Stein have survived, and the Göteborg museum contains a grand pianoforte and organ combined. This is a handsome instrument dated 1770; there are two keyboards of compass FF – f³; the upper is for the pianoforte and the lower for the organ. This latter contains four ranks of pipes, which are placed in the lower part of the case. Stein is well known on account of Mozart's interest in and use of his pianofortes. Their development and action are outside the scope of this book, and the subject has been dealt with in many works elsewhere; but these pianofortes are combined with both of the Stein harpsichords at present known, and form the *vis-à-vis* instruments described by Mozart.

The first example belongs to the Verona *Società Filarmonica*, who bought it from the maker in 1777; it is now preserved in the Museo Civico. It is rectangular, and contains at one end a single FF – f³ keyboard for the pianoforte, and two stop handles for the treble and bass dampers. At the other end of the case are three manuals of the same compass; of these the lowest is once again for the pianoforte, while the upper two command a harpsichord with four stops: $1 \times 16'$, $2 \times 8'$, $1 \times 4'$. The damper levers are duplicated at the harpsichord end of the instrument, where there are seven stop handles, a harp stop being present; the various manuals can be coupled. The harpsichord scaling is very unusual, as the four foot sounds on its own bridge at octave pitch for the lowest sixteen notes only, passing onto the eight foot bridge above this point and becoming a third unison. The sixteen foot is discontinued below C, there being no provision for it in the seven lowest notes.

Another *vis-à-vis* instrument by Stein is in the Conservatorio di San Pietro a Maiella in Naples. This was made in 1783,[1] and was given to the Conservatorio in the following year by the Emperor Joseph II of Austria, after being entertained at Naples by King Ferdinand (1751–1825).

The Stein business was carried on after the death of the founder by his daughter Maria Anna (Nannette), who appears in Mozart's letters. In 1793 she married a Stuttgart teacher and pianist, Johann Andreas Streicher, and together with him and her brother, with whom she was associated in business, she moved to Vienna whence many pianofortes issued bearing the new name.

Contemporary with Stein was the work of Joachim Swanen, probably an Alsatian, whose large pedal harpsichord of 1786 is in the Conservatoire des Arts et Métiers in Paris. This double manual instrument has the unusual keyboard compass of $5\frac{1}{2}$ octaves, EE – a³, and it is probable that key EE was tuned to CC. There are four rows of jacks and four sets of strings: $1 \times 16'$, $2 \times 8'$, $1 \times 4'$. There are also two octaves of *toe* pedals from EE, but these operate a hammer mechanism placed immediately beneath the harpsichord case. The harpsichord registers are worked by five pedals: four placed to the left and one to the right.

---

[1] The pianoforte is at one end, and a double manual harpsichord is at the other. The latter has two unisons, an octave, and two knee levers.

A handle on the right side, beneath the lower keyboard, lifts the pedal dampers. The instrument was restored in 1883 by Louis Tomasini, and it is now difficult to be sure which features are original.

DECORATION

The small German clavichords of the seventeenth century were very plain instruments. The outside of the case was usually left without any decoration, and in most of the less pretentious examples there was no decoration inside. But sometimes a picture is to be found inside the lid, often some biblical or mythical scene, usually painted in a somewhat crude manner. Sometimes prints were stuck inside the lid, a practice the writer has scarcely ever found elsewhere. These small clavichords were made without stands, as it was expected that they would be placed on a table or chair for playing. The keys often have boxwood naturals and ebony accidentals, but ebony naturals and ivory topped accidentals or *vice versa* are also found. These instruments are seldom signed or dated.

With the beginning of the eighteenth century the size of the clavichord began to increase; and a greater attempt to produce a decorative instrument manifested itself. The outside of the case of these large clavichords was generally painted; in the first half of the century the favourite style was a marbled or grained decoration, or one in imitation of tortoiseshell. The inside of the lid was from this time painted with much more care, landscapes, mythological subjects, and Chinese scenes being popular. These instruments were supplied with well made stands on cabriole legs and there was often a drawer for music. The small and undecorated clavichord was, of course, still made, and was used by those who could not afford a finer instrument, so it naturally retained its simple appearance. Decorated woods were not much used for veneer, as this was not a popular form of decoration for German instruments until the latter part of the century; but veneers occasionally make their appearance, as in the Hubert clavichord of 1783 owned by Messrs. Rushworth and Dreaper, and the Lemme of 1787 in the Heyer collection.

The keys of the large German clavichords and harpsichords are generally found to have ebony naturals and ivory topped accidentals. The Hass family, however, often covered the naturals with tortoiseshell, using ivory for the arcaded fronts. Then the accidentals were topped with ivory or with ivory and mother of pearl arranged in a series of squares, or with ivory inlaid with elaborate designs in tortoiseshell. Ivory naturals are also found, but usually in instruments which are either of restrained decoration, or else late models.

German harpsichords usually have a double curve to the bentside: the Hasses always use this, so do Zell, Brock and the Fleischers; but it is not universal. A feature of most of these instruments is the heavy stand, with legs turned and framed, and suggestive of a style a hundred years earlier. Fluted legs often appear on German clavichords from the 1780's.

The outside of the German harpsichord was sometimes painted in imitation of tortoiseshell, and Chinese decorative scenes were as popular as with the clavichords. Some instruments have plain painted cases, and plain wood is found in some examples; but as so many surviving German harpsichords seem to have been specially commissioned it is not surprising that they are often of very elaborate appearance. Lid paintings in two cases show musical instruments: in the one case, the Hieronymus Hass of 1723; in the other his harpsichord of 1740, which shows that instrument being presented to a lady with Hass standing next to it. Tortoiseshell and ivory were favourite materials with which to decorate the keyboard surrounds, particularly with the Hamburg makers; but marquetry was also employed for that purpose.

In harpsichords the soundboards were often painted with flowers and fruit, but this appears less often in German clavichords.

CHAPTER EIGHT

SCANDINAVIA, CENTRAL AND EASTERN EUROPE, SPANISH PENINSULA

The instruments coming from the groups of countries listed above are treated briefly in this chapter for three reasons. (1) In some cases the instrument making in a country was on so small a scale, and so few instruments have survived, that it is impossible to produce a detailed study of work which was, in fact, of little general musical importance. (2) In the case of Eastern Europe it has proved difficult to obtain direct access to such material as is preserved there. (3) The Spanish Peninsula, as so often, is the exception. Important problems of musical performance are inseparable from the instruments made in that part of Europe, but the amount of detailed information available at present is inadequate for more than the most superficial report.

SCANDINAVIA

We have already seen that German harpsichords and clavichords, chiefly of eighteenth century Hamburg manufacture, were imported into Scandinavia. In addition, during the early eighteenth century, native instrument making took root in these countries. In 1739 Niels Brelin, at one time pastor of Volstadt, near Carlstadt, published in the Stockholm *Vetenskaps Akademiens Handlingar* an account of his new plan for a harpsichord, which contained a special design of jack, and a set of sympathetic strings. In 1741 Brelin described, through the same medium, a clavicytherium with eight variations of tone, controlled by pedals. This suggests a general interest in, and experience of, instrument making; and from that time Baltic makers appear regularly.

The Nordiska Museum in Stockholm has a clavichord of 1742, compass C – d³, by Philip Jacob Specken, as well as a two manual harpsichord by this maker, with a five octave FF compass, and dated 1737. Pehr Lundborg of Stockholm has left three clavichords dated between 1787 and 1796, now in the Nordiska and Musikhistoriska Museums; all have a compass FF – a³, and the earliest example has octave strings in the bass. The latter Museum also has an organ and clavichord combined, a most unusual combination, made by Lundborg in 1772.

Lundborg's pupil, Mathias Peter Kraft, was Court instrument maker at Stockholm in 1780; there is a rectangular pianoforte by Kraft in the Göteborg Museum, dated 1802, and a five and a half octave clavichord, FF–c⁴, dated 1806, in the Nordiska Museum, Pehr Lindholm, of Stockholm (1742–1813) made numbers of clavichords of compass FF–c⁴, some with octave strings in the bass, and there are examples in The Historical Museum, Abo, Finland, in Copenhagen and elsewhere, made between 1776 and 1803. By the latter year Lindholm had taken into partnership H. J. Söderström, his son-in-law, who was maker of a clavichord dated 1816 which is now in the Nordiska Museum. This clavichord, also, has the five and a half octave compass which was becoming common in the early nineteenth century.

Harpsichord makers are further represented by Gottlieb Rosenau of Stockholm, who made a double manual harpsichord of 1786, with two unisons and an octave, and five octave FF compass, now in the Claudius collection in Copenhagen (plate 96). Johan Broman made a clavichord of 1756, and a five octave double manual harpsichord of 1756, which are in the Nordiska Museum. This harpsichord is unusual in that, while only an eight foot instrument as regards pitch, its length is eleven feet 9½ inches. There were other Swedish instrument makers working both in this period and also into the nineteenth century; they are mostly represented today by one or two clavichords each (plates 97 and 98).

Among Danish clavichord makers is M. Christensen of Copenhagen, by whom there is a clavichord dated 1759 in the National History Museum at Frederiksborg. In 1777 Johan Jesper Jørgensen of Odense made a clavichord, compass FF–f³, which is in the Musikhistorisk Museum, Copenhagen. H. P. Møller, an eighteenth century maker of clavichords and pianofortes in Copenhagen, was also a musical inventor; he founded the present day firm of Hornung and Møller, which, apart from pianoforte making, has revived the manufacture of harpsichords and clavichords. Moritz Georg Moshack also of Copenhagen, is represented by a clavichord, FF–f³, in the Norsk Folk Museum in Oslo.

A clavichord of four and a half octaves, C–f³, is preserved in the Oslo Folk Museum; it was made at Moss (Norway), and it is signed *H. Jansen, Hoc fecit, Moss, 1757.*

CENTRAL AND EASTERN EUROPE

Turning towards Central Europe, we find a considerable amount of work going on in Poland. Michael de Pilzna of Rzeszow worked in the fifteenth and sixteenth centuries as a clavichord maker in Cracow, and was followed in the latter century by Krzysztof Kiejcher. The seventeenth century saw Martin who worked in Cracow about 1609, Bernard Przeworski who died there in 1620, and Kasper Hauk. All these men are recorded by the National Museum, Poznan, as harpsichord, clavichord and spinet makers. This museum contains an anonymous eighteenth century harpsichord with two manuals, one of which has been fitted with hammer action; the maker's inscription is now partly illegible, but the instrument is believed to be of German or Polish origin. There is also a clavichord by Johann Christof Maywaldt of Weigandsthal, built in 1729, compass C–c³. A clavichord by Maywaldt, dated 1729, possibly the same instrument, is or was in the Schlesisches Museum, Wroclaw.

Mazlowski of Poznan was at work in the early nineteenth century. [1] Christian Gottlob

[1] Valdrighi.

Hubert (1714–1793), known as a German clavichord maker (page 106), was a Pole, born at Wschova, or Fraustadt as it became later on. In Danzig worked Paulus Steinicht, two of whose virginals, dated 1657 and 1661, are at Berlin, and also Delitz, whom Göhlinger (1910) records as a pupil of Zacharias Hildebrand (page 106) and a successful eighteenth century craftsman in Danzig.

Russia has proved elusive as regards native instrument makers; but her opera and court music in the eighteenth century, mostly supplied from Italy and Dresden, suggest that instruments may also have come from these sources. [1]

Advertisements announcing the sale of instruments appear from time to time in the Saint Petersburg and Moscow papers, in a manner reminiscent of France. Thus the *Saint Petersburg Gazette* for 2 November 1795 offers

'A large and complete harpsichord invented by the famous Ruckers of Antwerp in 1629, and perfected with new stops by Taskin in 1786.'

In Moscow there worked at this time two instrument makers: Poulleau and Johann-Christoph Hübner. In Saint Petersburg there was Kirschnigk, who made harpsichords and pianofortes combined with organs. More important was a Russian, Ivan Andréiévitch Batof (1767–1839), who was apprenticed to a Moscow instrument maker named Vladimirof. Batof later moved to Saint Petersburg where he made harpsichords and pianofortes, and also violins. An instrument maker called Meck worked in Moscow, and according to the *Moscow Gazette*, No. 17 of 1795, he made pedal harpsichords.

Robert Adam is known to have designed a harpsichord case for Catherine the Great in 1774, [2] but no evidence has been produced that the instrument was actually built. Certainly, however, harpsichords were exported from England to Russia, as Shudi's books record: '19 May 1772. Sent Mr. Lachicarsky's Harp^d on board a Rushian ship. 10 Aug 1773 Sent a double harpsichord to Rushia for Mr. Laperandor Lauknaitz', etc. and pianofortes followed at the end of the eighteenth century.

The collection of instruments formerly at the Hermitage has now been removed to the Institute for Scientific Research on the Theatre and Music in Leningrad (Saint Petersburg), where there are at least two early keyboard instruments: a very ornate three manual harpsichord, described as having 'five stops', and a clavichord by G. Lehner of Pressburg, compass FF–a³, dated 1816. The harpsichord is most elaborately painted, and has a heavily carved stand; but its origin is impossible to identify from photographs. The museum writes that it is 'reconstructed', but details are not available.

The Cesar Snoeck collection, which was dispersed from Ghent in three parts after 1902 (page 122), went to Berlin, to Brussels and to Saint Petersburg. The latter part consisted of 363 instruments, and these were acquired for Czar Nicholas II by General Baron de Stackelberg, the Director of the Imperial Chapel. Among them there was, however, only one keyboard instrument: an unsigned Italian spinet. This collection is now dispersed between Leningrad and the Museum of the Bolshoi Theatre in Moscow.

Czechoslovakia has various unidentified instruments in the Uměleckoprůmislové Museum

[1] Mooser.
[2] James, plate 53. The drawing is preserved in the Soane Museum, London.

at Brno, and there may be more in the Moravian Museum there. The National Museum at Prague has the collection of instruments from the Conservatoire, and probably those from the Premonstrate Monastery at Strahov. Johann Bohak was the maker of a clavichord dated 1794, now in the Royal College of Music in London. This maker may have come from Bohemia; the clavichord, which has a five octave compass from FF, has been mentioned in connection with Haydn. [1] Also from Bohemia was Ignaz Kunz who built the clavichord of 1821 in the National Museum at Prague. This instrument has a compass from $FF-a^3$ and was made at Jaroměr near Königsgraz.

Austrian instruments are very scarce. A harpsichord organ by Valentin Zeiss of Linz, dated 1639, is in the Museum Carolino-Augusteum, Salzburg. The keyboard compass is $C-c^3$, bass short octave, while that of the pedals is C – g. The harpsichord has two sets of strings. The Technisches Museum in Vienna has an unsigned clavichord, thought there to be Viennese, and dated about 1760; it is fretted, and has four and a half octaves of keys from C. The Ahlgrimm collection in Vienna has a clavichord, signed *C. G. Wien, 1789.* The National Museum in Prague has a clavichord from the Austrian Tyrol signed *Erzeuger Johann Baumgartner Bozen 1683*; the compass is $C-f^3$. The Kunsthistorisches Museum in Vienna has, or had, a spinet signed *Christoph Bock, Clavierstimer beider K. K. Hoftheater fecit ano 1804 in Wien*, but the writer has not been able to find it there.

Switzerland is unimportant in the history of early keyboard instruments. An example of Swiss work may be seen in a spinet in the Basel Musikhistorisches Museum which is signed *Johann Jacob Brosy Instrument und Orgelmacher in Basel 1775.* This has a compass of five octaves, and is very similar to spinets produced by Johann Heinrich Silbermann. Paul Brunold of Paris (1875–1948) owned a large double harpsichord of eighteenth century French appearance and design. He believed, though no inscription was visible, that this instrument, which came from the Château d'Oron in Switzerland, was the work of a Swiss, Antoine Watters, in 1737, and that it had been restored by one Fissot in 1762. But in view of the lack of evidence it is difficult to accept Brunold's attribution. Many details of Swiss instrument makers are given by Boalch and Hirt, to whom the reader is referred for information.

THE SPANISH PENINSULA

Keyboard instrument making was carried on in Spain as early as anywhere else; Van der Straeten [2] has recorded that before 1480 Sancho de Paredes, Chamberlain to Queen Isabella, owned two claviorgans. Another fifteenth century reference to that instrument was made by Fernández de Oviedo, [3] who recorded the construction of what he described as the first claviorgan to be seen in Spain. The maker's name was Moferrez, and he was known as The Moor of Çaragoça. A *clavicordia* by the Moor of Çaragoça is mentioned among the effects of Cardinal Juan Tavera, who owned a claviorgan and other *clavichordios* of unspecified make. [4]

[1] James, *Musical Times*, April 1930. [2] Vol. 7, page 248.
[3] *Anuario Musical*, Vol. 6, page 158. [4] *Anuario Musical*, Vol. 6, pages 157–8.

Nassare[1] tells us that the Spanish word *clavicordio* was generic, and that it covered all types of keyboard instrument:

'*Clavicordios* are of various different forms, varying both in size and in name; some are called *Claviorganos*, others *Clavicimbalos*, others *Clavicordios*, and others *Espinetas*.'

When, however, the clavichord is intended, Nassare makes it clear that the word *Manocordio* was generally used.

The appearance of keyboard instruments in inventories of the sixteenth century is not rare; thus, a harpsichord is recorded in an inventory, dated 1583, of the property of Archduke Albert of Spain:[2]

'A large *clavicordio* with two registers, bought from Juan Baptiste Quebon.'

Quebon was a harpsichord maker in Madrid.

Spain imported musical instruments from Antwerp in the sixteenth and seventeenth centuries, and a mid-sixteenth century virginal by Hans Bos of Antwerp, who is mentioned by Praetorius (see page 47), survives in the Convento de Santa Clara at Tordesillas. It bears the inscription *Huius instrumenti factor est Johannes Bossus, factor organorum.* In 1592 Hans Brebos (1567–1609) went out to Spain to build a new organ for Toledo Cathedral.[3] He stayed for the rest of his life, and was buried in Madrid at St. Martin's Church. Besides the Toledo organ Hans Brebos was repairer for the Queen's harpsichord at Valladolid; he built an organ for the Chapel Royal, Alcazar, and another for the Church of Our Lady, Madrid; he also made two regals for the Escurial, and a claviorgan for the Count of Nieve.

Among seventeenth century records, an inventory[4] of the effects of the Reverend Juan Canalies, the clergyman at Martorell, dated 12 August 1614, includes:

'Item, a musical instrument, vulgarly called *clavisimbol.*'

On 15 October 1634 Bartolomeo Jobernardi, an Italian musician working in the Chapel Royal, Madrid, dedicated his *Tratado de la Musica* to Philip IV. Tbe treatise remains in manuscript,[5] though extracts have now been printed,[6] and it contains an interesting description of a harpsichord which Jobernardi had planned. This instrument, called *cimbalo perfetto*, had one manual with fifty two keys, and, apparently, three unison registers. The author's nomenclature is very obscure, but it seems that the instrument was intended to have powers of *crescendo* and *diminuendo*, possibly by pedal control of the registers.

Few surviving Spanish harpsichords or clavichords are recorded at the present time, and we do not know how commonly these instruments were in use. Nassare tells us that claviorgans were rare, because of the scarcity of instrument makers, and that, for the same reason, there were few large harpsichords with three registers. He gives, however, a general picture of the Spanish instruments.

Claviorgans were usually built with an eight foot flute, a four foot, and, rarely, with a fifteenth as well. They were pitched a semitone lower than many other instruments, as they were used for accompanying the voice. Harpsichords were constructed with one, two, or

---

[1] Nassare (1724).
[2] Van der Straeten.
[3] Stellfeld.
[4] *Anuario Musical*, Vol. 5, page 211.
[5] National Library, Madrid, MS. 8931.
[6] *Anuario Musical*, Vol. 8.

three registers, of which one might have four foot pitch. Some were shaped like an imperfect triangle: the equivalent of our spinet. The *espineta* was also triangular, but was much smaller, and, clearly, this was a four foot instrument. The best plectrum for all these models was obtained from crow quill.

As regards the clavichord (*manocordio*), Nassare strongly advises its use; he says that it is the best practice instrument, essential for the cultivation of a sense of touch, and useful for organ students. The clavichord was customarily built with a compass of four octaves from C, with bass short octave, double strung, and fretted. Clavichords with quarter tones were occasionally made.

From inventories and from surviving examples it appears that the traditional Spanish harpsichord was an instrument with one manual only, and with two eight foot stops. Burney,[1] writing of his visit to Farinelli at Bologna in 1770, said that this singer's favourite instrument was his Florentine *piano forte* of 1730:

'The next in favour is a harpsichord given him by the late Queen of Spain, who was Scarlatti's scholar, both in Portugal and Spain; it was for this princess that Scarlatti made his two first books of lessons, and to her the first edition, printed at Venice, was dedicated, when she was princess of Asturias; this harpsichord, which was made in Spain, has more tone than any of the others. His third favourite is one made likewise in Spain, under his own direction; it has movable keys, by which, like that of Count Taxis, at Venice, the player can transpose a composition either higher or lower. Of these Spanish harpsichords the natural keys are black, and the flats and sharps are covered with mother of pearl; they are of the Italian Model, all the wood is cedar, except the bellies, and they are put into a second case.'

The inventory (appendix 18) of the keyboard instruments belonging to Queen Maria Barbara, of whom Burney speaks, includes Italian instruments as well as Spanish, and it is interesting to see that she had Italian pianofortes converted into harpsichords, a sign perhaps of their imperfections at that time (plate 102*a*).

The Museum of Musical History in Barcelona contains a six octave clavichord by Jozé Grabalos of Tarazona, together with two unsigned harpsichords which are said to be Spanish. One of these has a compass C – c³, bass short octave, and has two unisons and an octave; the other has a compass G – c³, bass short octave (38 keys), and two four foot stops only. The Museum also contains three harpsichords bought in Spain: a Carl Conradt Fleischer, Hamburg 1720, a Christian Zell, Hamburg 1737; the third is thought to be German but is unsigned.[2] In view of the scarcity of German harpsichords this suggests that German instruments may have been imported in the eighteenth century; and German origin is not unlikely for the second harpsichord in the Queen's inventory, which had four sets of strings.

Another Spanish claimant is an unsigned harpsichord in Taragoza, the property of D. Domingo Olleta y Mombiela. A signed instrument is the *Geigenwerk* of Fra Raymundo Truchado at Brussels (plate 103), and another is a clavichord at Berlin signed 'Dn Josef M...Madrid'.

[1] Burney (1771).
[2] This attribution has been made after careful examination by Frank Hubbard of Boston, Mass.

Instrument making in Portugal seems to have been identical with the work done in Spain. The Museum of the Conservatorio in Lisbon contains two harpsichords[1] by Joachim José Antunes, dated 1758 and 1789 (plates 99 and 101), and clavichords by M. de S. Carmo of Oporto, 1796, and Jacintho Ferreira of Lisbon, 1783 (plate 100). The similarity of the stands of the various instruments made in the Spanish Peninsula will be noticed.

In the Lisbon Conservatorio there is also a harpsichord by Henriques of Casteel, 1763. This instrument maker appears to have emigrated, as a harpsichord nameboard preserved in the Brussels Conservatoire is signed *Henricus van-casteel fecit Bruxellis 1778*. At Berlin there is a harpsichord by Manuel Anjos Leo of Beja, dated 1700. The compass is C – a³, and there are two unison registers.

The eighteenth century export of English harpsichords to Oporto is of interest, and a good many instruments must have gone out there. Shudi's books between 19 April 1773 and 5 March 1775 show the despatch of eleven harpsichords to that destination. Their present whereabouts is not, however, known.

[1] In Portugal, keyboard instruments with jack action were generally called *Espineta* or *Cravo*. But the word *Clavicordio* was also used.

CHAPTER NINE

THE NINETEENTH CENTURY

I n the preceding chapters we have watched the development of the early keyboard instruments, and have examined the characteristics of the various national schools of instrument making. We have seen that the harpsichord and clavichord existed, in forms we would recognize today, by the middle of the fifteenth century and probably earlier; we have also seen the decline of these instruments as the eighteenth century drew to its close. In this last chapter we shall witness their virtual extinction, together with the rise of the pianoforte, the formation of Instrument Museums, and finally the renaissance of harpsichord making.

The latest dated harpsichord known to survive is a double manual Kirckman, in private ownership in England, signed *Josephus Kirckman Londoni fecit 1800*. We have already seen (page 88) that the last Kirckman of all is thought to have been constructed in 1809. Hipkins tells us [1] that Clementi built his last harpsichord in 1802.

The establishment of the Paris Conservatoire in 1795 provided for six professors of the harpsichord, but a prize for harpsichord playing was awarded for the last time in 1798. By 1816 harpsichords were so little regarded that, during the cold weather of that year, the instruments which had been confiscated from the nobility during the Revolution (appendix 7), and were stored in the Conservatoire, were broken up and used for firewood. [2]

The spinet suffered the same fate as the harpsichord, and early nineteenth century examples are very rare. The latest dated spinet seems, very exceptionally, to be an Alessandro Riva of 1839, made at Bergamo; this is in the Heyer collection. The oblong virginal had been obsolete since the beginning of the eighteenth century.

The clavichord, judging from surviving examples, had twenty or thirty years more life than the harpsichord family. This may have been a result of its expressive powers, which are nearer those of a pianoforte than those of a harpsichord; but its low price was probably another factor. The latest example the writer can record is a large instrument made by Eric Wessberg of Stockholm in 1821, and now preserved there in the Nordiska Museum.

The pianoforte had been on the ascent since the second half of the eighteenth century. Cristofori's pioneer work in Florence was carried out between 1690 and 1730. In Germany Gottfried Silbermann first submitted his pianofortes to J. S. Bach in 1736, when he found them weak in tone and heavy in touch. Frederick the Great, however, had Silbermann's

[1] Hipkins (1896).   [2] Chouquet (1875).

119

pianofortes at Potsdam by about 1746, and Bach played on them when he visited the King in the following year. Friederici of Gera was building the instrument by this time, [1] and so was Hubert of Anspach. [2] In France Sebastian Erard was building pianofortes in the 1770's and Pascal Taskin was engaged in the same work in the 1780's. J. C. Bach arrived in London in 1759, and the pianoforte rapidly became fashionable. By 1760 Zumpe and about a dozen other German pianoforte makers had arrived in London.

In its early days the pianoforte was not regarded as something very different in conception from the harpsichord. Its purpose and particular quality was the dynamic control possible by touch alone. Beyond this the early examples were expected to sound rather like sensitive harpsichords, and were treated as such; but they were cheaper and easier to keep in order than their forerunner. These factors, assisted by the influence of fashion, produced vast numbers of pianofortes, chiefly in a conveniently small rectangular form. Shudi and Broadwood, if their harpsichords were consecutively numbered (which is uncertain), made 1155 examples during the sixty four years they were engaged on that work (1729–1793), while in the twenty years between 1782 and 1802 they produced some 7000 rectangular and 1000 grand pianofortes.

While the two types of instrument were similar in tone it was not very difficult for them to exist side by side; so the harpsichord makers exerted strenuous efforts to increase the expressive powers of their products, inventing Swell, Machine Stop, Celestial Harp, Knee Levers, strongly contrasted tone colours, etc. as we have seen. [3] These instruments, which we so much admire today, were of course quite unknown to the great harpsichord composers of the first half of the eighteenth century. Unlike the early pianoforte their cost rose as more complicated expressive mechanism was introduced, and this contributed to their very short musical life of only about forty years. The search on the part of the early pianoforte makers and composers for increased volume and dynamic possibilities rapidly blunted the tone of the new instrument; the harpsichord found the competition impossible, and its manufacture ceased.

The first public appearance of the pianoforte in England may have been on 16 May 1767, when Charles Dibdin accompanied Miss Brickler in a song from *Judith*, after the first act of *The Beggar's Opera* at Covent Garden. In the following year Johann Christian Bach used a Zumpe pianoforte as a solo instrument in a Benefit Concert for Fischer. There was an official pianist at Drury Lane in 1770, and the newcomer supplanted the harpsichord in the King's Band in London in 1795. [4] The general position at the turn of the century is demonstrated by the fact that when Dibdin sold his theatre in Leicester Place in 1805 and its contents were auctioned, a Shudi harpsichord was offered but there was no bid, though a Hancock grand pianoforte fetched £70.

[1] Two upright pianofortes (Pyramidenflügel) dated 1745 are preserved in the Brussels Conservatoire and in the Goethehaus, Frankfurt (see page 105).
[2] Meusel (1808–1814).
[3] It is interesting to observe that the fashionable trend in modern harpsichord making until recently stressed those very factors: complicated expressive mechanism, and strongly contrasted tone colours, which contributed to the fall of the harpsichord a hundred and sixty years ago.
[4] Harding.

HISTORICAL CONCERTS

The pianoforte was first mentioned in English printed music on the title page of John Burton's Sonatas, published in 1766 (*Ten Sonatas for the Harpsichord, Organ, or Pianoforte*); and for several years after this date the names of both instruments were commonly given on the title pages of keyboard music, the harpsichord being placed first. The pianoforte was first mentioned alone in the late 1770's, and it soon took precedence over the harpsichord where both were mentioned in a title.

Beethoven's early keyboard works were announced for *clavecin* in 1782 (Kinsky's WoO 63); *clavecin* or *pianoforte* is stipulated for three sonatas, opus 2 (1795); the latter instrument is first specified alone in 1799 for two solo sonatas, opus 14. In chamber music however the pianoforte had appeared alone in the trios, opus 1, published in 1795; but *clavecin* reappears from time to time in the early years of the following century.

Despite the attitude of up to date musicians, the old instruments lingered on in use, chiefly in out of the way places. In Eduard Devrient's recollections of Mendelssohn (1869), he tells us that in 1829 they called together on Carl Zelter (1758–1832), director of the Singakademie in Berlin, and Zelter was found sitting at his two manual harpsichord. Preserved in the *Museo Teatrale alla Scala* in Milan is an Italian polygonal spinet of crude workmanship on which Giuseppe Verdi, as a child in the 1820's, was taught to play.

Though, as Türk pointed out in his *Klavierschule* (1789), the rectangular pianoforte derives in form from the clavichord, and the grand pianoforte from the harpsichord, these classical instruments were forgotten as regards shape, and mechanism, and musical potential. During the eighty years from about 1800 the pianoforte underwent its great development into the kind of instrument we know today. During that period, also, keyboard virtuosity reached previously unknown heights, and public recitals were given in great numbers, and in a manner which had never been known before. None the less, despite the appearance of complete editions of the works of the most famous masters, it occurred to extremely few musicians that the harpsichord composers had laid out the text of their writing in a manner suitable to that instrument, but foreign to the best qualities of the pianoforte. There were, however, a few such men, and they appeared from time to time at the harpsichord in historical concerts and in lecture recitals.

In England, for example, Ignaz Moscheles (1794–1870) appeared on a number of occasions in harpsichord recitals, the first of which took place in May 1837. These were held at the Hanover Square Concert Rooms and in the Concert Room of the Italian Opera House, and Moscheles used a Shudi harpsichord of 1771. Charles Salaman (1814–1901) began a series of historical concerts in 1855; these were continued for several years, and were repeated privately to the Royal Family. Salaman used a Kirckman harpsichord of 1768 (page 60). Ernst Pauer (1826–1905) gave similar concerts between 1861 and 1867 in Willis's Rooms. Carl Engel (1818–1882), a German from Hanover, came to England about 1845 as a professional pianist, and formed a collection of early keyboard and other instruments on which he played and lectured regularly.

Almost contemporary with Engel was Arthur Hipkins (1826–1903), a highly competent pianist who worked with Messrs. Broadwood, and who formed his own collection of instruments at 100 Warwick Gardens, Kensington, on which he played in lecture recitals. It is revealing of the period, however, to note that, when Hipkins included the Goldberg Variations of J. S. Bach in his programme, he usually found it best to play only the Aria, the two manual variations, and the Quodlibet. On 7 June 1886 Hipkins lectured to the Musical Association in London, using five early keyboard instruments to illustrate the styles of the various leading schools of composition and instrument making; on that occasion Anton Rubinstein turned the pages of the music for him.

There were other harpsichord players as well, though they were essentially professional pianists. J. H. Bonawitz (1839–1917) gave three recitals on a Shudi harpsichord in 1886 at Princes Hall, and followed this by a new series at 175 New Bond Street. A Mr. Boscovitz did similar work at Steinway Hall.

The middle years of the nineteenth century saw a new phenomenon: the appearance of a large number of musical antiquarians who formed collections of early musical instruments, sometimes for themselves, sometimes for a museum. Some of these collections have been mentioned in earlier chapters, and at this point they may be examined more closely.

Carl Engel formed his large collection in his house at 54 Addison Road, Kensington; and this collection, which comprised many types of instrument, included several harpsichords and spinets, and four clavichords. The majority of these were acquired by the Victoria and Albert Museum in 1875; and they now form the basis of that collection which Engel had initially organized for the Museum, and of which his first catalogue had been published in 1870. A. J. Hipkins was intimately connected with the organization of the International Inventions Exhibitions, held in London in 1885, at which some hundred early keyboard instruments, drawn from all parts of Europe, were exhibited in the Royal Albert Hall.

Other collectors included Sir George Donaldson (1845–1925), whose collection is now in the Royal College of Music; Thomas Taphouse of Oxford (1838–1905), most of whose instruments were dispersed in 1896; Henry Watson of Manchester (1846–1911), whose keyboard instruments are divided between the Royal Manchester College of Music and the Manchester Central Library. Another Manchester collector, James Kendrick Pyne (1857–1938), formed a large collection when a young man, but sold it to Henry Boddington, a Manchester brewer, the catalogue appearing in 1888. This collection was later dispersed.

The idea of a museum of musical instruments for the *Conservatoire Royal de Musique* in Brussels was first discussed by the Belgian *Academie Royale* in 1846. Plans went ahead, and on the death of F. J. Fétis (1784–1871), the Director of the Conservatoire, his collection was bought for the new museum. The publication of the five volume catalogue began in 1880. Two other important collections were formed in Belgium, both the property of lawyers. Abel Régibo of Renaix formed a large instrumental museum, and a catalogue was issued in the year of his death, 1897, when the collection was dispersed by sale. A large part went to Brussels; but many instruments were bought by Régibo's competitor in this field: Cesar Snoeck of Ghent. Snoeck's collection was catalogued in two parts: a general catalogue appeared in 1894, and another, devoted to instruments from the Low Countries, was issued in 1903. This collection was sold in three main groups: in 1902 a part went to the *Hochschule für Musik* in Berlin; and in 1909 most of the remainder was bought by the

Brussels Conservatoire, and by Czar Nicholas II of Russia. This latter part is now dispersed between the Institute for Scientific Research on Theatre and Music in Leningrad (Saint Petersburg), and the Museum of the Bolshoi Theatre in Moscow.

In Germany the catalogue of the Instrumental Museum of the Berlin *Hochschule für Musik* first appeared in 1882. The collection was enlarged in 1888, and again in 1892, by the purchase of large groups of instruments from an unreliable collector and musical writer from Holland, Paul de Wit (1852–1925), who had made his headquarters in Leipzig. De Wit sold another collection in 1905, this time to Wilhelm Heyer of Cologne (1849–1913). The Heyer collection was moved to Leipzig in 1927. The collection at the *Hochschule*, badly damaged during the 1939 war, has now been reorganized, and is housed in the former Joachimsthal Gymnasium.

Count Giovanni Correr of Venice specialized in instruments of the sixteenth and seventeenth centuries, and his catalogue appeared in 1872. These instruments were mostly acquired by Brussels. In Florence the Kraus collection issued a catalogue in 1901, and was absorbed by Wilhelm Heyer in 1908. The faking of early instruments in Florence to meet the demands of all these collectors has already been discussed (pages 34 and 143–5).

America saw three important nineteenth-century enthusiasts, Morris Steinert, Hugo Worch and Mrs. Crosby Brown. Steinert's collection, catalogued in 1893, was later dispersed. In 1900 he gave many instruments to Yale University which, some sixty years later, also acquired those which had been sold by Steinert to Miss Belle Skinner. Others are now to be found at the Rhode Island School of Design in Providence. Worch, a successful piano dealer like Morris Steinert, formed a large collection of keyboard instruments which are now in the Smithsonian Institution in Washington. Mrs. Crosby Brown donated her collection of instruments in 1889 to the Metropolitan Museum of Art in New York, adding further instruments to it before the appearance of the catalogue, prepared under her direction, in 1904.

France is unusual in that plans for a museum of musical instruments were laid as early as 1795, when on 3 August the National Convention passed a law to establish such a collection. [1] Nothing was done however (apart from burning in 1816 some 376 old instruments, which included about 100 harpsichords) until 1861 when it was decided to put the plan into effect at the *Conservatoire National de Musique*. A catalogue was published in 1884. The first collection of M. Réné Savoye was sold in Paris in 1882, at which time his catalogue was issued.

This list of collections could be extended very considerably, since it notices some of the larger and more important museums only. A summary of important collections now available for study is given on pages 186 to 189.

A feature of the majority of these mid-nineteenth century instrumental museums was the preservation of their contents as objects of antiquarian interest only; thus very few of the instruments were in playing order. The debt which we owe to those collectors who preserved so many good classical instruments must not, however, be forgotten. But in Paris this

[1] Chouquet (1875).

period produced two skilled repairers who devoted much time to the restoration of early keyboard instruments.

Charles Fleury was a pianoforte maker who lived at 6 Boulevard Poissonnière. Among his restorations may be noted the Pascal Taskin harpsichord of 1786 in the Victoria and Albert Museum (1856), and the Hieronymus Albrecht Hass harpsichord of 1734 in the Brussels Conservatoire (1858).

A little junior to Fleury was an Italian who came to Paris: Louis Tomasini. A good many early instruments were restored by Tomasini, including (in 1883) the Joachim Swanen pedal harpsichord of 1786 in the *Conservatoire des Arts et Métiers*. Tomasini also built a few harpsichords himself, copying the eighteenth century French model.

There was at that time in Paris a distinguished pianist: Louis Diémer (1843–1919), who often appeared in concerts at the harpsichord. Diémer generally used the Pascal Taskin harpsichord of 1769 which had belonged to that instrument maker, and which was still in the possession of the Taskin family (plates 47 and 48). When in Brussels, however, Diémer used instruments from the Conservatoire museum there.

In 1882 the Taskin family sent their harpsichord to Tomasini for restoration; and on its return a request was received from Erard, the pianoforte maker, for permission to borrow the instrument for study, as plans were being considered for the commercial manufacture of harpsichords. The Taskin was accordingly lent to Erard, and used as the basic design for a new model. With this episode the commercial development of the modern harpsichord began.

APPENDIX ONE

BARTOLOMEO CRISTOFORI

On 23 September 1716 Bartolomeo Cristofori took charge in Florence of the musical instruments belonging to the Grand Duke Cosimo III of Tuscany, many of which had been left by his son, Prince Ferdinand, whose death had occurred in 1713. Among eighty-four instruments were forty-five keyboard instruments:

20 Harpsichords
16 Spinets
3 Clavichords
1 Organ with five stops
2 Small organs
1 Organ combined with a spinet
1 Organ combined with a harpsichord and two spinets
1 Organ and clavichord combined.

Apart from unsigned instruments there were:

A harpsichord by Baffo.
An ebony harpsichord with ivory keys by Cristofori.
A large spinet for the Theatre by Cristofori.
3 harpsichords with one stop each by Cristofori.
Another harpsichord with one stop by Cristofori.
An upright harpsichord by Cristofori.
A harpsichord by Domenico of Pesaro.
A large spinet by Domenico of Pesaro.
An organ and clavichord combined by Domenico of Pesaro.
An octave harpsichord with two stops by Domenico of Pesaro (see pages 30, 36 and 117).
A clavichord by Domenico of Pesaro.
A folding harpsichord made in France (probably by Marius, see page 55).
A harpsichord by Cortona of Rome.
A harpsichord from Antwerp, with two unisons, an octave, and two keyboards.
Two harpsichords by Girolamo Zenti.
Two spinets, one dated 1668, by Girolamo Zenti.
A spinet with two stops, by Giuseppe Mondini.

The following accounts, preserved in the Medici archives in Florence, throw further light on Cristofori's duties:

BARTOLOMEO CRISTOFORI

(1) Medici file 1073, No. 325.

12 August 1690

Owed to me, Bartolomeo Christofori, by the Treasury of His Serene Highness, Prince Ferdinando of Tuscany

For having a *cemballo* moved twice to the Piti Palace from my house	L	2 13	4
further for taking and bringing back one *cemballo* as above		1 6	8
For loading two instrument stands for Pratolino		1 10	0
For three vulture quills, and steel strings		1 3	4
For removing from Piti to my house three *cemballi* with their stands		2 13	4

6 November 1690

For moving a *cemballo* to the Palace	13	4
	———	
	10 0	0

(2) File 1073 No. 325.

15 August 1690

The Treasury of the Serene Prince Ferdinando of Tuscany owes me, Bartolomeo Christofori, for a new *spineta*

For getting ebony, fir, and poplar sawn up	L	12 10	0
For a pound and a half of fish glue		12	0
For ordinary glue and varnish		5	0
For brass pins, and iron pins		3	0
For five pieces of ivory		1 10	0
For nails, etc.		4	0
Salary and labour for ten months		172	0
For the cabinet maker		126	0

Total	336 0	0
My total work	700 0	0
	———	
Sum	1036 0	0

(3) File 1073. No. 325.

23 December 1690

I, Bartolomeo Cristofori, claim from the Treasury of the Serene Prince Ferdinando of Tuscany

For ten vulture feathers	L	2 10	0
For steel strings bought in Pisa		2 10	0
8 Aug. 1691 For twenty five vulture feathers		7 10	0
16 Aug. 1691 For loading three pairs of stands for the instruments at Florence and unloading them in Pratolino		4 13	4
1 Oct. 1691 For loading three stands in Pratolino and unloading them in Florence		5	0
11 Oct. For moving a *Cemballo* to Piti		1	0
For collecting the *Cemballo* of Cortona		21	0
For moving two *Cemballi* with their stands to Via della Pergola, and bringing them back to the house		4	0
15 March For fifteen vulture feathers		4	0
2 April 1692 For a music desk of Cypress to be sent to the Serene Electress of Hamburg		14	0

	———
	66 3 4

126

BARTOLOMEO CRISTOFORI

15 March 1692

For a new *Cemballo* with two stops

For home grown Cypress and getting it sawn up	L 14	0	0
For everything involving cabinet making	114	0	0
For the woodworker	40	0	0
For brass pins, iron pins, glue etc.	13	0	0
For my work	350	0	0
Total	597	3	4

(4) File 1073, No. 325.

1 July 1692

I, Bartolomeo Christofori claim the following from the Treasury of the Serene Prince Ferdinando of Tuscany for making a new *Cembalo* with two stops for the theatre.

For Cypress from Candia [in Crete] and for having it sawn up	L 45	0	0
For all kinds of cabinet work	144	0	0
For a Cypress rose	4	0	10
For the woodworker	35	0	0
For iron pins, brass pins, red felt, small nails, glue, etc.	18	0	0
For my work	350	0	0
Total	596	0	10
In addition for a music desk of Cypress inlaid with ebony.	18	0	0
For another music desk of Cypress, made for a *Cembalo* for the Roman Priest	14	0	0
For two desks for the above mentioned theatre *Cembalo*, one of Cypress, the other of fir, with their tin packing cases.	18	0	0
For a poplar stand for the above *Cembalo*	21	0	0
For various vulture feathers	5	0	0
For moving a *Cembalo* to the palace, and bringing it home again	1	6	8
Total	673	16	8

(5) File 1073. No. 325.

1 September 1693

I, Bartolomeo Cristofori claim from the Treasury of the Serene Prince Ferdinando of Tuscany, for a Cypress *spineta* with two stops, all inlaid with ebony.

For home grown Cypress, and getting it cut up.	L 5	10	0
For a Cypress rose	4	0	0
For nails, including getting them burnished	5	0	0
For brass, felt, leather, glue, nails, etc.	32	0	0
For the cabinet maker and assistant	339	0	0
For my work	800	0	0
	1185	10	0

4 November 1693

For remaking another *Cemballo* inlaid with ivory, ebony and green marble.

For two long sections of pear tree veneer	L. 8	0	0
For another piece of pear	1	6	8
For iron pegs, brass pins, felt glue, four pieces of ebony, tacks etc.	28	0	0
For the cabinet maker and assistant	146	0	0
For my work	420	0	0
	603	6	8

BARTOLOMEO CRISTOFORI

(6) File 1073, No. 325.

5 November 1693

I, Bartolomeo Cristofori, instrument maker, claim from the Treasurer to the Serene Prince Ferdinando of Tuscany

On 18 August 1692 for the visit to Pratolino in order to unload three instrument stands and take them to the Theatre together with a tip for the carriers.	L. 2	10	0
On 6 October for unloading two stands which arrived at my house from Pratolino	2	0	0
On 28 November for restoring a *spinetina*, remaking the keyboard, putting in bridges, strings, felt, and other work involving fifteen days.	45	0	0
Expenses for the *spinetina*	3	0	0
On 10 February, for a month and a half of my own work on an organ made of wood	105	0	0
Cost of kid leather	1	10	0
For brass wire and felt	2	15	0
For green silk ribbon, twenty yards	1	7	0
A months work for the assistant	30	0	0
For turning certain pipes for the organ	1	6	8
For glue		18	0
For twelve days work on the *cembalo* with bass octave (*ottava bassa*) by gierolamo [*sic*] Zenti in the apartment of His Excellency	36	0	0
Expenses for this *Cemballo*		15	0
For moving a *Cemballo* with its stand from Signor Giosefo Canovese's, and then taking it to San Firenze, and then bringing it to my house	2	3	4
1 April for restoring a *spineta* by Domenico of Pesaro, remaking the keyboard, new quills, strings, felt, and eighteen days work	53	0	0
Expenses relating to the *spineta*	5	0	0
25 June 1693, For twenty five vulture quills	6	5	0
For adjusting a keyboard of the organ at Pratolino, three days work with assistance	13	10	0
Cost of brass wire and felt	1	0	0
16 August for moving the *cemballi* at Pratolino for His Excellency	2	6	8
1 October for unloading the stands from Pratolino	2	10	0
	317	16	8

(7) File 1073 No. 325.

1 May 1694

I, Bartolomeo Cristofori claim from the Treasurer to the Serene Prince Ferdinando of Tuscany.

For adjusting a *spinetina* with gold strings	L. 28	0	0

25 June 1694

For remaking a *Cembalo* by Celestini with four stops,

Cost of Cypress from Candia	3	10	0
Scarlet felt	4	5	0
Glue and brass wire	2	15	0
Working time for three months for the assistant	117	0	0
For the apprentice	26	0	0
For my work	252	0	0
	405	10	0

128

BARTOLOMEO CRISTOFORI

15 July

For a music desk for the above *Cembalo*	L.	14	0	0
For having my present house repaired		113	0	0
For four curtains of material.		54	0	0

September 1694

For adjusting the two *cembali* by Gierolimo and the organ in the apartment of his Serene Excellency, fifteen days work with an assistant.	90	0	0

(8) File 1073 No. 325

1 Nov. 1696

I, Bartolomeo Cristofori, claim from the Treasurer of the Serene Prince Ferdinando of Tuscany.

10 Feb. 1693

For remaking a *spineta*, that is remaking an ebony keyboard, putting on bridges, all strings, felt, and quills, with all work for a month and with an assistant	L.	95	0	0
Expenses for the *spineta*		5	10	0
25 Feb for twenty four vulture quills		6	0	0
10 June 1696. For rebuilding a *cembalo* by Domenico of Pesaro bought by Signora Luzia, including remaking the keyboard and bridges, and a month's work with two assistants		112	0	0
Expenses for the *cembalo*		3	0	0
In addition a music desk of Candia Cypress inlaid with ebony for the *cembalo*		18	0	0
For removing the *cembalo* from the place it was bought to my house with its *claviorgano*, moving the *cembalo* to Pitti, and bringing it to my house again.		3	6	8
14 August. For loading a pair of instrument stands to be sent to Pratolino			10	0
16 August. For unloading two pairs of stands at Pratolino and carrying the *Cembali* to the theatre		1	10	0
30 October. Expenses for a *spinetina* bought from Berti the instrument maker for his Serene Excellency and sent to Maestro Pagliardi		30	0	0
26 October. For a poplar case for the *spineta* to send it to Rome for the use of Signor Raffaellino, musician.		15	0	0
December 1695. Cost of repairing fixtures in my house which his Excellency in his kindness is pleased to pay me for, and for timber and the cabinet maker		64	0	0
For two pieces of material		30	0	0
For eight pounds of wax		16	0	0
Ribbons and nails		5	0	0
August 1696. For repairing the mouldings on a *spinettina* assistant's expenses		3	0	0
For repairing a *cembalo* sent to Signor Pucini, work for three days with an assistant and expenses.		14	0	0
10 August. For repairing a hole in a *Cembalo* for Pratolino.			13	4
For packing three *cembali* and loading them		1	6	8
September Expenses at Pratolino for packing and loading the instruments		2	6	8
27 October Three ounces of brass wire sent to Poio Caiano			10	0
		426	13	4

BARTOLOMEO CRISTOFORI

(9) File 1073 No. 225.

10 August 1697

I, Bartolomeo Cristofori claim from the Treasury of the Serene Prince Ferdinando of Tuscany for work and expenses.

For an upright *Cembalo* with two stops, delivered on the above date.

For home grown cypress for the *cembalo*	L. 7	0	0
For iron pins, brass, felt, glue, etc.	13	0	0
For the cabinet maker and apprentice	170	0	0
For my work	560	0	0
For the expenses for Signor Niccola Onofrii paid by order of his Excellency for fifteen days in June 1697	40	0	0
Expenses in the country at Pratolino 1697	2	12	0
1 May 1698 For adjusting a *Cembalo* by Gierolimo Zenti with three stops, a month and a half work with an assistant	164	0	0
For a music desk of cypress painted black with gilt mouldings	18	0	0
For a new case for the *cembalo*	30	0	0
20 July 1698 For a new large *Cembalo* from GG chromatic with two stops	500	0	0
For a music desk of cypress inlaid with ebony for this *Cembalo*	18	0	0
	1522	12	0

(10) File 1073. No. 335.

The Treasury to the Serene Prince Ferdinando of Tuscany owes Bartolomeo Cristofori as follows

30 August 1698 For provisions for five months from the 1st of April 1698 to date at the rate of twelve scudi per month	60	0	0
Rent for the house for one year up to April 1698	24	0	0
	84	0	0

(11) File 1200. No. 392.

12 October 1711

The Treasury to his Serene Highness owes to Bartolomeo Cristofori for adjusting an ordinary *Cimbalo* by order of Signor Ant. Citerni, gentleman in waiting to the Serene Princess Eleonora, and replacing all strings, quills, felt, lengthening all the jacks, making a music desk, restoring the case as necessary.

Six days work with an assistant	25	0	0
Expenses for strings	2	0	0
Felt, quills, cypress for the music desk, etc.	2	10	0
	29	10	0

Additional details of the Medici instruments are given in Gai (1969).

APPENDIX TWO

THE CEMBALO ANGELICO
(Plate 17)

Lettera dell 'Autore del nuovo Cembalo Angelico
inventato in Roma nell 'anno MDCCLXXV.

In Roma Nella Stamperia di Giovanni Zempel.

Notice from the Publisher to
Players of Harpsichords

This letter by the inventor of the *Cembalo Angelico* has come into my hands. In it he explains with great accuracy to an Academician friend of his the rules to be observed in constructing such an instrument. I feel I would be rendering a welcome service to Harpsichord players by passing this letter on to the printing press. The ingenious *Cembalo Angelico* has been very much acclaimed by Musicians for its surprising sweetness and for the simplicity of its mechanism, and this can be adapted at very little expense to any Harpsichord fitted with jacks without in the least changing its ordinary structure. I am quite sure that wherever it is heard of all Harpsichord players will compete with one another to fit it to their instruments.

I am therefore offering to send to the same Harpsichord players and to Booksellers such copies of the present Instruction Book as they may ask of me, provided they send their letters postage paid, and make arrangements for me to receive here in Rome payment for the copies they have ordered. May you live in peace.

Most Esteemed Friend.

To satisfy your wish to know what the *Cembalo Angelico* is and in order to make its mechanism known to our Academy of Science, I will tell you that this invention which I made this year in Rome consists mainly of the easy and simple way I have discovered of substituting small velvet covered plectra for crow quills in the jacks. These imitate the touch of the tip of the most delicate finger, and they touch the strings by sliding over them, like a very small violin bow covered in velvet. Thus they render a mixed sound, which resembles partly that of the sweet Flute, and partly that of a silver bell when struck very lightly with a velvet covered hammer. The tone quality produced is most sweet and charming, and is far better than that of any other musical instrument so far invented, especially when the Harpsichord is played in the most silent surroundings, as in the depth of night.

For many years I have been searching for an easy way to sound the brass strings of the Harpsichord by means of rubbing or friction, so as to imitate the effect of violin bows on gut strings. But none of the many tests that I made really satisfied me, as they all lacked that simplicity which one must always aim at, especially when dealing with the mechanism of things that are in constant use, and because none of them proved suitable to the structure of the ordinary Harpsichord jack.

THE CEMBALO ANGELICO

Finally, on the 15th of February last, while I was having a new *Porta Armonica* made on the lines of the latest type I had perfected, I was able to imagine a velveted plectrum which, in the act of sliding over the brass strings, would pluck them and make them vibrate with that delicacy I wanted. I immediately thought of adapting this plectrum to the jacks of a Harpsichord, and this I succeeded in doing with such good results that, because the sound was so new and unbelievably sweet, I decided to name this Harpsichord *Angelico*.

In case you want to have this invention of mine put into practice, I will explain it to you in six separate articles. First: the ordinary mechanism of the jacks. Second: the structure of the new leather covered plectra which I have invented and which replace the crow quills. Third: the method of changing the registers, or stops of the Harpsichord. Fourth: the mechanism of the *sordine* on the Harpsichord. Fifth: the way to reduce mechanical noise from the jacks. Sixth: the particular attributes of the *Cembalo Angelico*.

ARTICLE 1

THE ORDINARY MECHANISM OF HARPSICHORD JACKS

To make it easier to understand how the leather plectra should be made, and how they should be placed in the jacks so that they should make the strings vibrate sweetly, it is advisable first of all to show you the ordinary and generally known mechanism of the jacks. In the attached diagram I have sketched the jack with all its component parts, which I will briefly enumerate.

In Figure I, *a b c d* is the rectangular piece of wood whose length from *a* to *c* is generally about 5 *once* of the Roman architectural palm. Its width from *a* to *b* is 3½ minutes of an *oncia* and its depth slightly over one minute.

It is already known that the Roman palm is divided into 12 *once*, and each *oncia* into five minutes, so that the whole palm is divided into 60 minutes. At the end of the diagram there is a scale of half a palm, that is to say of 6 *once*, each of which is divided into 5 minutes.

In Figure I, *e f* is the opening where you put the small piece of scarlet cloth which acts as a damper, and stops the vibration of the string after the return of the jack. *g h m l* is the opening in which the little wooden tongue *c d n r*, Figure II, is placed.

This little tongue is generally about 1½ *once* long from *c* to *n*, and 1½ minutes wide; and when making it it is usual to divide it in three parts. In the first part, between points *y* and *z*, a tiny hole is made in which either a pin or a small piece of wire is placed, and this serves as a pivot on which the little tongue moves. In the second part, at point *x*, there is a small transverse opening through which the crow quill which has to pluck the string is inserted. The tongue is thinned from *y* to *n*, and from *z* to *r*, so that its thickness towards *n* is reduced to the thinnest possble. Let us suppose therefore the tongue *c d n r*, Figure II, is placed in the opening *g h m l*, Figure I, and that the pin or axle is inserted in the hole *i*. One sees that the little tongue threaded on to the pin *i h* will fill the opening *g h m l*; and, since this aperture is tapered from *l* to *m*, it follows that, by putting the lower thinned portion of the tongue on this slope, the tongue will be parallel with the front side of the jack, as in Figure III, which represents a complete jack, with its crow quill *r*, and with its scarlet damper, *s*.

Furthermore it must be mentioned that the tongue *o p* when fixed on to the pin *m* can swing on it, so that the top end *o* moves back towards the opposite side of damper *s*; but this extremity *o* cannot move forward because the lower end *p* fits into, and is stopped by, the lower tapered end of the aperture. This is more clearly visible in Figure IV. While the tongue *o v t p*, which rotates on pin *m n*, and is thinned from *t* to *p*, and fits into the tapered part of the aperture *s r*, can rotate backwards from *g* to *o*, the extremity *o* cannot go forward in the opposite direction, because the lower end *p*, when striking the slanting edge *r*, cannot go any further back. At point *s* on the slanting edge there is a perpendicular hole into which is placed a piece of hen quill or a small brass

132

spring, held with a little gum or glue. The spring, pressing against the tongue at *v*, pushes it forward until its extremity *p* touches the slanting edge at *r*, and thus the tongue fills up the empty space in the aperture *g t s r*, as can be seen in Figure V. Here the small quill spring *a b*, slightly bent at one end *a*, presses against the tongue *c d* and keeps it true, in such a way that its top end does not go either one side or the other of the wood of the jack.

Since the jack is built in this way, and fitted with the crow quill *r*, Figure III, it will be seen that, when the jack moves upward from *b*, a taut string may be placed so that it can be plucked by the tip of the crow quill *r*. This quill will now come into contact with the string, because the top portion *o* of the tongue *o p* will be pushed forward towards *s*. But since this tongue cannot turn round any further than point *o*, owing to the lower tip *p* hitting the wood of the aperture in the jack, it follows that when the tongue is raised and the upper part of the crow quill touches the string at *r*, the tongue will not move. Thus the quill will be forced to bend until it is so short as to slip over the string, and at this point, owing to its elasticity, the quill will pluck the string, bringing fourth a loud and crude sound similar to that which one would obtain by plucking the same string with one's finger nail.

When the jack is lowered from *a* to *b*, and when the lower portion of the quill comes into contact with the same taut string, it need only just touch the string sufficiently to overcome the resistance of the small quill or brass spring, which presses on the back of the tongue. Since this resistance is of the slightest, it follows that, when the jack moves down from *a* to *b*, the quill *r* does not produce any sound from the string, or if it does it is so slight as to be imperceptible to human ears. This is because the quill or brass spring gives little resistance, and consequently the tip *o* of the little tongue moves back. The crow quill *r* passes under the taut string, touching it only lightly, and without producing any sound. If it did it would be silenced by the cloth damper *s*, the lower tip of which, pressing on the string as soon as the quill has passed under it, stops any vibration. But as long as the crow quill *r* is above the string the damper does not touch the latter. Consequently it follows that as long as the Harpsichord player presses a key the jack remains uplifted with damper *s* above the string, and the string maintains its vibrations and sound; but as soon as the player takes his finger off the key jack falls, and the damper deadens the sound. The quill *r* passes under the string, and the tongue *o p* returns in position level with the front of the jack. The player is again able to strike the note and make the same sound promptly and rapidly.

ARTICLE 2

STRUCTURE OF THE VELVETED LEATHER PLECTRA FOR JACKS

From the explanation of the mechanism of the jack, summarized in the preceding chapter, that of the new jack of the *Cembalo Angelico* will be obvious, since the only difference is that, while the tongue of the ordinary jack is provided with a crow or vulture quill, the tongue of the *Cembalo Angelico* is provided with a small piece of leather instead of quill, sharpened at the tip and covered with soft leather. I have called this the *Polpastrello*, and it is made as follows. A small piece of thin sole leather, long and rectangular, must be cut, similar to that shown in Figure VI, 4 minutes of a palm in length from *a* to *o*, $1\frac{1}{2}$ minutes in width from *a* to *b*, and about $\frac{1}{4}$ of a minute thick.

The top portion *a b n m* must be thinned from *m n* to *a b* in such a way that it becomes thinner towards *a b* like the blade of a knife, sharpened only on one side, but round and without an edge. The perfection of this leather lies in its tapering, because when the jack moves upwards the string must slide on this thinned and slanting edge, and this sliding on the jack, which resembles on a small scale the action of drawing a bow across a violin, makes the tone of the string similar to that of a sweet flute, and the rebound from the string of the rounded tip *a b* gives, as already said, that most delicate vibration which finally produces a silver tone similar to that of a small bell struck with a velvet covered hammer. Since it is of the utmost importance that this side *m n a b* should be tapered with the correct downward slant from *m n* to *a b* I will explain precisely this tapering and slant.

Let us suppose therefore that *d c e a* in Figure VII be the thickness of the sole leather, seen from the side. At the extremity *a c* of the sole, draw a vertical line *a c g* which leaves the line *a e*, forming a right angle of 90 degrees. With centre *a* construct the quadrant of a circle *e d f g*, and bisect this arc at point *f*. From point *f* draw a line *f b a*, which will give the correct slant of the tapered side of the sole at 45 degrees, and following this line cut with a small knife the upper angle of the sole *b c a*, and then this tapered side will give the true angelic tone on the string. But if this tapered side is given a slant of a more acute angle, the string will give a more resounding and a less sweet tone. In other words, by varying the angle of inclination of the tapered side of the leather plectrum, one can vary the vibration of the string in many ways. But according to various tests, made so as to obtain the true angelic tone, the tapered side must have a slant of between 45 and 50 degrees at the most.

Having tapered in such a way the top side of the small piece of leather at the correct slant, so as to soften its contact or friction with the string, its tip *a b m n* must be covered with soft glove leather, better thick than thin. The leather must be stuck on to the extremity *a b m n* with clove glue known as *Cervonia*, or with diluted glue, which must be thick and viscous, in the manner shown in Figure VIII, *c d e f*, noting however that the smooth side of the leather should be on the inside, and be stuck to the sole leather, while the rough side of the leather remains on the outside to touch the string. This rough side must be of soft grain like *Dante* leather, and somewhat pliable, because on this depends the delicacy of the tone of the string.

So as to prepare these leathers quickly and without great effort, take a piece of the above mentioned sole leather of any length, like the one *g h p q* in Figure IX, and, after tapering it from *i o* to *g h* as previously explained, it can be completely covered with a long strip of soft leather 2 minutes wide, glued on to the back of side *i o g h* in such a way that it covers the whole tapered side, as shown in Figure X, *r s t v*. When the glue or gum is well dried, as many leather plectra as fit into the width of the sole can be cut out with a knife on a small wooden table, by making, with or without a compass, the division points, and by drawing with a black lead pencil the corresponding lines *a h, b i, c l, d m, e n, f o, g p*, and these lines must be cut up with a penknife; thus the plectra will be made easily and quickly and will appear neater and more uniform. Before glueing the soft leather on to the hard leather, it should be noted that the top and lower surface of the latter should be scraped with the blade of a penknife to remove any roughness so that the glue can stick well; otherwise there is a risk that in cutting the plectra the soft leather may become unstuck from the hard. One must also be very careful when glueing the soft leather on to the back of the hard leather *r s t v* that the outer part of the leather should not become stained or spoilt in the glue or gum. If this happened, once the glue was dry, the plectrum on plucking the string would produce a crude sound almost similar to that of the crow quill.

It must be observed that if the back of the plectrum is covered with the soft and thick leather, namely of the thickness of one fifth of a minute of a palm, the plectrum produces from the string the true angelic tone, a full, round and very sweet sound. If on the other hand the plectrum is surfaced with a thinner leather, as used for gloves, it will produce a clearer, more silvery and stronger sound. The stronger tone can again be varied if the leather on the end part which touches the string is not scraped, and an acute angle is left on it without rounding it. From this it can be seen that everybody has the option to give his Harpsichord that sort of tone that pleases him most.

To place the plectrum in the tongue of the jack, one must widen the hole where normally the crow quill is placed as much as the wood of the tongue allows, making it of a size in proportion to the width of the plectrum, as shown in Figure XI. Here, in the opening *a b c o*, from *a* to *b* is nearly as wide as the tongue *d e f g*, while the opening from *a* to *c* is proportionate to the size of the plectrum. The leather has to be placed in this long and rectangular opening *a b c o*, and will have to be forced in, so it must be cut very exactly with a penknife; but it will have to be a little wider towards the end covered with soft leather, and be thinned at the opposite end *c d* Figure XII. The thinned end *c d* will then have to be put into the aperture in such a way that its other extremity *a b*, covered with soft leather, will remain outside the tongue on the front side of the jack, and will be of such a length that it can touch the string on the exact spot where it bends, namely on the slant of the thinned side. The exact spot on which the leather plectrum must touch the string is towards the middle of the slant of the thinned side, as can be seen in Figure XIII, in which the string *d c* is being touched by the leather plectrum *a b e f*. And since, as already explained, the plectrum must be forced into the aperture in the tongue, it is necessary to pull the tip *g h*, Figure XIV, with one's fingers, or with a pair of flat pliers or small pincers, without pushing it from the other end *ef* with one's fingers, because if this were done the sole would bend in front of the tongue, and consequently would lose its resistance and elasticity, both of which are necessary to give the string its correct vibration. After the plectrum has been pulled through with small pliers to the correct point, it must be held in position by means of a small wedge glued in place, so that it cannot move either by shortening or lengthening. This is done by inserting in the aperture of the tongue, at point *o* on top of the plectrum, a wooden wedge *m n*, with its tip pointing towards *o*. Care must be taken, when pushing this wedge, to hold the front part of the plectrum *e f* near to the tongue, so that the latter cannot move and the plectrum remains at the correct distance. When the plectrum is thus fixed, both this and the wedge behind the tongue at point *o* must be cut off with a pair of scissors. Figure XV shows the tongue *b c t v* with the plectrum and wedge cut at *r s*. It should be specially noted that such a cut is better done with scissors than with a knife, because the action of cutting with a knife would force the wedge on one side only and would slacken it, whereas this does not happen when using scissors, because the action of the scissors is equal both above and below the wedge and the plectrum.

ARTICLE 3

METHOD OF CHANGING THE REGISTERS OR STOPS
ON THE HARPSICHORD

It is fairly well known how the slides move, in which stand the jacks of a Harpsichord. They are commonly known as Registers or Stops.

Harpsichords with two registers nearly always have one movable and the other fixed (except for a few that have both registers movable). The movable register is used to pull back the jacks and to move the tips of the crow quills away from the strings, so that the other register plays by itself. Therefore in these Harpsichords the movable register must be left with the crow quills in it and the stationary register must be fitted with leather plectra.

Thus, when the stop with crow quills is moved back the register with leather is played by itself; both registers can be played together when the one with crow quills is pushed towards the strings.

When the register with leather plays together with the crow quill register, the roughness of the sound produced by the quills does not allow the ear to distinguish the angelic sound of the leather, and the sound as a whole is nearly the same as if both registers were equipped with quills. It is however a little fuller and sweeter, and has not got that tone without body which is known as *nasino*, and which is the ordinary defect of all Harpsichords with jacks equipped with crow quills.

If, after playing the two registers together, one with quills, the other with leather, one puts off the quill register and plays the leather register by itself, the tone of this latter is such a welcome change and sensation that it is surprising and moving.

THE CEMBALO ANGELICO

If both registers are equipped with leather the tone is much stronger and much fuller and has more body; but with ordinary jacks one cannot have the pleasure of hearing both registers with either quill or leather. In such a case, those who wish to have the variation are advised to have only one register with leather, whereas those who wish to obtain the perfect angelic tone are advised to put leather in both the registers.

Furthermore if one wishes to have the option of playing both registers, both with quill and leather, it becomes necessary to remake all the jacks with two tongues, moving in opposite directions, as shown in Figure XVI, where tongue $a\,n$ has a crow quill d, and tongue $g\,f$ has a leather e. The tip of the crow quill is placed at the front of the jack, while the leather faces in the opposite direction. With the jack made in this way, with two tongues, the following result will be obtained: when the register is pulled forward all the jacks will move near the strings in such a way that all the crow quills can touch and play their respective strings, and while the quill is near the string the leather of the same jack on the opposite side will not be able to touch its respective string or produce any sound from it. On the other hand when the register is pushed back, the leather on coming near to its string will be able to touch it and bring forth from it the angelic tone, while the crow quill, moving away from its string on the opposite side, will not touch it any longer and consequently will produce no sound. From this it follows that, when all the jacks of both registers are made with double tongues, on pulling forward both the registers all the crow quills will play according to the old system of quill Harpsichords, and when the same two registers are pushed back all the jacks of both registers will play with the leather plectra, and will form the new *Angelic* Harpsichord perfected, inside the same old crow quill Harpsichord.

A simple mechanism can be used to move the registers with one's feet, and this is illustrated in Figure XVII, in which $a\,b\,c\,d$ represents a portion of the left side of the case or body of the Harpsichord adjacent to the two registers of jacks $e\,f$ and $g\,h$. Let us suppose that the first of these registers $e\,f$ is movable from e to f, and *vice versa* from f to e. To give these two contrary movements to this register you need only make a small brass plate $o\,p\,q\,r$, attached by four small screws to the inside of the above mentioned side of the Harpsichord case. In the middle of this brass plate a small piece of iron or brass is soldered, about $\frac{1}{2}$ an *oncia* of a palm in length, to the end of which is attached the transverse piece of iron $l\,m\,n$, with its pivot at point s. This iron piece has two holes in it, one at each end, l and n, to which are attached two gut cords; and in hole n is placed a small nut which is fixed to the wood of the register $e\,f$, so that by moving the end n of the iron piece the register $e\,f$ also moves. A gut cord is fixed in hole l. This cord is then passed through hole t to bring it down outside the Harpsichord case towards the ground; finally another gut cord is attached to the screw at n, and this is also made to go outside the Harpsichord case through hole v. Cord $l\,t$ is attached near the ground to the piece of wood $x\,z$ of the pedal $z\,h$. The two ends of these pieces of wood [*sic*] are joined at z and h to the block of wood i, and the other two ends $x\,y$ remain free and a little above ground level. From this it is seen that if the Harpsichord player places his heel on the wooden block i, and with the tip of his toe presses on extremity x of wood $x\,z$, the chord $x\,t\,l$ will be pulled, and the end l of the iron piece pivoted on point s will move towards hole t; consequently the other end n of the same iron piece will move away from hole v, and by this action will push forward the whole register $e\,f$ with all its jacks. If the Harpsichord player then places the ball of his foot at point y on the wooden stick $h\,y$, cord $y\,v\,n$ will be pulled, and the end n of the iron piece, which is screwed to the register $e\,f$, will move back together with all the jacks. Thus with the greatest simplicity and ease the register can be moved backwards and forwards just as the player wishes.

It is advisable to place two small rings where the two gut cords press on the outer side of the two holes t and v in the Harpsichord case, so that the cords have less friction and the register can move more smoothly.

In the same way, and with the same mechanism, both the registers can be moved together, if the jacks are made with double tongues. If this is the case, you must join the two registers together by means of a small wooden cross bar, and lengthen the end *n* of the iron piece in such a way that it can be screwed in the middle of the cross bar. Thus, instead of only moving one register, the pedal mechanism will always move both registers at the same time.

THE MECHANISM OF THE SORDINE ON THE HARPSICHORD

The *sordine* of the Harpsichord is only a roll of soft woollen material, rather like a serpent in shape, and of the same thickness as a little finger. This roll is pressed against the strings of the Harpsichord near the little bridge [i.e. nut] to damp the vibrations. Thus, when the strings are touched, either by the crow quills or by the leather, the tone given out is nearly the same as that of a lute. The secret of the sordine consists in making the little cloth roll very soft, and in placing it in such a way that in the treble it touches the strings very close to the nut, and in the low notes at a distance of 2 minutes of a palm from the nut.

To make the little roll soft, take a small round stick or wire of the same thickness as the little finger, and round this sew a piece of flannel or other hairy wool. When it is all sewn on, the wire or stick must be pulled out and the hollow centre filled with horse hair, so that as well as being soft the roll may have elasticity.

In order to press this little wooden roll on the strings, glue it lightly underneath a long and rectangular wooden ruler, smoothed on its lower side, as shown in Figure XVIII. Here *a b c d* represents the ruler upside down, showing how the woollen roll *m n* should be attached, and where two little hooks *e* and *s* should be fixed; two gut cords should be tied to the latter so that the ruler can be pressed against the strings. From *a* to *b* this ruler should be a little longer than the whole nut of the Harpsichord, so that it can cover all the strings near the bridge, and the two ends can receive four steel wires that have to regulate the movement. For this purpose the ruler must have two holes at each end, as shown next to the two hooks *e* and *s*. When you have made the ruler, do as follows to put it into operation. In Figure XIX imagine that *a b* is the name board or end of the harpsichord from the front, and that *c d* is the nut with its brass pins. Let *f g* be the ruler, underneath which are the woollen roll and the two hooks. Let *e r s t* be the four holes in which are threaded four iron wires of the thickness of about one minute of a palm. The two wires, *s t*, are fixed on the board at *x*, and the other two, *e* and *r*, at *w*. Between the extremity *f* of the ruler and the board *a* two small brass springs are inserted on the two wires *e* and *r*, to keep the ruler lifted at *f*, and similarly between the ruler at *g* and the board at *b* two more similar springs are inserted on the two wires *t* and *s*, to keep the ruler lifted at *g*.

These four springs are only four thin brass wires, wound tightly round a little stick or piece of iron $1\frac{1}{2}$ minutes of a palm in thickness. In winding the brass wire be careful that the individual turns do not touch while on the little stick; hold the wire obliquely with a small interval between each wind.

After the brass wire has been wound tightly on the little stick in this way, it should be smoothed over with a small piece of wood, so that it can better assume the round shape of the little stick; this latter can then be pulled away, leaving the brass wire in its round shape, like a serpent. In this shape it can be compressed, and when the pressure is relaxed it automatically returns to its original shape as it was when it was wound round the little stick, and thus we have the effect of a very simple spring.

Apart from being most inexpensive these little springs have the advantage of being very long-lasting, because they do not easily lose their elasticity, and that is why they are widely used in Organs and in all mechanism that only needs weak springs.

THE CEMBALO ANGELICO

Now ensure that all four springs of the *sordine* will be of equal length and strength. Take a small stick of the same length as all four springs together, and wind round it the whole of the brass wire, of such a length that it can later be divided in four equal parts as required: see Figure XX. This brass spring must now be cut with scissors at points *a*, *b*, and *c*, so as to make four equal springs, which, when inserted on the four wires *e r t s*, Figure XIX, between ruler *f g* and the board *a b*, will keep the ruler lifted. But when the ruler is pressed near the nut *c d*, these springs will give way and compress; on releasing the ruler the springs will rebound. In this way the little wooden roll, glued under the ruler *f g*, will move either towards or away from the strings every time the ruler *f g* is moved down or up. To lower the ruler at its end *g*, you need only tie a gut cord on to its hook; this cord will then pass through a hole in the board or side of the Harpsichord, and will be attached at point *q* to the wooden bar *y q* of the pedal. By pressing with the ball of the foot on the stick at point *q*, the extremity *g* of the ruler will come near the strings, and by lifting the foot off the pedal at *q*, the elasticity of the brass wire springs will push back the extremity *g* of the ruler, and consequently, by means of the gut cord, the end of the pedal *q* will be lifted up again. By means of the same mechanism the opposite end *f* of the ruler can be moved. It is necessary for this movement to be executed by the player's right foot, because his left foot must be used to move the registers of the jacks. Therefore the iron piece *i h l m* must be placed underneath the Harpsichord case, and held in position by the two rings *h* and *l*, which are fixed into the case itself. The two ends of this iron bar must be upturned at points *i* and *m* to form a sort of lever.

At the end *i* of this iron bar there is a hole where the gut cord is attached, being also tied to the hook on the ruler at *f*. At the other end *m* of the same iron bar there is another hole, where the gut cord *m p* is fixed, and this is attached to the left hand wooden bar of the pedal at *p*.

It can be seen from this construction that by putting the foot on the piece of wood *z p* and pressing down at *p*, the end *m* of the iron bar will be lowered, as also will the other end *i* of the same bar; the extremity *f* of the ruler will thus come close to the strings. On the other hand, one can release the tip *p* by removing one's foot; the two springs inserted on the wires *e r* will then, because of their elasticity, lift up the end *f* of the ruler and with it the lever *i* of the iron bar; consequently the other lever *m* and the tip of the pedal *p* will also be raised.

From this simple and easy mechanism it can be understood that, by pressing with the tip of the right foot on the pedal bar at point *q*, the extremity of the ruler at *g* will be lowered, and the whole of the little woollen roll, by coming near to the high strings of the Harpsichord, will dampen their vibration, but will leave free the vibration of the low strings. And by pressing with the same foot on the other pedal bar at point *p*, the end *f* of the ruler will be lowered, and the little woollen roll will come down on the low strings of the Harpsichord, thus eliminating their vibration and leaving free that of the high strings. But by putting one's foot on both pedals at the same time, by means of the wooden cross bar 1 2, the whole ruler *f g* will be lowered and the woollen roll will eliminate by one and the same action the vibration of all the strings of the Harpsichord. It is therefore apparent that the player can operate the *sordine* either on the low notes only, or on the high ones, or on both together. Please note that, by pressing too hard with the tip of the toe on the pedal, the little woollen roll would press too hard on the strings, and would put them out of tune. To avoid this it is advisable to put two uprights made of thick iron wire in a vertical position on the board at points *n* and *o*, so that they act as checks to the ruler *f g* when it is pulled down. These checks will have to be made of such a height that they allow the exact lowering of the ruler necessary to dampen the vibration of the strings without putting them out of tune, and without eliminating the tone. It must furthermore be noted that the little wooden cross bar 1 2 on the pedal must not be securely fixed, but simply placed on top of the two pedals and held with string, so that each wooden pedal can be expressed independently to vary the *sordine*, either on the low notes or on the high notes, at the option of the player.

138

NOTES ON HOW TO MAKE THE JACKS FUNCTION SILENTLY

Since the tone of the *Cembalo Angelico* is very sweet, any sort of noise made by the jacks or the keys is insufferable. Therefore great care must be taken to observe the following points:

I. The keys of the Harpsichord must be well lined, both at the front and at the back, not only where they fall but also at the point where the jacks fall perpendiculary. The cloth that is used for lining must be soft and must possess a certain elasticity.

II. The holes in the middle of the key levers, through which pass the wires which act as pivot points, must not be too wide, or the keys when touched will clash with one another. To prevent the key levers making a noise at the point where they are pivoted, it is advisable to line these holes carefully with a little glove leather, which can easily be glued or gummed in them.

III. The small wooden blades which are inserted into the far ends of the key levers, and which move in the small grooves within the key frame to keep the keys apart, must be covered with thin and smooth glove leather, either glued or gummed on to them, so that despite the friction of wood against wood they shall not make a noise. To prevent the covering leather from getting stuck to the inner walls of the channels, it should be well smoothed or rubbed over with a little dry soap. If on the other hand one wishes to put a leather lining on the inner sides of the channels, rather than on the wooden blades, this will produce the same effect, provided there is no friction of wood against wood.

IV. Generally speaking the jacks are rather slack in the racks, from which it follows that the wood of the jacks knocking against the inner walls of the slots also creates an insufferable noise. There are two ways of preventing this. The first is to line the inside walls of the slots of the register with soft and smooth glove leather, and glue this lining on with a glue made from raw skins, *carniccio*. The second way is by facing the jacks with small strips of thin glove leather, smoothing these strips with an ivory stick, or with the blade of a knife, and rubbing them over with a piece of dry seasoned soap. When lining the slots or the jacks one must take care either to widen the slots or to thin the jacks a little, so that these can move up and down easily when the player moves the keys. To remedy the noise of the jacks all that is necessary is that wood should not touch wood in any way, and that the glove leather should be fixed as indicated, but always in such a way that the jacks can move freely in their slots. But of course it is well known that if there should be too much play serious trouble would arise, because the leather plectra, being unable to engage accurately with the strings, would not always touch them at the same points of their thinned sides. Consequently an unequal sound would result; when the jack plucked the string the tone would be too strong, and when it missed the tone would be too feeble: all this would have a very bad effect.

V. The wooden tongue which is in the jack must be lined on the bottom with a small piece of glove leather as shown in *t v*, Figure XV. Then, when the jack falls, the wood of the tongue when knocking against the wood of the aperture, at *s r*, Figure IV, will not make a noise. Before glueing the glove leather under the tip of the tongue at *p*, a layer of wood equal in thickness to the leather must be cut off the tongue, so that it will not go too far back at point *o*, and will not strike against the string behind it. This would otherwise happen when the leather plectrum, passing under the string as the jack came down, pushed back the upper part of the tongue.

VI. In its correct position the tongue should be parallel to the front side of the jack, without protruding either backwards or forwards. The leather plectrum must be hard, strong, and well beaten, and must be of the right size, without being too long, so that it will not produce a noise when it rebounds from the string. The quill which acts as a spring behind the tongue must have the right strength, because if the spring were too strong the leather plectrum would remain on top of the string when the jack fell, and if it were too weak the tongue, on the downward motion of the jack, would jolt back too violently, and in passing under the string would hit the string which is behind the jack with its back.

VII. It can sometimes happen, when the leather is not properly adjusted, and is not in its correct position, that the string gives forth a double, cracked, and jarring tone; and since this defect greatly prejudices the sweetness of the *angelico* tone, it must be avoided with the greatest care. Therefore we will briefly mention the causes which could produce this defect, and at the same time the ways in which they can be remedied.

THE FIRST CAUSE of such a defect is when the leather, having plucked the string, stops so close above it that the vibrating string can touch the leather from underneath. In such a case one must lift up or slightly thin the cloth which is stuck underneath the jack rail. When the defect is limited to a few jacks only it is necessary to lift these up a little by glueing on a small piece of wood, or by putting a little sealing wax under them, and at the same time cutting off a little of the wood from the upper part of the jack and the tongue, so that the leather will move a little higher above the string while it is vibrating.

THE SECOND CAUSE is when the scarlet damper is too long, and the string of the next note can touch the tip of the damper with its vibrations, and this creates a most unpleasant sound. The remedy for this is to cut the damper of each jack exactly and sufficiently to allow it to touch its own string without coming too near to the next one.

THE THIRD CAUSE is when the tongue of the jack, as the leather passes down under the string, strikes the next string which is behind the jack itself. This trouble can be remedied by placing the tongue in such a way that it is parallel to the front end of the jack. To bring its upper end further forward if necessary the tip of the tongue can even be thinned a little, if it is too thick. If these two remedies do not prove sufficient, it will be necessary to reinforce the quill spring behind the tongue, or to place a small piece of thin wire across the back of the jack, thus allowing the tongue to bend backwards only as far as is necessary to allow the leather to pass under the string, but without touching the next one behind it. It should be noted that in those Harpsichords that have their registers all in one piece, it sometimes happens that the tongue is prevented from moving far enough back to allow the jack to pass under the string, owing to the lower tip of the tongue hitting the front wall of the slot. To remedy this it is necessary to cut off a little of the wood on the tongue towards the lower tip; otherwise the slot can be widened slightly, so that the tongue shall have enough room to move.

THE FOURTH CAUSE is when the plectrum is too weak and too long; then, apart from producing very little tone, it causes the string to hiss and shake when the jack falls, because the leather has to slide over the string before going down under it. This defect can be cured or prevented by making the plectrum of strong, hard, and resilient leather, which should have been soaked and well beaten with a hammer, in the same way as is done by shoemakers; then the leather will be much harder and of greater consistency, and can consequently be kept shorter and nevertheless have a sufficiently strong tone.

It can also happen that the string gives forth the same hissing tone because it is not true and is also too thin. In this case it is quite easy to change the string and replace it with a good one of the correct thickness. It should be noted that the whole Harpsichord should be provided with thick strings rather than thin ones; therefore the Harpsichord with a short scaling, and consequently provided with thick strings, produces the *angelic* tone far better and renders it more perfect.

Briefly, one must take care that, as far as possible, neither the keyboard nor the jacks make the slightest noise, because the effect of the *Cembalo Angelico* depends to a great extent on this.

140

THE CEMBALO ANGELICO

SPECIAL VALUES OF THE CEMBALO ANGELICO

Amongst the many advantages of the *Cembalo Angelico* the following are of special value:

I. The tone of the *Cembalo Angelico*, as already explained, is the sweetest so far discovered in any musical instrument, and this unusual sweetness goes particularly well with delicate voices. Consequently this Harpsichord is excellent for accompanying such voices, when singing, as we say, *a mezza voce* in rooms.

II. One can play either soft or loud on the *Cembalo Angelico*, as on hammer Harpsichords (*Cembali a martelli*). When one touches the key lightly the sliding of the velvet like plectrum on the brass string gives a soft and extremely sweet tone, with very little attack; when one touches the same key with strength and violence the same leather produces a tone three times louder and stronger. Therefore sonatas and more especially *cantabili*, which require some expression, can be played on this Harpsichord with very good effect.

III. The hammer Harpsichords generally have four defects which cannot be remedied.

THE FIRST is the slowness of the hammers which cannot respond with the necessary speed in trills, and in playing *fuse*, that is to say double notes in short time; therefore Sonatas which require great agility of the hands cannot be played on these Harpsichords.

THE SECOND is the complete lack of sound when a key is only lightly pressed. This happens because if the key lever is not struck the hammer does not strike the string, therefore there is only an empty sound. And this imperfection is most noticeable when playing *Adagio delicato* on the hammer Harpsichord.

THE THIRD is the difficulty of damping the vibration of the strings, which at the best make a sibilant noise, which is confusing and offending to the ear.

THE FOURTH is the insufferable noise made by the keys, the levers, and the hammers, particularly in those Harpsichords which are built according to the invention of the immortal Bortolo Fiorentino, (i.e. Bartolomeo Cristofori) which are otherwise most clever. It is true that this imperfection has up to a point been remedied in the modern hammer Harpsichords built in England, in which the inventor instead of using three levers uses only two; but by remedying one defect he has increased the other fault, because when gently touching the keys in *Sonate cantabili* the hammers do not produce any sound. On the contrary in the *Cembalo Angelico* there are none of the above mentioned imperfections, because the leather plectra respond with the same speed as the crow quills in ordinary Harpsichords. By touching the keys gently the leather easily produces a soft and most delicate sound, and never leaves an empty tone as the hammers do. The damping of the sound is the same as in quill Harpsichords, that is to say it is easy, simple, and quick. And the noise of the keys and the jacks can be eliminated easily and simply, as has been explained in the preceding Article.

IV. In the same Harpsichord, without any change from the structure of the ordinary Harpsichord, one can have six changes of tone: the harmony of a strong tone with the crow quills together with the sound of the leather plectra, to accompany Symphonies in orchestras. That of a medium tone with quills together with leather sweetened with the *sordine*, to accompany Airs in Chamber music. That of a single register with quills, without the *sordine*. That of the *angelic* tone, to accompany delicate voices and for solo performances of chamber music.

Finally that of the *angelic* tone with the *sordine*, which imitates the tone of a most delicate Lute. All these changes, as already explained, can be obtained by means of a very simple mechanism and at a minimum of expense. Further, if the jacks are made with double tongues, as explained in Article III, apart from the above mentioned changes one can also have the *Cembalo Angelico* with two registers of jacks, and also the ordinary Harpsichord with two registers of crow quills.

V. By making the leathers, as explained, with the acute angle on the top, and by covering them with thin glove leather, one can obtain the harmony of a middle tone, in between the *angelic* and the quill tone, which will be just a little stronger than the quill, but will have the delicacy of a sweet flute in the higher notes, and in the middle ones will give a natural imitation of a hunting horn sounded in the distance. And, by varying the angle and the leather of the plectrum, many other different tones can be obtained at the option of the music lover.

VI. The leathers, apart from being exceedingly easy to make and to place in the jacks, are not liable to be attacked by worms, as happens with crow or vulture quills. They can also be made at very little expense, by using the little pieces of thin sole leather discarded by shoemakers, and by similarly making use of the small pieces of leather discarded by glove makers, or by using the leather from old gloves. From this it can be seen that without expenditure, and with only a few days' work, every music lover will be able to adapt his own Harpsichord to give these most agreeable changes of tone.

Here, my dear friend, is all the mechanism of my *Cembalo Angelico* explained in detail. I have also made a Pedal to enable one to play it like an Organ, by touching the key levers of the low notes with the foot, those of the middle notes with the left hand and those of the high notes with the right hand, thus having complete and perfect harmony. I will not add here the mechanism of the pedal, since it differs little from that of ordinary organ pedals, which is quite well known to you. The only difference is that, for greater beauty of appearance, I have covered my pedal mechanism with a little case, from which emerge as many pedals as there are trackers; by pressing these pedals with the foot the trackers are lowered, thus playing the respective bass notes without the mechanism being visible. The upper part of the trackers of the same pedal, which by means of thin gut cords are attached to the respective keys, are all set in a small frame which is fixed by two screws underneath the Harpsichord case, and by means of this simple mechanism the whole pedal may be removed and lifted off with the greatest ease.

And wishing that this little invention of mine may meet with your acceptance and that of our respected Academy, I embrace you with the most affectionate friendship.

Rome, 22nd of July, 1775.

APPENDIX THREE

SOME KEYBOARD INSTRUMENTS OFFERED FOR SALE BY LEOPOLDO FRANCIOLINI OF FLORENCE

(Undated catalogue, *c.* 1900, in the Library of the Brussels Conservatoire Museum, Vol. 170, No. 166)

The writer has not been able to assess the extent of Leopoldo Franciolini's work as a faker, nor that of his sons, as he has failed to discover a complete set of this man's catalogues. The catalogue referred to above contains, however, the keyboard instruments in Schedule A below. Bearing in mind the fact that Italian spinets and harpsichords are generally unsigned, the list presents highly suspicious features; and a considerable proportion of the names included are known only through Franciolini, and lack independent corroboration. This list is included in order to warn students of the care which must be taken when identifying Italian musical instruments (of any type) and accepting as authentic their inscriptions and makers' names.

The prices of these instruments vary, for the smaller examples, between 200 and 400 lire. The clavicytherium of 1587, and the cimbalone of Ferrini, 1699, cost 1000 lire. The cimbalone of Remoti, now in the Württembergisches Landesgewerbemuseum, Stuttgart, cost 3000 lire.

This catalogue was published from Piazza Santa Maria Novella 6.

Mr. John Morley possesses another catalogue issued by Franciolini, this time from Via de'Benci 14. These keyboard instruments are shown in Schedule B below. Their prices, marked in ink in the catalogue, do not correspond with those given above.

SCHEDULE A

(Some inscriptions in abbreviated form [?])

1. Clavicytherium, Petrus de Paulus, 1587.
2. Cimbalone, 3 manuals, Simone Remoti, 1602.
3. Cimbalone, 1 manual, Antonius Migliai Florentinus, 1617.
4. Cimbalo, 1 manual, Attus Gheerdinck me fecit anno 1603.
5. Cimbalone, Dominicus Pisaurensis, 1622.
6. Cimbalone, Io Bartolomeo Andressi F.A. 1769 Napoli.
7. Cimbalo, Nicolaus De Quoco fecit 1680.
8. Cimbalo, Jacobus Rodulphus di Zentis fecit anno domini 1650.
9. Cimbalo, Nicolaus Bertius Florentinus 1682.
10. Spinetta, Ioannes di Perticis 1672.
11. Cimbalone, Ioannes di Perticis 1672.
12. Spinetta, Alessandro Trasuntini 1604 [restored by Milesi 1820].
13. Spinetta, Antonius Bononiensis, 1600.
14. Cimbalo, Ioannes Gilius fecit Romae 1610.
15. Clavicordio, Gaspare Assalone fecit in Romae 1732.
16. Spinetta, Ioannes Baptista Giusti Lucensis faciebat 1679.

17. Cimbalo, Nicolaus de Quoco, 1640.
18. Clavicordio, unsigned.
19. Cimbalo, Vincetius [*sic*] Sodi Florentinus fecit anno Domini 1778.
20. Spinetta, Antonius Bentes Brexia anno Domini 1580.
21. Cimbalo, Elpidius Gregori e Selfidio Fecit 1691. [*see* No. 44.]
22. Spinetta, Agostinus Federicius fecis [*sic*] in Pisis Anno 1767.
23. Spinetta, Rinardo Beretoni fecit anno 1738.
24. Spinetta, A. Santinus 1571.
25. Spinetta, Agostinus Federigus fecit in Pisis 1786.
26. Spinetta, Marcus Gianninus faciebat Florentiae anno 1570.
27. Cimbalo, Giacumas Gherardus 1663 Bononiae.
28. Spinetta, Viti de Trasuntinus fecit anno Domini 1601.
29. Spinetta, Ioannes Landi fecii Sena 1670.
30. Spinetta, Stefanus Bolcionius Pratensis 1629.
31. Cimbalo, Hieronimus de Zentis Viterbiensis 1633.
32. Spinetta, Petrus Scappa Mediolani, 1670.
33. Spinetta, Dominicus Venetus 1560.
34. Cimbalo, Horatius Albana, 1645.
35. Spinetta, Joseph Mondini, 1660.
36. Spinetta, Petrus Germanni 1750.
37. Cimbalo, Niccolo Campi 1632 Florenza.
38. Spinetta, Petrus Vimercati fecit Brixiai anno Domini MCXC [*sic*].
39. Cimbalo, Bartolomeo Stephanini 1646.
40. Cimbalo, Vincentius Pratensis 1613.
41. Cimbalo, Joannes Baptista Giusti Lucensis 1677.
42. Spinetta, Horatius Albana 1589.
43. Spinetta, Antonius Bononiensis 1592.
44. Cimbalo, Opus Elpidii Gregorii et Sancta Elpidis Caefani Quarta Katena Areminis 1779.
45. Cimbalone, Giovanni Ferrini Florentinus 1699.
46. Cimbalo, Joseph Tunonus fecit Bononia in Platea Paraglionis anno domini 1637.
47. Spinetta.

Schedule B

1. Cimbalo, *Viti de Trasunitinis 1591*, Lire 400.
2. Cimbalone, *Simono Remoti, fecit anno 1602*, Lire 400.
3. Clavicetro [upright harpsichord], Lire 500.
4. Cimbalone, *Dominicus Pisauiensis fecit 1622*, Lire 400.
5. Cimbalo, *Ionnes Gilius fecit Romae Anno 1610*, Lire 400.
6. Spinetta, *Ioes Karest De Colonia Fecit 1550*, Lire 500.
7. Spinetta, *A. Bartoli* 1777, Lire 300.
8. Cimbalo, *Christophorus Rigunini fecit 1602*, Lire 300.
9. Spinetta, *Antonius Bati fecit in Arezzo, 1691*, Lire 300.
10. Cimbalone, *Ionnes de Perticis fecit Anno Domini 1672 Florentinus*, Lire 400.
11. Mezzo Cimbalo, Louis XV, Lire 300.
12. Cimbalone, *Bartolomeo Cristofori fece in Firenze, 1689*, Lire 600.
13. Cimbalone, *Ionnes Baptista Giusti Lucensis Faciebat anno 1673*, Lire 400
14. Spinetta, *Ionnes Patavini decti Hongari 1540*, Lire 200. [*see* page 36.]
15. Spinettina a Ottavino, *Girolamo Zenti 1676*, Lire 200.

LEOPOLDO FRANCIOLINI OF FLORENCE

16. Spinettina a Ottavino, *Pasquino Querci fiorentino fece 1615*, Lire 300.
17. Spinettina a Ottavino, *Adriano Parronchi restaurò nel 1841 in Prato*, Lire 200.
18. Clavicordo, painted and gilded, ebony inlaid with ivory, and with the arms of the Medicis, and two roses, Lire 600.
19. Spinettina, *Ioseph Bonos et Cortona*, Lire 200.
20. Cimbalone, *Ioannes Antonius Baffo Venetus fecit 1581*, Lire 400.
21. Cimbalo, *Ioseph Mae De Coccinis Bononiensis Opus 1706*, *D.O.D.*, Lire 300.

APPENDIX FOUR

ORIGINAL REGULATIONS FOR INSTRUMENT MAKERS
ENTERING THE GUILD OF SAINT LUKE IN ANTWERP, 1557

The Ledgers for 1557 give the facts as follows:
(Ledgers, vol. 1, 206.)

'Item, this same year the makers of harpsichords petitioned the Gentlemen of the City that they wished to be admitted into our Guild, and that those after them should have to make a test piece, viz. a harpsichord (*clavesimbaele*) well quilled and well strung, and they have provided one of the chambers for the test piece; and, the Gentlemen having agreed to their request, they have been admitted into our Guild and have paid the requisite dues.'

The full text of the ordinance is as follows:

'We, Jan van Immerseele, sheriff of the City of Antwerp and margrave of the land of Ryen, and we, burgomasters, aldermen and councillors of the aforementioned City of Antwerp, make it known and certify as the truth, that Messrs. Joost Carest, Marten Blommesteyn, Jacop Theeuwes, Aelbrecht van Neers, Hans d'orgelmakere, Christoffel Blommesteyn, Ghoosen Carest, Jacop Aelbrechts, Marten van der Biest and Lodewyck Theeuwes, all harpsichord makers, dwelling within the City, having unanimously acquainted us by supplication that they had recently met and communicated with the deans, sworn councillors and common fathers of St. Luke's Guild in this City, having discussed and agreed with same, that they, the supplicants were all willing and prepared to enter the aforementioned Guild, if they were to be granted and permitted the following points and articles which they had jointly drawn up and which are set out below, so that among them and those who are to come after them in the art of making harpsichords and other similar musical instruments there should be order and policy, as exist among the other trades and guilds of this City; whereupon the abovementioned deans, sworn councillors and common fathers of the aforementioned Guild, realizing that the points and articles in question had a bearing upon the ordinances and permits of us aforementioned, dare not co-opt the aforementioned petitioners freely into their guild without previous consent and ordinances on our part; as a result of which the aforementioned supplicants and along with them the abovementioned Guild of St. Luke, unanimously and in all humility and reverence, prayed us and desired that we, taking everything into consideration, should, to the advancement and increase of the above Guild, consent to the abovementioned course, and in doing so agree to the wishes of the supplicants and those to come after them, and grant them the following points and articles, and embody these in the proper form.

'Having considered the above petition and the points it puts forward, and being inclined to grant the supplicants' desire it being deemed reasonable, we have granted them herewith the following:

(1) In the first place, that the abovementioned supplicants shall be bound to appear forthwith before the abovementioned Guild of St. Luke, and each one of them to swear a suitable oath and pay the requisite fees;

146

(2) Furthermore, that the same supplicants, as free masters and guild brothers of the above-mentioned Guild, within this City and its Liberties, shall remain free and unhindered to carry out their abovementioned trade of making and selling harpsichords (*clavisimbalen*) and similar musical instruments, as was their wont before, without having to submit any test piece whatsoever.

(3) Furthermore, that these same supplicants and also those who after them shall be freely received in the abovementioned Guild as makers of harpsichords (*clavicymbelmakers*) shall enjoy and use all such privileges and liberties as the aforementioned Guild now enjoys and later may obtain, in all ways and manners as the other free masters and brothers of the Guild are wont to and shall enjoy, in conformity with the ordinances and privileges now existing and at any later date to be promulgated.

(4) It is to be understood that in future, after the abovementioned supplicants have been freely admitted into the Guild of St. Luke, only such may be admitted as have made by hand the following test piece, and that at the house of an assessor as described below, who will have to provide him with all the necessary materials and tools, *viz.* a square or long (*gehoecte*) *clavisimbale* [*sic*], five feet long or thereabouts, or longer should he so desire, well and truly fashioned, in the correct shape and proportions, and in accordance with its nature being sound in tone and properly quilled and strung.

(5) Furthermore, the above prescribed test piece having been completed, it will have to be taken to the chamber of the above Guild, where the prescribed assessors, in the presence of the deans and sworn councillors of the above Guild and in that of two or three free *clavicymbelmakers*, shall inspect and test same, and declare upon oath whether or not the test piece has been made in accordance with the prescribed articles, and declare truthfully and without deceit whether he who has made it should be accepted a free harpsichord maker in the abovementioned Guild.

(6) Furthermore, in case the abovementioned test piece be passed, the assessor, in whose house it has been made and who has provided the materials and tools required for its manufacture shall have and retain the *cembalo* for his materials and trouble, without having to pay aught to the person who made it for his labour.

(7) And in case the test piece be rejected, the person who made it shall have to remove it and pay for and make good the materials and tools the assessor has provided.

(8) Furthermore, that every year the deans and sworn councillors of the abovementioned Guild of St. Luke shall, from among the harpsichord makers (*klavierbouwers*), choose and appoint two suitable and able assessors, who shall be bound to visit tests in progress and report upon same in a way conforming to the manner above laid down and upon the oath which they shall have sworn to that end.

(9) Furthermore, that in future no one within this City and its Liberties shall be entitled to carry on the trade of making harpsichords (*clavicymbels*) or similar musical instruments and afterwards sell them, unless he be first freely admitted into the abovementioned Guild of St. Luke, having paid the requisite dues and performed the prescribed test, upon pain of fine and forfeit, and any who will be found to have contravened this ordinance for each occasion to be fined the sum of six Guilders Carolus, and that in three parts, one third to the sheriff, one third to the City, and one third to the abovementioned Guild.

(10) Furthermore, that each free harpsichord maker (*clavicymbelmaker*) of this City shall be bound and liable to provide each musical instrument by him manufactured with his own mark, distinctive sign or emblem, and such applied in the most obvious place, before ever he sells it or distributes it, upon pain of a fine of two Guilders Carolus, to be levied for each single instrument he should have sold contrary to this ordinance, the fine to be paid in three parts as above.

ORIGINAL REGULATIONS FOR INSTRUMENT MAKERS

'We reserve the right to ourselves and to those after us in our office at any time to add to, delete from, interpret, increase, diminish and/or change any point in this ordinance as may be deemed fit and suitable without fraud or ulterior motive. . . .

'Given on the 28th day of March, in the year of Our Lord 1575, Brabant style. (signed) Van Asseliers'.

APPENDIX FIVE

DOUBLE VIRGINALS

1. Martin van der Biest, 1580. Germanisches Museum, Nürnberg.
2. Hans Ruckers, 1581. Metropolitan Museum, New York.
3. Ludovic Grauwels, 1600. Metropolitan Museum, New York.
4. Hans Ruckers, undated. Yale Collection, New Haven.
5. Hans Ruckers, undated. Castello Sforzesco, Milan.
6. Hans Ruckers, 1610. Conservatoire, Brussels.
7. Hans Ruckers, 1620. Conservatorio, Lisbon.
8. Jan Ruckers, 1623. Harding Museum, Chicago.
9. Andries Ruckers, 1644. Heyer Museum, Leipzig.

HARPSICHORD AND VIRGINALS COMBINED

1. Hans Ruckers, 1594. 1 manual harpsichord. Berlin.
2. Jan Ruckers, undated. 1 manual harpsichord. Berlin.
3. Jan Ruckers, 1619. 2 manual harpsichord. Conservatoire, Brussels.
4. Jan Joseph Coenen, 1734. 2 manual harpsichord. Plantin Moretus Museum, Antwerp.

The following examples of the double virginal, and the combination of harpsichord with virginal, can no longer be traced, and may have been destroyed.

De Briqueville quotes the following sales in Paris:

1. Large spinet by Andries Ruckers with a smaller spinet which can be placed above the former in order to give two keyboards. L300. 25 July, 1771.

2. An excellent harpsichord enclosing a spinet, the masterpiece of Ruckers, richly ornamented and decorated with a painting by Watteau, which represents a concert of animals. 30 Dec., 1767.

3. An excellent harpsichord built by Ruckers in two sides; it forms an oblong rectangle with 4 [sic] keyboards, and is beautifully painted. L1000. 2 May, 1768.

4. Harpsichord by Andries Ruckers made in 1606 [sic] with a fine spinet by the same maker enclosed inside it. Pictures by Watteau and superb gilding. The stand is completely gilded. Price 100 Louis. 20 Dec., 1778.

The Duke of Chandos (chapter 5) possessed at Cannons:

5. "A four-square harpsichord, 2 rows of keys at one end, a spinet on the side; painted on the lid, Minerva and the nine Muses, by A. Tilens, 1625, made by J. Ruckers, Antwerp."

Kinsky (1910) p. 76, says:

6. "A fine two manual spinet by Jan Couchet (Antwerp 1640) a nephew of Hans Ruckers the elder, is in the Boers Collection at the Rijksmuseum, Amsterdam."

There is no trace or record of such an instrument, however, in the museum records.

APPENDIX SIX

LETTERS BETWEEN DUARTE AND HUYGHENS

First letter from G. F. Duarte to Constantijn Huyghens.
Original at Leiden University Library
'Sir, having received your honour's pleasing (communication) of Feb. 27th, I shall refer in answer to the problem of the large harpsichords (*clavesinglen*) with one full keyboard down to the octave of G sol re ut[GG]. May it please you to know of the nephew of the late Joannis Ruckarts, one named Couchet, who has worked for the aforementioned uncle for sixteen years and whom I have found of a very studious disposition, to which my instruction contributed not a little, *viz.* in the matter of investigations which his aforementioned uncle never troubled about, for the rapid action of the touch must be studied if the larger instruments are to respond and obey readily, and the subtleties and delicate points are to be discovered in matters of length of quills, keyboard and jacks, and the thickness and length of the strings, all these being matters which it would take too long to relate. The extreme extent of the length of the large harpsichords is 8 ft. or thereabouts; the tone *Corista* with 3 registers, i.e. 2 strings in unison and one in the octave. These can be played all three together, or each string separately, together with the octave or without the octave, like the ordinary harpsichords which your honour mentions, but which have a better harmony by reason of one string which, not being plucked, is made to vibrate on its own account, thus making a sweet, soft harmony to the continuous sound of its counterpart, which does not occur if the three strings are all being played at the same time. Of the 2 strings in unison the one is somewhat sharper than the other, which also causes a pleasing sweetness, the one having being made a large straw's width longer than the other. The virtue of the instruments is also that the strings are made louder, thinner and longer rather than thick, so that it is possible to play these 3 strings in five or six different ways, and they must be well nigh as soft in touch as those in a small harpsichord, in which resides the greatest art, though few of the masters know it, that is to say in so far as it concerns the large instruments. Of these so far only four have been made, the last ones being the best and sold for about 300 and afterwards for 20 to 30 guilders less, so that one would have to make them specially. Now, as concerns the small harpsichords (*steertstukxkens*) with unison or with an octave, that is to say each made according to predilection, they are usually one tone higher, as I invented them at one time, to be used in small chambers for playing courantes, allemandes and sarabands. If your honour wishes to command me in this as in other matters I shall ever show myself to be, dear Sir,
In Antwerp, March 5th, 1648

Your humble servant,
G. F. Duarte.'

Second letter
'Sir, I have received your extremely pleasant (communication) of the 27th of the previous month of April, and have understood your honour's intention to be that you desire a harpsichord (*steert stuck*) with unison and a full keyboard, like that of Mrs. Swan, but in length like the one Mr.

150

Couchet has sent to one called Pater, about which I have spoken to the aforementioned Couchet by often calling upon him at his house as he also calls on me. Now, as regards making the instrument two tones lower than that of Mrs. Swan, that can hardly be, and is in no way the fashion nor suitable for any concert of voices. On the other hand I can provide one of the natural tone of this country which is called *Chorista*, which happens to be one tone lower than that of Mrs. Swan's, used for ordinary voices, and the one of the same lady is good for voices singing high, and for the playing of allemandes and courantes. Of that same tone, I have at my disposal some four or five, apart from my harpsichord (*clavesingel*), the pitch of which is a *Chorista* of the correct tone. That is how your honour's will have to be, and it must also be somewhat longer than Pater's. I having recently come to the conclusion that each frontmost string of the pair, the one which sounds sharp, must be plucked by the second jack, and the other string, which inclines somewhat more, by the front jack, as this gives a different harmony; we have recently tried it out with a harpsichord. Please lift the jackrail of Pater's harpsichord, and consider this point by watching the vigorous plucking of one note, whereupon your honour will immediately understand my meaning, such matters and others being too subtle for long writing, and never having been investigated by other masters, as they are felt only by reason of very rapid performance, to which the common instruments respond but badly. Your honour will ever freely command me according to your wishes and without standing upon ceremony, and will ever find me ready to be
In Antwerp, May 3rd, 1648.

G. F. Duarte.'

Third letter

'Sir, I have received your very pleasing (communication) of the 13th inst. in which you thank me for the fine things which your honour's son is supposed to have heard here at our place, which even so were not in conformity with your honour's great merits and the obligation I have in serving your honour. The harpsichord will be ready this week, with pitch of the lowest ordinary tone *Chorista* which is made, a full keyboard down to the octave of ef fa ut [FF] and up the cadence of the la sol re [d³]. I doubt not that your honour will be pleased with the lid, white inside, as is also the ground under the strings and the front above the keyboard, which will be all painted according to your honour's wishes, the edge of the yellow piece gilt right round, as also the jackrail, which will be finished this week. I hope it will be at your honour's before your departure for Cleves where your honour is to go.
In Antwerp, July 19th, 1648.

G. F. Duarte.'

Fourth letter

'Sir, This is solely to inform your honour that the harpsichord has now been made, and is acquiring a sweet and lovely harmony, much praised by all the connoisseurs. Mr. Couchet has put his utmost ability into it, especially the keyboard, which is very light for two large strings. He will send it to your honour tomorrow or the day after. It cannot be given for less than 30 Pounds Flemish. It is eight feet long. I had told him 28 Pounds Flemish, so he will have to be satisfied. Your acknowledgement of receipt and your feelings concerning the instrument will be welcome to
Antwerp, July 30th 1648.

G. F. Duarte.'

AN INVENTORY OF HARPSICHORDS CONFISCATED FROM THE NOBILITY, ETC.,

during the French Revolution, and catalogued under the direction of a *Commission temporaire des arts*. See Bruni (1890), and page 119.

Description	*Owner, or place where found*
1. A harpsichord, painted green, with gilt panels. No key.	Caillebeau
2. A very bad triangular spinet.	Rue de Grenelle 370.
3. A gilt harpsichord with arabesques on it. By *Andreas Ruckers me fecit Antverpen.*	Pignatelli Rue des Piques 29.
4. A harpsichord, painted white, with gilt and carved legs, rebuilt by Pascal Taskin in 1778.	Quinski Rue Dominique 1522.
5. A harpsichord, painted grey, gilt panels, rebuilt by Pascal Taskin in Paris, 1778.	,, ,,
6. A harpsichord in plain wood.	Cossé-Brissac Rue de Grenelle 72.
7. An unsigned harpsichord, gilded and painted with arabesques.	Montmorency
8. A harpsichord, painted black, with gilt panels, by *Andreas Ruckers me fecit Antverpiae 1638.*	Croix d'Havre.
9. A harpsichord, painted black, with gilt panels, by *Andreas Ruckers me fecit Antverpiae, 1616.*	Lauragnais Rue de Lille.
10. An unsigned harpsichord, painted red, with gilt stand.	Orsay Rue de Varenne.
11. A green harpsichord, gilt panels, no Key.	Caumont—La Force Rue de Grenelle Saint Germain 367
12. A harpsichord, painted black, gilt flowers, by *Joannes Ruckers me fecit Antverpiae.*	Gilbert de Voisins Rue d'Enfer.
13. A harpsichord by *Hans Ruckers, 1606,* painted black, with gilt flowers, and carved stand.	Noailles-Mouchy Rue de l'Université 193.
14. A spinet dated 1726.	,, ,,
15. An unsigned harpsichord, painted green, gilt panels.	Thiroux-Mondésir.
16. A harpsichord, painted green, gilt panels, enlarged by *Pascal Taskin, Paris, 1776.*	La Borde.
17. A harpsichord, painted green, gilt panels, the legs broken, repaired by *Nadreau,* made by *Pascal Taskin, 1774.*	,, ,,
18. A harpsichord in walnut, made in 1769 at Strasburg by *Jean Henri Silbermann.*	Maubec.

INVENTORY OF HARPSICHORDS CONFISCATED FROM THE NOBILITY

Description	Owner, or place where found
19. A superb harpsichord in mahogany, gilt panels, carved and gilt stand, no music desk or maker's name.	Clermont d'Amboise.
20. A small harpsichord to place underneath (*pour mettre dessous*).	„ „
21. A grey harpsichord, unsigned.	De Celles.
22. A grey harpsichord, by *Antoin Valter, 1725*.	Femme Roux.
23. A harpsichord, painted green, gilt panels, dated 1645.	Surgères Rue de la Ville-Lévêque 1298.
24. A harpsichord, painted black, gilt panels, by *Pascal Taskin, élève de Blanchet, en 1770. No. 15*.	Menus-Plaisirs.
25. A harpsichord, painted with flowers, enlarged by *Pascal Taskin, 1774*.	„ „
26. A harpsichord, painted yellow and with figures on it, by *Joannes Ruckers me fecit Antverpiae No.1*.	„ „
27. A harpsichord, painted black, gilt panels, by *Antoine Valter, 1724*.	„ „
28. A harpsichord, painted black, with gilt panels and flowers, unsigned, marked No. 29.	„ „
29. A spinet, painted black, gilt panels, unsigned.	„ „
30. A harpsichord, gilt and painted, by *Hans Ruckers me fecit Antverpiae*, enlarged by *Pascal Tasquin* [*sic*] Paris, 1771.	Bacquencourt Rue Bergère 1001.
31. A harpsichord, painted grey, gilt panels, by *Joseph Treyer*, known as *L'Empereur*, Paris 1770. Value 250 francs.	La Chapelle Faubourg Montmartre, 26.
32. An unsigned harpsichord, painted and gilt.	Bouthillier.
33. A harpsichord, painted black, gilt panels, by *Johannes Ruckers me fecit Antverpiae*.	Xavier.
34. A harpsichord, painted black, gilt panels, unsigned.	Xavier.
35. A harpsichord, painted black, gilt panels, by *Antonius Valter*.	Grimm.
36. An English harpsichord by *Thoaner, 1772*, value 2,000 francs.	Spanish Ambassador Rue de l'Université
37. An English harpsichord in mahogany, quite new, by *Johannes Broadvood* [*sic*], *Londini fecit 1789*, value 2,000 francs.	Ecuries de Chartres.
38. A harpsichord, painted red, stand carved and gilt, unsigned, coming from Noailles, value 400 francs.	Maison de Séquestre de Saint-Priest.
39. A harpsichord, painted yellow with flowers, no stand, coming from Saint-James, by *François Blanchet*, 1749, value 90 francs.	Faubourg du Roule.
40. A harpsichord, painted green, with gilt panels, unsigned, value 250 francs.	The Emigrant Lostange Rue de la Madeleine.
41. A harpsichord, painted, rebuilt by *Baltazard Peronard*, 1777, value 500 francs.	Durney Rue de la Loi 152.
42. A harpsichord, painted black, gilt panels, unsigned.	Breteuil.
43. A very fine harpsichord by *Joannes Ruckers me fecit Antverpiae 1637*.	Disney Fitch, the English Emigrant, rue d'Anjou, Faubourg Saint-Honoré, 973.
44. A harpsichord, painted black, gilt panels, unsigned, value 300 francs.	Lucerne (emigrated), Rue de Thorigny, Maison de Juigné au Marais.

INVENTORY OF HARPSICHORDS CONFISCATED FROM THE NOBILITY

Description	Owner, or place where found
45. A harpsichord, painted green, gilt panels, unsigned, marked No. 1630 [the date ?].	Femme Mirecourt (emigrated) Rue Merry, 77.
46. A harpsichord, painted black, gilt panels, by *Henri Hemsch*, Paris, 1763, value 300 francs.	Maison Vente (*ex* Farmer General) Rue Gramont 12.
47. A harpsichord, painted grey, gilt panels, unsigned, value 150 francs.	Vilgnier (condemned) Rue des Capucines.
48. A harpsichord, yellow, gilt panels, unsigned, marked 1621 (the date ?) value 400 francs.	Femme Marbeuf (con-demned) at Chaillot.
49. An unsigned harpsichord, painted grey, gilt decoration (*filets dorés*), value 200 francs.	Maison Thuezi [*sic*] emigrated, Rue Guenegaud.
50. A full size spinet (*à grand ravalement*), painted black, with gilt decoration (*filets*), value 250 francs.	Thelis, emigrated. Rue du Cherche-Midi.
51. A harpsichord in bad order, painted black, unsigned, owned by the condemned Vallot.	,, ,,
52. A harpsichord, painted grey, and shaped like a chest (*cassette*), made by *Baillon*, frontboard missing, value 60 francs.	Femme Jaucourt (emigrated) Rue de Babylone.
53. A harpsichord in walnut, unsigned, value 300 francs.	D'Avrincourt [*sic*] Rue Dominique, Faubourg Germain, 1045.
54. A harpsichord by *Ruckers*, painted *Merd'oie*, gilt decoration (*filets*), value 600 francs.	Ménage de Pressigny (condemned) Rue des Jeuneurs 25.
55. An unsigned harpsichord, painted black.	Jeringhaus [*sic*] (emigrated) Rue Dominique 205.
56. A harpsichord by *Henri Hemsch*, 1763.	Lowendal Rue du Faubourg-Montmartre, 1039.
57. A harpsichord, painted red, by *Henri Hemsch*, value 800 francs.	Maison de Croi [*sic*] Rue du Regard.
58. A harpsichord, painted grey, gilt panels, by *Joannes Germain*, value 400 francs.	Lusignan (emigrated) Rue Dominique-d'Enfer.
59. A harpsichord, painted red, by *Henry Hemsch*, value 400 francs.	Oppède, Rue du Vieux-Colombier, 746.
60. A spinet painted black, unsigned, value 60 francs.	,, ,,
61. A harpsichord, painted grey, gilt panels, by *Baltazard Peronard* 1760, belonging to the emigrant La Mark, value 600 francs.	Maison Ci-Devant Bourbon, Rue du Faubourg Honoré.
62. A bad harpsichord by *Ruckers*, painted black, gilt panels, all the legs broken, belonging to the emigrant Durfort, value 200 francs.	Maison de Ci-Devant Conception, Rue Honoré.

APPENDIX EIGHT

THE MUSICAL INSTRUMENTS OF KING HENRY VIII

From an Inventory of the Guarderobes, etc., 1547
(Brit. Mus., Harl. 1419)

Stuffe and Implements at GRENEWICHE.
In the Kynges priuey Chambre.
f. 54. One paier of Regalles with the case.

In the Kynges Withdrawing Chambre.
f. 56. One faire Instrument being Regalles and Virgynalles.

In the Kynges Gallery.
f. 57b. A paier of Virgynalles.

In the Closet over the Waterstewe.
f. 59. A Horne of Iverey.

AT WESTMINSTER.

In the Study nexte tholde Bellechambre.

f. 155b. An Antique horne garnisshed with Siluer guilte with a Bawdrike likewise garnisshed.
f. 156b. ii hornes copper guilte enameled grene and redde.

Instruments at Westminster in the charge of Philipp Van Wilder

DOUBLE REGALLES

f. 200. FIRSTE a paire of double Regalles with twoo Stoppes of pipes couered in purple vellat all over enbrawdered with Venice gold and damaske pirles hauing the Kinges Armes and badges likewise enbrawdered standinge uppon a foote couered with fustian of Naples and garnisshed with redd ribon the same foote beinge the Case for the same Regalles.

Item. A paire of double Regalles with twoo Stoppes of pipes couered with purple vellat all over enbrawdered with Venice golde and damaske pirles hauing the Kinges Armes and badges likewise enbrawdered standinge upon the Case of the same couered with fustian of Naples.

Item. A paire of double Regalles of latten with iii Stoppes of pipes couered with purple vellat enbrawdered all over with damaske pirles and Venice golde and the Cover thereof the inner parte covered with crimeson vellat likewise enbrawdered with damaske pirles hauing a stele Glasse in the same and the Kinges Armes and Quene Janes Armes likewise enbrawdered with a cover the pipes couered with crimeson vellat likewise enbrawdered hauing a rose crowned upon the same standinge upon a foote of wainscott painted in Rabeske woorke wherein liethe the Bellowes,

Item. A paire of double Regalles with viii halfe Stoppes and one hole stoppe of pipes, of woodde

155

gilte siluered and painted with Rabeske woorke and histories havinge the Kinges Armes with a gartire supported by his graces beastes painted and gilt uppon the trimmer of the same standinge uppon a foote of woode beinge painted wherein liethe the Bellowes.

Item. A paire of double Regalles with iii stoppes of pipes, of woode vernisshed yellowe and painted with anticke woorke hauinge the Kinges Armes and Quene Janes armes with twoo playinge uppon a lute and a harpe and twoo singinge painted uppon the same standinge uppon a foote of wainscott painted yellowe with anticke woorkes wherein liethe the Bellowes: the same hath but two stoppes of pipes and thother Stoppe is but a Cimball.

SINGLE REGALLES

Item. One paire of single Regalles with iii stoppes of pipes, of woode vernisshed yellowe standinge uppon a frame of woode withe iiii pillors: it hathe but one Stoppe pipe of tinne one Regall of Tinne and a Cimball.

f. 201.—Item. One paire of single Regalles with twoo Stoppes of pipes, of woode vernisshed yellowe and painted with blacke Rabeske woorke standinge uppon a foote of wainscott the Bellowes liynge in the same: it hathe but one Stoppe of pipes of woode with a Cimball of Tinne and the Regall of papire.

Item. Twoo paire of single Regalles euerie of them with vi halfe stoppes of brase pipes, of woode gilte and painted and hauinge the Kinges Armes within a gartier and badges painted uppon the Bellowes standinge uppon a foote of woodde like a Cheste painted blacke.

Item. V small single Regalles twoo of them beinge in Cases of Timbre couered with leather and thother iii in cases of Timbre not couered.

Item. One paire of single Regalles with twoo Stoppes of pipes of timbre and one Stoppe of pipes of Tinne, of woode painted with blacke Rabeske woorke and vernisshed standinge uppon a foote of wainscott wherein liethe the Bellowes: the same hathe but one Stoppe of pipes of woode the Regall of papire and hathe a Cimball.

Item. One paire of single Regalles with iiii Stoppes of pipes, of woode vernisshed yellowe and painted with blacke anticke woorke standinge uppon a foote of wainscott the Bellowes lieing in the same: it hathe but one Stoppe of pipes of woode a Cimball of Tinne and a Regall.

Item. One paire of single Regalles with twoo stoppes of pipes couered with grene vellat and garnisshed on the foreparte with a narrow fringe Venice golde standinge uppon a foote of wainscott painted grene with the Bellowes liinge in the same havinge a Cimball.

Item. One paire of single Regalles with vii halfe Stoppes of pipes, of woode vernisshed yellowe and painted with blacke Rabeske woorke with a foote of wainscott unpainted wherein liethe the Bellowes: the saide vii stoppes are but vii Registers diuided in three Stoppes with a Cimball.

VIRGYNALLES

Item. An Instrumente with a single Virginall and single Regall withe a Stoppe of timbre pipes, of woode vernisshed grene and redde.

Item. An Instrumente with a double Virgynall and a double Regall with iii Stoppes of pipes, of woode painted with grene Rabeske woorke with a foote of wainscott and the Bellowes lyinge in the same

Item. An Instrumente that goethe with a whele without playinge uppon, of woode vernisshed yellowe and painted blewe with vi round plates of siluer pounced with anticke garnisshed with an edge of copper and guilte.

Item. Twoo paire of double Virgynalles thone covered with blacke Leather and the lidde lined with grene bridges Satten and thother covered with redde leather.

Item. A paire of double Virgynalles couered with blacke Leather partelie siluered the lidde lined with grene bridges satten.

Item. A paire of double Virgynalles of Cipres in a case of wainscot.

Item. A paire of single Virgynalles covered with redde leather and the lidde with grene bridges Satten.

Item. Twoo paire of single Virgynalles thone of them havinge keies of Ivorie and thother of Boxe with twoo Cases to them of redde leather partelie gilte and lined with blacke vellat.

Item. A paire of single Virgynalles couered with grene bridges Satten with iii Tilles in them.

f. 202.—Item. Twoo paire of single Virgynalles couered with blacke Leather.

Item. One paire of single Virgynalles couered with redde Leather.

Item. A paire of single Virgynalles with pipes underneth and in a case of timbre couered in blacke Leather.

Item. A paire of single Virgynalles couered with redde leather partelie guilte.

INSTRUMENTS OF SOUNDRIE KINDES

Item. A paire of Claricordes couered with gilte leather.

Item. A paire of Claricordes couered with leather siluered.

Item. xix Vialles greate and small with iii cases of woodde couered with blacke leather to the same.

Item. Foure Gitterons with iiii cases to them: they are caulled Spanishe Vialles.

Item. Twoo Gitteron pipes of Ivorie tipped with silver and gilte: they are caulled Cornettes.

Item. xiiii Gitteronne pipes of woodde in a bagge of Leather: they are caulled Cornettes.

Item. A Gitteron and a Lute beinge in a Case Cheste fashion of Timbre couered with leather.

Item. xxiii Lutes with xxiii Cases to them.

Item. v Cases with fflutes and in euerie of iiii of the saide Cases iiii flutes and in the vth three fflutes.

Item. One Case furnisshed with xv fflutes in it.

Item. One Case with tenne flutes in it: the same are caulled pilgrim Staves and the same case furnisshed conteinethe butt vi hole pipes.

Item. One case with vii fflutes in hitt.

Item. v fflutes of Ivorie tipped with golde enameled blacke with a Case of purple vellat garnisshed at both thendes with Silver and guilte: the same Case furnisshed conteinethe but iiii hole pipes.

Item. Foure fflutes of Ivorie tipped with golde in a Case covered with grene vellat.

Item. One case with vii Crumhornes in it.

Item. One case with vi recorders of Boxe in it.

Item. viii Recorders great and smale in a Case couered with blacke Leather and lined with clothe.

f. 203.—Item. Twoo base Recorders of waulnuttre, one of them tipped with Siluer: the same are butt redde woodde.

Item. Foure Recorders made of okin bowes.

Item. vi Recorders of Ivorie in a case of blacke vellat.

Item. One greate base Recorder of woode in a case of woode.

Item. Foure Recorders of waulnuttre in a case couered with blacke vellat.

Item. ix Recorders of woode in a case of woode.

Item. A Pipe for a Taberde in a Case of blacke leather.

Item. viii Shalmes in iii Cases couered with leather.

Item. A case with vii Shalmes in it: the same case furnisshed conteineth but v whole pipes caulled pilgrim Staves.

Item. A case with a Shalme of Boxe in it.

Item. One Shalme of woode.

Item. A Baggepipe with pipes of Ivorie, the bagge couered with purple vellat.

f. 204b.—FYRSTE one newe paire of double Virgynalles couered with blacke leather with smale roses printed and gilte upon it the lidde lined with grene satten and garnisshed upon with redde silke Ribonne lozenge wise.

Item. Another newe paire of double Virgynalles vernisshed yellowe and painted all ouer with redde rabeske woorke the lidde beinge lined with purple serrconet and havinge the Kinges armes painted and guilte in the middes of hit.

Item. A little paire of Virgynalles single couered with redde leather in a Case of woode couered with blacke lether.

Item. Twoo faire paire of newe longe Virginalles made harpe fasshion of Cipres with keies of Ivorie havinge the Kinges armes crowned and supported by his graces beastes within a gartier guilte standinge ouer the saide keies with twoo caeses to them couered with blacke leather the inner partes of the liddes to the saide caeses beinge of wallnuttre with sondrie antickes of white woode wroughte in the same.

f. 205.—Item. A Case couered with crimeson vellat hauinge locke and all other garnisshements to the same of Siluer gilte with viii recorders of Iuerie in the same Case the twoo bases garnisshed with Siluer and gilte.

Item. One case of blacke leather with viii recorders of boxe.

Item. A case of white woode with ix recorders of boxe in the same.

Item. A case couered with blacke lether with vii recorders of woode in it.

Item. A little case couered with blacke lether with iiii recorders of Iverie in it.

Item. One flute and vi phiphes of blacke Ibonie tipped withe Siluer thone of the phiphes lackinge a tippinge at one ende in a bagge of redde leather.

Item. iii fflutes of glasse and one of woode painted like glasse in a Case of blacke leather.

Item. iii fflutes of woode in a case of blacke leather.

Item. iiii fflutes in a redde leather bagge.

Item. A case with iiii Crumhornes in it.

Item. Another case with vii Crumhornes in it.

Item. v shorte Instruments caulled Dulceuses in v seuerall cases to them couered with blacke leather.

Item. viii Dulceuses couered with blacke leather, some of them havinge tippinges of Silver.

Item. iiii bagge pipes with pipes of Ivorie.

Item. A litle Venice lute with a case to the same.

Item. Sondrie bookes and skrolles of songes and ballattes.

Item. An olde chest couered with blacke fustian of Naples.

Item. A chest collored redde with vi Vialles havinge the Kinges Armes.

AT HAMPTON COURTE

In the Privey Chambre

f. 243b. One payre of portatives with the Kynges and Quene Janes Armes.

In the next bedchambre.

f. 245b. A paire of Virgynalles the case covered with blacke Lether.

In the long Galorie

f. 247. A paire of Regalles in a case coured with crimeson vellat.

Seven paires of Virginalles in cases of printed lether.

A paire of Virginalles facioned like a harp.

f. 247b. A case of printed lether with vii crokhornes of Ivorie.

THE MUSICAL INSTRUMENTS OF KING HENRY VIII

In another Chambre

f. 248. One paire of portatives covered with crimeson Satten and embrawdered with passumynt of golde and Silver standing upon a square table of wainscotte.

In the Quenes Galorie

f. 249b. Paire of Regalles in a case of lether.

AT WYNSORE

f. 315. One doble Regall with doble pipes painted and gilte with Antique woorke with a greate Rose painted and gilte uppon the foreparte of the foote thereof.

AT THE MORE

Soundrie parcelles

f. 340. One olde paire of Regalles broken in peces.

F. 340b. Two paires of olde Virginalles.

AT NEWHALL

f. 362. A paire of faire greate Organes in the Chappell with a curten afore them of lynnen clothe staynd redd and blewe paned.

A paire of Virginalles verye olde and broken.

One olde Lute.

AT NOTYNGHAM CASTELL

f. 367. An olde paire of Organes.

The Guarderobe of THE ROBES

HORNES

f. 408b. A Horne of Brasse garnisshed with nedle worke with a Bawdricke of Stole worke.

Item. A Horne of Saintte Cornelis couered with grene vellat.

Item. A Horne garnisshed with Silver with a grene Coursse sett with Bullions of Silver.

Item. A litle White Horne garnisshed with golde, the Bawdrick of blacke Corssey: the saide Bawdrick tied together with a buckle of golde and euerie ende the Corsse a Tape of golde with a paire of couples of silke and golde.

Item. A horne coured with grene satten garnisshed with silver the Bawdericke of grene silke and Venice golde.

Item. One blacke horne garnisshed with silver and guilte with a Bawdricke of redde Corssey.

Item. Three white hornes garnisshed with Silver their Bawdrickes of silke.

Item. One white horne slewed with silver and guilte.

Item. A great blacke base horne slewed with silver.

Item. A horne of brasse guilte.

Item. A great white horne graven with Antique wourk garnisshed with silver and guilte with a bawdrick of grene vellat with buckles and studdes of silver and guilte and a coller of Stole worke with turret buckle and pendaunt silver and guilte.

Item. iii blacke hornes garnisshed with silver and guilte two havinge Cheines of silver guilte.

Item. One white horne garnisshed with silver guilte with a Cheine of silver guilte.

159

THE MUSICAL INSTRUMENTS OF KING HENRY VIII

f. 445. A paire of Organes standinge in the Chapple.

AT WESTMINSTER

In the lytle Studye
f. 473. An antique horne garnisshed with silver gilte with a Bawdricke likewise garnisshed.

An Inventory taken at WESTMINSTER, 1550

f. 762. One case of Cornettes of v covered with blacke leather and a locke and a keye to it.

APPENDIX NINE

KING CHARLES I'S HARPSICHORD
Extracted from Original Papers Relating to RUBENS
W. N. SAINSBURY.

Page 208–210 Transcripts.

CCIII

B. GERBIER to Sec. Sir F. WINDEBANK.
Brussels Jan. 20/30 1637–8

Right Honnorable

The Virginall I do pitch upon is an excellent peece, made by JOHANNES RICKARTS at ANTWERP. Its a dobbel steart stick as called hath foure registers, the place to play on att the side. The Virginal was made for the latte Infante, hath a faire picture on the inne side of the Covering, representing the Infantas parke, and on the opening, att the part were played a picture of RUBENS representing Cupid and Psiche, the partie asks £30 starling. Those virginals which have noe pictures cost £15:– Your Honr will have time enuf to consider on the sum, cause I can keepe the Virginal long enuf att my house.

I take my leave and rest
Your Honrs etc.

B. GERBIER.

CCIV

Sir F. WINDEBANK to B. GERBIER.
WESTMINSTER, February 2, 1637–8

Sir:—

You are pleased to give me a testimony of yor care of my privat little businesse concerning the virginall for which I retourne yu my most affectionat thankes.

If the instrument for sounde and goodnesse, be right, I do not much respect the accessories of ornament or paintings, and therefore if you can meete wth a very good one plaine and wthout these curiosities, I shold rather make choice of such a one. But I will advise wth your good frende and myne Mr. NORGAT, whose skill in these businesses is excellent and then I will take the liberty to acquaint you with my further desires. Presenting my true love to you and making it my suite to you to use me as freely as by your many civilities you have obliged me to be (Sr)

Your most faithful true servant,

FRAN WINDEBANK

CCV

Sec. Sir F. WINDEBANK to B. GERBIER
(Extract)
WESTMINSTER, July 29, 1638.

Sir,

The virginall which you sent me is com safe, and I wish it were as usefull as I know you intended it. But the workman, that made it, was much mistaken in it, and it wantes 6 or 7 keyes, so that it is

161

utterly unserviceable if either he could alter it or wolde change it for another that may have more keyes, it were well: but as it is our musick is marr'd. Neverthelesse, I am exceedinglye behoulding to you for it and acknowledge as many thankes to be due to you, as if it had bene the most exquisit piece in the worlde. In that quality I beseeche you (Sr) comaunde

Your most faithfull and obliged
true frende to serve you

FRAN WINDEBANK

CCVI

B. GERBIER to Sec. Sir F. WINDEBANK
(Extract)
BRUSSELS July 28/Aug. 7, 1638.

Right Honnorable,

I have your honors letter to me of 20/30 July, to which I have no more to say but that I must take patience, the virginall proves not according expectation. Iff your honor causeth the same sent to me agayne well conditioned and a just measure of the keyes desired annother virginall to be; I will cause this to be sould as itt can annother made forthwith by Mr. RUKAERTS the same and the best master here, who saith this virginall cannot be altered, and none else made here on saille.

Humbly take my leave and rest your honour, etc.

B. GERBIER.

On 3 August, 1638, Sec. WINDEBANK writes to GERBIER from HAWES HILL: 'For the virginall I desire you not to trouble yourself seeing the fault was myne that did not give better instruction.'

APPENDIX TEN

SHUDI HARPSICHORDS WITH 5½ OCTAVES

No.	Date.	
496	1765	Wroclaw Castle Museum (formerly owned by Frederick the Great).
511	1766	Potsdam. Specially made for Frederick the Great. No. 512 disappeared in
512	1766	1945, and was reported in the Moscow Conservatoire 1950–1955.
625	1770	Benton Fletcher Collection, Fenton House, London.
639	1771	Messrs. Broadwood, London.
686	1773	St. Michaels College, Tenbury, Worcestershire.
691	1773	Musée du Conservatoire, Brussels. Made for Empress Maria Theresa.
762	1775	Kunsthistorisches Museum, Vienna, lent by Gesellschaft der Musikfreunde. Made for Haydn.
919	1782	Victoria and Albert Museum, London.
938	1782	Duke of Devonshire, Chatsworth, Derbyshire.
—	—	Mrs. Mary Potts, Cambridge. [Unsigned.]
—	—	Viscount Scarsdale, Kedleston, Derby. [Unsigned.]

APPENDIX ELEVEN

CONDITIONS RELATING TO BURKAT SHUDI'S RETIREMENT

After John Broadwood's marriage to Barbara Shudi in 1769 he was taken into partnership by his father-in-law. In March 1771, however, Burkat Shudi retired, having reserved a certain income from his business, and went to live in Charlotte Street, Tottenham Court Road, where he died on 19 August 1773.

John Broadwood and Sons have the Deed of Grant with Reciprocal Covenants, dated 7 March 1771, signed by Shudi and Broadwood, in which the former

'hath agreed to yield up his business in his trade of an Harpsichord Maker to the said John Broadwood during the joint lives of the said Burkat Shudi and the said John Broadwood solely to make and vend a certain piece of mechanism or machinery for the improvement of the Harpsichord for the sole making and vending of which the said Burkat Shudi hath obtained his Majesty's Letter Patent.'

This mechanism or machinery was Shudi's Venetian Swell, the Patent for which is dated 18 December 1769 and entitled, 'A piece of Mechanism or Machinery by which the Harpsichord is very much improved.'

Shudi binds himself not to set up business in opposition to Broadwood, with this proviso:

'except the selling such Harpsichords as the said Burkat Shudi is now possessed of which it is agreed between the said parties that it shall be lawful for the said Burkat Shudi to do at his conveniency and discretion.'

In consideration of this Broadwood agrees to pay his father-in-law a fixed sum of £25 p.a., and definite Royalties varying with the type of instrument sold:

'for every double keyd. Harpsichord with five stops and common pedal and the said piece of mechanism or machinery . . . the sum of sixteen guineas.'
'for every double keyd. Harpsichord with four stops and the said piece of mechanism and machinery . . . the sum of fourteen guineas.'
'For a double keyd. Instrument with five stops and a common pedal without the said piece of mechanism or machinery . . . twelve guineas.'

There is a lease of the Great Pulteney Street premises granted by Shudi to Broadwood, also dated 7 March 1771. Broadwood can have the whole building

'except sufficient and convenient room in the said messuage for the Harpsichords now belonging to the said Burkat Shudi until such time as the same shall be sold and particularly the use of the Dining Room for the new Harpsichords belonging to the said Burkat Shudi.'

APPENDIX TWELVE

HANDEL'S HARPSICHORD

The association of surviving objects with celebrated historical figures has always been a source of pleasure and awe, often interpreted as inspiration. Thus we find relics of the cross and of the saints and martyrs, beds in which Queen Elizabeth the First slept, trees in which King Charles the Second hid, and endless instruments claimed as the personal favourites of musicians, scientists and surgeons. And generally, in proportion as the validity of the claim is in doubt, so the partisans mass their forces.

Handel has received much attention where musical instruments are concerned. Every organ by Snetzler or Bernard Smith, which the composer could have played on, is described as his favourite organ or special design, and domestic instruments of smaller kinds have been similarly treated. A John Hitchcock spinet, No. 1656, in the Royal College of Music, a clavichord in the County Museum, Maidstone, and two Flemish harpsichords, have been given greatest attention. Here we will examine the claims of the latter two instruments.

Handel's will is dated 1 June 1750 (he died in 1759), and one paragraph only refers to musical instruments:

'I give and bequeath to Mr. Christopher Smith my Large Harpsichord, my little House Organ, my Musik Books, and five hundred Pounds sterl:'

Several codicils were added in the next nine years, but the only other musical instrument to appear is mentioned in the third codicil, dated 4 August 1757:

'I give to John Rich Esquire my Great Organ that stands at the Theatre Royal in Covent Garden.'

After Handel's death, which occurred on 14 April 1759, his Executor sold much of the contents of his house in Great Brook Street (now Brook Street), and an inventory was prepared on 27 August 1759. There are no musical instruments in this inventory.

Much concern has been caused by the fact that Handel left such brief reference to his instruments. No doubt, as with any other busy professional, a number of instruments passed through his hands during his life, and others were hired for special purposes, as was done quite commonly at that time, and is quite commonly done today. The lack of detailed references in Handel's will is nothing to cause suspicion; wills do not enumerate everything; much is left out, and executors generally search in vain for something which is specifically mentioned. Handel may quite possibly have given away instruments before his death, or his executors may have disposed of instruments after his death. It does not follow that we must have a record of such transactions.

Let us now examine the two claimants for the title, 'my Large Harpsichord', quoted above.

1. Harpsichord inscribed *Ioannes Ruckers me fecit Antwerpiae 1612.*

This harpsichord is Crown Property, and is lent to the National Trust, at Fenton House, Hampstead.

There are two manuals: compass GG – f³, chromatic, but without GG♯. There are three registers: one unison common to both manuals, and a unison and an octave for the lower maunal. The trade mark of Hans Ruckers (H.R.) is in the soundboard, but the date is recorded nowhere but on the nameboard. This nameboard is not original, since the harpsichord has been widened some six inches in the treble, probably in England in the mid eighteenth century, when the inscription was first replaced and the decoration extended.

This harpsichord was found in a very derelict condition at Windsor Castle in 1883, and was repaired by Messrs. Broadwood for the International Inventions Exhibition of 1885. The keys and stand, which were missing, were replaced at that time. The exhibition catalogue, by A. J. Hipkins, refers to this instrument on page 63:

'Double Harpsichord, by Hans Ruckers. 1612. From Windsor Castle. The "large harpsichord" in Handel's will may have been this instrument. The keyboards are new.'

The instrument was then lent to the Victoria and Albert Museum and acquired a label stating that it was 'bequeathed by Handel to George II'.

In 1950–1951 the harpsichord was restored, and the old decoration: dark green outside, vermilion and gold leaf inside, was removed to effect various repairs. The case was then painted black outside, with red and gold paint inside.

This harpsichord is 7′6″ long.

2. Harpsichord inscribed *Andreas Ruckers me fecit Antverpiae 1651*.

This harpsichord is in the Victoria and Albert Museum, and was presented by Messrs. Broadwood in 1868 as 'Handel's Harpsichord'.

There are two manuals: compass GG – f³, chromatic, but without GG♯. There are three registers: a unison common to both manuals, and a unison and an octave for the lower manual.

This harpsichord was originally a one manual instrument. In eighteenth century England it was enlarged, the treble extended some four inches, and the instrument lengthened seven inches to include a second manual. The keyboards date from that restoration, as does the nameboard. The A. R. rose in the soundboard, and the date 1651 which is painted there, probably record the work of Andries Ruckers the younger.

This harpsichord is 6′8″ long.

The length of each instrument is important, though more so in the case of the 1612 harpsichord which claims in particular to be the 'Large Harpsichord' mentioned in the will; however, it is not large for 1750, and it is very difficult to suppose that Handel would have considered it so. A fourth row of jacks for a lute stop, and a length of about eight feet, would more reasonably constitute the large model of that time.

The possible association of this harpsichord with Handel's will is obtained in this way. Handel left his 'Large Harpsichord' to his old friend Christopher Smith. In Smith's will, first published by James S. Hall in *Musical Times*, March 1955, he left to his son, John Christopher Smith, who had been Handel's assistant:

'All my Musick Books and Pieces of Musick whether Manuscript or otherwise which were left to me in and by the last Will and Testament of my Friend George Frederick Handel deceased And also all my other Musick and Books of Musick both in print and manuscript and all my Instruments of Musick which I shall be possessed of at the time of my decease.'

Here the 'Large Harpsichord' is lost from sight. In 1799 a book was printed called *Anecdotes of George Frederick Handel and John Christopher Smith* (London. Bulmer and Co.). There it was stated that the Younger Smith presented to King George the Third 'the rich legacy which Handel had left him', which included his manuscript book, his bust by Roubiliac, and his harpsichord. The bust by Roubiliac is at Windsor Castle today.

It is not at present possible to offer a closer connection than this between the unidentified 'Large Harpsichord' and the moderate size Ruckers found at Windsor Castle.

HANDEL'S HARPSICHORD

Let us now turn to the Andries Ruckers of 1651, which was presented to the Victoria and Albert Museum by Messrs. Broadwood in 1868 as 'Handel's Harpsichord', and with which were presented various documents in support of the title.

Messrs. Broadwood bought the harpsichord from Mr. Hooper, a pianoforte tuner of Winchester, in 1852.

Mr. Hooper obtained it from the Cathedral organist, Dr. Chard (1765–1849).

Dr. Chard obtained the harpsichord on the death of a Prebendary of the Cathedral, the Reverend Mr. Hawtrey, to whom it had belonged.

Mr. Hawtrey acquired it from a surgeon, Mr. Wickham, who had obtained the instrument from the Dowager Lady Rivers. She was stepdaughter of John Christopher Smith.

To record all this properly, Dr. Chard addressed himself to the Reverend George Cox, Rector of St. Michael's, Winchester, who was the Dowager Lady Rivers' brother, and step-son of Christopher Smith.

The Rev. G. Coxe, Twyford, Rector of St. Michael's, Winchester.
My dear Sir,

Will you oblige me by certifying (if I am correct) the following:

The celebrated Mr. Smith (or Schmidt) was Handel's private friend and amanuensis. This said Mr. Smith was presented by Handel with his favorite fine double-keyed harpsichord, made by the best maker of the day, Andreas Ruckers of Antwerpia, 1651. This said instrument you have heard repeatedly Mr. Smith play on. Mr. Smith was father in law [sic] to you as well as your sister the late Dowager Lady Rivers; and at his death the said harpsichord, together with a large collection of Handel's oratorios, etc. etc., MSS., came into the hands of the Dowager Lady Rivers. This instrument was parted with to a Mr. Wickman, surgeon, who parted with it to the Rev. W. Hawtrey, Prebendary of Winchester Cathedral, upon the death of whom I purchased it at the sale of his effects; and in my possession it still remains. Is not this the identical instrument now spoken of? Your early answer to these queries, as the only living witness, will oblige.

Dear Sir,
Yours faithfully,

G. W. Chard.

P.S. Will you oblige me by certifying on this sheet of paper, and returning it?

Answer

I certify that the above statement is correct, as far as my knowledge goes.

George Cox.
Twyford, May 13th, 1842.

Witness to the above signature:
    Susanna Gregg
    James Harris.

It should here be recorded that the harpsichord is not mentioned in John Christopher Smith's will (he died in 1795) nor in Lady Rivers' (she died in 1835); but it has already been said that wills are by no means always reliable on such points.

The claim of the 1612 Ruckers from Windsor rests on the assumption that the younger Smith in fact received Handel's 'Large Harpsichord' on his father's death, that he gave it to the King at Windsor, and that this is the very instrument. There have been other harpsichords at Windsor Castle: for example a Shudi of 1740, thought to have belonged to Frederick, Prince of Wales, (died 1751) son of King George the Second, and now in Kew Palace. So the Ruckers, to establish its claim, must obtain the disqualification of any other instruments which have been at Windsor. Identification of the harpsichord by name and date from some contemporary document would solve this point. But hearsay and speculation confuse the issue.

HANDEL'S HARPSICHORD

The claim of the 1651 Ruckers is, on the surface, rather more definite. But it is very difficult to associate this small instrument with the description 'Large Harpsichord'.

Attention is drawn to the design by Sir James Thornhill (plate 62) for the lid of a harpsichord in Handel's possession, and it is explained that the shape of this lid makes it impossible that the instrument could have been either of the Ruckers claimants. It is highly improbable that the instrument could, on account of its shape, have been the Shudi advertised for sale in 1788 (page 81). The most probable English maker for a harpsichord with this double curve lid is the Hitchcock family.

In the portrait of Handel by Mercier, owned by the Earl of Malmesbury, which is reproduced in Dale (1913), the composer is seated at a harpsichord with keys of the distinctive design particularly associated with the Hitchcocks. This harpsichord has, however, only one manual, and can scarcely have been a 'Large Harpsichord'.

It will be clearly seen that our knowledge (as opposed to our imagination) is at present inadequate to solve this problem. Factual discoveries may help us, but false statements and inventions of the kind which surround the spurious Bach harpsichord and some of the aspiring Mozart pianofortes should have no place in our investigations.

APPENDIX THIRTEEN

AFFIDAVIT RELATING TO JOSHUA SHUDI

John Broadwood & Sons possess a copy of the following affidavit, sworn on 12 Jan. 1767 by three of Shudi's apprentices, Clark, Nixon and Broadwood. It throws some light on Joshua Shudi about whom very little is known. From this affidavit it appears that Burkat Shudi made four harpsichords for the King of Prussia. Today we have only records of three: a harpsichord dated 1765 and formerly in Breslau Castle, and two of 1766 which Shudi sent to Potsdam (appendix 10).

Andrew Clark, of the parish of St. James, in the liberty of Westminster and county of Middlesex, Harpsichord-maker, Thomas Nixon of the same place, Harpsichord-maker and John Broadwood, of the parish of St. Ann, Soho, in the said county, Harpsichord-maker, severally make oath, and say, and first this deponent Andrew Clark saith, that he, this deponent hath worked for Mr. Burkat Shudi, Harpsichord-maker, to her Royal Highness the Princess Dowager of Wales upwards of nine years. And this deponent John Broadwood, saith, that he, this deponent, hath worked for the said Burkat Shudi ever since the middle of September, one thousand seven hundred and sixty one. And this deponent, Thomas Nixon, saith, that he, this deponent, hath worked for the said Burkat Shudi about two years. And these deponents, Andrew Clark and John Broadwood, further say, that one Joshua Shudi came to live with the said Burkat Shudi sometime in the winter of the year one thousand seven hundred and sixty one, to the best of these deponents remembrance and belief, the said Joshua Shudi having then lately quitted the sea, as these deponents were informed and believe. And these deponents, Andrew Clark and John Broadwood farther say, that they deny that the said Joshua Shudi did begin and end the Harpsichords which the said Burkat Shudi sold to his Prussian Majesty, or any of them. And these deponents can the better depose, as aforesaid, for that the greatest part of the work of the said Harpsichords was done by these deponents Andrew Clark and John Broadwood, under the direction of their said master Burkat Shudi; and particularly this deponent, John Broadwood, perfectly remembers his having glewed up the sounding boards of all the said Harpsichords, and his having assisted his said master Burkat Shudi in putting the sounding-board (after this deponent had wrought and finished the same under the immediate direction of this deponent's said master Burkat Shudi) into the first of the said Harpsichords sold to his Prussian Majesty, as aforesaid. And this deponent Thomas Nixon, farther saith, that the greatest part of the first of the said Harpsichords was done before this deponent began to work for the said Burkat Shudi; but this deponent did see the said Andrew Clark and John Broadwood do the greatest part of the work of the other three Harpsichords which were sold to his Prussian Majesty. And these deponents, Andrew Clark, and John Broadwood, farther say, that the said Joshua Shudi, during the whole time that he lived with the said Burkat Shudi never did begin and finish any one harpsichord, to the best of these deponents knowledge and belief. And this deponent, Thomas Nixon, saith, that the said Joshua Shudi never did begin and finish any one Harpsichord during the time that this deponent hath worked for the said Burkat Shudi.

	Andrew Clark
Middlesea ⎱ Sworn before me	Thomas Nixon
to wit ⎰ Jan. 12, 1767	John Broadwood.

G. Wrighte

169

AN IMPROVED METHOD OF QUILLING A HARPSICHORD
BY F. HOPKINSON, ESQUIRE

[Communication to the Philosophical Society, Philadelphia]
(See plate 52)

Read Dec. 5, 1783.

Much of the pleasure and effect in performing on a harpsichord depends on the equality of what is called *the touch*; and this is principally owing to a continuance of uniformity in the spring of the little quills, which by their impulse set the strings in vibration. These quills, in the present manner of applying them, will not retain their elasticity for any length of time, but require constant repair; which is one of the most troublesome and difficult operations in keeping the instrument in order. To remedy this inconvenience, I have sought for a substitute for the crow quill, and tried a variety of substances, but without success. I then considered whether an improvement might not be made in the application of the quills themselves, and to this purpose I examined the cause of the quills being so liable to break, and observed that the piece of quill is thrust through a small hole in the tongue of the jack, projecting only about a quarter of an inch beyond the face of the tongue: That this quill is too short to yield in all its parts, and so act properly as a spring; but bends only at the place where it issues from the hole in the tongue, and works up and down as upon a hinge, in that place; and *there only* is the quill ever known to break.

Thus in Plate 52A, Figure 6, *a*, is the tongue, *b*, the quill fixed firmly in it, which being too short to act fairly as a spring, will bend only at *c*, when it is forced to pass the string; and by repeated exercise must necessarily break in that part, as any spring would do if compelled to act in the same manner.

But if this quill could be made longer, or applied so that its spring should be part of a curve, it would probably preserve its elasticity for any length of time, as other springs do.

To effect this I have constructed the tongue and applied the quill as represented in figure 7, where *a*, is the tongue, the top of which is rounded off; the quill is firmly fixed in the hole at *c*, as usual, but instead of passing through a length sufficient to strike the string, it is cut off even with the face of the tongue at *f*. The quill thus fixed with its polished face downwards, is bent upward round the top of the tongue, and then proceeds horizontally the proper length; being kept in the horizontal position by the little wire staple *e*, being firmly driven into holes drilled for the purpose, but not so far as to pinch the quill against the top of the tongue; a little space being left for the quill to play in.

From this construction it is manifest, that the spring of the quill will be in its whole length, but chiefly in the curve *c*, *d*; and that a quill so applied will act fairly as a spring, and may be expected to retain its elasticity for years, subject to no variations but such as may be occasioned by alterations in the state of the air, to which all known substances are more or less liable.

Read, 1784.

In the beginning of last winter, I had the honour to lay before the society an improved method

AN IMPROVED METHOD OF QUILLING A HARPSICHORD

of quilling a HARPSICHORD. Wishing to bring my discovery to the test of full experiment and to the judgment of abler critics, I forwarded a description and a model of my improvement to a friend in London, requesting that it might be submitted to the examination of proper judges, and directing, in case it should be approved of, that an instrument made by one of the first artists and quilled according to my proposed method, should be sent to me. I have accordingly received an excellent double harpsichord, made by Messrs. *Shudi* and *Broadwood* of London, and quilled according to my method; with this difference, I had rounded off the top of the tongue, and bending the quill over it, kept it in a horizontal position by means of a small wire staple; as will be more fully understood by referring to my former description. But Mr. *Broadwood* has left the tongue of its full length and usual form: But made the hole, in which the quill is commonly fixed tight, so large, that the quill has free room to play therein; and then fixing the quill below, has bent it round and brought it through this hole; which renders a staple unnecessary; the top of the tongue answering the same purpose. The principle on which the improvement depends is the same in both; but his is the best method of executing it.

He informs, however, that one inconvenience occurs *viz.* the quills being so forcibly bent in the curved part, are liable, in some instances, to spring back, and so become not only too short to reach the string it should strike, but the projection of the curve will be apt to touch the string behind it, when the stop is pushed back.

To explain this, let *a*, *b*, figure 8, represent the tongue, *c*, *d*, *e*, the quill, firmly fixed at *c*, then bent upwards and brought through a hole, which is large enough for the quill to play freely therein. But the curved part of the quill at *d*, being so forcibly bent, will in some instances spring back (as represented in the figure) not keeping close to the back of the tongue, as it should do: And as there is no waste room, the curve *d*, will be apt to touch the string behind it, when the stop is pushed back, I acknowledge that this inconvenience occurs in some few instances in the instrument Mr. *Broadwood* has sent me; but would observe that as it does not *always* happen, it is a fault in the execution and not in the principle. Yet, as it may be difficult to guard against it, I have considered how this evil may be effectually prevented.

Instead of punching the small hole, in which the quill is to be fixed, straight through the tongue, let it be punched slanting downwards; this will relieve the quill from that strained position which causes it to spring back. According to the first mode of application the curve formed by the quill will be as at *a*, figure 9, in the second as at *b*. I have constructed many tongues in this way, and found none of them liable to the inconvenience complained of, or shewing any tendency whatever to spring back; but to remove all jealousy on this head, should any remain, it will be easy to drive a small wire staple against the bottom of the curve behind, which must effectually retain it close to the back of the tongue.

I mention this expedient of the wire staple merely with a view of removing all doubt; but I do not think it necessary; the objection being perfectly remedied by the other method: To prove this, I have cut out the entire block between the two holes, in the manner of a mortise, and drove a pin across the upper part of it. I then caused the quill to lie in this slanting mortise, and bending it round brought it over the pin; and I found it would remain perfectly at ease in its birth, although not pinched or restrained in any part; *a*, figure 10, represents the tongue in front, and *b*, the mortise, of which the slanting shape cannot be seen in this view; but will be better understood by observing the position of the quill in figure 11, where *a* is a profile of the same tongue, *b*, *c*, the quill lying on the mortise, and *d*, the pin over which the top of the quill passes.

I have need to apologize to the society for directing so much of their attention, to an object which may appear to some to be of little importance. To the musical tribe, however this improvement will present itself in a different light. Many persons who play very well on the harpsichord, are not able to keep the instrument in order: And to send for a person to repair the quills and tune the instrument as often as it shall be necessary, is not only troublesome and expensive, but such assistance is not always to be had, especially in the country. And for these reasons many a good harpsichord or spinnet lies neglected and the scholar loses the opportunity of practice. To such persons a method of quilling that shall seldom want repair is a *desideratum* of no small importance. And this, I flatter myself I have accomplished.

The difficulty of *quilling* being thus removed, I considered in what manner *tuning* might be made easy to the practitioner in music. Harpsichords are tuned by means of *fifths* and *thirds*; but such is the musical division of the monochord as to make it necessary, that none of these *fifths* or *thirds* should be perfect; an allowance must be made; and to do this with judgment, so that the chords may be good and the instrument be in tune, requires much attention and practice. Of the numbers that play, there will not be found one in an hundred that can tune a harpsichord. To render this task easy, I have procured *twelve tuning forks*, for the *twelve semitones* of the octave; these I had perfectly tuned; and as they will not be sensibly affected by any change of weather, they remain as standards. I take it for granted that any person at all accustomed to musical sounds can tell when one tone is *in unison* with another; and that a very little practice will enable him to tune one sound *an octave* to another, these conchords are so manifest that they cannot easily be mistaken. There is then nothing to be done but to tune the twelve strings in unison with the twelve forks; this will fix the scale, or temperature for one octave, which is the whole difficulty; the rest of the instrument is easily tuned by unisons and octaves to the scale, so ascertained.*

Having, I hope, fully accomplished the design I had in view when I turned my thoughts to this subject, I shall now take leave of it; and shall be highly gratified if I find others benefited by my attentions, although in a matter of no very serious import.

Nov. 1784.

* My set of forks are tuned from the middle C sharp to the C above, inclusive.

DESCRIPTION OF A FURTHER IMPROVEMENT IN THE HARPSICHORD

Read January 28, 1786.

IN a former paper read before the society, respecting an improved method of quilling a HARPSICHORD, I made some apology for troubling you with a subject not strictly within the limits of your view as a philosophical society, and which might appear to some of small importance. At the same time I took formal leave of a pursuit which had accidentally engaged my attention, and which I had obtruded upon your's. Notwithstanding this, I find myself under a necessity of again requesting your indulgence, whilst I describe a discovery I made in August last, of a still further improvement to the same purpose.

Having succeeded to the extent of my expectation in a more advantageous way of applying the crow quill in common use in a harpsichord, I thought to rest content with that improvement; which had principally for its object the duration of the quill's elasticity, and of course the duration of equality of touch. But notwithstanding the long established prejudice in favour of the crow quill, and the prevailing opinion that no substance can supply its place to advantage, I think a candid critic will allow that one of the following positions is founded in fact, and the other in reason.

First. Although the three stops of a harpsichord should be quilled to the best advantage, the result of the whole will be an observable jingle or tinkling between the quills and wires, which depreciates the dignity and sweetness of the instrument. The best harpsichords are so censurable for this imperfection, that the *Forte Piano*, which is free from it, stands a chance of rivalling that noble instrument, for this cause only; being far inferior in every other respect.

Second. Is it not reasonable to suppose that so long a string, so advantageously stretched over so large a box, should yield a greater body of tone, than that which is produced by the impulse of a quill? If the quill be made very stiff, this will render the touch disagreeable and encrease the jingle, but not add to the *body* of tone. One reason why the quill does not draw a fuller tone from the string, I suppose to be the smallness of its contact. The back of a quill is a portion of a circle, the extended string is a right line, and a circle can touch a right line only in a point; the contact therefore must be so small, that mere strength of impulse is not sufficient to put the string into full vibration.

The method I am now to describe of quilling, or rather *tonguing* a harpsichord, I have found by experiment, to draw forth the powers of the instrument to a surprising effect, causing it to yield a full and pure body of tone, free from all jingle and very pleasant to the ear.

N.B. What hath hitherto been called the tongue of the jack, I shall denominate the *palate*; and the substitute I have made for the quill, I shall call the *tongue*. The propriety of this will appear in the description.

Plate 52A. Let A, figure 12, represent the palate in front, with a mortise cut through it for the tongue to work in. B, is the tongue, having two small holes drilled through it, one in the centre of its motion and the other at a little distance behind, for the reception of one end of a wire spring hereafter mentioned.

Figure 13, is the palate in profile, with the tongue properly mounted and moveable on the centre pin. This figure also shews how the palate must be hollowed in behind to expose the root of the tongue, and the small hole in it for the reception of one end of the wire spring.

Figure 14, is a back view of the palate, shewing the groove in which the hair spring of the jack lies, and a small wire staple at *b*, to which the lower end of the steel spring is to be fastened.

Figure 15, is the spring which is to govern the tongue. It must be of fine steel wire, somewhat annealed by being forcibly rubbed between pieces of leather or cork, and is formed by winding the wire backwards and forwards with a tight hand, over pins driven deep and firm into a piece of wood. As the palate must play freely within the fork or jaws of the jack, the windings of the spring must not exceed the width of the palate. The upper end of the spring being run through the small hole in the root of the tongue and bent round, so as to secure it, and the superfluous part cut off; the lower end of the same spring must be run under the little staple (*b*, figure 14,) and bent upwards with a gentle strain, so as to hook it on and secure it to that staple; the spring will then operate with all its elasticity, and the tongue will be subjected to its operation.

Figure 17, represents the palate in a back view with the zig zag spring fastened by one end to the root of the tongue, and by the other to the little staple.

To prevent the tongue from rising by force of the spring above a horizontal position, there must be a wire staple driven in the front of the palate immediately above the tongue (as at *a*, in figure 12 and 13;) and the tongue, if of wood, should be armed with a small piece of soft leather just under the staple, to prevent noise.

It must be left to future experiment to determine the most proper of all substances of which the tongue should be made; different substances drawing different tones from the string. After many essays to this purpose, I have concluded to furnish my harpsichord in the following manner.

The tongues of the first unison are of *Ben sole-leather*. Those of the second are of a soft leather faced with Morocco, such as is frequently used in harpsichords, though applied in a different way, and the tongues of the octave are of wood, such as pear tree, laurel, or any wood of an even grain and not too hard in substance. But all mounted on springs, as above described, and their faces well polished with black lead where they come in contact with the strings.

My reasons are. The sole-leather produces a full, sweet and vigorous tone from the first unison. The second unison, which is the piano of the instrument when the pedal is pressed, is furnished with Morocco leather, which draws a full but more soft and smothered tone from the string. And the octave is struck with wooden tongues for the sake of vivacity and brilliancy, which is the genius of that stop; yet I am not sure but that the octave also had better be struck with sole-leather, like the first unison.*

A harpsichord thus furnished, will produce a body or quantity of sound, and a purity of tone, that will astonish at the first hearing, much resembling the diapason stop of an organ. And it is manifest that if the touch be well regulated at first, it will not afterwards be subject to alteration for a long course of time. The touch is in part regulated by the strength of the serpentine spring and the number of its zig zag evolutions; and in part by the manner of rounding off the tip of the tongue; for the tip of the tongue must not be cut off square, (in which case, the string would leave the tongue too abruptly and cause a disagreeable twang,) but should be slanted off from underneath, and its extreme point rounded and well polished by rubbing it very hard with a piece of black lead. As to the strength of the spring, four sizes of wire, *viz.* from no. 4 to no. 8, will be sufficient for the whole instrument; but the touch is more immediately regulated by rounding off the tips of the tongues by the pressure and polish of the black lead, more or less, as occasion shall require. When the tongues are of wood, a stroke or two of a fine file will be necessary to take off the square edge left by the knife, previous to the polishing it with the black lead.

After all, a harpsichord just furnished in this way, will not be so pleasant to the touch or to the ear as it will be after a few weeks use; when the strings will, by repeated friction, have rounded off and polished the tips of the tongues, and have made for themselves a broad bearing or contact, which cannot perhaps be so accurately produced by any care of the workman.

Lastly, it is scarce necessary to observe that the serpentine spring and the root of the tongue must be comprised within the thickness of the jack; otherwise they will be apt to interfere with the string behind, when the stop is pushed back.

F. HOPKINSON.

* Because, after the stroke has been given, the wooden tongue repassing the string, yet in vibration, makes a jingle, which the leather tongues do not.

AN IMPROVED METHOD
OF QUILLING A HARPSICHORD

[See plate 52B]

The strings of a Harpsichord are made to vibrate by the impulse of small pieces of a crow-quill: these, from the manner in which they are applied, are compelled to perform their office to such disadvantage that many become weak and fail, with little use, and what is called *the touch* of the instrument, becomes thereby unequal and disagreeable both to the performer and hearer; unless frequently repaired, which is one of the most troublesome and difficult operations in keeping the instrument in order.

I attempted, two or three years ago, to remedy this imperfection. My first idea was to encrease the length of quill, that it might act more like a spring than it can do in the way it is now applied. I effected my purpose, by mounting the quill in the manner represented by fig. I. By this means the spring of the quill was advantageously encreased without its horizontal length, which from the construction of the instrument cannot be more than about 1-4th of an inch. AB fig. I. is the tongue of the jack in profile, C is the quill fixed tight in a hole punched slanting downwards through the tongue according to the dotted line. The quill is then bent upwards and made to pass through another hole D, punched through the upper part of the tongue, and then proceeds horizontally the necessary length. This last hole is made large enough for the quill to have free play in it, so that the spring of the quill may be in the curve CD; which will not break or fail by any service it has to perform.

This contrivance seemed to answer very well; but it was objected, that the quill being thus forcibly bent, was apt to spring back, in some instances, so that not only the point of the quill became too short to reach the string it should strike, but the curved part would interfere with the string next behind it. And although, in the experiment, this inconvenience rarely occurred, and was rather a fault in the execution than in the design, yet the project was not adopted because of the uncertainty.

My next device was to throw aside the quills altogether; and taking hard and well seasoned soal leather, I cut therefrom the intended *tongues*,* which I mounted on springs as in fig. 2. Where A is the palate seen in profile, having a mortoise [*sic*] cut through it for the reception of the leathern tongue B, which is moveable in the mortoise on a small pin; C is a back view of the same palate, showing the zig-zag spring by which the tongue is governed. The spring is of fine wire, and is fastened by one end to the root of the tongue, as at D, and by the other to a small staple at E.

This contrivance produced in effect an admirable fulness of tone, and promised permanency, because the elasticity required is not in the tongue which gives the stroke, but in the wire spring, which, if properly annealed, will not be likely to fail.

The objection was, that the touch was not so lively and agreeable as that of the common quill; but principally that the machinery was too complex and delicate for general use.

Both these methods are fully described in the second volume of the transactions of the American philosophical society of Philadelphia.

Encouraged by at least a partial success, I again endeavoured to attain the object I had in view, and flatter myself that I have now fully succeeded.

The desideratum is, a substance to supply the place of the crow-quill, sufficiently elastic for the purpose, which shall afford an easy and brilliant touch, shall draw a full and pure tone from the string, be applied with as much simplicity as the common quill, and be permanent in itself.

After fair experiment and a long trial, the following method of *tongueing* a harpsichord hath been found to answer all the above requisites.

I took what is called *velvet-cork*, of the best kind, free from dolts, cracks or blemishes. I cut this cork into plates, about one quarter of an inch thick, and glued upon them thin and well polished leather; from these plates I cut the tongues, and pressed them tight into mortoises cut for the purpose through the palates, in the same manner, and with the same ease that the common quill is fixed in the little hole punched for its reception. The cork must then be shaved off underneath, slanting from the point, where it must be very thin, to the face of the palate, and then nibbed like a pen to the proper length. The touch may afterwards be nicely regulated by shaving away more of the cork from underneath, if requisite, with a sharp pen-knife or a fine file.

REMARKS

I. The *cork* (as before observed) must be of the kind called *velvet-cork*, of an elastic substance, and free from imperfections of every kind.

II. The *Leather* should be thin, well stretched, and of a polished surface—That which I used was stripped from the cover of a bound book, which answered very well, after I had scraped and well washed its under surface.

III. The *paste* or *glue*. In my first experiment I made common glue pretty thin, and with this I glued the leather on the cork; but found afterwards, that in very dry and frosty weather, the touch became harsh and disagreeable, because glue in such weather becomes as hard as horn. I then

* What is commonly called the tongue, I shall now call *the palate*, and my substitute for the crow-quill I shall denominate the tongue.

dissolved a little isinglass, or fish glue, in hot water, and with the addition of some flour I made a moderately thin paste; and with this I pasted the leather upon the cork, putting the plates under a press till dry: and found it to answer well.

IV. In cutting the tongues from these plates of cork faced with leather, care must be taken that the grain of the cork shall run lengthwise from end to end, and not across the tongue. The reason is plain.

I have found these tongues to answer every requisite. The cork is sufficiently elastic for the service it is to perform, and affords a lively and pleasant touch. The polished leather presents a most agreeable surface of contact with the metal string, and shields the cork, which would be soon cut through by the string. The tone produced is full, and very pure, being perfectly free from that *clicking* noise which the strokes of a quill unavoidably produce, and which has been justly complained of in the best harpsichords. And lastly, the tongue thus made will be durable, I may judge if from the experience of eighteen months and almost daily use, very few having failed in that time, and those only where there was some imperfection in the cork, or the grain lay across the tongue. But when this happens, nothing is easier than to cut and shape a new tongue from the plate of cork and leather, which may be fitted to the mortoise and adjusted in as little time as a common quill and with as little trouble. Harpsichords, quilled in the usual way, may be furnished in the manner now recommended, by dismounting the palates and cutting mortoises of a proper size; the little hole in which the quill has been fixed serving for the upper limit of the mortoise in which the cork tongue is to be fitted.

1787.

APPENDIX FIFTEEN

LETTERS BETWEEN HOPKINSON, JEFFERSON, AND BURNEY

Thomas Jefferson
   to
Francis Hopkinson

Paris, September 25, 1785

Dear Sir,—My last to you was of the 6th of July. Since that, I have received yours of July the 23d. I do not altogether despair of making something of your method of quilling, though, as yet, the prospect is not favourable. I applaud much your perseverance in improving this instrument, and benefiting mankind almost in spite of their teeth. I mentioned to Piccini the improvement with which I am entrusted. He plays on the pianoforte, and therefore did not feel himself personally interested. I hope some better opportunity will yet fall in my way of doing it justice. I had almost decided, on his advice, to get a pianoforte for my daughter; but your last letter may pause me, till I see its effect. . . .

Hopkinson to Jefferson

Philadelphia, September 28, 1785

. . . I am sorry my Improvement in Quilling a Harp.^{d} has cost you so much Trouble—I resign my Expectations from that Source. I have since made a further & more important Improvement. I have long suspected that the Quill did not draw the full Power of Tone from Strings so long & so advantageously stretched, & on Experiment find my Conjecture was right. My Harp.^{d} has not now got a single Quill in it, & for Richness of Tone & the Body or Quantity of Sound it yields, exceeds any Instrument of the Kind I ever heard. The enclosed Model will give you a full Idea of the Contrivance & save the Trouble of Descriptions. My Harp.^{d} is at present furnished thus: The First Unison with sole-Leather, well rubb'd with black-Lead, the Second Unison, a kind of soft Morocco Leather, for the Piano of the Instrument, & the Octave with wooden Tongues polish'd with black Lead, for giving Vivacity to the whole—All mounted on Springs, according to the Model —I say nothing as to the admirable Result—Let Experiment determine.

Hopkinson to Jefferson

Philad^a Octr 1785

Dear friend,

It is not long since I wrote to you & forwarded another Package (I think the third) of our News Papers, and at the same Time sent you a Model of my last Improvement in the Harpsichord. The Effect produced by furnishing an Instrument in that way is truly astonishing. I have discovered the Reason—It causes the Instrument to sound the Octave below the Tones produced by the Quill. The full Tone of the Harp.^{d} has never yet been drawn forth. The Quill on Account of it's Substance,

& the Smalness of it's Contact with the String, being only in a Point (because the Back of a Quill is a Portion of a Circle) has not been sufficient to put the String in a uniform Vibration thro'out it's whole length. It vibrates in two halves, & those halves vibrate in contrary Directions—so that the Tone produced will be only the Octave above that of the whole string. My Method draws forth the full, clear & genuine Tone. . . .

Hopkinson to Jefferson

Philadelphia, December 31, 1785

. . . I wrote you some Time ago an Account of my Discovery of a new Method of drawing the Tone from a Harps.ᵈ—I believe I sent you a Model. I am much pleased with this Invention—it answers to admiration—I have instructed an ingenious workman here, & he is engaged in altering the Harps.ᵈ of this City according to my Plan—If you should ever have the Opportunity of having a Harp.ᵈ so furnished you will be surprised at the Effect. All the Jingle, so much complained of in that instrument is removed. The Tone is full, round, & Mellow, &, in the Bass, very like the Diapason Stop of an Organ—I am confident that the power of the Instrument was never before drawn forth. Crow Quills will herafter be totally thrown aside—I sent this Discovery to a friend in England —he was to offer it for 50 Gˢ but writes in answer that my Invention has been anticipated—I see I am to be defrauded both of the Money & Credit—but I will have the Matter investigated.

Jefferson to Hopkinson

Paris May 9, 1786

. . . I am just returned from a trip to England. I was in the shop of Mr. Broadwood the maker of your Harpsichord, and conversed with him about your newest jack. He shewed me instruments in his shop with precisely the same substitute for the quill, but I omitted to examine whether it had the same kind of spring on the back. He told me they had been made some time before your model came over; & I now recollect that when I advertised your improvement of the quill here, a workman sent me a jack with buff leather as a substitute for the quill. Walker's celestine stop is indeed a divine thing: a band of a simple silk thread is made to pass over a pulley on the right and another on the left, so that one string of the band is almost in contact with the strings of the harpsichord. It is kept in motion by a treadle as in a flax wheel. A set of hammers is placed just above the band, and one end of each hammer being thrust up by it's corresponding jack, the other is pressed down on the band, between the two unison strings of that note, so as to make it strike them and no others. The band being always in motion, it is as if you drew a fiddle bow over those strings, and produced a tone as different from the ordinary one of the harpsichord, as is that of a violin. To prevent the pressure of the hammer from impeding the motion of the band, a friction wheel is placed transversely in the end of every hammer, precisely in the point of contact. The whole can be shifted out of the way by a touch of the foot, & leaves the harpsichord in it's usual state. It suits slow movements, and as an accompaniment to the voice, can be fixed in any harpsichord, being under a patent, costs 8. guineas. I wait till I hear more particularly from you as to your last improvement before I order a harpsichord for my daughter. . . .

Jefferson to
John Paradise, London.

Paris May 25, 1786

Dear Sir

. . . I have yet another favour to ask which is to get Kirkman to make for me one of his best harpsichords with a double set of keys and the machine on the top resembling a Venetian blind for giving a swell, the case to be of mahogany, solid not vineered, without any inlaid work but deriving all from the elegance of the wood. I would wish entirely to avoid a complication of stops, wishing to have such only as are most simple & least liable to be put out of order as the instrument is to go to a country and to a situation where there will be no workman but myself to put it in order. When done I shall be glad to have a celestini apparatus put to it by Mr. Walker. I hope by that time he will have brought to perfection some method of giving it movement by a spring or a weight, or by some other moves than the foot or hand. I confide so much in Dr Burney's judgment & knowledge of musical instruments, and his interest too with Kirkman, that tho' I have no right to ask either myself, from the momentary, yet pleasing, acquaintance I contracted with him, I will however resort to your better acquaintance to interest him in advising or directing for the best. On receiving advice of the time when the instrument will be ready, I will take care to place the money in time in London & to direct it's package & conveiance.

Burney to Paradise.

London. June 19*th* 1786

Dear Sir

I beg you will acquaint Mr Jefferson that he flatters me very much by his remembrance, & that I shall have great pleasure in executing the commission with Kirkman. I went to him immediately on receiving your note, and have bespoke a double Harpsichord of him, which is to fulfill, as nearly as possible, every Idea & wish contained in Mr Jeffersons Letter. The machine for the Swell resembling a Venetian blind, will be applied; the stops & machinery for moving them & the swell will be perfectly simple & unembarrassing to the Tuner, the Lid of the Case will be of solid mahogany; but the sides cannot if the wood is beautiful: as the knots & irregularities in the grain, by expanding & contracting different ways, will prevent the Instru*mt* from ever remaining long in tune; but Kirkman will answer for securing the sides from all effects of weather & climate, by making them of well-seasoned oak, & veneering them with thick fine, long mahogany, in one Pannel. By this means he has sent Harp*ds* to every part of the Globe where the English have any commerce, & never has heard of the wood-work giving way. The Front will be solid, & of the most beautiful wood in his possession. The instrument will be ready to deliver in ab*t* 6 weeks; & the price, without Walker's machine, and exclusive of packing-case & Leather cover, will be 66 Guineas. The Cover & packing-case will amount to a*bt* 2gs & 1/2. A desk to put up in the Harp*d* will not be charged separately, but be reckoned a part of the Instrum*t*.

With respect to Walker's Celestine Stop, I find that Kirkman is a great enemy to it. He says that the Resin used on the silk thread that produces the tone, not only clogs and occasions it to be frequently out of order; but, in short time, adheres so much to the strings as to destroy the tone of the instrument. This may be partly true, & partly his prejudice. I am not sufficiently acquainted with this stop to determine these points; but I will talk with Walker on the subject, & try to discover whether he admits the difficulties or can explain them off; & whether he has found out any such method of giving motion to this *Bowstring* as suggested by Mr Jefferson.

Ma Lettre tire en longueur; but being unfortunately out of the reach of a conversation with your very intelligent correspondent *viva voce*, I was ambitious to let him know that I intend heartily into the business in question, & give him all the information in my power on each particular article of his commission.

I am, dear sir, with very sincere regard, & most respectful compliments to Mr Jefferson, your obedt and most humble servant.

Chas Burney.

179

LETTERS BETWEEN HOPKINSON, JEFFERSON, AND BURNEY

Jefferson to Burney.

Paris July 10, 1786.

Sir

I took the liberty, through Mr. Paradise, of asking your advice in the matter of a harpsichord. He has transmitted me a letter you were pleas'd to write him on that subject. The readiness with which you have been so good as to act in this matter excites my utmost gratitude, & I beg you to accept of my thanks for it. The objection made by Kirkman to the resin of Walker's bowstring has some weight, but I think by wiping the strings from time to time with a spunge moistened in water or in some other fluid which will dissolve the resin without attacking the metal of the strings, the evil may be relieved. It would remain to use Walker's stop sparingly, but in the movements to which it is adapted I think it's effect too great not to overweigh every objection. That it should be worked however either by a weight or a spring is very desirable. The constant motion of the foot on a treadle diverts the attention & disipates the delirium both of the player & hearer. Whenever either yourself or Mr. Paradise will be so good as to notify me that the Instrument is ready, with information of the cost of that, it's appendages, packages & delivery at the waterside, I will send by return of the post a banker's bill for the money with directions to whom to deliver it. Are organs better made here or in London? I find that tho' it is admitted that London workmen make the best harpsichords & Pianofortes, it is said the best organs are made here. I omitted in London to visit the shop of any organ-maker, but you are so much the better judge, that your decision would be more satisfactory. Indeed if it would not be too great a liberty I would ask the favor of your description of a proper organ for a chamber 24 feet square & 18 feet high, with the name of the best workman in that way in London. I feel all the impropriety of the freedom I am taking, & I throw myself on your goodness to pardon it. The reading your account of the state of music in Europe had prepared one to expect a great deal of pleasure from your acquaintance; and the few moments I was as happy as to pass with you, were a proof that my expectations would have been fully gratified, had not the shortness of time which obliged me to hurry from subject to object deprived me of opportunities of cultivating your acquaintance. I must be contented therefore with offering you my hommage by letter, & assuring you of the esteem & respect with which I have the honour to be Sir,

Your most obedient
& most humble servant
Th. Jefferson

Paradise to Jefferson, Paris.

July 28, 1786

'. . . Doctor Burney, who was with me a few days ago, desired me to acquaint you, that, in consequence of the letter with which he has been honoured by you he went to Kirkman's to enquire what state the double harpsichord was in, which he had bespoken for you; and though he found it on the stocks, he was informed that it would be near a fortnight before it could be played on in the way of trial. This being the case the Doctor will pospone his answer to your Excellency's letter till it is finished, and ready for Mr. Walker's Machinery, with whom he will have a conference previous to the instrument's being placed in his hands; the result of which shall be communicated to you, as well as the Doctor's opinion of the comparative excellence of French and English organs. He went out of Town the day after I had the pleasure of seeing him, for about a fortnight, and begged that these particulars may be communicated to you as a preface to the letter which he shall write at his return. . . .'

LETTERS BETWEEN HOPKINSON, JEFFERSON, AND BURNEY

Dr. Charles Burney to Jefferson

London, Jany 20*th*
1787

Sir

Few things have given me more concern that the not being able sooner to give you a satisfactory acc*t* of the Harp*d* & the Machinery, w*ch* I had the honour to bespeak for you last Summer. I visited Kirkman from time to time whenever I came to town, & saw the Instrum*t* in every Stage of its construction. The wood was chosen with great care; the Lid is solid, as you desired, & no part has been veneered or inlaid that *cd* possibly be avoided, or *wch cd* receive the least injury from climate. I got the Instrum*t* out of Kirkman's hands very completely finished, as far as concerned his part of the business, in autumn; & by a little management prevailed on him to send it to Walker, with tolerable good-humour. Walker undertook to place his Machine for the Celestini Stop upon it, with great readiness, finding for whom the Instrumt was made: as I discovered that he had had the honour of conversing with you *abt* the difficulties & objections on the subject of his Stop. I was glad of this, as it made him more alert & Saliticious to execute his part well. He told me that he had little doubt but that he cd put his machinery in action by clock-work, with very little use of a pedal, I let him alone to meditate & work at his leisure till the month of November, when I began to be uneasy, lest you *cd* imagine the commission had been neglected on my part. Walker was still in high spirits a*bt* the success of his new Machine, & only waited for the Clock-maker's part of the work. Last month the new Machine was applied, & though infinitely superior to the old, the motion given to it by a slight stroke or pressure of the foot, was not so desirable as I wished, or as Walker expected. He had difficulties in placing, & covering his machine, after it was made; as well as in regulating its operations. At length, after long delay some occasioned by real difficulties, & others by having like all his brethren, projected too many pursuits at a time, the machine has re*cd* all the perfection he can give it. He has promised to describe its powers & the means of exhibiting them, in a paper w*ch* will accom*py* the Instru*mt*, The Rosin will, he says, be easily brushed off the strings if adhesion from damp is not suffered to take place, by neglecting to clean the strings too long. As a Harp*d* I never heard a better instru*mt* or felt a more even & pleasant touch. The Tone is full, sweet, & equally good through the whole scale. And as to Walker's Stop, it is much more easily used than any I ever tried. It will not suit strings of execution, but is not confined to mere psalmody, as was the Case at the first invention. The machine Bow is sooner & more easily brought into contact than formerly, & is not so subject to produce a *Scream* by over pressure of the keys. It is perfectly sweet, & at a little distance *Organic*: that it reminds one of the best & most expressive part of an organ, the Swell. On the degree of pressure depends, not only the durability of tone, but its force. It will require much exercise to find out, & display, all the beauties of this Stop. You, Sir, are speculative musician sufficient to know the truth of this assertion, & to avail yourself of it. As to the Question you ask concern*g* the propensity of organs made in England or France? I can only answer that as far as I have seen, heard or examined, the mechanism of the English is infinitely superior as well as the tone of the solo stops, given the org. builder here, is a very ingenious & experimental man, & not only makes dayly discoveries & improvements himself, but readily adopts those that may be made or recommended to him by others. *Pour la forme* & ornaments The Fr. will doubtless beat us; mais, *pour le fond*, I think we always had, & still *have* it all to nothing against the rest of Europe. We are notorious for want of invention yet give us but a principle to work on, & we are sure of leaving an invention better than we find it. I write now in too great a hurry to describe the contents of such a Chamber org. as you have in meditation. Ab*t* £100 w*d* I think supply all that is wanting in such an Instru*mt*, sev*l* stops, well-varied, & chosen, will produce better Effects in a small space, than crowds of such coarse or

181

unmeaning pipes as are usually crammed into Chamber organs of any size. If I can be of the least further use in this or any other commission in my power, I beg you not to spare me, being with great respect & regard, Sir,

> Yours obedient
> & most humble Servant
> Chas Burney.

Jefferson to Burney.

Paris Feb. 12, 1787

Sir

I have been honoured with your favour of the 20*th* of January, and am now to return you my sincere thanks for your very kind attention to the instrument I had desired. Your goodness has induced you to give yourself a great deal more trouble about it than I would have presumed to propose to you. I only meant to intrude on your time so far as to give a general instruction to the workmen. Besides the value of the thing therefore, it will have an additional one with me of the nature of that which a good catholic affixes to the relick of a saint. As I shall set out within three or four days on a journey of two or three months I shall propose to Col Smith, if the instrument is not already embarked, not to send it till about the 1*st* of April when it will be less liable to be injured by bad weather. A friend of mine in America (the same who improved the quilling of the harpsichord) writes me word he is succeeding in some improvements he had proposed for the Harmonica. However imperfect this instrument is for the general mass of musical compositions, yet for those of a certain character it is delicious—we are all standing a tip-toe here to see what is to be done by the assembly of Notables—nothing certain has yet transpired as to the objects to be proposed to them. The sickness of the ministers continues to retard the meeting. I have the honour to be . . .

[Originals in Library of Congress]

APPENDIX SIXTEEN

BACH'S MUSICAL INSTRUMENTS

'Details of the Estate left by the late
Mr. Johann Sebastian Bach
formerly Cantor at the Thomas-Schule in
Leipzig, departed in God July 28, 1750'

Section VI: INSTRUMENTS

1 veneered Clavecin (*fournirt Clavecin*), which if possible is to remain in the family	80 rt.	–gr.	–pf.
1 Clavecin	50		
1 ditto	50		
1 ditto	50		
1 ditto, smaller	20		
1 Lautenwerck	30		
1 ditto	30		
1 Stainer violin	8		
1 less valuable violin	2		
1 violino piccolo	1	8	
1 Braccia	5		
1 ditto	5		
1 ditto	–	16	
1 Bassetgen	6		
1 Violoncello	6		
1 ditto	–	16	
1 Viola da gamba	3		
1 lute	21		
1 Spinettgen	3		

371 rt. 16 gr. –pf.

Johann Cristoph Bach had received from his father before his death three claviers with a set of pedals, and these are not therefore included in the inventory. Whether these were clavichords or harpsichords, and whether the pedals were simple pull-downs or a separate instrument is unknown; and speculation will not solve that problem.

[*See* Philipp Spitta's *J. S. Bach*. 2 vols. Leipzig. 1873–1880]

APPENDIX SEVENTEEN

J. A. STEIN

This list of instruments is cited by Hertz (1937) as coming from the workshop of Johann Andreas Stein in 1750. It must be remembered, however, that Stein was born in 1728; and the list is formidable for one aged twenty-two. It is possible that some error has crept into the date; but this list is none the less interesting as an example of the yearly output of one of the best known eighteenth century German makers, whatever the actual year may have been.

1 Flügel H. Schw. ger Kaufba [Kaufbeuren]	75
1 Clavecin Coleg. Beckenhaus	160
1 Flügel H gramer (?)	60
1 dito Frau Ober Postmst.	75
1 dito Christ. Gignoux	50
1 dito H v. Ranner	75
1 dito Frau Jacob v. Amann	75
Forte Piano H Knäferle	75
ditto einem Geistlichen	75
Clavecin Ihro Durchlaucht den Fürst alhir	250
Clavecin Ihro Durchl. Fürst v. Elwang [Ellwangen]	170
ein dito Frau v. Adelman	200
Clavecin der Traunerin vor welcher sich jederman zu hüten weiss (?)	200
Clavecin H Patricij	180
Clav. H. v. Erdel würtzb.	200
Forte P. Erzbischof Salzb.	200
Forte P. H. v. Kühner Memmingen	250
F.P.H. Hofmarchal	60
F.P.H. Liebert	75
Gross Flügel Bischof	140
Flügel Fraul. v. rechberg	75
Flugel Grafin glaris inspruck	200
Flugel Frau v. Aman	60
Flugel Fräul. v. Münich	75
F.P. Herrn Liebert	200
F. H. v. Horns Stein	81
Frau rentmeister Augsb.	60
Fo Pian H. Professor Bade Freyburg	230 oder 250
Flügel I H graf München	150
Forte piano H Ott Zürch	400

APPENDIX EIGHTEEN

INVENTORY OF KEYBOARD INSTRUMENTS
BELONGING TO QUEEN MARIA BARBARA OF SPAIN
(1712–1758)

Madrid, Library of Royal Palace VII E 4 305: Testament of Maria Barbara of Braganza. Appended inventory of estate. Fol. 228r to fol. 231r.

1. Pianoforte made in Florence, the whole interior of cypress, the case of black poplar coloured with dark green (*palosanto*), keyboard of boxwood and ebony, with fifty six keys, turned legs of beech.
2. Quilled harpsichord of walnut, with five registers, and four sets of strings, keyboard with fifty six keys of ebony and mother of pearl, legs of pine in three columns with carving.
3. Quilled harpsichord, the case of white poplar, the interior of cedar and cypress, with sixty one keys of ebony and mother of pearl, turned legs of beech.
4. Quilled harpsichord, formerly a pianoforte, made in Florence, the interior of cypress, the exterior coloured green, with fifty six keys of ebony and bone, on turned legs of beech.
5. Another quilled harpsichord in the same style and green colour, also made in Florence and formerly a pianoforte, with fifty keys of ebony and bone, on turned legs of beech.
6. Quilled harpsichord of walnut with three sets of strings, fifty eight keys of ebony and bone, on turned legs of beech.
7. Quilled harpsichord made in Flanders, in a dark lacquered case, three sets of strings, keyboard ebony and bone, on turned legs of beech.
8. Quilled harpsichord of walnut with three sets of strings, keyboard with fifty six keys of ebony and bone, on turned legs of beech.

Dr. Gregorio Garcia de la Vega is present and states that, in addition to the harpsichords listed above, Her Majesty left four others: two at Aranjuez, and two at San Lorenzo, of which he has details, and in accordance with which now ... they are listed.

9. Pianoforte, made in Florence, of cypress, coloured pink, keyboard of boxwood and ebony, forty nine keys, on turned legs of beech, at Aranjuez.
10. Quilled harpsichord, exterior of white poplar, interior of cedar and cypress, two sets of strings, keyboard of ebony and mother of pearl with sixty one keys, on turned legs of beech, at Aranjuez.
11. Pianoforte of cypress coloured green, keyboard of boxwood and ebony, with fifty four keys, on turned legs of beech, at the Royal seat of San Lorenzo.
12. Quilled harpsichord, case of white poplar, interior of cedar and cypress, keyboard of ebony and mother of pearl with sixty one keys, on turned legs of beech, at San Lorenzo.

For the Spanish text *see* Kirkpatrick (1953), Appendix IIIB.

COLLECTIONS OF EARLY KEYBOARD INSTRUMENTS

The following list of collections is not intended to be complete. Its purpose is to draw attention to the most interesting groups of instruments only. Collections which have been dispersed are not recorded. When there is a published catalogue the author's name and the date are given; details of the work can then be found in the list of books. A note is included of any special item or field for which a collection is noted.

AMSTERDAM Rijksmuseum. A small collection of Flemish instruments.

ANTWERP City Museums. Very rich in the work of the Ruckers family. The collections are controlled from the Vleeshuis, where most of the instruments are kept. Independent of the City museums is the collection of instruments in the Koninklijk Vlaams Conservatorium, and the harpsichord spinet in the Plantin Móretus Museum.

BAMBERG, *see* NÜRNBERG.

BARCELONA, Museo de Musica, Avenida República Argentina 1. This collection contains a harpsichord by Christian Zell of Hamburg, a Spanish clavichord by Grabalos of Tarazona, and other instruments.

BASEL, Historisches Museum. Catalogue by Karl Nef (1906).

BELLE SKINNER COLLECTION, *see* NEW HAVEN.

BENTON FLETCHER COLLECTION, *see* LONDON.

BERLIN, Musikinstrumentenmuseum (Institut für Musikforschung), Joachimsthal Gymnasium. This is the remains of the collections formerly in the Hochschule für Musik, and in the Schlossmuseum. The greater part was destroyed between 1939 and 1945, but much of importance remains. Catalogues by Fleischer (1882), Sachs (1922), Alfred Berner (1952), Irmgard Otto (1968).

BETHERSDEN, Colt Collection. While principally devoted to early pianofortes, this collection includes a Joseph Mahoon, London, double harpsichord of 1738, a Kirckman single of 1750, and possibly the last Kirckman harpsichord made, a double of 1800.

BOSTON, Mass. Museum of Fine Arts. Here is the greater part of Canon Galpin's collection, which includes a double Kirckman harpsichord of 1798, and an Andries Ruckers virginal of 1610. Catalogue by Bessaraboff (1941).

BROADWOOD COLLECTION, *see* LONDON.

BRUGES, Hôtel de Gruuthuse. A Hans Ruckers polygonal spinet, 1591, and an Andries Ruckers single manual harpsichord of 1624.

BRUSSELS, Conservatoire Royal de Musique. This one is of the largest and most important collections of all. It is rich in Flemish work of all periods, and also in Italian Instruments. France is poorly represented; from England there is a $5\frac{1}{2}$ octave Shudi harpsichord of 1773, and a virginal by Gabriel Townsend dated 1641; from Germany there is a sixteen foot Hieronymus Hass harpsichord of 1734, and one of his clavichords dated 1744. Catalogue by Mahillon.

CHARLOTTENBURG, *see* BERLIN.

CHICAGO, George F. Harding Museum. This contains a double virginal by Jan Ruckers of 1623.

CLAUDIUS COLLECTION, *see* COPENHAGEN.

COLLECTIONS OF EARLY KEYBOARD INSTRUMENTS

COLOGNE, Heyer Collection, *see* LEIPZIG.

COPENHAGEN, Carl Claudius Collection. Catalogue by Claudius (1931).

COPENHAGEN, Musikhistorisk Museum. There is a double manual harpsichord by Hieronymus Hass dated 1723, and a clavichord of 1755 by his son. Catalogue by Hammerich (1909).

CROSBY BROWN COLLECTION, *see* NEW YORK.

DEUTSCHES MUSEUM, *see* MUNICH.

DONALDSON COLLECTION, *see* LONDON.

DUBLIN, National Museum. Harpsichord and spinet by Weber of Dublin, upright harpsichord by Rother of Dublin, and other instruments.

EDINBURGH, Russell Collection. This collection, formed by the author, was presented to the University of Edinburgh in 1964. The instruments are representative of most significant countries and periods, including examples from the Antwerp workshops, and harpsichords by Hass, Kirckman, Shudi and Taskin. Catalogue by Newman and Williams (1968).

EISENACH, Bachmuseum. Various keyboard instruments including an eighteenth century German double manual harpsichord. Catalogue by Breidert and Freyse (1939).

ERLANGEN, *see* NÜRNBERG.

FLORENCE, Conservatorio 'Luigi Cherubini'. A large general collection including a few keyboard instruments by Italian and English makers. Catalogue by Gai (1969).

FORSYTH COLLECTION, *see* MANCHESTER.

FRANKFURT-AM-MAIN, Historisches Museum. Catalogue by Epstein (1927).

GEMEENTEMUSEUM, *see* HAGUE.

GÖTEBORG, The Museum. A Hieronymus Hass harpsichord of 1721, a Gottfried Silbermann spinet of 1723, a Stein organ and pianoforte combined, dated 1770, and other instruments. Catalogue by Thulin (1931).

HAGUE, Gemeente-Museum. A good general collection, representative of the Low Countries in particular. (A new catalogue by Dr. C. von Gleich is forthcoming.)

HARDING MUSEUM, *see* CHICAGO.

HEYER COLLECTION, *see* LEIPZIG.

HOLYOKE, Mass., *see* NEW HAVEN.

LEIPZIG, Heyer Collection, Stadtgeschichtliches Museum. This famous Collection formerly belonged to Wilhelm Heyer of Cologne. It was presented to Leipzig in 1927 by H. Hinrichsen. Its many riches are described in the 3 volume catalogue by Kinsky (1910–1916).

LENINGRAD (Saint Petersburg), Institute for Scientific Research on Theatre and Music. Here are kept the instruments formerly at the Hermitage.

LISBON, Conservatorio Nacional. A large general collection containing harpsichords and clavichords of Portuguese origin, a Longman and Broderip harpsichord, a double virginal by Hans Ruckers, dated 1620, etc. There is no catalogue available though a general description of the collection was published in the *Boletin do Conservatorio Nacional*, Lisbon, 1946–1947.

LIVERPOOL, Rushworth and Dreaper Collection. A small general collection. There is no detailed catalogue, but a small pamphlet is available.

LONDON, Broadwood Collection. The property of John Broadwood & Sons, this collection contains five Shudi and Broadwood harpsichords, a Thomas Hitchcock spinet, etc. There is no up to date catalogue.

LONDON, Donaldson Collection, Royal College of Music. Catalogue by Donaldson.

LONDON, Benton Fletcher Collection, at Fenton House. Particularly rich in English instruments. Catalogue by Russell (revised edition 1969).

LONDON, Victoria and Albert Museum. An important collection, rich in Flemish, Italian and English instruments, besides a clavichord by Barthold Fritz, and a harpsichord by Taskin. Catalogue by Engel (1874). A new (1968) catalogue by Russell (and others).

COLLECTIONS OF EARLY KEYBOARD INSTRUMENTS

MANCHESTER, Henry Watson Collection. This is divided between the Central Library, Manchester, and the Royal Manchester College of Music.

MANCHESTER, Forsyth Collection, 126/8 Deansgate. Contains English harpsichords, and a Hass clavichord.

METROPOLITAN MUSEUM, *see* NEW YORK.

MILAN, Castello Sforzesco. A large general collection, including a number of exceptional Italian instruments, such as a two-manual harpsichord by Pietro Todini of 1675, a Taskin double harpsichord of 1780, and a 16th-century Hans Ruckers double virginal. Catalogue by Gallini and Gallini (1963).

MUNICH, Deutsches Museum von Meisterwerken der Naturwissenschaft und Technik. A large and important collection, very well kept. It contains the sixteen foot recording pianoforte harpsichord of Merlin. There is no up to date catalogue.

NAPLES. Conservatorio di Musica S. Pietro a Maiella. The museum contains an Andries Ruckers double manual harpsichord of 1633, a Stein harpsichord and pianoforte combined, dated 1783, etc.

NEUPERT COLLECTION, *see* NÜRNBERG.

NEW HAVEN, Conn., Yale University Collection of Musical Instruments. Originally formed by instruments donated by Morris Steinert in 1900, the collection has been augmented by many accessions, including the entire Belle Skinner Collection, formerly at Holyoke, Massachusetts, in 1960, and now contains a total of 26 harpsichords and 7 clavichords. Makers represented include Blanchet, Hass, Kirckman, Leversidge, Ruckers and Taskin. Catalogue of the Belle Skinner Collection (1933). Checklist (1968).

NEW YORK, Crosby Brown Collection, Metropolitan Museum of Art. A most important collection covering every period and country. Catalogue of 1903 and guide by Winternitz (1961).

NÜRNBERG, Germanisches Nationalmuseum. The Neupert and Rück collections (formerly in Bamberg and Erlangen, respectively) have now been incorporated in the museum. The collection includes a double virginal of 1580 by van der Biest, a virtually pristine Ruckers of 1637, a Carlo Grimaldi of 1697, and a Gräbner double harpsichord of 1782. Checklist and history of the Neupert instruments by van der Meer (1969). Guide by van der Meer (1971).

OSLO, Kunstindustrimuseet. There is a single manual harpsichord, attributed to the Hass family.

OXFORD, Ashmolean Museum. There is a Kirckman harpsichord of 1772, and an Adam Leversidge virginal of 1670. Catalogue by Boyden (1969).

OXFORD, Taphouse Collection. This is largely dispersed, but a few instruments are on loan to the University Faculty of Music.

PARIS, Conservatoire National de Musique. A fine general collection containing first class instruments from France, the Low Countries, Italy and England. Catalogue by Chouquet (1875).

PARIS, La Comtesse de Chambure. A fine small collection, containing a virginal of 1598 by Hans Ruckers, seventeenth and eighteenth century French harpsichords, a pianoforte by Stein, etc.

PRAGUE, National Museum. Some of the instruments are illustrated in Buchner.

PROVIDENCE, Rhode Island School of Design, A part of the Morris Steinert collection.

ROME, Museo Nazionale. This collection was purchased from Dr. Evan Gorga by the Italian Government, and includes the Hans Müller, Leipzig, harpsichord of 1537.

RÜCK COLLECTION, *see* NÜRNBERG.

RUSHWORTH AND DREAPER COLLECTION, *see* LIVERPOOL.

SMITHSONIAN INSTITUTION, *see* WASHINGTON.

STOCKHOLM, Musikhistorisk Museet. Here is a large collection of instruments, chiefly from the Baltic countries. There is no up to date catalogue.

STOCKHOLM, Nordiska Museet. A collection of Baltic instruments, including clavichords and harpsichords.

COLLECTIONS OF EARLY KEYBOARD INSTRUMENTS

STUTTGART, Württembergisches Landesgewerbemuseum. Catalogue by Josten (1928).

TAPHOUSE COLLECTION, *see* OXFORD.

VIENNA. Gesellschaft der Musikfreunde. The instruments are on loan to the Kunsthistorisches Museum, and include Joseph Haydn's Shudi harpsichord of 1775.

VIENNA. Kunsthistorisches Museum. The collection contains the instruments mentioned above, but is particularly rich in early pianofortes. Catalogue by Luithlen (1966).

WASHINGTON, Smithsonian Institution. An important general collection. Checklist (1967) and guide by Hoover (1969).

WATSON COLLECTION, *see* MANCHESTER.

BOOKS OF REFERENCE

ADLUNG, Jacob (1768): *Musica mechanica organoedi.* . . . 2 vols. Berlin, F. W. Birnstiel. (Facsimile: Kassel, Bärenreiter, 1961.)

AGRICOLA, Martin (1529): *Musica instrumentalis deudsch.* . . . Wittenberg, George Rhaw. (Reprint: Leipzig, Breitkopf, 1896.)

ALDRICH, Henry, and TALBOT, James: Christ Church Library, Oxford. Music MS. 1187. (Partial reprint in: Hubbard (1965), 260 ff.; see also Mould (1968).)

ANTEGNATI, Costanzo (1608): *L'arte organica.* Brescia, 1608. (German translation: Magonza, 1938.)

ARNAULT, Henri: Bibliothèque Nationale, Paris, MS. fonds Latin 7295. (Edition by G. le Cerf and E.-R. Labande for Editions Auguste Picard, Paris, 1932.) (An account of this MS. by Cecil Clutton appeared in *Galpin Soc. Jl.* No. 5, 1952.)

BARNES, John (1966): *Two Rival Harpsichord Specifications.* London, *Galpin Soc. Jl.* No. 19, 1966.

BERG, A. E. (1907): *Writings of Thomas Jefferson.* Washington, D.C.

BERNER, Alfred (1952): *Die Berliner Musikinstrumentensammlung: Einführung mit historischen und technischen Erläuterungen.* Berlin.

BESSARABOFF, Nicholas (1941): *Ancient European Musical Instruments:* . . . *in the Leslie Lindsay Mason Collection at the Museum of Fine Arts.* Boston, Harvard University Press.

BIERDIMPFL, K. A. (1883): *Die Sammlung der Musik-Instrumente des Bayerischen National-Museums.* Munich.

BLANKENBERG, Quirin van (1739): *Elementa Musica.* . . . Hague, Laurens Berkoske.

BLUME, Friedrich, ed. (1949 ff.): *Die Musik in Geschichte und Gegenwart. Allgemeine Enzyklo-pädie der Musik.* . . . 14 vols. Kassel, Bärenreiter.

BOALCH, Donald (1956): *Makers of the Harpsichord and Clavichord, 1440–1840,* London, George Ronald.

BOSTON, John (1954): *An English Virginal-Maker in Chester, and his tools.* London, *Galpin Soc. Jl.* No. 7, 1954.

BOTTRIGARI, Hercole (1594): *Il Desiderio overo de' concerti di varii strumenti musicali.* Venice. (Facsimile: Berlin, Martin Breslauer, 1924.) (English translation by Carol MacClintock, Rome, American Institute of Musicology, 1962.)

BOUMAN, A. (1949): *Orgels in Nederland.* Amsterdam, Allert de Lange.

BOYD, M. C. (1940): *Elizabethan Music.* Philadelphia.

BOYDEN, David D. (1969): *Catalogue of the Hill Collection of Musical Instruments in the Ash-molean Museum, Oxford.* London, Oxford University Press.

BREIDERT, Friedrich, and FREYSE, Conrad (1939): *Verzeichnis der Sammlung alter Musikinstru-mente im Bachhause zu Eisenach.* Leipzig, Breitkopf and Härtel.

BRELIN, Niels (1741): *Svenska Vetenskaps Akademiens Handlingar.* Stockholm.

BRICQUEVILLE, Eugène de (1908): *Les ventes des instruments de musique au XVIIIe siècle.* Paris, Fischbacher.

BROWN, Mrs. John Crosby (1903–1914): *Catalogue of Keyboard Musical Instruments in the Crosby Brown Collection.* 6 vol., New York, Metropolitan Museum of Art.

BOOKS OF REFERENCE

BRUNI, A. (1890): *Un inventaire sous le Terreur.* . . . Paris, Chamerot.

BUCHNER, Alexander (n.d.): *Musical Instruments through the Ages.* (Translation by Iris Urwin.) London, Spring Books.

BURBURE, Léon de (1863): *Recherches sur les facteurs de Clavecins* . . . *d'Anvers* . . . , Brussels, Hayez. (Reprinted from: *Bulletin de l'Académie Royale de Belgique*, 2nd series, Vol. 15, No. 2, 1863.)

BURNEY, Charles (1771): *The Present State of Music in France and Italy*..., London, T. Becket & Co.

BURNEY, Charles (1773): *The Present State of Music in Germany, The Netherlands, and the United Provinces.* . . . London, T. Becket & Co.

CELLES, François Bédos de (1766–1778): *L'Art du Facteur d'Orgues.* 4 Parts. Paris. (Facsimile: Kassel, edited by Christhard Mahrenholz, 1935–1936.)

CEMBALO ANGELICO (1775): *Lettera dell' autore del nuovo Cembalo Angelico inventato in Roma nell'anno MDCCLXXV.* . . . Rome, Giovanni Zempel.

CERONE, Pietro (1613): *El Melopeo y Maestro. Tractado de musica theorica y pratica.* Naples.

CERVELLI, Luisa (1967): *Conservato a Roma il più antico clavicembalo tedesco,* . . . Rome, Edizione Palatino.

CHOUQUET, Gustave (1875): *Le Musée du Conservatoire National de Musique.* Paris, Didot. (New edition 1884, with supplements by Léon Pillaut in 1894, 1899, 1903.)

CLAUDIUS, Carl (1931): *Carl Claudius' Samling af gamle Musikinstrumenter,* Copenhagen.

CLOSSON, Ernst (1910): *Pascal Taskin. Sammelbände der Internationalen Musikgesellschaft*, XII (1910–1911).

CORRER, Giovanni (1872): *Elenco degli strumenti musicali antichi da arco, fiato, pizzico e tasto, posseduti dal Nob. Conte Giovanni Correr.* . . . Venice.

CORRETTE, Michel (1753): *Le maître de clavecin.* . . . Paris.

DALE, William (1913): *Tschudi the harpsichord maker.* London, Constable.

DENSMORE, Francis (1927): *Handbook of the collection of musical instruments in the United States National Museum.* Washington, U.S. Government Printing Office.

DENT, Edward (1949): *Notes on Continuo-playing.* London, *Monthly Musical Record*, Vol. 79, No. 906.

DEUTSCH, Otto Erich (1955): *Handel, a documentary biography.* London, A. & C. Black.

DEVRIENT, Eduard (1869): *Meine Erinnerungen an Felix Mendelssohn-Bartholdy.* . . . Leipzig.

DIDEROT, Denis (1751–1772): *Encyclopédie, ou Dictionnaire Raisonné des Sciences, des Arts et des Métiers.* 35 vols. Paris.

DONALDSON, George (1899): *Catalogue of the musical instruments and objects forming the Donaldson Museum* (in the Royal College of Music). London.

DOUWES, Klaas (1699): *Grondig ondersoek van de toonen der musijk.* . . . Franeker (in Friesland), A. Heins.

ELLIS, Alexander John (1880): *History of Musical Pitch.* London. (Summary in: Helmholtz (1885), 493 ff.).

ENGEL, Carl (1874): *A descriptive catalogue of the Musical Instruments in the South Kensington Museum.* 2nd ed., London.

ENGEL, Carl (1879): *Some account of the clavichord.* . . . London, *Musical Times*, July 1879.

ENGEL, Carl (1942): *Some Letters to a namesake.* New York, *Musical Quarterly*, Vol. XXVIII, July, 1942.

EPSTEIN, Peter (1927): *Katalog der Musikinstrumente im Historischen Museum der Stadt Frankfurt-am-Main.* Frankfurt.

ERNST, Friedrich (1955): *Der Flügel Johann Sebastian Bachs.* Frankfurt, C. F. Peters.

FÉTIS, Franz Joseph (1860–1881): *Biographie universelle des musiciens* (2me éd.). . . . 10 vols. Paris, Firmin Didot.

191

BOOKS OF REFERENCE

FLEISCHER, Oscar (1882): *Führer durch die Sammlung der Königlichen Hochschule für Musik in Berlin*. Berlin.

FORKEL, Johann Nicolaus (1802): *Über J. S. Bach's Leben, Kunst and Kunstwerke*. Leipzig.

FRITZ, Barthold (1756): *Anweisung wie man Claviere, Clavecins, und Orgeln, nach einer mechanischen Art, in allen zwölf Tönen gleich rein stimmen könne, das aus solchen allen sowohl dur als moll wohlklingend zu spielen sey*. . . . Leipzig, Breitkopf.

GAI, Vinicio (1969): *Gli strumenti musicali della corte medicea e il Museo del Conservatorio 'Luigi Cherubini' di Firenze*. Florence, Licosa.

GALLINI, Natale and Franco (1963): *Museo degli strumenti musicali. Catalogo*. . . . Milan, Castello Sforzesco.

GALPIN, Francis (1910): *Old English Instruments of music*. London, Methuen. (4th ed., revised by Dart, 1965.)

GALPIN, Francis (1937): *A textbook of European Musical Instruments*. London, Williams & Norgate.

GERBER, Ernst Ludwig (1790–1792): *Historisch-biographisches Lexicon der Tonkünstler*. . . . 2 vols. Leipzig, Breitkopf. (New ed. 4 vols. 1812–1814, Leipzig.)

GÖHLINGER, Franz August (1910): *Geschichte des Klavichords*. Basel, Birkhäuser.

GOUGH, Hugh (1954): *Clavichord*. London, *Grove's Dictionary*.

GROVE, George (1954): *Dictionary of Music and Musicians*, 9 vols. 5th ed. by Eric Blom. London, Macmillan.

HALFPENNY, Eric (1946): *Shudi and the Venetian Swell*. London, *Music and Letters*, July, 1946.

HAMMERICH, Angul (1911): *Das Musikhistorische Museum zu Kopenhagen*. . . . (German translation) Copenhagen.

HARDING, Rosamond (1933): *The Piano-forte*. . . . Cambridge University Press.

HELMHOLTZ, Hermann L. F. (1885): *On the Sensations of Tone*. . . . 2nd English ed., translated and with additional notes by Alexander J. Ellis, London, Longmans Green. (Reprint: New York, Dover Publications, 1954.)

HERTZ, Eva (1937): *J. A. Stein: ein Beitrag zur Geschichte des Klavierbaues*. Wolfenbüttel & Berlin, Kallmeyer.

HESS, Joachim (1774): *Disposition der merkwaardigste Kerk-Orgelen, welke in ons Nederland, als mede in Duitsland en elders aangetroffen worden*. Gouda, J. van der Klos.

HESS, Joachim (1779): *Korte en eenvoudige Handleyding tot het Leeren van t' Clavecimbel of Orgel-Spel*. . . . Gouda, Johann van der Klos.

HIPKINS, A. J. (1885): *Guide to the Loan Collection* (of the International Inventions Exhibition, London), *and list of Musical Instruments*. . . . London, William Clowes.

HIPKINS, A. J. (1886): *The Old Clavier or Keyboard Instruments; their use by composers, and technique*. London, *Proceedings of the Musical Association*, Vol.12.

HIPKINS, A. J. (1888): *Musical instruments, historic, rare, and unique*. . . . (Plates by William Gibb.) London, A. & C. Black. (Re-issue: 1921.)

HIPKINS, A. J. (1896): *A description and history of the Pianoforte and of the older Keyboard stringed instruments*. London, Novello. (There is an undated revised edition.)

HIRT, Franz Josef (1955): *Meisterwerke des Klavierbaues*. . . . Olten, Urs Graf-Verlag.

HOOVER, Cynthia, ed. (1967): *A Checklist of the Keyboard Instruments*. . . . Washington, Smithsonian Institution.

HOOVER, Cynthia (1969): *Harpsichords and Clavichords*. Washington, Smithsonian Institution.

HUBBARD, Frank (1950): *Two Early English Harpsichords*. London, *Galpin Soc. Jl*. No. 3, 1950.

HUBBARD, Frank (1956): *The* Encyclopédie *and the French Harpsichord*. London, *Galpin Soc. Jl*. No. 9, 1956.

HUBBARD, Frank and HARDOUIN, P. J. (1957): *Harpsichord Making in Paris: Part I, Eighteenth Century*. London, *Galpin Soc. Jl*. No. 10, 1957.

BOOKS OF REFERENCE

HUBBARD, Frank (1965); *Three Centuries of Harpsichord Making.* Cambridge, Mass., Harvard University Press.

JAMES, Philip (1930): *Early Keyboard instruments.* London, Peter Davies.

JEANS, Susi (1950): *The Pedal Clavichord and other Practice Instruments of Organists.* London, *Proceedings of the Royal Musical Association,* Vol. 77.

JOBERNARDI, Bartolomeo (1634): *Tratado de la Musica.* National Library, Madrid, MS. 8931. (Extracts printed in *Anuario Musical,* Vol. 8.)

JOSTEN, Hanns H. (1928): *Württembergisches Landesgewerbemuseum. Die Sammlung der Musikinstrumente.* Stuttgart.

KINSKY, Georg (1910): *Musikhistorisches Museum von Wilhelm Heyer. Vol. I.* Cologne, Wilhelm Heyer.

KINSKY, Georg (1924): *Zur Echtheitsfrage des Berliner Bach-Flügels.* Leipzig, Bach-Jahrbuch, 1924, Breitkopf & Härtel.

KINSKY, Georg (1930): *A History of Music in Pictures.* London, J. M. Dent.

KIRCHER, Athanasius (1650): *Musurgia universalis sive ars magna consoni et dissoni.* Rome.

KIRKPATRICK, Ralph (1938): *The Goldberg Variations, edited for the harpsichord or piano.* New York, Schirmer.

KIRKPATRICK, Ralph (1953): *Domenico Scarlatti.* Princeton University Press.

KLOTZ, Hans (1934): *Über die Orgelkunst der Gotik, der Renaissance und des Barock.* Kassel, Bärenreiter.

KRIEGER, Johann (1699): *Anmutige Clavierübung.* Nürnberg.

LAFONTAINE, H. C. de (1909): *The King's Musick.* London, Macmillan.

LAMBRECHTS-DOUILLEZ, Janine, ed. (1971): *Colloqium-Restauratieproblemen van Antwerpse klavecimbels.* Antwerp, Ruckers Genootschap.

LANFRANCO, Giovan Maria (1533): *Scintille di musica.* ... Brescia, Britannico.

LEMME, F. C. W. (1802): *Anweisung und Regeln zu einer zweckmässigen Behandlung englischer und deutscher Pianofortes und Klaviere.* Brunswick.

LLOYD, Ll. S. (1954): *Acoustics, Standard Pitch.* London, *Grove's Dictionary,* 5th ed.

LÖHLEIN, Georg Simon (1773): *Clavier-Schule.* ... Leipzig.

LOUBET DE SCEAURY, Paul (1949): *Musiciens et facteurs d'instruments de musique sous l'Ancien Régime: statuts corporatifs.* Paris, Pedone.

LUITHLEN, Victor, and WEGERER, Kurt (1966): *Katalog der Sammlung alter Musikinstrumente I. Teil Saitenklaviere.* Vienna, Kunsthistorisches Museum, Neue Burg.

MACQUOID, Percy, and EDWARDS, Ralph (1954): *The Dictionary of English Furniture.* 2nd edition. 3 vols. London, Country Life.

MAEYER, René de (1969): *Exposition des instruments de musique des XVIème et XVIIème siècles* ... Brussels, Musée Instrumental.

MAHILLON, Victor (1893–1922): *Catalogue descriptif et analytique du Musée Instrumental du Conservatoire Royal de Musique de Bruxelles.* 5 vols. Brussels and Ghent.

MARCUSE, Sibyl (1960): *Musical Instruments at Yale* .... New Haven, Yale University Art Gallery.

MARCUSE, Sibyl (1964): *Musical Instruments—a Comprehensive Dictionary.* New York, Doubleday, 1964; London, Country Life Press, 1966.

MARPURG, Friedrich Wilhelm (1754–1778): *Historisch-kritische Beyträge zur Aufnahme der Musik.* 5 vols. Berlin.

MARPURG, Friedrich Wilhelm (1762): *Die Kunst das Clavier zu spielen.* (4th ed.) Berlin.

MARPURG, Friedrich Wilhelm (1755): *Anleitung zum Clavierspielen.* ... Berlin.

MATTHESON, Johann (1713): *Das neu-eröffnete Orchestre (Orchester).* ... Hamburg.

MATTHESON, Johann (1722–1725): *Critica Musica.* ... 2 vols. Hamburg.

BOOKS OF REFERENCE

MATTHESON, Johann (1740): *Grundlage einer Ehrenpforte*. Hamburg. (Reprint: Berlin Liepmaunssohn, 1910.)

MEER, J. H. van der (1966): *Beiträge zum Cembalobau im deutschen Sprachgebiet bis 1700*. Nürnberg, *Anzeiger des germanischen National-museums*, 1966.

MEER, J. H. van der (1969): *Die klavierhistorische Sammlung Neupert*. Nürnberg, *Anzeiger des germanischen Nationalmuseums*, 1969.

MEER, J. H. van der (1971): *Wegweiser durch die Sammlung historischer Musikinstrumente*. Nürnberg, Germanisches Nationalmuseum, 1971.

MEEÙS, Nicolas (1970): *Le clavecin de Johannes Couchet, Anvers, 1646*. Brussels, *Bulletin No. 1 du Musée Instrumental de Bruxelles*, 1970.

MENDEL, Arthur (1948): *Pitch in the Sixteenth and Early Seventeenth Centuries*. New York, *Musical Quarterly*, Vol. XXXIV.

MENDEL, Arthur (1949): *Devices for Transposition in the Organ before 1600*. Copenhagen, *Acta Musicologica*, Vol. 21, 1949.

MENDEL, Arthur (1955): *On the Pitches used in Bach's Time*. New York, *Musical Quarterly*, Vol. XLI, 1955.

MERSENNE, Marin (1636–1637): *Harmonie Universelle.* . . . Paris, Pierre Ballard. (English translation of the books on instruments by R. E. Chapman, The Hague, Nijhoff, 1957.)

MEUSEL, Johann Georg (1808–1814): *Teutsches Künstlerlexicon*. 3 vols., 2nd ed. Lemgo.

MOOSER, R. A. (1950–1955): *Annales de la musique . . . en Russie au XVIIIe siècle*. 3 vols. Geneva.

MOULD, Charles (1968): *James Talbot's Manuscript* (*Christ Church Library Musical Manuscript 1187*). London, *Galpin Soc. Jl.* No. 21, 1968.

NASSARE, Pablo (1724): *Escuela musaic, segun la practica moderna, dividida en primera, y segunda parte*. Zaragoza.

NEF, Karl (1906): *Katalog der Musikinstrumente im Historischen Museum zu Basel*. Basel.

NEUPERT, J. C. (1938): *Führer durch das musikhistorische Museum Neupert in Nürnberg*. Nürnberg.

NEUPERT, Hanns (1969): *Das Cembalo*. Kassel, Bärenreiter, 4th ed. 1969. (English translation: *Harpsichord Manual*, by F. H. Kirby.)

NEUPERT, Hanns (1952): *Vom Musikstab zum modernen Klavier*. Berlin, Otto Krause.

NEUPERT, Hanns (1965): *Das Klavichord* (3rd ed.) (English translation by A. P. P. Feldberg, *The Clavichord*.) Both Kassel, Bärenreiter, 1965.

NEVEN, Armand (1970): *L'Arpicordo*. Basel, *Acta Musicologica*, Vol. XLII, 1970.

NEWMAN, Sidney and WILLIAMS, Peter (1968): *The Russell Collection and Other Early Keyboard Instruments in St. Cecilia's Hall, Edinburgh*. Edinburgh University Press.

NORLIND, Tobias (1939): *Systematik der Saiteninstrumente*. (*Musikhistorisches Museum, Stockholm*.) 2 vols. Hanover, Albert Küster.

OTTO, Irmgard (1968): *Das Musikinstrumenten-Museum Berlin*. Berlin, Staatliches Institut für Musikforschung.

PARIS (1900): *Exposition Universelle Internationale. Musée rétrospectif de la Classe 17, Instruments de musique.* . . . Paris.

PETRI, Johann Samuel (1767): *Anleitung zur practischen Musik, vor neuangehende Sänger und Instrumentspieler*. Lauben.

PIERRE, Constant (1893): *Les facteurs d'instruments de musique, les luthiers, et la facture instrumentale: précis historique*. Paris, Sagot.

POLS, André M. (1942): *De Ruckers en de Klavierbouw en Vlaanderen*. Antwerp, de Nederlandse Boekhandel.

PRAETORIUS, Michael (1619): *Syntagmatis musici . . . tomus secundus de organographia.* . . . Wolfenbüttel, Elias Holwein. (Facsimile: Kassel, Barenreiter 1929.)

PROFETA, Rosario (1942): *Storia e letteratura degli strumenti musicali*. Florence, Marzocco.

PULITI, Leto (1874): *Cenni storici della vita del . . . Ferdinando dei Medici . . . e della origine del pianoforte*. Florence, *Atti dell' Accademia del R. Istituto Musicale*. . . . 12th year.

PYNE, J. Kendrick (1888): *Catalogue of musical instruments principally illustrative of the history of the pianoforte, the property of Henry Boddington*. Manchester.

RÉGIBO, Abel (1897): *Catalogue d'une . . . bibliothèque musicale et d'une collection d'antiquités*. Renaix.

REICHARDT, Johann Friedrich (1774–1776): *Briefe eines aufmerksamen Reisenden*. Frankfurt and Leipzig.

REPHANN, Richard (1968): *Checklist*. New Haven, Yale Collection of Musical Instruments.

REYNVAAN, Joos Verschuere (1795): *Muzykaal Kunst-woordenboek*. . . . Amsterdam, W. Brave.

RIMBAULT, Edward Francis (1860): *The pianoforte . . . with some account of the clavichord, the virginal, the spinet, the harpsichord, etc.* London, R. Cocks.

RIPIN, Edwin M. (1967): *The French Harpsichord before 1650*. London, *Galpin Soc. Jl.* No. 20, 1967.

RIPIN, Edwin M. (1967): *The Early Clavichord*. New York, *Musical Quarterly*, Vol. LIII, 1967.

RIPIN, Edwin M. (1968): *The Two Manual Harpsichord in Flanders before 1650*. London, *Galpin Soc. Jl.* No. 21, 1968.

RIPIN, Edwin M. (1969): *The Couchet Harpsichord in the Crosby Brown Collection*. New York, *Metropolitan Museum Journal*, Vol. II, 1969.

RIPIN, Edwin M. (1970): *A Reassessment of the Fretted Clavichord*. London, *Galpin Soc. Jl.* No. 23, 1970.

RIPIN, Edwin M., ed. (1971): *Keyboard Instruments—Studies in Keyboard Organology*. Edinburgh University Press.

ROMBOUTS, T., and LERIUS, T. van (1864–1872): *De liggeren en andere historische Archieven der Antwerpsche St Lucasgilde*. 2 vols. Antwerp.

RUSSELL, Raymond (1954): *List of Instruments made by the Ruckers Family*. London, *Grove's Dictionary*, Vol. 7. pp. 304–324.

RUSSELL, Raymond (1956): *The Harpsichord since 1800*. London, *Proceedings of the Royal Musical Association*, Vol. 82.

RUSSELL, Raymond (1957): *Catalogue of the Benton Fletcher collection of Early Keyboard Instruments*. . . . London, Country Life Press for the National Trust (revised ed. 1969).

RUSSELL, Raymond (1968): *Victoria and Albert Museum Catalogue of Musical Instruments: Vol. I. Keyboard Instruments*. London, H.M.S.O.

SACHS, Curt (1922): *Sammlung alter Musikinstrumente bei der Staatlichen Hochschule für Musik zu Berlin. Beschreibender Katalog*. . . . Berlin, Julius Bard.

SACHS, Curt (1940): *The History of Musical Instruments*. New York, Norton; London, Dent, 1942.

SASSE, Konrad, ed. (1966): *Katalog zu den Sammlungen des Händel-Hauses in Halle, 5. Teil-Musikinstrumentsammlung—Besaitete Tasteninstrumente*. Halle, Händel-Haus.

SAVOYE, (1882): *Catalogue des instruments de musique*. . . . Paris.

SCHLICK, Arnold (1511): *Spiegel der Orgelmacher und Organisten*. . . . Heidelberg. (Reprinted in modern German by Ernst Flade: Mainz, Paul Smetz, 1932.)

SCHLOSSER, Julius (1920): *Die Sammlung alter Musikinstrumente. Beschreibendes Verzeichnis*. (Kunsthistorisches Museum.) Vienna, Anton Schroll.

SCHOTT, Howard (1971): *Playing the Harpsichord*. London, Faber; New York, St. Martin's Press.

SHORTRIDGE, John D. (1960): *Italian Harpsichord Building in the 16th and 17th Centuries*. Washington, *Smithsonian Institution Bulletin*, No. 225, 1960.

SKINNER, William (1933): *The Belle Skinner Collection of Musical Instruments*. Holyoke.

BOOKS OF REFERENCE

SNOECK, César (1894): *Catalogue de la collection d'instruments de musique anciens ou curieux de C. C. Snoeck*. Ghent.

SNOECK, César (1903): *Catalogue de la collection d'instruments de musique flamands et néerlandais de C. C. Snoeck*. Ghent.

STEINERT, M. (1893): *Catalogue of the M. Steinert Collection of Keyed and Stringed Instruments*. New Haven, Conn.

STEINERT, Morris (1900): *Reminiscences of Morris Steinert, compiled and arranged by Jane Marlin*. New York and London, Putnam.

STELLFELD, J. A. (1942): *Bronnen tot de geschiedenis der Antwerpsche clavecimbel- en orgelbouwers in de XVIe en XVII eeuwen*. Antwerp, Drukkeri Gresseler.

STRAETEN, Edmond van der (1867–1888): *La musique aux Pays Bas*. . . . 8 vols. Brussels. (Reprint: New York, Dover Publications, 1968.)

SUMNER, W. L. (1962): *The Organ*. London, MacDonald, 3rd ed.

THULIN, Otto (1931): *Historiska Avdelningen, Göteborgs Museum. Musikinstrument*. Gothenburg, Elanders Boktryckeri.

TÜRK, Daniel Gottlob (1789): *Clavierschule*. Leipzig and Halle. (2nd ed. 1802.) (Facsimile: Kassel, Bärenreiter, 1962.)

UFFENBACH, Zacharias von (1753–1754): *Merkwürdige Reisen durch Niedersachsen, Holland und Engelland*. Frankfurt. (Translation: *London in 1710*, by W. H. and W. C. J. Quarrell. London.)

UNIVERSAL DIRECTOR (1763): London, J. Coote.

UPDIKE, Daniel Berkeley (1922): *Printing Types*. . . . Oxford University Press.

VALDRIGHI, Luigi Franceso (1884): *Nomocheliurgografia antica e moderna, ossia elenco di fabbricatori di strumenti armonici*. . . . With 5 suppls. Modena, Società Tipografica.

VANNES, René (1951): *Dictionnaire universel des luthiers*. 2nd ed. Brussels, Les Amis de la Musique.

VICENTINO, Nicola (1555): *L'antica musica ridotta alla moderna prattica*. Rome.

VICENTINO, Nicola (1561): *Descrizione dell'arciorgano, nel quale si possono eseguire i tre generi della musica diatonica, cromatica, ed enarmonica*. Venice.

VIRDUNG, Sebastian (1511): *Musica getutscht*. . . . Basel. (Facsimiles: Berlin, Robert Eitner, 1882; Kassel, L. Schrade, 1931.)

WALTHER, Johann Gottfried (1732): *Musikalisches Lexicon*. . . . Leipzig, Wolffgang Deer. (Facsimile: Kassel, Bärenreiter-Verlag, 1953.)

WERCKMEISTER, Andreas (1681): *Orgelprobe*. . . . Frankfurt and Leipzig. (2nd ed. 1698.)

WINTERNITZ, Emanual (1961): *Keyboard Instruments in the Metropolitan Museum of Art*. New York, Metropolitan Museum.

WIT, Paul de (1892): *Perlen aus der Instrumentensammlung Paul de Wit*. Leipzig.

WOODFILL, Walter (1953): *Musicians in English Society from Elizabeth to Charles I*. Princeton University Press.

ZARLINO, Gioseffe (1558): *Istitutioni armoniche*. . . . Venice.

ZIMB: *Zeitschrift für Instrumentenbau*. Leipzig, 1880–1943.

ZIMG: *Zeitschrift der Internationalen Musikgesellschaft*. Leipzig, 1900–1914.

INDEX

Italic numerals denote plates or plate commentaries.

INDEX

INDEX

Longshall, J., 86
Longside, 20, 94, *66, 67*
Loosemore ,J., 86
Lorillart, M., 55
Los Angeles, 69, 70, 73
Lostange, 153
Louis XI, King of France, 53
Louis XIV, King of France, 55
Louis XV, King of France, 59
Lucca, 143, 144
Lucerne, M., 153
Lugt, D. van der, 50
Lukey, 83, 84
Lundborg, P., 112
Luscinius, 95
Lusignan, 154
Lute, 104, 157, 158, 159, 183
  Tone imitated by harp stop, 71, 137, 141
Lute stop, 15
  English, 49, 70, 78, *1, 61*
  Flemish, 49
  German, 49, 102, *86, 88*
  Italian, 28 *31*
Lute strings 65
Lyons, 62
Lyme Park, 74, *63*
Lyrichord, 84, 89
Lyster, Mr., 87

M. Don Josef, 117
Macdonnell:
  A., 87
  D., 87
  J., 87
Mace, T., 70, 71, *55*
Machine stop, 34, 79, 80, 81, 82, 84, 87, 90, 120, *72, 75*
Mack, H. L., 106
Maddey, 86
Madrid:
  Chapel Royal, 116
  Church of Our Lady, 116
  Don Josef M., 117
  Museo del Prado, 45
  Royal Palace Library, 185
  St. Martin's, 116
Maffei, S., 37
Magdeburg, 95
Mahieu, J., 49
Mahillon, V., 186
Mahogany, 82, 91–2, 94, 153, 179
Mahoon, J., 84, 93
Maidstone, 165
Maine, Henry de la, 87
Maler, S., 27
Malmsbury, Earl of, 168, *62*
Manchester, 86
  Cathedral, 13
  Central Library, 81, 122, 188
  Royal College of Music, 122, 188
Manichord, 21, 54, 87
Manners, Lady Luisa, 83
Manocordio, 116, 117
Maplewood, 92
Marbeuf, 154
Marbling, 51, 52, 110, *28*

Maria Barbara, Queen of Spain, 38, 117, 185
Maria Theresa, Empress, 163
Marius, J., 55, 57, 125, *45*
Markneukirchen, 104
Marpurg, F. W., 30, 107
Marquetry, 70, 83, 92, 93, 94, 111, *43, 59, 66, 67*
Marseilles, 62
Marsham, A., 65
Martin, 113
Martorell, 116
Marx, O., 39
Mary, Queen of Scots, 67
Mattheson, J., 105
Maubec, 152
Maywaldt, J. C., 113
Mazlowski, 113
Mears, Mr., 76
Meccoli, Federigo, 38
Meck, 114
Medici, Cosimo III de, 37, 125
Medici, Ferdinando de, 37, 57, 125–130, 145
Meerane, 105
Meeùs, N., 45
Meidling, A., *81A*
Meissen, 87
Melville, Sir James, 67
Memmingen, 184
Mendel, A., 18, 45
Mendelssohn, F., 121
Menus-Plaisirs, 59, 153
Mercator, M., 87
Mercier, P., 168, *62*
Merde d'oie, 63, 154
Merlin, J. J., 85, 86, 188
  his Invalid Chair, *79*
Mersenne, M., 30, 54
Metropolitan Museum, New York, 29, 30, 31, 38, 42, 43, 46, 47, 62, 88, 93, 99, 106, 149, 188
  Collection formed, 123
Meusel, J., 120
Mezzo Cimbalo, 144
Michigan University, 29, 37, 38
Migliai, A., 143
Milan, 37, 60–1, 121, 144, 188
Milchmeyer, P. J., 106
Milesi, 143
Milton, Massachusetts, 91
Minnesingers, 23
Mirecourt, 154
Mirouet, M., *36*
Modena, 27
Moermans, H., 42
Moferrez, 115
Møller, H. P., 113
Mombiela, D. O. y, 117
Mondini, G., 125, 144
Monochord, 22, 23, 95, 96
Montmorency, 152
'Moor of Çaragoça,' 115
More, the, 67, 159
Morley, John, 143
Mornington, Lord, 87
Mors, A., 41
Moscheles, Ignaz, 121

Moscow, Bolshoi Theatre, 114, 123
Moscow Gazette, 114
Moshack, M. G., 113
Moss, 113
Mother of Pearl, 110, 117, 185 *85, 86, 94*
Mottoes for decoration, 51, 52, *24, 27, 31*
Mountjoy, Lord, 68
Mount Vernon, 88, 89
Mozart, W. A., 109
Müller, Hans, 27, 95
Munich, 106, 184, 188, *81B*
Muselar, 21, 47
Museums, Formation of, 119, 121–123, 186–9
Musical Association, 122
Music desks, 94, 126, 127, 129, 130, 153, 179, *72, 75*

Nadreau, 152
Nails, 126, 127, 129
Namur, 43
Naples, 30, 109, 143, 188
Naples Fustian, 155, 158
Nasino, 135
Nassare, Pablo, 116, 117
Naubauer, F., *see* Neubauer
Neers, A. van, 146
Nef, K., 186
Nepridi, *see* Pedrini, T.
Nesle, J., 32
Nettlefold Castle, 83
Neubauer, Charlotte, 84
  F., 84
Neupert Collection, 29, 35, 38, 39, 105, 187, 188, *91*
Newhall, 67, 159
New Haven, 188
New York, 88, 104, 188
Nicholas II of Russia, 114, 123
Nieve, Count of, 116
Nixon, T., 169
Noailles, 152, 153
Nomenclature:
  Clavichord, 21, 23, 66, 116, 117
  Harpsichord, 21, 96, 108, 116
  Spinet and Virginal, 20, 21, 47, 66, 95, 96, 116
Norgate, E., 69, 161
Normanton, Lord, 87
Norton, W., 65
Nottingham Castle, 159
Nürnberg, 188
  Germanisches Nationalmuseum, 188, *91, 92*
Nürnbergisch Geigenwerck, 97
Nut, 14, 28, 56, 66, 78
Nyack, 35

Oak, 46, 63, 75, 91–3, 179, *57*
Obert, 62
Octave strings, *see* Clavichord, Harpsichord, Spinet, Virginal, Four foot stop
Odense, 113
Olive wood, *93*
Oncia, 132, *17*

203

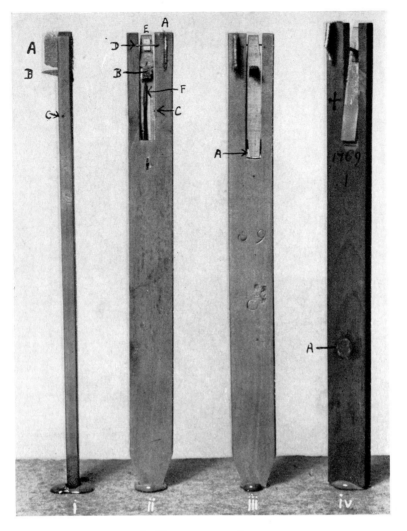

1. HARPSICHORD JACKS

(i) The left side.
    A. The Damper.
    B. The Plectrum (of leather).

(ii) The back.
    A. The Damper.
    B. The Plectrum.
    C. The Pivot Pin for the Tongue.
    D. The wire to limit the backward movement of the Tongue and Plectrum.

C. The end of the pin on which the Tongue pivots.

E. The Tongue, bearing near the top a pad of white buff leather. The latter reduces the sound caused by the Tongue striking the wire D.

F. The upright spring of hog's bristle which holds the Tongue in a vertical position.

(iii) The front.
    Note the lower part of the mortice, A, which is cut at an angle, to limit the forward movement of the Tongue and Plectrum.

    The above three jacks are taken from the Lute register of a Jacob Kirckman harpsichord of 1755 (Plates 66–68). [Actual Height: 5″.]

(iv) The Plectrum and Tongue are here shown pressed back into the position of escapement, assumed when the plectrum falls past the string on the release of a key. This jack is from the upper keyboard register of a Pascal Taskin harpsichord of 1769 (Plates 47–48). The plectrum is of quill. Observe the lead weight, A, to assist the prompt return of the jack: a rare feature in old harpsichords, but sometimes found in the upper keyboard jacks.

2. HARPSICHORD WITH SHORT AND BROKEN OCTAVE FROM C

Key E   sounds C.   Key F♯ (back) sounds F♯.
 ,,   F♯ (front) ,,   D.   ,,   G.   ,,   G♯.
 ,,   G♯ (front) ,,   E.   ,,   G♯ (back)   ,,   G♯.
 ,,   F   ,,   F.
and thence upwards chromatically.
See page 17.

Harpsichord by Faby of Bologna, 1677.

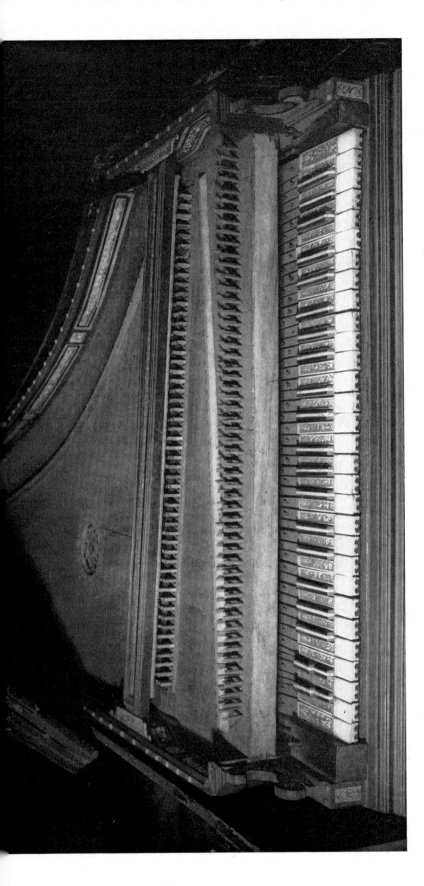

3. HARPSICHORD WITH SHORT AND BROKEN OCTAVE FROM GG

Key BB   sounds GG.   Key C♯ (back) sounds C♯.
 ,, C♯ (front) ,, AA.   ,, D   ,, D.
 ,, D♯ (front) ,, BB.   ,, D♯ (back) ,, D♯.
 ,, C   ,, C.
 and thence upwards chromatically.
 See page 17.

Harpsichord by Faby of Bologna, 1691.

Conservatoire, Paris

4. CLAVICHORD ACTION

Observe:

    A. The Tangents.   B. The Dampers.

See page 22.

Clavichord by Gottfried Horn, 1790.

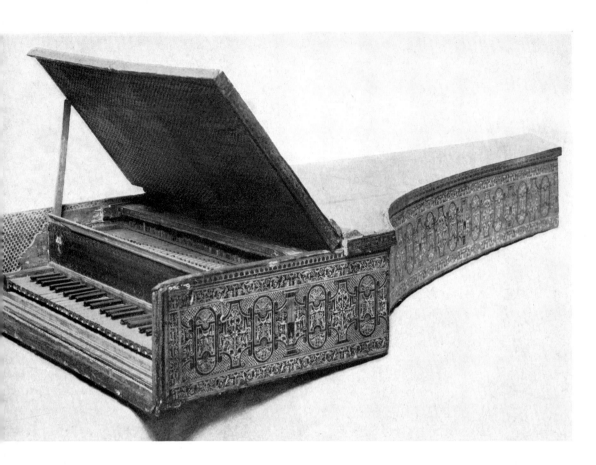

5. Harpsichord by Jerome of Bologna, 1521

This is the earliest domestic keyboard instrument at present known, the inscription and date of which are accepted as authentic. Above the keyboard, on a panel of gilt tooled leather, is stamped:

Hieronymus Bononiensis faciebat Romae MDXXI

and also the following elegiac couplet:

Aspicite ut trahitur suavi modulamine vocis
Quicquid habent aer sidera terra fretum.

The harpsichord is built of cypress wood; and, in typical Italian manner, it can be removed from the outer case, which is covered with gilt tooled leather and lined with green velvet.

Dimensions: 6′ 3″ × 2′ 7½″ × 0′ 8″.

Victoria and Albert Museum

6. SOUNDBOARD OF PRECEDING
HARPSICHORD

Compass: C – d³, bass short octave. Boxwood naturals, ebony accidentals.

Two eight foot sets of strings, and two rows of jacks which are permanently fixed 'on'.

Scaling: C: 57½″, c²: 10½″, d³: 4½″.

Plucking point: C: 5¼″, d³: 1¼″.

The underside of the instrument is cut away beneath the lowest fourteen keys to admit cords or trackers, originally attached to pedals, though these are now missing. This use of Italian harpsichords and spinets as practice instruments for organists is not uncommon.

Observe the angle in the base of the bridge, (A), a typical Italian feature. The rose, (B), is of varnished leather.

Victoria and Albert Museum

(This photograph was made before restoration by Andrew Doug in 1964. Details of the alteratio made in the course of the instrumen history are given in Russell's ca logue of this collection on pp. 29–3

7. Harpsichord by Baffo of Venice, 1574

Compass: C – f³ chromatic. A chromatic bass, though rare, is occasionally to be seen in sixteenth century Italian instruments.

Two eight foot sets of strings, and two rows of jacks which are fixed 'on'.

Scaling: C: $74\frac{1}{2}''$, c²: $13\frac{1}{2}''$, f³: $4\frac{1}{2}''$.

Plucking Point: C: $6\frac{1}{2}''$, f³: $1\frac{3}{8}''$.

Observe the angle in the bass of the bridge, (A), the carved wood rose, (B), and the diagonally placed jacks, (C), which are typical Italian features.

The harpsichord has been removed from the outer case.

Dimensions: $7' 1'' \times 2' 8\frac{3}{4}'' \times 0' 7\frac{1}{2}''$.

Victoria and Albert Museum

(This photograph was made before restoration by John Barnes in 1964. Details of the alterations made in the course of the instrument's history are given in Russell's catalogue of this collection on pp. 34–35.)

8. ORGAN HARPSICHORD (CLAVIORGAN) BY BERTOLOTTI OF VENICE, 1585

There is one keyboard, with boxwood naturals and ebony accidentals, compass GG – c³, bass short octave. This is the compass of the harpsichord. The organ extends from C to c³. The harpsichord has one set of strings each at eight foot and four foot pitch, and two sets of jacks. The four foot bridge, A, and the eight foot bridge, B, will be noted. The two sets of jacks are moved by the two hand stops, C.

Scaling: Eight foot: GG: $73\frac{1}{4}''$, c²: $9\frac{3}{4}''$, c³: $5\frac{1}{8}''$.
                Four foot: GG: $41\frac{5}{8}''$, c²: $5''$, c³: $2\frac{3}{8}''$.

Plucking   Eight foot: GG: $5\frac{1}{2}''$, c³: $1\frac{1}{2}''$.
Point: Four foot: GG: $5\frac{1}{2}''$, c³: $1\frac{3}{4}''$.

The organ by Gottlob W. S. Gut (1657 or 1677?) is German and has three ranks of pipes controlled by the levers at D: a four foot wood, a quint wood, a two foot metal.

Dimensions: $7'\ 3\frac{1}{4}'' \times 2'\ 9\frac{1}{4}''$. The harpsichord is $7\frac{1}{4}''$ deep.

Conservatoire, Brussels

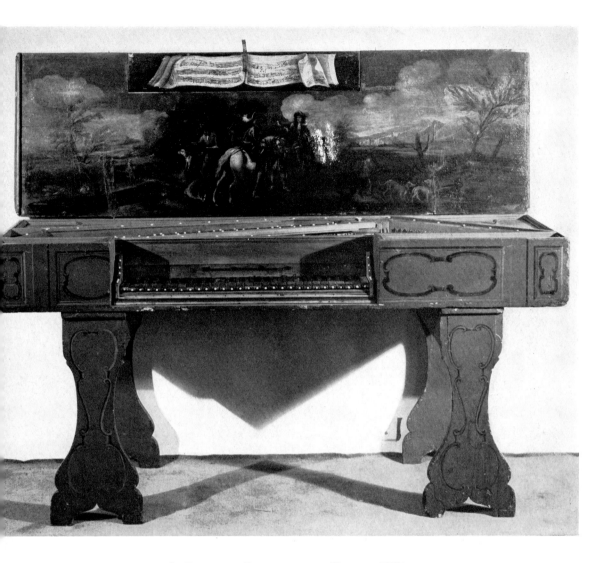

9. Spinet by Bertolotti of Venice, 1585

The instrument is made of cypress wood, and is contained in an outer case from which it can be removed in the usual Italian manner. The outer case is painted dark green.

Observe the decorative use of ivory headed studs, and the inscription branded above the keyboard. Both are typical Italian features.

Dimensions: $5'\ 6\frac{1}{2}'' \times 1'\ 9'' \times 0'\ 8''$.

Russell Collection, Edinburgh

10. SOUNDBOARD OF PRECEDING SPINET

Compass: C – f³, bass short octave. This compass together with one pitched a fourth below, GG – c³, bass short octave, are the two basic Italian keyboard compasses; but that illustrated here is much the more common.

Scaling: C : 50½", c² : 13", f³ : 5".

Plucking
Point: C : 9½", f³ : 3¼".

The lowest key is provided with a slot for an extra jack, marked A, together with wrestpin (B), nuts (C and D), and hitch pin (E), for an extra string, thereby facilitating an additional tonic or dominant note in the bass.

Observe the jacks which pass directly through slots cut in the soundboard, and not through a slide; also the five sided spinet with projecting keyboard, which is contained in a rectangular outer case, the surplus space being enclosed to form boxes with lids.

Russell Collection, Edinburgh

11. CLAVICHORD, SIXTEENTH CENTURY
Probably Italian workmanship

Compass: C – c³, bass short octave, 45 keys.

This clavichord is fretted (page 24), and has 19 pairs of strings which are allotted thus:

1st pair : C.
2nd ,, : F.
3rd ,, : D.
4th ,, : G.
5th ,, : E.
6th ,, : A.
7th ,, : B♭.

8th pair : B.
9th ,, : c, c♯, d.
10th ,, : d♯, e, f, f♯.
11th ,, : g, g♯, a.
12th ,, : b♭, b, c¹, c¹♯.
13th ,, : d¹, d¹♯, e¹.

14th pair : f¹, f¹♯, g¹, g¹♯.
15th ,, : a¹, b¹♭, b¹.
16th ,, : c², c²♯, d².
17th ,, : d²♯, e², f², f²♯.
18th ,, : g², g²♯, a².
19th ,, : b²♭, b², c³.

Dimensions: 3′ 3″ × 0′ 11¾″ × 0′ 5½″

Heyer Collection, Leipzig

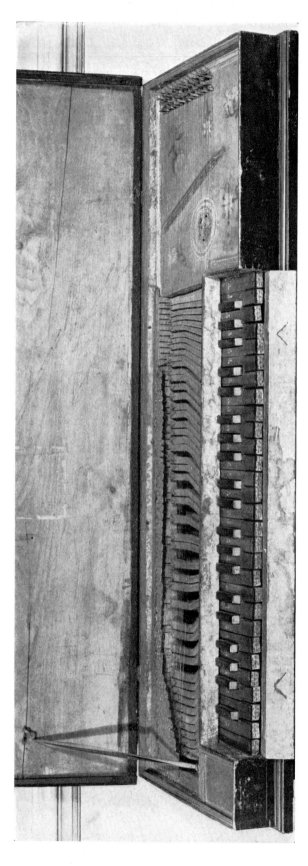

12. CLAVICHORD, SEVENTEENTH CENTURY
Probably Italian workmanship

Compass: C – c³, chromatic, but lacking C♯, 48 keys.

This clavichord is fretted, and the 23 pairs of strings are allotted thus:

1st pair : C.	9th pair : A.	17th pair : f¹, f¹♯, g¹, g¹♯.
2nd „ : D.	10th „ : B♭, B.	18th „ : a¹, b¹♭.
3rd „ : D♯.	11th „ : c, c♯.	19th „ : b¹, c², c²♯.
4th „ : E.	12th „ : d, d♯, e.	20th „ : d², d²♯, e².
5th „ : F.	13th „ : f, f♯, g.	21st „ : f², f²♯, g².
6th „ : F♯.	14th „ : g♯, a, b♭.	22nd „ : g²♯, a², b²♭.
7th „ : G.	15th „ : b, c¹, c¹♯.	23rd „ : b², c³.
8th „ : G♯.	16th „ : d¹, d¹♯, e¹.	

Dimensions: 3′ 10¾″ × 1′ 1″.

Conservatoire, Brussels

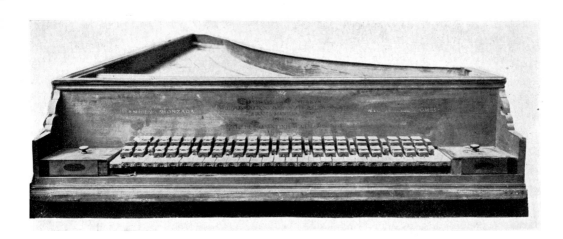

13A. ARCHICEMBALO BY VITO TRASUNTINO OF VENICE, 1606

13B. SOUNDBOARD OF PRECEDING ARCHICEMBALO

This instrument was constructed as an experimental harpsichord capable of diatonic, chromatic, and enharmonic tuning.

Compass: $C - c^3$.

One eight foot register and one set of jacks. Each accidental key (as the expression is understood in terms of the normal keyboard) is divided into four keys; and between each *b* and *c*, and each *e* and *f*, is inserted an extra accidental key divided into two keys. Thus the four octave keyboard contains thirty two keys to each octave, a total of one hundred and twenty five keys.

With this instrument is a tetrachord, or quadruple monochord (not shown), with intervals marked on it, to assist in tuning.

Conservatorio G. B. Martini, Bologna   *On loan to Museo Civico, Bologna*

14. OCTAVE SPINET, SIXTEENTH OR SEVENTEENTH CENTURY

Though unsigned this is probably an Italian instrument.

A typical small spinet of indeterminate pitch, but approximately four foot.

Charles Burney, writing of his tour in Italy in 1770, said: 'To persons accustomed to English harpsichords, all the keyed instruments on the continent appear to great disadvantage. Throughout Italy they have generally little octave spinnets to accompany singing, in private houses, sometimes in a triangular form, but more frequently in the shape of our old virginals; of which the keys are so noisy, and the tone is so feeble, that more wood is heard than wire' (page 30).

Conservatoire, Brussels

15. UPRIGHT HARPSICHORD, PROBABLY SEVENTEENTH CENTURY

Compass: C – c³, bass short octave.

Two eight foot sets of strings, and two rows of jacks. Both registers can be put 'on' or 'off' by means of hand stops (now broken) at A.

There is a harp stop to damp one eight foot. which is controlled by the hand stop at B.

Deutches Museum, Munich

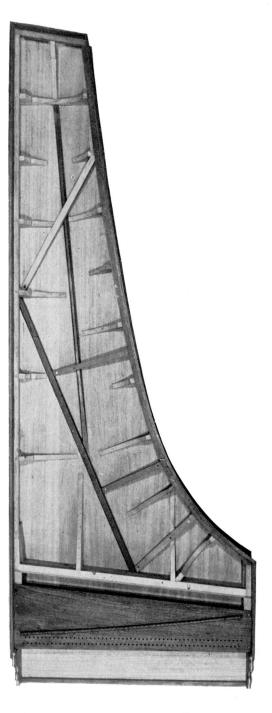

16. INTERIOR OF HARPSICHORD, ITALIAN TYPE

This view shows the interior of a modern harpsichord, built by Hugh Gough of London in 1956, on traditional Italian lines. The photograph shows the instrument, as viewed from above, before the insertion of the soundboard. The 'buttress' system of bracing, designed to enable the case to withhold the tension of the strings, can be clearly seen.

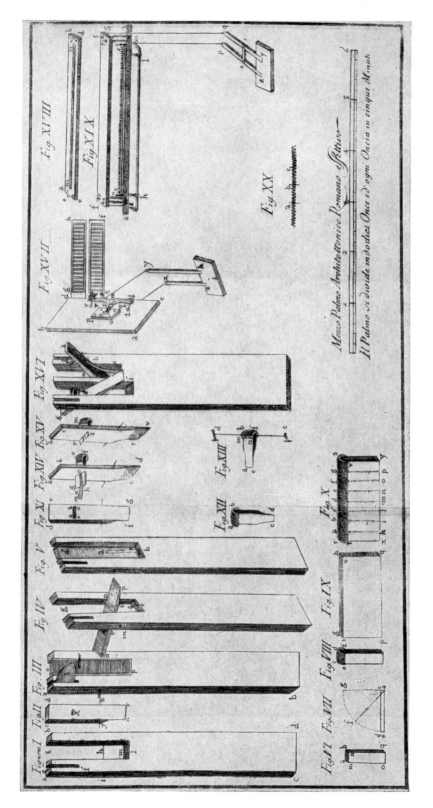

17. Cembalo Angelico (Appendix 2)
[An *Oncia* = ¾ inch.]

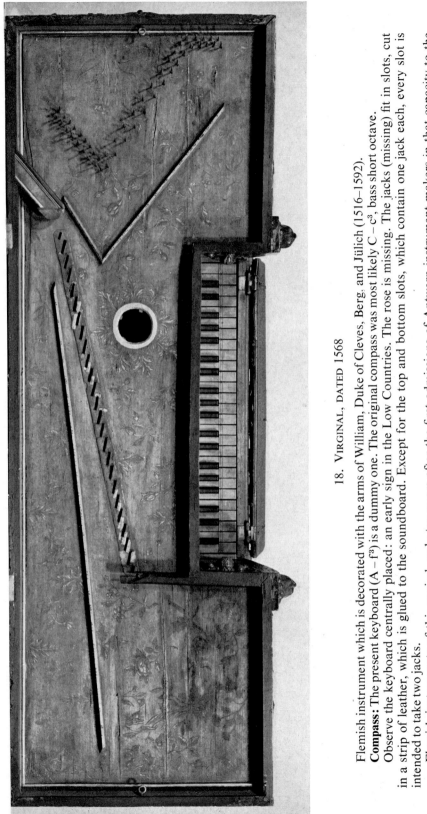

18. VIRGINAL, DATED 1568

Flemish instrument which is decorated with the arms of William, Duke of Cleves, Berg, and Jülich (1516–1592).

Compass: The present keyboard (A – f³) is a dummy one. The original compass was most likely C – c³, bass short octave.

Observe the keyboard centrally placed: an early sign in the Low Countries. The rose is missing. The jacks (missing) fit in slots, cut in a strip of leather, which is glued to the soundboard. Except for the top and bottom slots, which contain one jack each, every slot is intended to take two jacks.

Flemish instruments of this period, only ten years after the first admissions of Antwerp instrument makers in that capacity to the Painters' Guild of Saint Luke, and ten years before the admission of Hans Ruckers, are very rare.

Scaling: (assuming C – c³ compass). C: 51", c²: 13¼", c³: 7⅞".

Plucking Point: C: 14", c³: 4½".

Dimensions: 5' 7" × 2' 4" × 1' 4".

Victoria and Albert Museum

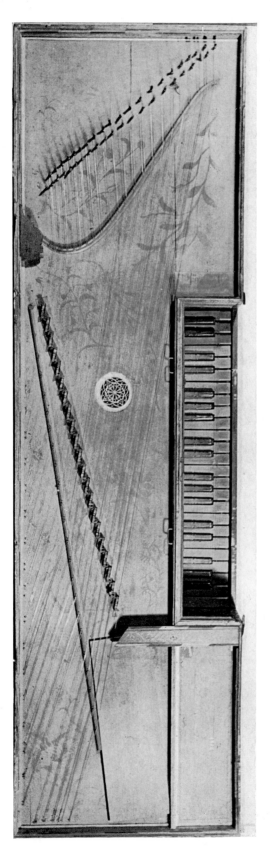

19. VIRGINAL BY HANS GRAUWELS, LATE SIXTEENTH CENTURY

Hans Grauwels was Master of the Guild of Saint Luke in 1579.
This early Flemish virginal, like that in Plate 18, retains the old central keyboard.

Compass: C – a², bass short octave. Boxwood naturals, ebony accidentals.

Scaling: C: $49\frac{1}{4}''$, c²: $13\frac{1}{2}''$, a²: $6\frac{7}{8}''$.

Dimensions: 5' $0\frac{1}{4}'' \times 1'$ 6" $\times 0'$ $8\frac{1}{2}''$.

Conservatoire, Brussels

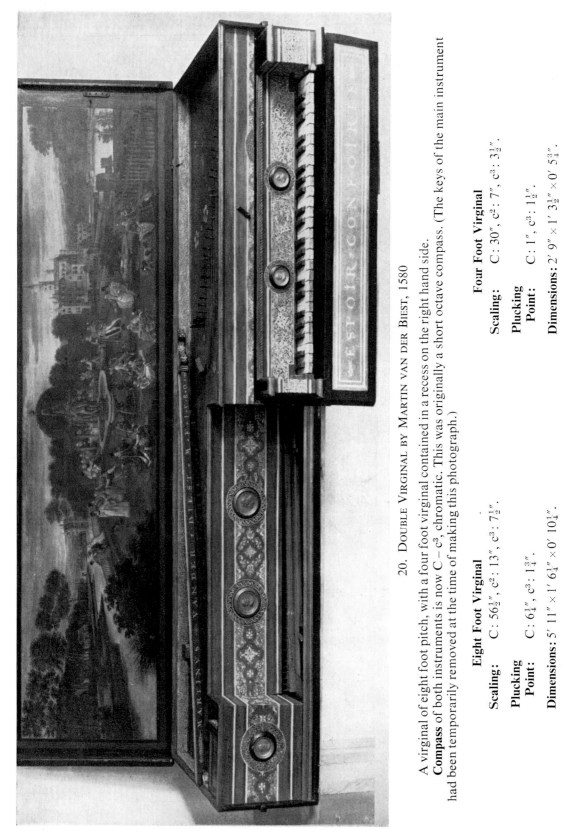

20. Double Virginal by Martin van der Biest, 1580

A virginal of eight foot pitch, with a four foot virginal contained in a recess on the right hand side.
Compass of both instruments is now C – c³, chromatic. This was originally a short octave compass. (The keys of the main instrument had been temporarily removed at the time of making this photograph.)

Eight Foot Virginal

Scaling: C: $56\frac{1}{2}$", c²: 13", c³: $7\frac{1}{2}$".

**Plucking
Point:**   C: $6\frac{1}{4}$", c³: $1\frac{3}{4}$".

Dimensions: 5' 11" × 1' $6\frac{1}{4}$" × 0' $10\frac{1}{4}$".

Four Foot Virginal

Scaling: C: 30", c²: 7", c³: $3\frac{1}{2}$".

**Plucking
Point:**   C: 1", c³: $1\frac{1}{2}$".

Dimensions: 2' 9" × 1' $3\frac{1}{2}$" × 0' $5\frac{3}{4}$".

This instrument was built for Alessandro Farnese, the Stadthalter of the Netherlands (1546–1592). Martin van der Biest joined the Guild of Saint Luke as one of the original instrument maker members in 1557–8. In 1575 he attended the wedding of Hans Ruckers in the O.L.V. Church (Onze Lieve Vrouw) in Antwerp.

21. HARPSICHORD BY JEAN-CLAUDE GOUJON, 1749

Until recently this harpsichord was thought to be an instrument of 1590 by Hans Ruckers, as the inscriptions on nameboard and jackrail indicate. When necessary repairs were made to the soundboard, a pencilled signature of the well-known French maker Goujon was discovered on the four-foot hitchpin rail. It is known that, while harpsichords signed 'Goujon' sold for 250 livres, those further embellished with the name of the great Hans Ruckers fetched 350 livres. Such 18th-century fakery of Ruckers instruments was limited neither to the Goujon workshop nor to France.

But one should not despise this harpsichord because of its dubious origins. It is an excellent example of a fine 18th-century French instrument in the style of a Flemish one which has been enlarged (*mis à grand ravalement*), a harpsichord of superb tone and touch in the best contemporary tradition.

Dimensions: 7′ 9″ × 2′ 10½″ × 0′ 11″.

Conservatoire, Paris

22. KEYBOARDS OF PRECEDING HARPSICHORD

Compass: FF – f³, chromatic. The keys are eighteenth century French work, and are typical in style; the naturals covered with ebony and faced with arcaded boxwood fronts, the accidentals topped with slips of ivory.

Goujon cleverly pretended that the original compass had been 4½ octaves, GG – c³, bass short octave. Thus, when extended to five octaves, the instrument would necessarily have been widened. A tell tale join in the front board, marked A, and extending down to a point just to the right of the word *Antverpiae*, can be seen. There is, however, no join in the jackrail or nameboard; hence these, together with the inscription, would have dated from the ostensible reconstruction or *ravalement*.

Observe the Flemish paper, block printed, which decorates the frontboard and appears as if matched carefully during the operation of *ravalement*. This particular design is uncommon, but appears in two other harpsichords known to the writer: a Jan Ruckers of 1618 which is on loan from Schloss Kappenberg, Westphalia, to the Museum für Kunst und Kulturgeschichte, Dortmund, and a Jan Ruckers of 1638 (Plate 34).

The registers of this harpsichord are worked by knee levers, and three of the five, marked B, can be seen. They are similar to those used by Pascal Taskin.

Conservatoire, Paris

During *ravalement* a Flemish harpsichord would have been lengthened some five inches, and widened about three inches, but the careful extension of the *tempera* decoration would have hidden this.

Observe: A. The date 1590, placed on a small white scroll. But this particular background for the date was chiefly used by Andries Ruckers, not by Hans.

B. The rose, or trade mark, which incorporates the initials H. R., is made of papier-maché and not gilded metal, as in authentic specimens.

There are three sets of strings: two unisons and an octave, and four rows of jacks as follows:

1. Eight foot quill (Upper keyboard).
2. Four foot quill (Lower keyboard).
3. Eight foot quill (Lower keyboard).
4. Eight foot buff leather (Lower keyboard).

Rows 3 and 4 attack the same set of strings, but the different plectrum and point of attack provide a contrast in tone colour.

Scaling: Eight foot: FF: $71\frac{1}{4}''$, c^2: $13\frac{7}{8}''$, f^3: $4\frac{3}{8}''$.
Four foot: FF: $46\frac{1}{2}''$, c^2: $7\frac{1}{4}''$, f^3: $2\frac{3}{4}''$.

Conservatoire, Paris

SCIENTIA·NON·HABET·INIMICVM·NISI·INGNORANTEM

1591

24. Hexagonal spinet by Hans Ruckers, 1591

This is the only polygonal spinet by a member of the Ruckers family which is known to the writer. It was undoubtedly inspired by the conventional Italian instruments of this type.

Compass: $C-c^3$, bass short octave, the standard Ruckers compass for virginals and single manual harpsichords. The jackrail and many jacks are missing. The bridge is a replacement, and is not in the original position.

Scaling: C : 56″, c^2 : $14\frac{1}{8}$″, c^3 : $6\frac{3}{4}$″.

The plain keyboard, with ivory topped naturals and ebony accidentals, is that normally made in the Ruckers workshops. The outside of the case is painted dark green. The interior is decorated with the Antwerp block printed paper so much used on keyboard instruments. The pattern is black, printed on white paper. Details are picked out with vermilion or green. This paper was usually varnished, and this has often led to the mistaken idea that the paper itself was yellow. The sea horse design here shown was very popular, and is perhaps the most common of all.

The inscription—with its unorthodox spelling—was a favourite decoration in the Low Countries at this time. The writer has not been successful in tracing the origin of this quotation which was also known in Spain: *Nunca han tenido, ni tienen las artes otros enemigos que los ignorantes* (Updike (1922) title page).

Length: 5′ $7\frac{1}{4}$″.

Hôtel de Gruuthuuse, Bruges

25. VIRGINAL BY HANS RUCKERS, 1598

This is the model with keyboard to the left, the jacks consequently attacking the strings close to the nut. There is about one virginal of this model to every two with the keyboard to the right.

This example is unusual only in that the compass is GG – c³, bass short octave, instead of the normal C – c³, bass short octave.

Observe the spacing of the inscription, which starts with high letters, well spaced, but ends with smaller letters crowded together. This curious feature is the rule with original Ruckers inscriptions.

Scaling: GG : $54\frac{3}{4}''$, c² : $12\frac{3}{16}''$, c³ : $6\frac{3}{16}''$.

Plucking
Point: GG : $5\frac{1}{2}''$, c³ : $2\frac{1}{2}''$.

Dimensions: $5'\,5\frac{1}{2}'' \times 1'\,6\frac{7}{8}'' \times 0'\,9\frac{1}{2}''$.

See plate 27.

La Comtesse de Chambure, Paris

26. VIRGINAL BY HANS RUCKERS, 1604

Here the keyboard is to the right, the jacks attacking the strings some way from the nut. This model is twice as common as that shown in Plate 25.

The H.R. rose is in the soundboard, but the authentic jackrail (not shown) bears the startling inscription *Ioannes et Andreas Ruckers fecerunt*. It is evident that Andries Ruckers, then twenty five years old but not yet a member of the Guild of Saint Luke, assisted his father in the construction of this virginal.

Observe the original batten (marked AB) affecting lower part of the compass only, and probably intended for accompaniment purposes. It is furnished with metal hooks in place of felt or leather pads: the *Arpichordum* of Praetorius (pages 46 and 97).

Scaling: C: $47\frac{1}{2}''$, c^2: $13''$, c^3: $6\frac{1}{4}''$.

Plucking Point: C: $17''$, c^3: $2\frac{1}{2}''$.

Dimensions: $4' \, 8'' \times 1' \, 7\frac{1}{4}'' \times 0' \, 8\frac{1}{2}''$.

Conservatoire, Brussels

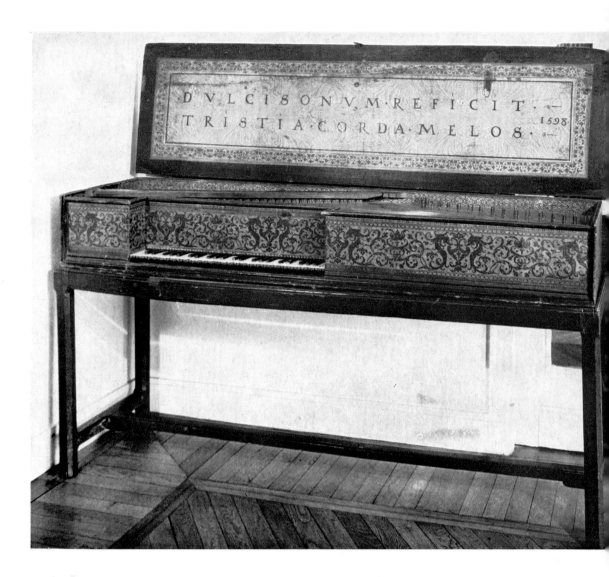

27. VIRGINAL BY HANS RUCKERS, 1598
(See Plate 25)

Here is shown the general appearance of a Flemish virginal of late sixteenth or early seventeenth century construction, decorated with printed papers.

Above the paper which decorates the keyboard recess is written:

François Chappelle a refait cette épinette et
Luy a donne de l'armonie 1739.

The stand is not original.

La Comtesse de Chambure, Paris

28. Virginal by Andries Ruckers, 1611

The case is covered with paint, each surface being marbled within a plain painted border. In this case the marbled panels are red and brown, the surrounding border being dark green. Painted casework in imitation of marble or wood was a popular form of decoration for keyboard instruments in the Low Countries.

The elaborate and original stand will be noted.

The jackrail of this virginal bears the inscription: *Ioannes Ruckers fecit Antverpiae*, but the soundboard contains the rose of Andries Ruckers.

The keyboard is to the right.

Compass: $C - c^3$, bass short octave.

Scaling: $C: 59''$, $c^2: 13''$, $c^3: 6\frac{7}{8}''$.

Dimensions: $5' \ 7\frac{1}{2}'' \times 1' \ 7\frac{1}{2}'' \times 0' \ 9\frac{1}{2}''$.

Vleeshuis, Antwerp

29. DOUBLE VIRGINAL BY HANS RUCKERS, 1610

The case of the large virginal has been crudely restored, and the old decoration, stand, and inscription, replaced. Much of the decoration of the octave instrument is, however, old.

The original compass of both virginals: C – c³, bass short octave, has been extended to C – f³, chromatic. The necessary alterations to the instruments for securing this increased compass made it impossible to fit the octave virginal into the traditional left hand part of the main instrument. The recess was therefore closed, and the octave instrument placed permanently above the eight foot virginal, in the correct position for their use together.

Conservatoire, Brussels

30. ACTION OF PRECEDING DOUBLE VIRGINAL

The octave virginal has been turned up to show the simple action for simultaneous use of the two instruments.

The jacks of the eight foot virginal (A to B), on rising when a key is depressed, press on the underside of the keys of the octave virginal (C to D) through a channel cut through the base of the latter instrument, thus causing it to speak.

All double virginals seem to have been constructed for use in this way, and the system is mentioned by Praetorius. In some cases, however, the system has later been modified.

Eight foot virginal

Scaling: C: $59\frac{3}{4}''$, c²: $14\frac{1}{2}''$, f³: $5\frac{1}{8}''$.

Dimensions: $5' 7'' \times 1' 9'' \times 0' 10\frac{1}{2}''$.

Four foot virginal

Scaling: C: $27\frac{1}{2}''$, c²: $7\frac{1}{16}''$, f³: $2\frac{1}{4}''$.

Dimensions: $2' 8\frac{1}{2}'' \times 1' 4\frac{1}{4}''$ (excluding keyboard) $\times 0' 5\frac{3}{8}''$.   *Conservatoire, Brussels*

31. Double virginal by Jan Ruckers, 1623

This instrument exhibits all the features of the Ruckers double virginals unaltered.
As in five of the six other examples by this family, the main keyboard is to the right of the instrument.

Compass of each instrument: C – c³, bass short octave.
Note the paper, covered with patterns incorporating sea horses, on the front of the main virginal.
The interior of the lid is inscribed:

Audi vide et tace si vis vivere in pace.

The drop front contains:

Omnis spiritus laudet Dominum

Harding Museum, Chicago

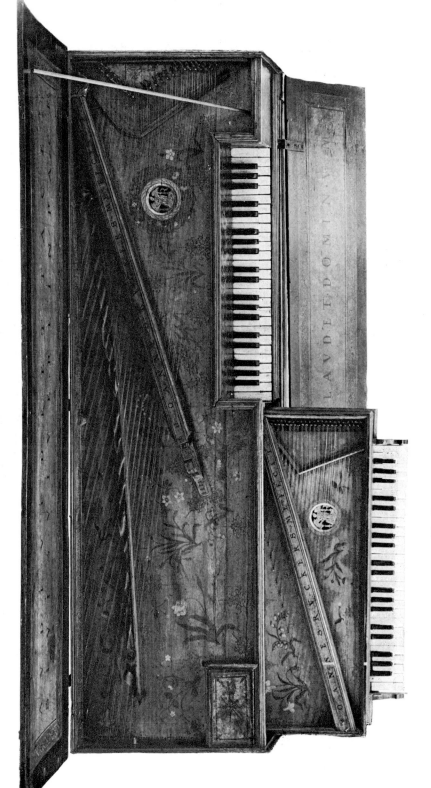

32. SOUNDBOARD OF PRECEDING DOUBLE VIRGINAL

The rose in each soundboard is the less common of the two chief designs used
by Jan Ruckers, who employed three forms in all.
Note the two jackrails bearing their original and ill spaced inscriptions:

Ioannes Ruckers me fecit.

Harding Museum, Chicago

33. Transposing Harpsichord by Jan Rucke[r] 1638

This harpsichord preserves its original k[ey]boards placed a fourth apart in pitch, and it see[ms] to be the only double manual Ruckers which s[till] preserves this transposing device virtually intact.

There is one eight foot and one four foot of strings, and, as no coupling is possible betw[een] the two keyboards, four rows of jacks are necess[ary] to enable the player to use both registers on eit[her] manual. There is a harp stop of buff leather for [the] eight foot, and this draws in halves, breaking [be]tween $c^1\sharp$ and d^1.

Observe the extra string for each $e\flat$ on b[oth] keyboards (A): a primitive attempt to overcom[e a] deficiency in mean tone tuning (page 46).

The upper keyboard is the main keyboa[rd] sounding at normal pitch. The lower manual i[s a] fourth away in pitch. Thus key c^3 on the up[per] keyboard sounds that note, while key f^3 on [the] lower manual, which also plucks the top string[s of] the instrument, must also sound c^3. There a[re] however, five extra notes for the lower manual [to] allow a short octave tuning from GG, and th[ese] notes are GG, AA, BB, F$\sharp$, G$\sharp$.

Scaling: Eight foot: GG : $66\frac{3}{4}''$, C : $65\frac{3}{4}''$, 14'', c^3 : $6\frac{7}{8}''$.
Four foot: GG : $37\frac{3}{4}''$, C : $3($
c^2 : $6\frac{7}{8}''$, c^3 : $3\frac{1}{4}''$.

Plucking Point: (The eight foot jacks on each k[ey]board are nearer the player t[han] the four foot jacks.)
Eight foot: (Upper Manual) $5\frac{1}{2}''$, c^3 : 2''.
Four foot: (Upper Manual) $2\frac{1}{8}''$, c^3 : $1\frac{1}{8}''$.
Eight foot: (Lower Manual) G[G] $6\frac{7}{8}''$, c^3 : $3\frac{1}{4}''$.
Four foot: (Lower Manual) G[G] $3\frac{1}{2}''$, c^3 : $2\frac{3}{8}''$.

Dimensions: $7'\ 4'' \times 2'\ 7'' \times 0'\ 10\frac{1}{2}''$.

Russell Collection, Edinbu[rgh]

34. KEYBOARDS OF PRECEDING HARPSICHORD

Compass of upper manual: C – c³, bass short octave. This is the standard compass for original Ruckers virginals and single manual harpsichords.

Compass of lower manual: GG – c³, bass short octave. The compass *appears* to be C – f³, bass short octave, but is in fact that given above, since the lower manual plucks the same two sets of strings as the upper manual.

The bass keys of the lower manual act as follows:

Key E sounds note GG, available on lower manual only.

,,	F	,,	,,	C,	,,	,, both manuals.
,,	F♯	,,	,,	AA,	,,	,, lower manual only,
,,	G	,,	,,	D,	,,	,, both manuals.
,,	G♯	,,	,,	BB,	,,	,, lower manual only.
,,	A	,,	,,	E,	,,	,, both manuals.
,,	B♭	,,	,,	F,	,,	,, both manuals.
,,	B	,,	,,	F♯,	,,	,, lower manual only.
,,	C	,,	,,	G,	,,	,, both manuals.
,,	C♯	,,	,,	G♯,	,,	,, lower manual only.

Russell Collection, Edinburgh

35. Keyboards and keyframes of preceding harpsichord

Plate 34 has shown the relative pitch level of the two keyboards with particular explanation of how this works in the short octave. It is obvious that, since the two keyboards share the same strings, the keys of both manuals must be in alignment with these strings. This presents no difficulty where there is chromatic sequence in the larger part of the compass; but in the bass the short octave system throws the keys and strings out of alignment. Hence, on the upper manual, keys E, F♯, and G♯, which sound C, D and E, are built crooked in order to get in alignment with keys F, G, A, of the lower manual, which also sound C, D, and E.

The five keys which are absent from the upper keyframe are present on the lower manual to give notes GG, AA, BB, F♯, and G♯.

Observe the style of the ordinary Ruckers keyboard. Note also that 'A 41' is written in ink on the top key of the upper manual. This appears on top and bottom keys of the lower manual, on both keyframes, on all four slides, and on the jackrail. A similar system of numbering appears on most Flemish instruments of this period, but the writer has not succeeded in establishing the significance of the marks.

Russell Collection, Edinburgh

36. Harpsichord by Hans Ruckers, 1616

This instrument preserves a stand of a general design favoured in Antwerp for the more elaborately decorated instruments (see Plate 28). The case is painted dark green, with panels of gold.

Observe the four stop levers, direct extensions of the slides, which project from the right of the case (A).

There are two sets of strings: one unison and one octave; and four rows of jacks: a unison and an octave set for each keyboard.

This double manual harpsichord was originally constructed as a transposing harpsichord with the two manuals a fourth apart; but, most unusually, the keyboards were constructed with chromatic basses instead of the almost invariable short octave. The keyboards have since been brought into alignment, and the original keys replaced. The present compass is $FF - b^2$ (no $b^2\flat$), 54 keys.

Dimensions: $7' \ 4'' \times 2' \ 9'' \times 0' \ 10\frac{1}{2}''$.

M. Mirouet, Paris

37. HARPSICHORD BY ANDRIES RUCKERS, 1627

Compass: F – f³, bass short octave.

There are two sets of strings, and two rows of jacks: one each at eight and four foot pitch.

The scaling is such that the pitch level of the instrument is between eight and four foot pitch. Hence the note sounded on depressing a key is at about the level obtained on an instrument of the usual C compass.: *i.e.* key f² sounds note f².

Scaling: Eight foot: F: $34\frac{3}{4}''$, f²: $9\frac{1}{4}''$, f³: $4\frac{1}{2}''$.
Four foot: F: $21\frac{3}{8}''$, f²: $4\frac{1}{2}''$, f³: $2\frac{1}{4}''$.

An examination of the keys and keyframe show that at some time the keys were arranged to give a compass of C – c³, bass short octave. The instrument would then have sounded about a fourth above the keyboard compass: *i.e.* key c² sounded f².

Observe that at one time there was a second row of eight foot pins.

Dimensions: $4'\ 0\frac{1}{2}'' \times 2'\ 3\frac{1}{4}'' \times 0'\ 7\frac{1}{2}''$.

Gemeentemuseum, Hague

This is a double manual harpsichord which bears the rose of Andries Ruckers and the date 1608.

The bottom boards have been removed for the photograph. The four struts, marked A, are normally secured to the bottom of the instrument.

B. The box, opening to the longside, intended for storing the tuning hammer, spare wire and quill, etc.

C. The four foot hitchpin rail.

D. The large transverse cut off bar, which limits the area of soundboard influenced by the four foot bridge. It will be understood that the latter is placed in the centre of a section of soundboard the boundaries of which are marked by the cut off bar on one side and the four foot hitchpin rail on the other.

Similarly the eight foot bridge stands mid way between the four foot hitchpin rail and the bentside. The area of soundboard sensitive to each bridge is thus carefully controlled.

E. The four soundbars placed at right angles to the longside.

F. The rose.

G. The wrestplank.

Russell Collection, Edinburgh

39. HARPSICHORD AND SPINET BY JAN COENEN, 1734

This instrument has been in the home and printing works of the Plantin Moretus family in Antwerp since it was made. It is the work of Jan Joseph Coenen, organist of Roermund Cathedral. The design was probably copied from a similar model by the Ruckers family who occasionally made these instruments (Appendix 5).

Note the stop levers, which are direct extensions of the slides (A).

Above the keys of the harpsichord is written:

> *Joannes Josephus Coenen presbyter et organista cathedralis me fecit.*

Over the keys of the spinet is written:

> *Ruraemundae A° 1735*

The roses of both instruments are made of gilded tin and bear the date 1734.

The instrument was damaged during the 1939–45 war, at which time one of the roses was destroyed. It has since been restored.

Plantin Moretus Huis, Antwerp

40. Soundboard of preceding instrument

The Harpsichord

Compass: $GG - c^3$, bass short octave.

There are two unisons, one octave, and four rows of jacks:

Row 1: four foot on the upper keyboard.
Row 2: eight foot on both keyboards.
Row 3: four foot on the lower keyboard.
Row 4: eight foot on the lower keyboard.

All the jacks are quilled, excepting those of the lower eight foot, which are provided with plectra of buff leather—probably original.

Scaling: Eight foot: GG: $67\frac{1}{4}''$, c^2: $13\frac{7}{8}''$, c^3: $6\frac{7}{8}''$.
Four foot: GG: $38''$, c^2: $6\frac{1}{2}''$, c^3: $3\frac{5}{8}''$.

The Spinet

Compass: $C - c^3$, chromatic, but lacking $C\sharp$.

Scaling: C: $44''$, c^2: $12\frac{7}{8}''$, c^3: $6\frac{3}{4}''$.

Observe the common hitchpin rail to both instruments, (AB), and the large box for tuning key, spare parts, etc. (C).

Plantin Moretus Huis, Antwerp

41. Upright harpsichord by Albert De Lin

This instrument, though undated, is of mid eighteenth century origin.
Albert De Lin was a successful instrument maker at Tournai. His dated work is from 1750–1770, and consists of spinets, harpsichords, and upright harpsichords. This instrument has two unison registers.

Gemeentemuseum, Hague

42. HARPSICHORD, MID SEVENTEENTH CENTURY

Seventeenth century French harpsichords are very scarce.

The example shown here was formerly the property of M. P. Quereuil, and was exhibited at the International Exhibition of 1900 in Paris.

It passed into the Léon Savoye collection, and was sold when the collection was dispersed in 1924. This instrument was destroyed in the bombing of Rotterdam in 1940.

There were two manuals, **compass:** FF – c³, chromatic. The instrument had two unisons and an octave.

The painting bore the inscription:

Le Roy pingebat, 1685

43. HARPSICHORD BY VINCENT TIBAUD OF TOULOUSE, 1679

This harpsichord is provided with a turned and framed stand, as is the instrument shown in Plate 42. The interior is richly decorated with marquetry.

Compass: GG – c³, broken octave. Two unisons, one four foot.

Scaling: Eight foot: GG: 61″, c²: 12¾″, c³: 6½″.
               Four foot: GG: 37¼″, c²: 6″, c³: 2⅞″.

Plucking   Eight foot: GG: 5½″, c³: 2¼″.
Point: Four foot: GG: 4⅛″, c³: 2″.

Inscribed over the keyboards:

Fait par moy Vincent Tibaut A Tolose 1679

Dimensions: 6′ 10″ × 2′ 6″ × 0′ 9″.

Conservatoire, Brussels

44. SPINET SIGNED RICHARD, AND DATED 1690

This instrument is shown as a typical example of the late seventeenth century French spinet.

The inscription must however be treated with suspicion. It reads:

Fait à Paris par Richard rue du Pan praes St. Nicolas du Chardonnet. 1690

Richard who lived at the above address seems to have left the following examples of his work:

1. An octave spinet of 1672 at Berlin.
2. A signature of 1688, recording repairs carried out on the Hans Ruckers harpsichord of 1613, now in the Rhode Island School of Design, U.S.A.
3. A spinet dated 1693 in the Paris Conservatoire.

This spinet passed through the hands of Marcel Salomon, rue Boissy-d'Anglas, Paris, in the 1920's, and is now believed to be in private ownership in Montreal.

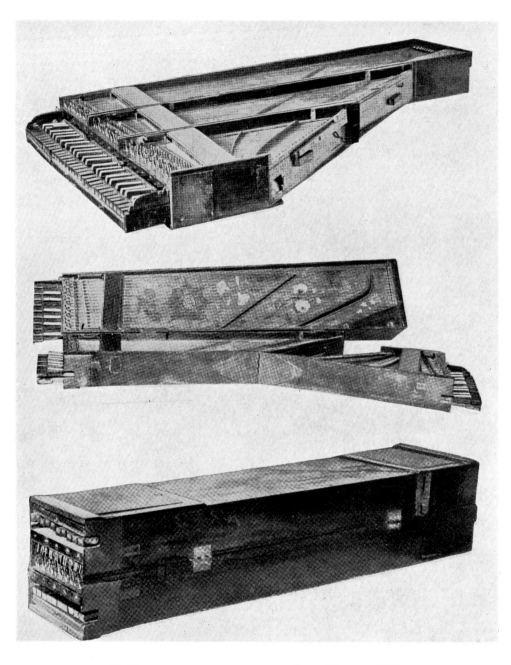

45. TRAVELLING HARPSICHORD BY JEAN MARIUS, 1713

This is the *Clavecin Brisé* which Jean Marius built between 1700 and 1720 under a Royal Patent dated 18 September, 1700.

Compass: GG – e³, broken octave. The key E♮ is broken, giving BB at the front and E♭ at the back.

There are two unisons and an octave.

Dimensions: Open: 4′ 8″ × 2′ 5″ × 0′ 4¾″.
Closed: 4′ 3¾″ × 1′ 2¼″ × 0′ 9½″.

Heyer Collection, Leipzig

46. Spinet, late eighteenth century

This spinet is a good example of the decoration of keyboard instruments popular in France in the second half of the eighteenth century. A spinet of similar design and decorated with fluted legs is in the Yale Collection, New Haven. That instrument was made by Pascal Taskin in 1778.

The spinet illustrated here is apparently unsigned and undated. It was formerly in the possession of Marcel Salomon, rue Boissy-d'Anglas, Paris.

47. HARPSICHORD BY PASCAL TASKIN, 1769

This harpsichord is an excellent example, both as a musical instrument and a piece of furniture, of the large standard French harpsichord of the eighteenth century.

The outside of the case is pale green with panels in gold; the inside is pale chocolate lacquer.

The keyboards have the conventional French decoration: ebony natural keys with arcaded boxwood fronts, and accidentals topped with ivory.

Pascal Taskin was born at Theux near Liége in 1723, and came to Paris as a boy to study harpsichord making with the Blanchets. He married the widow of François Blanchet the younger, became the best known French instrument maker of his day, and died in Paris on 9 February, 1793.

This harpsichord seems to have been Taskin's own instrument, as the writer obtained it from the Taskin family in France, in whose possession it had been throughout the nineteenth century.

Dimensions: $7' \, 8\frac{1}{2}'' \times 3' \, 1\frac{1}{4}'' \times 0' \, 11''$.

Russell Collection, Edinburgh

48. SOUNDBOARD OF PRECEDING
HARPSICHORD

The soundboard and wrestplank
are painted in *tempera* with conventional designs. The gilt rose contains
the initials P.T., and round it is written
Pascal Taskin élève de Blanchet. The date
is painted on the soundboard, and also
appears on the top and bottom jack of
each register (Plate 1(iv)) and on the top
and bottom key of each manual.

Upper Manual: $1 \times 8'$ (quill), Harp.

Lower Manual: $1 \times 8'$ (buff leather),
Harp, $1 \times 4'$ (leather),
Coupler.

Scaling: Eight foot: FF: $69\frac{1}{4}''$, c^2:
$14''$, f^3: $5\frac{1}{2}''$.
Four foot: FF: $42\frac{1}{4}''$, c^2:
$6\frac{1}{2}''$, f^3: $3''$.

Plucking Eight foot: FF: $6\frac{1}{4}''$, f^3:
Point: $1\frac{3}{4}''$.
Four foot: FF: $3\frac{1}{2}''$, f^3:
$1\frac{1}{4}''$ (middle row).

Russell Collection, Edinburgh

49. Harpsichord by Pascal Taskin, 1786

The stand with fluted legs is gilt. The outside of the case is painted black with decoration in gold. The inside of the case has Chinese designs in gold on a coral pink ground.

Over the keys is written:

Fait par Pascal Taskin à Paris 1786

Behind the nameboard is written:

Refait par Charles Fleury facteur de pianos à Paris au 1856 *Fleury*

This harpsichord is of very small proportions, and one octave of keys measures only $4\frac{3}{4}$ inches, against Taskin's normal $6\frac{1}{4}$ inches. The height is only 29 inches.

The keyboard is too small for the adult hand, and the writer supposes that this harpsichord must have been made for some (perhaps noble) child.

Dimensions: 5′ $11\frac{1}{2}$″ × 2′ 9″ × 0′ 8″.

Victoria and Albert Museum

50. Soundboard of preceding harpsichord

Compass: EE–f³. This is very unusual, and it is probable that key EE was tuned to sound CC. This low key EE appears in the Taskin spinet of 1778 in the Yale Collection, in an undated Andries Ruckers harpsichord in the Rhode Island School of Design, and in the harpsichord of 1786 by Joachim Swanen in the Conservatoire des Arts et Métiers, Paris. It is not otherwise known to the writer.

The harpsichord has two unison stops, and one harp stop.

Scaling: EE: $57\frac{1}{2}''$, c²: $13''$, f³: $4\frac{3}{4}''$.

Plucking Point: EE: $4\frac{3}{8}''$, f³: $\frac{5}{8}''$.

String gauge numbers are marked on the nut as follows:

EE: 0	BB♭: 2	E: 4	d♯: 6	c²♯: 8
GG: 1	C♯: 3	G♯: 5	e¹: 7	g²♯: 9

Both Corrette (1753) and Diderot (1753) give details of stringing for harpsichords but the two scales differ from one another, and are anyway intended for instruments of a more standard scaling than this. Of course neither of the two sources quoted above expresses the size of wire in exact terms of diameter; hence we cannot make use of their tables.

Victoria and Albert Museum

51. Interior of harpsichord by Nicolas and François Blanchet, 1730

The bottom boards have been removed to obtain this photograph.

It will be seen that the French system of bracing the interior of their instruments was derived from the design of the Flemish harpsichords (Plate 38).

This system was also followed in Germany, but in England it was modified (Plate 74).

Charles Fisher, Framingham Center, Mass.

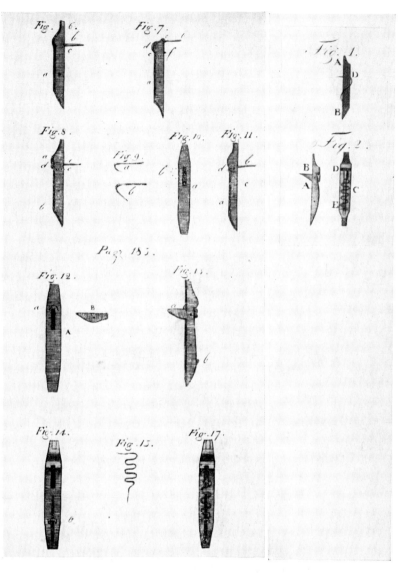

52 A   52 B

52A. EXPERIMENTAL PLECTRA BY FRANCIS HOPKINSON (Appendix 14)
52B. EXPERIMENTAL PLECTRA BY FRANCIS HOPKINSON (Appendix 14, page 174)

53. ORGAN HARPSICHORD (CLAVIORGAN) BY LUDOVIC THEEUWES OF LONDON, 1579

Theeuwes was a Fleming who was admitted to the Guild of Saint Luke in Antwerp in 1557, and who ten years later was working as virginal maker in the parish of Saint Martin's le Grand in London. He was the son of Jacob Theeuwes whose name appears in the Antwerp archives from 1533 as a harpsichord maker (*clavesymbelmaker*).

This harpsichord stands on an organ with which it was originally combined; however only three wooden organ pipes now remain, and the stickers which formerly ran between the keyboard and the organ have also vanished. There are five stop levers for the organ on each side of the keyboard.

Observe the arms of the families Hoby and Carey. During a cleaning of the case work in 1947 these were cleaned away, revealing the arms of the Roper family. The instrument bears the inscription:

Lodowicus Theeuwes me fesit 1579.

Victoria and Albert Museum

54. SOUNDBOARD OF PRECEDING INSTRUMENT

The pivot rail of the keyboard shows a compass of C – c³, chromatic. The keys are missing. Formerly one accidental key was preserved, and this was topped with small squares of ebony and boxwood, alternately placed. A similar decoration has been used on the virginal by Thomas White, 1653, at Hardwick Hall.

The harpsichord had two unisons and an octave. An unusual feature of the three registers is that the upper jack slides are fixed, but the lower guides move: the reverse of the usual construction. These guides were controlled by three hand stops. It is probable that the four foot jacks were placed in the centre row, since that guide is lower than the other two.

The original four foot bridge and nut are missing, as is the lower half of the original eight foot bridge. Between each pair of pins on the eight foot bridge is screwed a brass pin (marked C) shaped like an inverted L. The purpose of these is as yet unknown.

One jack (marked A) remains, and this is pierced for quill. Observe the free soundboard on which the eight and four foot nuts are placed (B), the oak wrestplank being only large enough to contain the three rows of wrestpins. This is reminiscent of Italian practice, and is very rarely seen in Flemish or English harpsichords.

Scaling: Eight foot: C: 60″ (approx.), c²: 14″, c³: 7″.

Dimensions of harpsichord: 7′ 0″ × 2′ 11″ × 0′ 9″.

Victoria and Albert Museum

55. HARPSICHORD BY JOHN HAWARD, 1622

This is the earliest seventeenth century English harpsichord, and, apart from the Theeuwes instrument of 1579 (Plates 53 and 54), the earliest English domestic keyboard instrument of any kind at present recorded.

No other instruments by this maker seem to have survived, and very little information about him is available. In 1649 he was resident in the parish of Saint Helen, Bishopsgate; the date of his death is not known. Thomas Mace (*Musick's Monument* (1676) p. 235) mentions John Hayward [*sic*] in connection with harpsichord pedals, but it is unlikely that he was alive at the time Mace was writing. Haward's possible relationship to the virginal makers Charles Haward (fl. 1660–1687) of Aldgate Street, and Thomas Haward (fl. 1656–1663) of Bishopsgate and Saint Giles Cripplegate, has not been established.

The harpsichord here shown is in a plain oak case. Round the inside are painted Latin mottoes in green and yellow, but these are no longer decipherable. The lid is missing. Over the keyboard is written:

Johannes Haward fecit Londini MDCXXII.

Note the fine arcaded stand.

Dimensions: $8' \, 2'' \times 2' \, 9\frac{1}{4}'' \times 0' \, 9\frac{3}{8}''$.

Lord Sackville, Knole Park, Sevenoaks

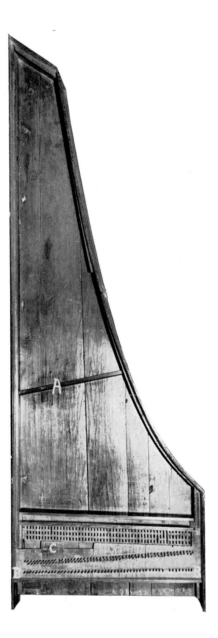

56. Interior of preceding harpsichord

The soundboard is missing. One transverse strut remains (A), but there were at one time four. This is reminiscent of the construction of Flemish harpsichords (Plate 38).

The keyboard is missing, but it had a compass of 53 keys. There were three sets of strings; and a glance at the wrest plank shows that one of these (B) was longer than the other two. Hence their pitch may have been: 1×16, 2×8; 1×8, 2×4; or $1 \times 10\frac{2}{3}$, 2×8. Bearing in mind that this was the period of transposing harpsichords the quint pitch of one set of strings is not improbable.

It can be seen (C) that the nut for the two shorter registers stood on free soundboard, a feature characteristic of Italian harpsichords and of the Theeuwes of 1579 (Plate 54). Another Italian feature is the position of the jacks, which are further (by only an inch) from the player in the bass than in the treble.

Lord Sackville, Knole Park

57. VIRGINAL BY STEPHEN KEENE, 1668

This is a typical example of the ordinary virginal built in England from 1640–1675. Though the decoration seems elaborate it is in fact the standard decoration found on all English virginals. The instrument is also very standardized, and it suggests that they derive from the Ruckers virginals, which were doubtless imported into this country in the early part of the century.

The English virginals are built in oak cases; the drop front is attached; the lid is sometimes convex, but is often plane. Gilt embossed paper decorates the front parts of these instruments and lines the interiors, and this is often embossed with Royal heads and coats of arms, taken from coins and medals. The writer is sorry to convey the bad news that this does not in any way mean that the instruments belonged to members of the Royal Family. The inside of the lid and the drop front are normally painted with conventional groups of figures and landscapes (often described as St. James's Park), and these decorations are often painted in *tempera*.

Dimensions: 5′ 11¼″ × 1′ 9½″ × 0′ 10″.

Russell Collection, Edinburgh

58. SOUNDBOARD OF PRECEDING VIRGINAL

The keyboard is placed to the left, and this seems to be characteristic of all the English virginals.

Note the four roses of carved wood, and the box on the left of the keyboard (marked A) for spare parts, etc.

This virginal has an unusually large compass: FF – d³, without FF♯. Only one other example known to the writer descends to FF, and that is the Robert Hatley of 1664 in the Benton Fletcher Collection which ascends to c³. The more general keyboard is from GG, bass short octave. In four examples the compass ascends to f³. However the 57 key compass of the instrument here illustrated is the largest known to the writer.

Stephen Keene was a virginal and harpsichord maker in Threadneedle Street. Signed instruments date him as working between 1668 and 1719.

Scaling: FF: 64″, c²: 11¼″, d³: 5″.
Plucking
  Point: FF: 6″, d³: 2″.

Russell Collection, Edinburgh

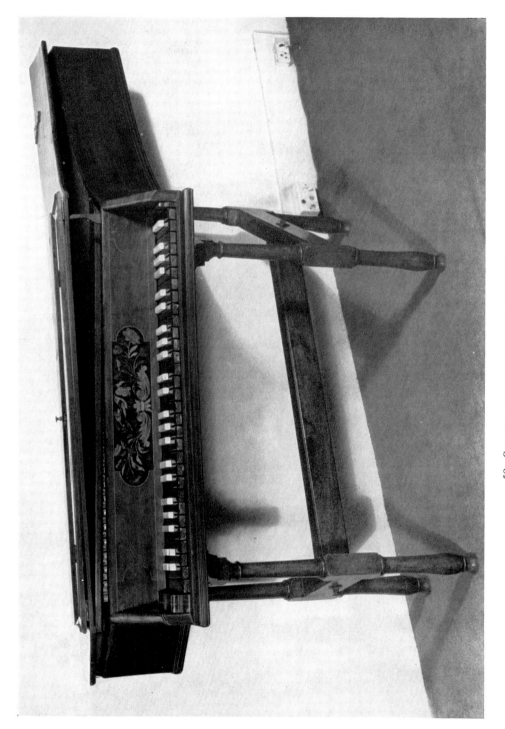

59. SPINET, LATE SEVENTEENTH CENTURY

Here is the ordinary transverse spinet which supplanted the rectangular virginal, as the most common English domestic keyboard instrument, in the last third of the seventeenth century. In the eighteenth century English harpsichord making became a flourishing trade, but the spinet remained popular as the equivalent of the upright pianoforte of today: the model used by those who did not want to be put to the inconvenience and expense of the large instrument. The case is oak. Note the marquetry over the keys, which was common decoration in this type of instrument. The keyboard with black naturals was not much used in England after the beginning of the eighteenth century.

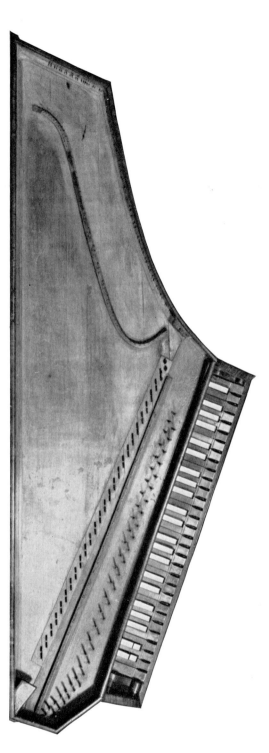

Scaling:
  GG: $51\frac{1}{2}''$, c^2: $10''$, d^3: $4''$.

Plucking Point:
  GG: $4\frac{1}{4}''$, d^3: $1\frac{3}{4}''$.

60. Soundboard of preceding spinet

Compass: GG – d^3, broken octave.
  Originally this keyboard extended to c^3 only, but by reducing the treble key block it proved possible at some time to extend the compass.

Russell Collection, Edinburgh

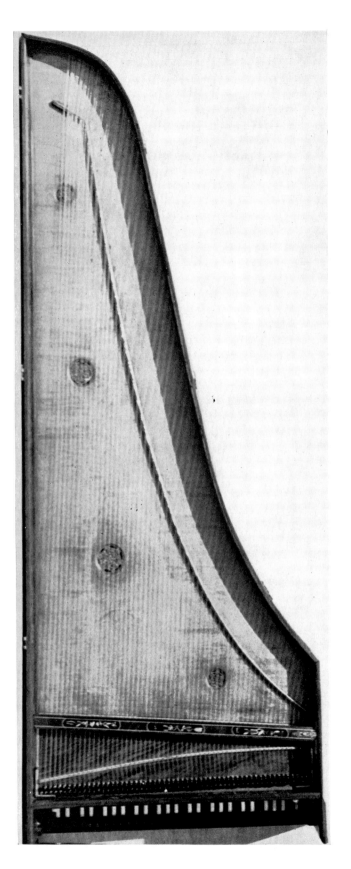

61. Harpsichord by Charles Haward, 1683

This is the only recorded English harpsichord belonging to the last quarter of the seventeenth century.

The four roses are reminiscent of the English virginal (Plate 58). Italian influence is noticeable in the design of the instrument, the short treble and the long bass scaling, the bridge which is angled in the bass, the jack slide diagonally placed, the two unison registers only.

The maker's name is written on the soundboard near the jacks:

Carolus Haward Londini 1683

Compass: FF – d³, chromatic, but without FF♯.

This harpsichord has, at some comparatively early time, undergone restoration, since there are signs which show that it once contained a lute stop. This must have been a very early example; lute stops are not found at all regularly in harpsichords until the second quarter of the eighteenth century, and this example was removed in the pre pianoforte period.

Charles Haward lived in Aldgate Street and was certainly at work between 1660 and 1687. Samuel Pepys visited him in 1668 and ordered a spinet (page 72).

Sir William Worsley
Hovingham Hall, Yorkshire

62. DESIGN BY THORNHILL FOR THE LID OF A HARPSICHORD OF HANDEL

This design is by Sir James Thornhill (1675–1734), and it bears the note 'Mr. Handel has or had the Harpsichord this design was made for'.

This instrument cannot now be traced, and no account of the harpsichord has survived. The double curve lid narrows down the probable makers to one of the Hamburg families (Hass or Zell) and to the Hitchcocks. Handel may have possessed a German harpsichord, and his early years were spent in Hamburg. But it is perhaps more likely that this instrument was a Hitchcock. The Earl of Malmesbury owns a portrait of Handel by Mercier, showing the composer at a single manual harpsichord. The instrument has a GG keyboard, decorated with the elaborate use of ivory and ebony generally employed by Hitchcock (Plates 64 and 65). That instrument may have been the harpsichord for which this drawing was prepared. There is no evidence that the painting was made.

Fitzwilliam Museum, Cambridge

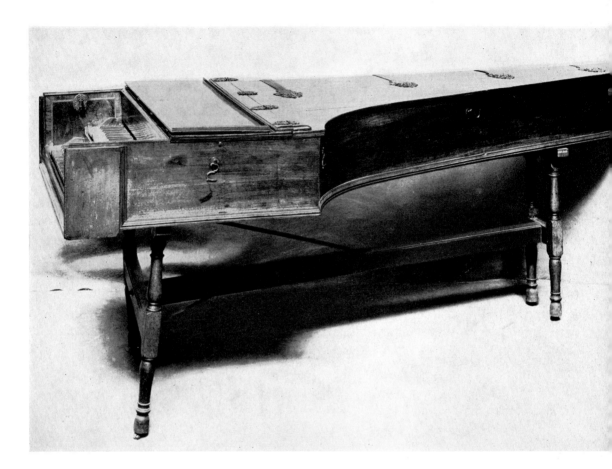

63. Harpsichord by Thomas Hitchcock, early eighteenth century

This harpsichord is from the London workshop of the well known family of spinet makers who are known to us as Thomas Hitchcock (the elder), his son Thomas Hitchcock (the younger), and the latter's son, John Hitchcock. Many Hitchcock spinets have survived, but only two harpsichords: this instrument, and one by John Hitchcock which is at Lyme Park, Cheshire.

The case is of walnut. Note the unusual double curve bentside, and the stand with turned legs. Over the keyboard is written:

Thomas Hitchcock fecit Londini.

There is no date recorded on the instrument, which probably belongs to the first quarter of the century. The bracing follows the Italian system.

Dimensions: 7′ 9½″ × 3′ 0¼″ × 0′ 9¼″.

Victoria and Albert Museum

64. SOUNDBOARD OF PRECEDING HARPSICHORD

There are several unusual features.

Observe the graining of the soundboard, diagonally placed; the four foot hitchpin rail (marked A); the compass, GG – g³, chromatic, so common in English spinets but rare in harpsichords; the elaborate accidental keys which contain a slip of ivory—a Hitchcock speciality, though occasionally used by Shudi, Snetzler, Kirckman and others.

A section of wrestplank (marked B C D), triangular in shape, contains the eight foot wrestpins. This is joined to that part beyond, which contains the eight foot nut, the four foot bass wrestpins, and the lute slide, (marked D E F B); and this latter part seems to have been made as a spinet wrestplank, being adapted for use in a harpsichord by the addition of B C D. This would point to the small amount of harpsichord making carried out by the Hitchcocks.

There are two unisons, an octave, and there is a lute stop for the upper manual.

Scaling: Eight foot: GG: 68″, c²: 13″, g³: $4\frac{1}{2}$″.
Four foot: GG: $46\frac{1}{2}$″, c²: $6\frac{1}{4}$″, g³: $2\frac{1}{8}$″.

Plucking Point: Eight foot: GG: $8\frac{3}{4}$″, g³: $2\frac{1}{8}$″.
Four foot: GG: $4\frac{7}{8}$″, g³: $1\frac{3}{4}$″. (back row).
Lute: GG: $3\frac{1}{8}$″, g³: $\frac{1}{2}$″.

Victoria and Albert Museum

65. SPINET BY THOMAS HITCHCOCK, EARLY EIGHTEENTH CENTURY

The case is walnut with boxwood inlay. Note the keyboard: compass GG – g^3, the natural keys covered with ivory and with arcaded ivory fronts, the accidentals of ebony with a central ivory slip. Note also the stand with turned legs.

Above the keyboard is the maker's inscription:

Thomas Hitchcock Londini fecit N 1241.

The spinets of the Hitchcock family usually bear the maker's number which has sometimes been mistaken for a date, though the latter is very seldom given. Inside these instruments the workman's name is often to be found, usually on the top or/and bottom key and jack.

Scaling: GG: $59\frac{1}{2}''$, c^2: $10\frac{7}{8}''$, g^3: $3\frac{3}{4}''$.

Plucking Point: GG: $7''$, g^3: $2''$.

Russell Collection, Edinburgh

66. Harpsichord by Jacob Kirckman, 1755

Jacob Kirckman was an Alsatian, born in 1710. He came to England as a young man, and his dated work covered the period 1750–1790. From 1772 nearly all his instruments were signed jointly with his nephew Abraham. After Jacob Kirckman's death in 1792 the firm continued, turning in time to pianoforte making.

The instrument here shown is typical of the double manual English harpsichord of the period, though the decoration is unusually elaborate. Of the hundred or so surviving Kirckmans only two or three are quite so elaborate in appearance.

The case is of cross banded walnut, with boxwood stringing and inlay. The keyboard surround, jackrails, and case lining, are covered with marquetry on a sycamore ground. Over the keys is the maker's monogram and the inscription:

Jacobus Kirckman Londini fecit 1755.

The carved stand with claw and ball feet is a very unusual luxury in a harpsichord of this period, but much more unusual is the longside (Plate 67) which is veneered as the rest of the instrument. Of Kirckman's other marquetry harpsichords only two or three seem to have this feature. The longside was almost always left plain, for standing against the wall.

Dimensions: 8′ 0″ × 3′ 0½″ × 0′ 11¾″.

Russell Collection, Edinburgh

67. HARPSICHORD BY JACOB KIRCKMAN, 1755

The decorated longside can here be seen. Though a very rare feature in harpsichords of the early and middle eighteenth century, it appears more regularly in instruments at the end of the century (often in unpretentious cases), and also in the $5\frac{1}{2}$ octave harpsichords of Shudi (Appendix 10). The natural keys have boxwood moulded fronts—a very usual English keyboard.

Russell Collection, Edinburgh

68. SOUNDBOARD OF PRECEDING HARPSICHORD

Compass: FF – f³, without FF♯.

There are two unisons and an octave.

The four stop levers control (from left to right):

1. Lute (Upper manual).
2. Four foot (Lower manual).
3. Eight foot (Both manuals).
4. Eight foot (Lower manual).

Note the rose with initials I.K., and the walnut veneer on the wrestplank—a common English feature. In England, however, soundboards were not decorated.

Scaling: Eight foot: FF: $70\frac{1}{4}''$, c^2: $13\frac{1}{2}''$, f³: $5\frac{1}{4}''$.
Four foot: FF: $41\frac{1}{2}''$, c^2: $6\frac{1}{2}''$, f³: $2\frac{1}{2}''$.

Plucking Eight foot: FF: $7\frac{3}{8}''$, f³: $1\frac{7}{8}''$.
Point: Four foot: FF: $4\frac{1}{4}''$, f³: $1\frac{3}{4}''$.
Lute: FF: $2\frac{5}{8}''$, f³: $\frac{3}{8}''$.

String gauge numbers are stamped on the nut as follows:

Eight foot:

13 FF	11 BB♭	9 D	7 B♭	5 c¹
12 AA♭	10 C	8 F♯	6 f♯	4 c²

Four foot:

11 FF	9 BB♭	7 G	5 b
10 GG	8 D	6 f	4 c²

It is not possible to interpret these numbers with accuracy and certainty in terms of the diameter of the wire (page 19).

Russell Collection, Edinburgh

69. SPINET BY JOHN HARRISON, 1757

The ordinary eighteenth century English spinet, which served the purposes of the upright pianoforte of today.

The case is cross banded mahogany. The natural keys have ebony moulded fronts. Above the keyboard is inscribed:

Joannes Harrison Londini fecit 1757.

Length: 5' 10".

Russell Collection, Edinburgh

70. SOUNDBOARD OF PRECEDING SPINET

Note the common English spinet compass: GG – g³, chromatic.
The wrestplank is veneered.

Scaling: GG: $58\frac{1}{2}''$, c²: $10\frac{1}{8}''$, g³: $3\frac{1}{4}''$.

Plucking
Point: GG: $6\frac{1}{8}''$, g³: $1\frac{1}{2}''$.

Note the short treble scale which is a special feature of these instruments.

Russell Collection, Edinburgh

71. HARPSICHORD BY JACOB AND ABRAHAM KIRCKMAN, 1772

The decoration of this instrument is a very usual one for the period. The case is crossbanded mahogany, with boxwood stringing. The lid is solid mahogany. The stand is the usual model. The longside is not veneered. The keyboard surround is veneered with panels of burr walnut, cross banded with tulip wood.

Dimensions: 7′ 8″ × 3′ 4$\frac{1}{4}$″ × 1′ 0$\frac{1}{2}$″.

Mrs. Gilbert Russell

72. Keyboards of preceding harpsichord

The instrument is a standard model, with the exception of the compass, which is FF – c³, (no FF♯). The usual upper limit to the keyboard is f³. The keyboard is the usual English design: natural keys covered with ivory and with moulded boxwood fronts, accidentals of ebony. The top five keys are most unusual in that this decoration is reversed. The purpose of this extended keyboard with reversed key decoration above g³ is not clear; and there does not seem to be any contemporary music which demands it.

The stop levers, from left to right, are as follows:

1. Machine stop (for use in conjunction with the pedal—see page 80).
2. Harp stop of buff leather (upper manual).
3. Lute (upper manual).
4. Four foot (lower manual).
5. Eight foot (both manuals).
6. Eight foot (lower manual).

The four foot breaks back an octave, taking on unison pitch, for the five highest notes.

Note the adjustable music desk, an unusual feature in harpsichords of this period.

Mrs. Gilbert Russell

73. SOUNDBOARD OF PRECEDING
HARPSICHORD

Scaling: Eight foot: FF: 68″, c^2
$13\frac{1}{2}″$, c^4: $3\frac{3}{8}″$.
Four foot: FF: $40\frac{1}{2}″$, c^2
$6\frac{3}{4}″$, c^4: $3\frac{1}{2}″$.

Plucking   Eight foot: FF: $7\frac{1}{4}″$, c^4
Point: $1\frac{1}{2}″$.
Four foot: FF: $4\frac{1}{4}″$, c^4
$\frac{3}{4}″$.
Lute: FF: $2\frac{5}{8}″$, c^4: $\frac{3}{8}″$

String gauge numbers are marked on
the nut as in the Kirckman of 1755 (Plate
68). Gauge number 4 is used from c^2 to c^4

Mrs. Gilbert Russell

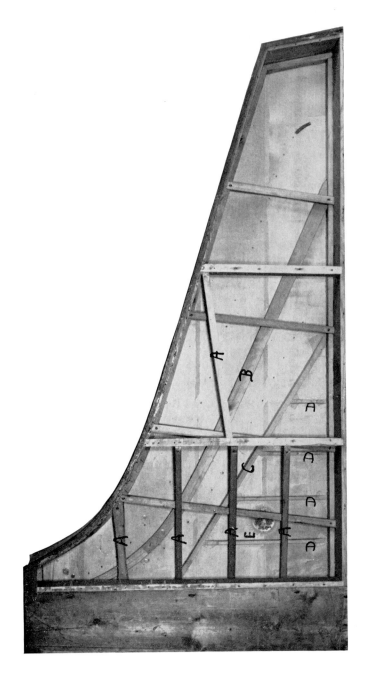

74. INTERIOR OF PRECEDING HARPSICHORD

The bottom boards, which are normally attached to the case work and cross braces, thus forming an important feature in the strength of the frame, are removed for this photograph.

The English system of building the frame of the harpsichord derived from the Low Countries (Plate 38), an influence which continued in France and Germany (Plate 51). In England, however, braces running lengthways down the harpsichord were added to the Flemish scheme. These are marked A.

Observe : B. Four foot hitch pin rail.
    C. Large transverse cut off bar. (See Plate 38.)
    D. Four soundbars.
    E. The rose.

Mrs. Gilbert Russell

75. HARPSICHORD BY SHUDI AND BROADWOOD, 1782

The case, lid, and stand, are of mahogany, with cross banding of satinwood. The music desk is of mahogany.

This was the largest model harpsichord made in England. A list of such instruments still known to exist is given in Appendix 10.

Note the two pedals. That on the left operates the mechanism of the Machine stop; the right hand pedal opens the Venetian Swell shutters (marked A).

Dimensions: 8′ 9″ × 3′ 4½″ × 1′ 0¾″.

Victoria and Albert Museum

Compass: CC – f^3, chromatic.

There are two unisons and one octave.

The stop levers, from left to right, are:

1. Machine stop.
2. Lute (upper manual).
3. Four foot (lower manual).
4. Harp (lower manual).
5. Eight foot (both manuals).
6. Eight foot (lower manual).

Scaling: Eight foot: CC: 83″, c^2: 13$\frac{3}{4}$″, f^3: 5″.

Four foot: CC: 46″, c^2: 6$\frac{1}{2}$″, f^3: 2$\frac{1}{2}$″.

Plucking Point: Eight foot: CC: 9$\frac{1}{2}$″, f^3: 2″.

Four foot: CC: 5$\frac{3}{4}$″, f^3: 1$\frac{7}{8}$″.

Lute: CC: 4$\frac{5}{8}$″, f^3: $\frac{1}{2}$″.

Though the scaling of these large Shudis is fairly constant, the plucking point is closer to the nut in the early models. The example of 1770, number 625 (Benton Fletcher Collection), has:

Plucking Point: Eight foot: CC: 7$\frac{1}{4}$″, f^3: 2″.

Four foot: CC: 4$\frac{1}{4}$″, f^3: 1$\frac{3}{4}$″.

Lute: CC: 2$\frac{1}{2}$″, f^3: $\frac{1}{2}$″.

String Gauge numbers are marked on the nut:

Eight foot:		
15 CC.	11 BB♭.	7 c.
14 EE♭.	10 C.	6 f.
13 FF♯.	9 E♭.	5 b.
12 GG♯.	8 F♯.	4 c^2.

Four foot:		
12 CC.	9 C♯.	6 c♯.
11 FF♯.	8 F.	5 f♯.
10 AA.	7 B♭.	4 c^1.

Victoria and Albert Museum

77. Upright harpsichord by Ferdinand Weber of Dublin, 1764

A curious feature of Dublin instrument making was the construction of upright harpsichords. The date is pencilled on the rear of the soundboard.

An example by Henry Rother of Dublin, *c.* 1775, is preserved in the National Museum in Dublin. That instrument has one manual with a compass FF – g³, chromatic, but without FF♯. It contains two unisons and an octave.

The instrument here shown was sold by Sotheby & Co. of London on 29 June, 1956.

78. SOUNDBOARD OF PRECEDING INSTRUMENT

The compass is GG – g^3; and this g^3 should be noted, as it was an Irish speciality in harpsichords, whereas in England it was almost completely confined to spinets. (Page 76.)

There are two unisons, a four foot, and a harp; the strings of the four foot have their own nut, but share the eight foot bridge.

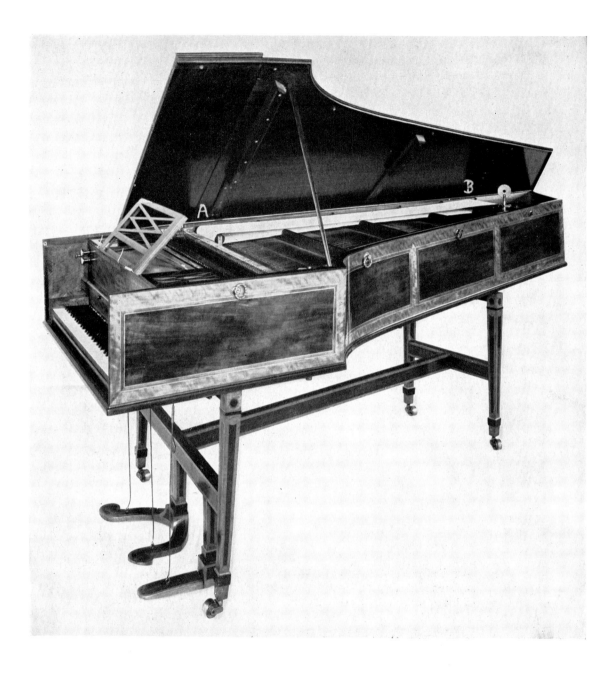

79. Harpsichord and pianoforte by Joseph Merlin, 1780

The maker of this unusual instrument was born near Liége in 1735, and came to England in the Spanish Ambassador's Court in 1760. It is not known where Merlin learned his instrument making, but he took out a patent for the combination here shown in 1774. Merlin was a friend of many well known men in London, and among these was Charles Burney for whom he constructed a six octave pianoforte from CC. Merlin's inventive mind turned to other things than the harpsichord, and his Invalid Chair is still in wide use.

This instrument is signed

Josephus Merlin Privilegiarus Novi forte piano No. 80 *Londini* 1780.

Compass: FF – f³, chromatic.

The harpsichord has three sets of strings: sixteen foot, eight foot, four foot, and three rows of jacks. Of these the eight and four foot are quilled, and the sixteen foot has buff leather plectra. The sixteen foot jacks are nearest the player, the eight foot in the middle, and the four foot nearest the soundboard. Each register has its own soundboard bridge, but the sixteen and eight share the same nut.

There is a harp for the eight foot, and also a Celestial Harp stop. This mechanism is a very thin rod which runs beside the eight foot jacks, and which, on moving the appropriate stop lever, lifts up the entire row of jacks and holds them clear of the strings, which are left free to vibrate in sympathy with the rest of the instrument. This invention was applied to English harpsichords from time to time, but never achieved great popularity. Pascal Taskin in Paris sometimes used a mechanism of a different design, and worked by a knee lever, to produce the same effect.

This is the only old English harpsichord known to the writer which possesses an original sixteen foot stop.

The pianoforte is provided with one set of eight foot strings of its own, but the hammers strike both this and the harpsichord eight foot strings. This action is down-striking, and is worked by means of extensions above the sixteen foot jacks.

Besides all this there is a **recording machine,** built into a large frame which fits above the soundboard. It consists of a long roll of paper which passes over a roller at each end of the frame (marked A and B). The rollers and paper can revolve by means of clockwork. There are prolongations above each four foot jack connected, by means of trackers, with a row of pencils placed near the roller B. When a note is depressed the appropriate tracker draws its pencil towards the paper on the drum (and thus towards the player), and the note and its duration are recorded. The shorthand result has then to be deciphered. This original mechanism was very damaged when the instrument was acquired by the Museum, and it was reconstructed by Seiffert of Leipzig.

Above the keyboard are five stop levers. On the left a small lever brings the recording machine into action, while two larger handles control the harpsichord unison and octave. The two stop handles on the right control the Celestial Harp and the Welsh Harp (as the normal harp stop is called).

Of the three pedals that on the left controls the sixteen foot, the centre pedal brings the pianoforte action on, while the right hand pedal puts it off. This latter pedal may be a later addition.

Scaling:	Sixteen Foot:	FF : 81″, c² : 17½″, f³ : 7½″.
	Eight Foot:	FF : 68½″, c² : 13″, f³ : 4½″.
	Four Foot:	FF : 43″, c² : 6½″, f³ : 2½″.
Plucking Point:	Sixteen Foot:	FF : 10″, f³ : 1¾″.
	Eight Foot:	FF : 10¾″, f³ : 2½″.
	Four Foot:	FF : 9¾″, f³ : 2¼″.

Deutsches Museum, Munich

80. SPINET BY SAMUEL BLYTHE OF SALEM, MASSACHUSETTS, 1789

A large part of the demand for early keyboard instruments in America was met by import from England. This spinet, however, is an example of American work, derived from the English instruments of the time. While there are other American spinets of this period, there is some doubt as to whether any original harpsichords have survived.

Essex Institute, Salem, Massachusetts

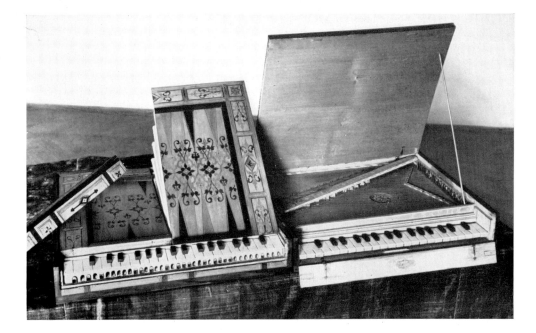

81A. Spinet and Regal, by Anton Meidling, 1587

This is a regal and a small spinet of approximately four foot pitch, which are hinged together. When closed the two instruments form a type of backgammon board.

Compass: F – a², without F♯, G♯, and g²♯.

This instrument came from the castle of Archduke Ferdinand of Tyrol at Ambras.

Kunsthistorisches Museum, Vienna

81B. Spinet, sixteenth century

This spinet fits like a drawer into an elaborate cabinet. The pitch is approximately four foot.

Compass: C – a², bass short octave, without g²♯.

Bayerisches Nationalmuseum, Munich

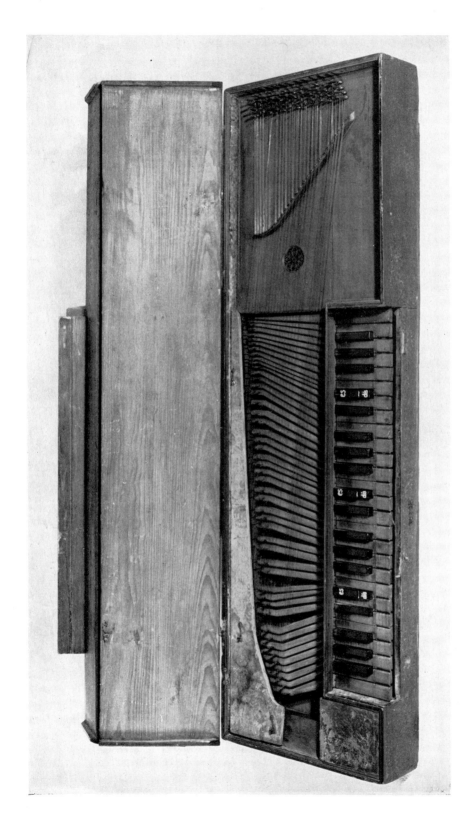

82. CLAVICHORD, PROBABLY SIXTEENTH CENTURY

These early clavichords are often impossible to assign with certainty to German or Italian origin, or to a definite period in the sixteenth or seventeenth centuries.

This example is fretted. **Compass** C – c³, bass short octave. Each E♭ key is divided into two keys: a front and a back part, a feature not uncommon in instruments built in the period of mean tone temperament, when this attempt was made to counter the dissonant interval between keys E♭ and A♭.

These small instruments were often made without a stand, and were put on a

83. CLAVICHORD BY JOHANN WEISS, 1702

Compass: C – c³, chromatic, but without C#. The clavichord is fretted. Note the carved keys provided for each pair of natural key semitones.

Deutsches Museum, Munich

84. UPRIGHT HARPSICHORD BY MARTIN KAISER, LATE SEVENTEENTH CENTURY

This instrument was built for Emperor Leopold I (1640–1705). It is contained in an elaborate ebony case, inlaid with silver and tortoiseshell.

Compass: GG – c³, chromatic, but without GG♯.

Over the keyboard is inscribed:

Martinus Kaiser Ser. Electoris Palatini Instrumentorum
Opifex Et Huiusmodi Inventor.

There are two unison registers. The layout is very unusual, as the longest strings are placed in the centre, with the short strings on either side. As a result the keys are not in alignment with the strings they control, and the lower part of the case contains a complicated, but beautifully made, system of trackers, stickers, and rollers to overcome the difficulty.

Scaling: GG: 66″, c²: 14⅛″, c³: 6½″.

Plucking Point: GG: 5¼″, c³: 1¾″.

Kunsthistorisches Museum, Vienna

85. Harpsichord by Hieronymus Hass, 1734

This is the work of the elder of the two Hasses, who together have left more signed instruments, both harpsichords and clavichords, than any other German makers, and who may be considered the first of their profession in that country.

The unusual length of the right hand key cheek: 3 ′ 3″, is due to the presence of a sixteen foot register with its own soundboard.

Note the double curve bentside, a Hamburg speciality, which can also be associated with Christian Zell and the Fleischers.

The outside of the case is painted cream, with brown and gold mouldings. The lid painting suggests the style of that in the Hass of 1740 (Plate 87).

The natural keys are covered with ivory, and have ebony arcaded fronts. The accidentals are inlaid with mother of pearl and tortoiseshell. Tortoiseshell and ivory decorate the keyboard surround. The maker's inscription is written in ink on the soundboard:

Hieronymus Albre Hass fecit Hamburg. Anno 1734.

This inscription is repeated on a plate, probably of later date, on the right upper keyblock. On the left upper keyblock another plate records:

Restauré par Fleury facteur de pianos à Paris en 1858.

(Plate 49 and page 123.)

The soundboard bears the inscription in ink:

Restauré et perfectionné par Fleury facteur de pianos à Paris en 1858.

Dimensions: 8′ 9″ × 3′ 0½″ × 0′ 11¼″.

Conservatoire Brussels

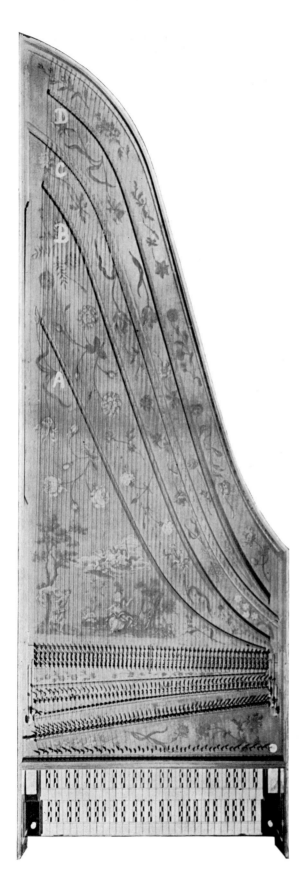

86. SOUNDBOARD OF PRECEDING HARPSICHORD

Compass: GG – d³, chromatic.

There are four sets of strings: a sixteen foot, two unisons, and a four foot.

The five stop levers, from left to right are:

1. Eight foot (both manuals).
2. Four foot (Lower manual).
3. Eight foot (Lower manual).
4. Sixteen foot (Lower manual).
5. Lute (Upper manual).

There are harp stops for the lower manual unison and sixteen foot. The upper manual can be coupled to the lower by pulling the latter towards the player, but this movement will only couple the lute, since the upper eight foot always plays from both manuals when drawn. Originally there was no coupler, but the dogleg jacks could be disconnected by pulling the lower manual forward.

Scaling: Sixteen foot: GG: 84″, c²: 28″, d³: 13½″.

Eight foot: GG: 68½″, c²: 13½″, d³: 6¼″.

Four foot: GG: 46½″, c²: 6¾″, d³: 3″.

Plucking Sixteen foot: GG: 11½″, d³: 6″.
Point: Eight foot: GG: 7½″, d³: 3¾″.
Four foot: GG: 4″, d³: 1½″.
Lute: GG: 1¾″, d³: ¼″.

Observe: A. Four foot bridge.
B. Eight foot bridge.
C. Eight foot hitchpin rail.
D. Sixteen foot bridge standing on its own soundboard.

Conservatoire, Brussels

87. Harpsichord by Hieronymus Hass, 1740

This instrument seems to be old Hass's *magnum opus*, and it is the most elaborate harpsichord known to the writer.

The whole case is painted in imitation of tortoiseshell, and on this Chinese scenes in gold are imposed. The main picture in the lid shows a scene in which the harpsichord is being presented to a lady, Hass standing beside it. Unfortunately the writer has not been able to identify the original owner. The keyboard surround is inlaid with ivory and tortoiseshell; the natural keys are covered with the latter material and have arcaded ivory fronts; the accidentals are ivory inlaid with tortoiseshell.

The maker's signature is in ink on the soundboard:

Hieronymus Albr. Hass in Hamb. Anno 1740.

There are three manuals. **Compass** FF – f³, chromatic, without FF♯. The lowest manual can be pushed into the instrument like a drawer if not wanted. If pulled out its full course the middle keyboard is coupled down to it, but if drawn about $\frac{1}{2}''$ short of this the lowest manual is independent. The exact position is marked by dark strips of wood let into the upper surface of its kevblocks, which are not visible if the manual is uncoupled (marked A, Plate 88). The top manual can be coupled to the middle by pushing the former in about $\frac{1}{2}''$, but this only couples the lute stop, as the upper eight foot is common to the top and middle manuals if drawn.

Dimensions: 9' 3" × 3' 3¼" × 1' 2".

Rafael Puyana, Paris

88. Keyboards of preceding harpsichord

There are five sets of strings: sixteen foot, two unisons, four foot, and two foot (up to c¹ only), and six rows of jacks.

The jacks in order from the player to the soundboard, are:

1. Lute (Top manual).
2. Eight foot (Top and middle manuals).
3. Four foot (Middle manual).
4. Eight foot (Middle manual).
5. Sixteen foot (Lowest manual).
6. Two foot (Lowest manual).

This numbering is shown against the appropriate stop levers.

There is a harp stop for the sixteen foot.

Scaling:
Sixteen foot: $FF : 84''$, $c^2 : 28''$, $f^3 : 11\frac{1}{4}''$.
Eight foot: $FF : 70\frac{1}{2}''$, $c^2 : 13\frac{1}{2}''$, $f^3 : 5\frac{1}{4}''$.
Four foot: $FF : 46\frac{1}{2}''$, $c^2 : 8\frac{1}{2}''$, $f^3 : 3\frac{1}{4}''$.
Two foot: $FF : 31\frac{3}{4}''$, $c^1 : 6\frac{1}{2}''$.

Plucking Point:
Sixteen foot: $FF : 11\frac{1}{2}''$, $f^3 : 6\frac{1}{4}''$.
Eight foot: $FF : 6\frac{1}{8}''$, $f^3 : 2\frac{3}{8}''$.
Four foot: $FF : 2\frac{1}{4}''$, $f^3 : 1''$.
Two foot: $FF : 4\frac{1}{4}''$, $c^1 : 4''$.

Observe: A. The marks which are visible when the lowest manual has engaged the middle manual.
B. Two foot bridge.
C. Four foot bridge.
D. Eight foot bridge.
E. Eight foot hitchpin rail.
F. Sixteen foot bridge on its own soundboard.

Rafael Puyana, Paris

89. Pedal clavichord by Johann Gerstenberg, 1760

Instruments such as this were used in Germany as practice instruments by organists, since churches were unheated and organs were silent without the help of manual labour for blowing. This instrument is unusual in having two manuals. Each of the manual clavichords possesses two eight foot strings for each note; the pedal instrument has two eight and two sixteen foot strings for each note.

Heyer Collection, Leipzig

90. PEDAL CLAVICHORD BY GLÜCK

The pedal board is a modern replacement, and it has one string to each note. The pedal clavichord itself is placed upside down, so that its soundboard is above its strings.

Deutsches Museum, Munich

91. SPINET BY JOHANN HEINRICH SILBERMANN, 1767

This spinet was made by the nephew of Gottfried Silbermann, the famous Dresden organ builder. Apart from the seven recorded instruments of this model which the younger Silbermann has left (pages 104 and 105), there are practically no other German spinets.

Neupert Collection, Germanisches Nationalmuseum, Nürnberg

92. Harpsichord by Carl Gräbner, 1782

German harpsichords are scarce, as only about twenty are at present recorded; however four have survived from the workshops of the Gräbner family of Dresden. The writer has not seen the inscription on this harpsichord, which is said to be somewhere inside.

Compass: FF – f³ chromatic.

Upper Manual: $1 \times 8'$.

Lower Manual: $2 \times 8'$, $1 \times 4'$.

Though the upper eight foot plays from both manuals, a lower manual coupler is present.

Scaling: Eight foot: FF: 74″, c²: 12¾″, f³: 5″.
Four foot: FF: 49″, c²: 6¼″, f³: 2¼″.

Plucking Point: Eight foot: FF: 6″, f³: 1½″.
Four foot: FF: 4¾″, f³: 1⅛″ (middle row).

Dimensions: 8′ 2″ × 3′ 2″ × 0′ 11″.

Rück Collection, Germanisches Nationalmuseum, Nürnberg

93. CLAVICHORD BY JOHANN HASS, 1767

This is typical of the large eighteenth century German clavichord.
The case is painted brown in imitation of wood. The keyboard surround and
inside of the case are veneered with olive wood.

The natural keys are covered with tortoiseshell and have arcaded ivory fronts;
the accidentals are covered with slips of tortoiseshell and mother of pearl

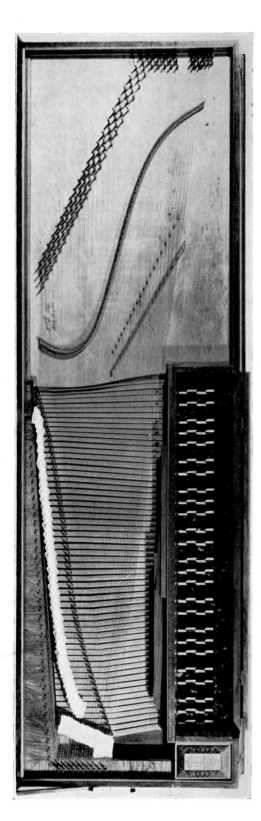

94. SOUNDBOARD OF PRECEDING CLAVICHORD

Compass: FF – f³ chromatic. The handsome appearance of Hass's keyboards are a special feature in most instruments from the Hamburg workshop. Note the engraved lid to the box at the bass end of the keyboard.

There are two unison strings to each note throughout the compass, and there is a four foot string as well for the lowest twenty keys. There is a second soundboard beneath the keys.

Scaling: Eight foot: FF: $58\frac{1}{2}''$, c²: $11\frac{3}{8}''$, f³: $4\frac{1}{8}''$.
Four foot: FF: $44\frac{1}{4}''$, c: $23\frac{1}{2}''$.

String Gauge numbers are written against the eight foot wrest pins as follows:

FF 000.	BB 0.	F♯ 2.	f 4.	c² 6.
AA♭ 00.	E♭ 1.	B♭ 3.	c¹ 5.	e³♭ 7.

It has not proved possible to express these numbers in terms of the diameter of the wire.

Dimensions: 5′ $8\frac{1}{4}''$ × 1′ $9\frac{1}{4}''$ × 0′ 7″.

Mrs. Gilbert Russell

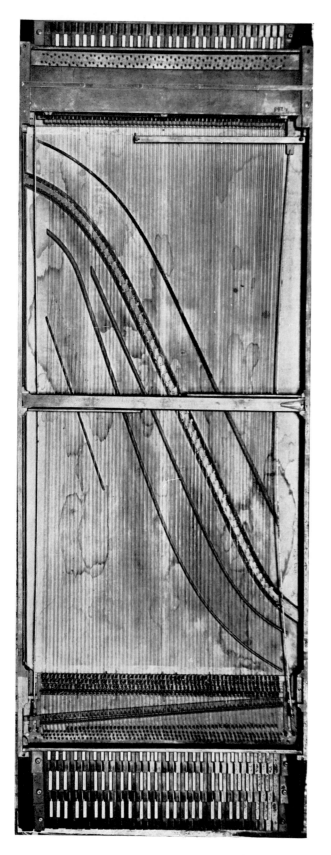

95. Harpsichord and pianoforte by Johann Stein, 1777

At one end is a grand pianoforte, doubl[e] strung throughout its compass, with two han[d] stops for treble and bass dampers.

At the other end is a two manual harp[si]sichord, with a third (lowest) keyboard whic[h] controls the pianoforte by stickers.

The two instruments share a hitchpin rail[.]

The harpsichord has four sets of strings[,] a sixteen foot, two unisons, and a four foot[.] All four rows are played from the middle key[-] board, and only one unison from the uppe[r] manual.

There is a harp stop for one eight foot.

Five hand stops control these five harp[-] sichord registers, and two more duplicate th[e] two pianoforte damper stops.

The sixteen foot is discontinued for th[e] lowest seven notes, stopping at C. The fou[r] foot is discontinued above A when it goe[s] onto the eight foot bridge as a third unison[.] Thus it has only sixteen notes at octave pitc[h] on its own bridge.

Scaling: Sixteen foot: C: $59\frac{1}{2}''$, c^2[:] $21\frac{1}{2}''$, f^3: $10\frac{1}{2}''$.
Eight foot: FF: $65''$, c^2[:] $12\frac{3}{4}''$, f^3: $4\frac{3}{4}''$.
Four foot: FF: $52\frac{3}{4}''$.

This instrument is stated to have bee[n] made in 1777 for the Società Filarmonica of Verona, who still own it.

The plain wood case stands on six turned legs.

Dimensions: $9'\ 5'' \times 4'\ 0'' \times 0'\ 10\frac{1}{2}''$.

Castelvecchio, Verona

96. HARPSICHORD BY GOTTLIEB ROSENAU OF STOCKHOLM, 1786

Compass: FF – f³, chromatic.

There are two unisons and an octave, and three sets of jacks.

The upper manual can be coupled to the lower by pushing inwards.

The case is decorated with red paint, and the interior of the lid with scenes in gold on a blue ground.

Note the double curve bentside, a common feature in Scandinavia as in Hamburg, whence this characteristic probably derived.

Dimensions: 9′ 2″ × 3′ 6″.

Claudius Collection, Copenhagen

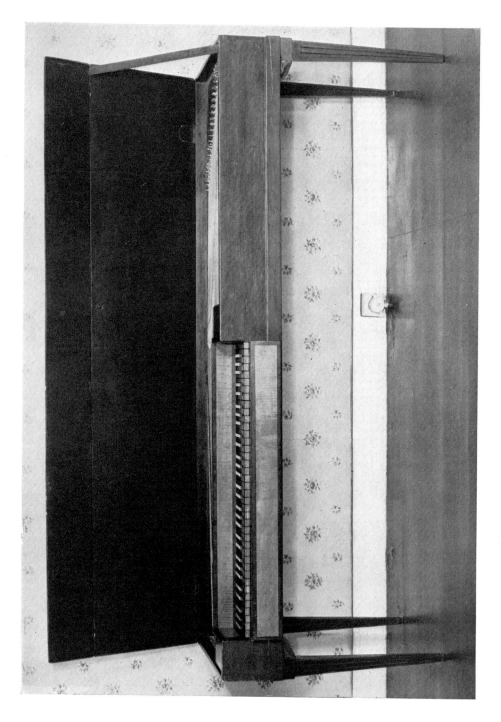

97. CLAVICHORD BY GEORGE RACKWITZ OF STOCKHOLM, 1796

Note the compass of this late instrument:

FF – c^4, chromatic.

There are two unison strings for each key, and an octave string as well for the lowest twenty keys.

Scaling: Eight foot: FF: 67$\frac{1}{4}$", c^2: 12$\frac{3}{4}$", c^4: 3$\frac{1}{4}$".

                  Four foot: FF: 49", c: 24$\frac{1}{4}$".

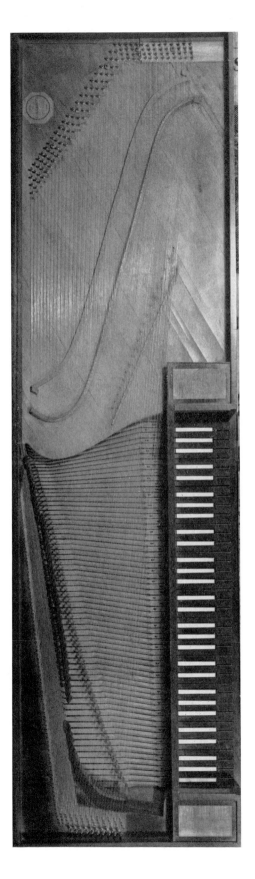

98. SOUNDBOARD OF PRECEDING CLAVICHORD

The maker's label on the wrestplank states:

No. 22 af G. C. Rackwitz i Stockholm 1796

The Galpin Society

99. Harpsichord by Joachim Antunes of Lisbon, 1758

Compass: C – e³, chromatic.

There are two eight foot registers.

Note the stand, carved in a manner apparently very usual in the Spanish peninsula.

Conservatorio, Lisbon

100. Clavichord by Jacintho Ferreira of Lisbon, 1783

Conservatorio, Lisbon

101. Harpsichord by Joachim Antunes of Lisbon, 1789

Compass: FF – a^3.

There are two unison registers.

Conservatorio, Lisbon

102A. HARPSICHORD, PROBABLY OF EIGHTEENTH CENTURY SPANISH ORIGIN

This instrument was acquired by the late Arnold Dolmetsch on the understanding that it had come from Spain. The style of the stand is clearly a confirmation of this (Plates 99, 100, 101). At that time the instrument contained hammer action, but Dolmetsch, who was certain that this was a later modification, rebuilt the instrument with jack action and two unison stops.

The stand and borders of the instrument are painted red, the panels enclosed by the latter are blue with gilt decoration.

In private ownership in Scotland

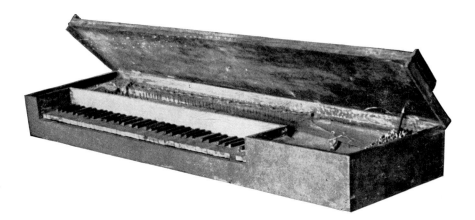

102B. CLAVICHORD BY JOSÉ GRABALOS OF TARAZONA, EIGHTEENTH CENTURY

Observe the very large compass: FF – f⁴, six octaves.

Museo de Musica, Barcelona

103. Geigenwerck by Raymundo Truchado
Spanish, 1625

Compass: C – c³, bass short octave. The strings are excited by the action of resined wheels, operated by the handle on the right. Apparently the instrument was intended for standing on a low table; hardly, perhaps, to facilitate the performer sitting on the floor, as has been suggested.

Conservatoire, Brussels

DATE DUE

APR 24 1975	JUN 0 1 2002	
NOV 3 75		
MAY 24 76		
APR B 78		
JUN 28 79		
APR 7 80		
84 SO 330		
AUG 1 1983		
OCT 2 2 1984		
MAY 2 0 1985		
MAR 2 7		
MAR 1 3 1996		

GAYLORD   PRINTED IN U.S.A.

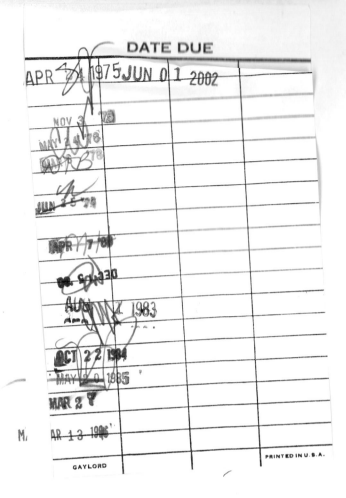

ML
651
R96
1973

Russell, Raymond.
    The harpsichord and clavichord; an introductory study, by Raymond Russell. 2d ed., rev. by Howard Schott. New York, W. W. Norton ₍1973₎

    208 p. illus., 103 plates. 26 cm. $18.75

    "Collections of early keyboard instruments": p. 186–189. Bibliography: p. 190–196.

    1. Harpsichord. 2. Clavichord.   **I. Title.**

ML651.R88 1973b   786.2'21   73–174157

274182 ISBN 0-393-02174-2   MARC

    Library of Congress   73 ₍4₎   MN